1-2-3® Release 3.1 QuickStart

2nd Edition

Que® Development Group

Text and graphics pages developed by
David P. Ewing and Katherine Murray

Revised for 2nd Edition by
Joyce J. Nielsen and Rick Winter

que®

CORPORATION

LEADING COMPUTER KNOWLEDGE

Publisher
Lloyd J. Short

Acquisitions Manager
Terrie Lynn Solomon

Product Director
Joyce J. Nielsen

Production Editor
Nancy E. Sixsmith

Editors
Ann Holcombe
Robin Drake

Technical Editors
Robert Walker
Jerry Ellis

Technical Support
Timothy S. Stanley

Indexer
Susan VandeWalle

Production Team
Jeff Baker
Claudia Bell
Brad Chinn
Jeanne Clark
Martin Coleman
Scott Cook
Sandy Grieshop
Denny Hager
Betty Kish
Bob LaRoche
Michele Laseau
Sarah Leatherman
Howard Peirce
Cindy L. Phipps
Tad Ringo
Johnna Van Hoose
Lisa A. Wilson

Contents at a Glance

Table of Contents

6   Modifying a Worksheet 195

7   Using Functions 229

Acknowledgments

Que Corporation thanks the following individuals for their contributions to the second edition of this book:

David Ewing, for providing valuable insight, support, and direction during the developmental phase of this book.

Terrie Lynn Solomon, for coordinating the authoring team for this book, and for managing the communications and materials sent to and from the authors.

Joyce Nielsen, for her thorough developmental work and authoring, and for ensuring high quality and technical accuracy in the final manuscript.

Rick Winter, for providing both original and revised material that adhered to the QuickStart format, and for doing so in a timely manner.

Nancy Sixsmith, for preparing the manuscript for production, and for carefully tracking the project through the production process.

Mary Bednarek, for her project and editorial management skills, as well as her troubleshooting expertise.

Ann Holcombe, for copy editing the original manuscript, and *Robin Drake* for proofing the final version.

Robert Walker and *Jerry Ellis*, for their dedication to ensuring the book's technical accuracy. Thanks also to Jerry for assisting with figure creation.

Tim Stanley, for writing the appendix of this book, and for providing valuable and reliable technical support.

Stacey Beheler and *Karen Opal*, for their prompt and efficient editorial support throughout the project.

Kathie-Jo Arnoff, for her ongoing work on the development of the QuickStart series.

Karen Bluestein, for providing valuable contributions to the final book design.

The Que Production Department, for their skillful talents in producing a high-quality text that meets Que's standards of excellence.

Trademark Acknowledgments

Introduction

If you are new to Lotus 1-2-3—and have access to Release 3 or 3.1—this book is for you. *1-2-3 Release 3.1 QuickStart*, 2nd Edition, helps you grasp the basics of using 1-2-3—enabling you to begin creating your own worksheets (or modify existing worksheets created by others) with a minimum of effort. You don't even need to be familiar with computers—keyboard basics are covered, as well as how to install 1-2-3 if it is not already installed on your computer.

1-2-3 Release 3.1 QuickStart, 2nd Edition, is a step forward in the evolution of how a book is organized and structured. The book uses a tutorial approach, taking you through important concepts step-by-step, describing all the fundamentals you need to know about the program. The text supplies essential information and provides comments on what you see. Many illustrations help guide you through procedures or clarify difficult concepts.

Learning any new program can be an intimidating experience. *1-2-3 Release 3.1 QuickStart*, 2nd Edition, is designed to help shorten your learning curve by allowing you to learn basic concepts quickly. Whether you are new to 1-2-3 or have tried unsuccessfully to learn the program, you will find *1-2-3 Release 3.1 QuickStart*, 2nd Edition, a quick way to learn the fundamentals of 1-2-3.

What Does This Book Contain?

The chapters in *1-2-3 Release 3.1 QuickStart*, 2nd Edition, are organized to take you from basic information to more sophisticated tasks, including printing presentation-quality reports and creating graphs.

Chapter 1, "An Overview of 1-2-3," shows you the wide range of 1-2-3's capabilities. You explore how 1-2-3 can be used for spreadsheet, graphics, and database applications.

Chapter 2, "Getting Started," explains how to start and leave 1-2-3, and teaches you the basics about using the keyboard and a mouse, understanding the screen display for single- and multiple-worksheet applications, and utilizing 1-2-3's help features.

Chapter 3, "Introducing Worksheet Basics," teaches you about the fundamental tasks of using a spreadsheet. You learn how 1-2-3 fits into the realm of integrated software and discover how to enter and edit data, move around in the worksheet, select commands from menus, and save and retrieve files.

Chapters 4, 5, and 6 cover all the basic concepts you need to begin creating 1-2-3 worksheets. Chapter 4, "Working with Ranges," teaches you how to use the range commands and specify ranges, and shows you step-by-step how to perform formatting tasks. Chapter 5, "Building a Worksheet," shows you how to use the worksheet commands to improve the appearance of the worksheets you develop. And Chapter 6, "Modifying a Worksheet," explains how to modify your worksheet by moving and copying cell contents, and finding and replacing the contents of cells.

Chapter 7, "Using Functions," introduces you to 1-2-3's selection of built-in functions for performing a variety of calculations. Among the functions illustrated are those for performing mathematical, statistical, and logical calculations.

Chapter 8, "Printing Reports," shows you how to set print specifications and organize your data for printing. You also learn to hide columns and rows, control paper movement, enhance a report by adding headers and footers, and change the page layout.

In Chapter 9, "Printing with Wysiwyg," you learn about the Release 3.1 add-in feature Wysiwyg, which provides a "What-you-see-is-what-you-get" display. Wysiwyg offers presentation-quality printing techniques such as the use of different font styles and sizes, including graphs along with data in your printed output, and shading, outlining, or underlining selected ranges.

Chapter 10, "Managing Files," describes how to use passwords to protect your worksheets, how to work with multiple files in memory, and how to link cells between different files. This chapter also explains how to delete and list your files, as well as how to import files from other software programs (such as dBASE) into 1-2-3.

Chapter 11, "Creating and Printing Graphs," teaches you how to produce graphs with 1-2-3. This chapter takes you from selecting graph types to adding titles and legends and other options. In addition, you learn to set and change print specifications and save graphs before printing.

Chapter 12, "Enhancing Graphs with Wysiwyg," shows you how to use the Release 3.1 Wysiwyg add-in to greatly enhance your 1-2-3 graphs by adding colors and freehand objects, editing text, resizing the graphs, and rotating objects.

Chapter 13, "Managing Data," explains how to use 1-2-3 for database management. You learn to create and modify a database, sort and search specific records, and work with external databases from other programs.

Chapter 14, "Understanding Macros," gives you an introduction to the concept of simple keystroke macros. The chapter teaches you to plan, position, create, name, and edit simple macros. Also included are macros you can use to start your own macro library.

The book concludes with an appendix that shows you how to install 1-2-3 Release 3.1.

Who Should Use This Book?

1-2-3 Release 3.1 QuickStart, 2nd Edition, is designed to be a quick guide for new 1-2-3 users. Whether you are sitting down with 1-2-3 for the first time or have tried many times to learn enough about 1-2-3 to use it efficiently, *1-2-3 Release 3.1 QuickStart*, 2nd Edition, gives you enough information to get you started quickly. The book highlights important concepts and takes you through important information by providing steps and explanations interwoven with examples and illustrations.

What Do You Need To Run 1-2-3 Release 3.1?

There are no prerequisites for using this book or for using 1-2-3. The assumption is, of course, that you have the software, the hardware, and a desire to learn to use the program.

The system requirements for running 1-2-3 Release 3.1 include the following:

- At least an IBM AT or compatible computer. This includes computers with 80286, 80386, 80386SX, and 80486 microprocessors.
- A hard disk drive with at least 5M available disk space.
- DOS version 3.0 or later.
- At least 1M of available RAM. If you frequently keep other programs in memory while using 1-2-3 (such as pop-up menus and desktop utilities), you may need at least 2M of available RAM.
- An EGA, VGA, high resolution CGA, or Hercules graphics adapter for the Wysiwyg display.
- *Optional*: A printer. Refer to the Lotus 1-2-3 Release 3.1 documentation for a complete list of supported printers.
- *Optional*: A mouse, mouse software, and a graphics monitor and graphics card that support the use of a mouse.

What Is New in 1-2-3 Release 3.1?

This book discusses some of the new features available with Release 3.1 of 1-2-3. This version of 1-2-3 has been enhanced with such additional features as the following:

- Wysiwyg, a what-you-see-is-what-you-get spreadsheet publishing add-in, is the primary new feature of Release 3.1. Wysiwyg lets you add different fonts, shadow boxes, colors, boldface, underlining, outlining, and shading to selected ranges of data. Graphics can be greatly enhanced by resizing and rotating images, adding objects and freehand drawings, and selecting from a palette of 224 colors. You can combine text and graphics on one page and the image you create on the screen matches your printed output.
- Mouse support, which (with Wysiwyg in memory) enables you to use a mouse to select commands and files, move the cell pointer, and specify ranges.
- Microsoft Windows-compatibility, which enables you to access 1-2-3 from within the Windows environment.
- Virtual-memory management, enabling you to build even larger worksheets without having to add memory to your system.

Note: All of the significant enhancements added to Release 3 are included with Release 3.1. These include the following capabilities: multiple worksheets within a single file, multiple files in memory, viewing three worksheets or files on-screen, creating instant graphs, the ability to read data directly from other database programs, background printing, search and replace, and keystroke recording for building macros quickly.

Learning More About 1-2-3

After you learn the fundamentals presented in this book, you may want to learn more advanced applications of 1-2-3. Que Corporation has a full line of 1-2-3 books you can use. Among these are the following:

Using 1-2-3 Release 3.1, 2nd Edition, is a reference book that provides comprehensive coverage of all aspects of using 1-2-3 (Releases 3 and 3.1) and Wysiwyg. A quick command reference and tear-out command chart are included with this book.

1-2-3 Release 3.1 Quick Reference is an affordable, compact reference to the most commonly used Release 3.1 commands and functions. This is a handy book to keep near your computer when you need to quickly find the purpose of a command and the steps for using it.

1-2-3 Database Techniques contains concepts and techniques to help you create 1-2-3 database applications. With an emphasis on Release 3 features, this book introduces database fundamentals, compares 1-2-3 with traditional database programs, offers numerous applications tips, and discusses add-in programs.

All of these books can be found in better bookstores worldwide. In the United States, you can call Que Corporation at 1-800-428-5331 to order books or to obtain further information.

Where To Find More Help

You can use 1-2-3's context-sensitive Help feature to answer some of your questions while working with 1-2-3. Using Help is explained and illustrated in Chapter 2, "Getting Started." Also, you can refer to the appropriate sections of the Lotus documentation provided with the 1-2-3 program.

Should all else fail, contact your computer dealer, or Lotus Customer Support at 1-800-223-1662. In Canada, contact Lotus Customer Support at 1-800-668-8236.

For more information on how to use DOS commands, new computer users can benefit from reading Que's *MS-DOS QuickStart*, 2nd Edition.

Conventions Used in This Book

A number of conventions are used in *1-2-3 Release 3.1 Quickstart*, 2nd Edition, to help you learn the program. This section provides examples of these conventions to help you distinguish among the different elements in 1-2-3.

References to keys are as they appear on the keyboard of the IBM Personal Computer and most compatibles. The function keys, F1 through F10, are used for special situations in 1-2-3. In the text, the function key name and the corresponding function key number are usually listed together, such as Graph (F10).

Direct quotations of words that appear on the screen are spelled as they appear on the screen and are printed in a `special typeface`. Information you are asked to type is printed in **boldface**. The slash and the first letter in each command from the 1-2-3 menu system also appear in boldface: **/R**ange Format Currency. Also, the colon and the first command letter of Wysiwyg commands are in boldface: **:T**ext Edit. Elements printed in uppercase include range names (SALES), functions (@SUM), modes (READY), indicators (CAP), and cell references (A1..G5 and B:C4).

Conventions that pertain to macros deserve special mention here:

1. Single-character macro names (Alt-character combinations) appear with the backslash (\) and single-character name in lowercase: \a. In this example, the \ indicates that you press the Alt key and hold it down while you also press the A key.

2. 1-2-3 menu keystrokes in a macro line appear in lowercase: /rnc.

3. Range names within macros appear in uppercase: /rncSALES.

4. In macros, representations of direction keys, such as {DOWN} and {NEXTSHEET}; function keys, such as {CALC}; and editing keys, such as {DEL}, appear in uppercase letters and are surrounded by braces.

5. Enter is represented by the tilde (~).

When two keys appear together and are hyphenated, such as Ctrl-Break, press and hold down the first key as you also press the second key. Other key combinations, such as Alt-F4, are pressed in the same manner. When two keys appear together and are not hyphenated, such as End Home, the first key is pressed and released before the second key is pressed.

Within the tables and step-by-step instructions, some keys appear similar to actual keys on the keyboard. Blue lines point out the most important areas of the illustrations.

Examples that use a mouse are provided as an alternative to using the keyboard to perform a similar function. A mouse is not required to use Release 3.1 and Wysiwyg efficiently. However, with practice, you may find that using a mouse will allow you to complete routine tasks more quickly and accurately.

Note: All screens included in this book were captured with the Wysiwyg add-in active. Most screens also display a worksheet grid (added with the Wysiwyg command **:Display Options Grid Yes**). Chapter 2 explains how to load Wysiwyg into memory temporarily, as well as how to configure your system to load and invoke Wysiwyg automatically each time you start 1-2-3.

An Overview of 1-2-3

1

Before you put your fingers on the keyboard to start using 1-2-3, you need to know the range of capabilities of this software package. If you are inheriting a spreadsheet created by someone else, coming up to speed with 1-2-3 may require little more of you than simply entering data. If, on the other hand, someone has handed you the 1-2-3 package and said, "Prepare a sales forecast for product A," your task may seem a bit intimidating. Whether you are an experienced or a novice spreadsheet user, this chapter shows you some of the many features of 1-2-3 and describes how they can fit into your day-to-day tasks.

As you read through this chapter, ask yourself which of the 1-2-3 features you will use most often. Will you be maintaining an accounts receivable spreadsheet? Will you perform consolidations with 1-2-3's capability to work with multiple worksheets in a single file and multiple files in your computer's memory? Perhaps your department is in charge of setting up a database to track inventory. Will you be responsible for printing reports and graphs? Whatever the application, read the appropriate overview sections closely, and look for chapter references at the ends of these sections for the chapters in the book that deal more specifically with that topic.

Learning how 1-2-3 functions as a spreadsheet

Understanding basic spreadsheet concepts

Discovering the graphics capabilities of 1-2-3

Knowing how 1-2-3 handles data management tasks

Introducing macros as timesaving shortcuts

1

Key Terms in This Chapter

Electronic spreadsheet	The electronic replacement for the accountant's pad.
Worksheet	The 1-2-3 spreadsheet.
Wysiwyg	An acronym for "what-you-see-is-what-you-get"—the name of the spreadsheet publishing add-in provided with Release 3.1.
Direction keys	The keys that allow movement within the 1-2-3 worksheet—including PgUp, PgDn, Home, End, Tab, and the arrow keys.
Cell	The intersection of a row and a column in the 1-2-3 worksheet.
Cell pointer	The highlighted bar that allows you to enter data within the worksheet area.
Formula	An action performed on a specified cell or group of cells. For example, +A1+B1 sums the contents of cells A1 and B1.
Function	A shorthand method of using formulas. For example, instead of typing the formula +A1+B1+C1+D1+E1, you can use the @SUM function @SUM(A1..E1).
Command	A menu selection used to carry out an operation within the worksheet.

Whether you are an experienced computer user who is new to 1-2-3, or you are using a computer for the first time, you can quickly grasp the fundamentals of 1-2-3. If you start by learning the most basic concepts of 1-2-3 and then gradually build on your knowledge and experience, you will be amazed by how easily you can learn the program. If, however, you jump right in and start using string functions or macros right away, you may find yourself running into snags. This book uses an easy, step-by-step approach to demonstrate the fundamental tasks you can perform with 1-2-3.

What Is a Spreadsheet?

Sometimes known as a ledger sheet or accountant's pad, a spreadsheet is a specialized piece of paper on which information is recorded in columns and rows. The multiple worksheet and file capabilities of Releases 3 and 3.1 extend this analogy further—providing multiple accounting worksheets that you can use simultaneously. Spreadsheets usually contain a mix of descriptive text and accompanying numbers and calculations. Typical business applications include balance sheets, income statements, inventory status reports, sales reports, and consolidations that use multiple worksheets.

Although you may be unfamiliar with business applications for spreadsheets, you already use a rudimentary spreadsheet if you keep a checkbook. Similar to an accountant's pad, a checkbook register is a paper grid divided by lines into rows and columns. Within this grid, you record the check number, the date, a transaction description, the check amount, any deposits, and a running balance.

NUMBER	DATE	DESCRIPTION OF TRANSACTION	PAYMENT/DEBT (−)	FEE (IF ANY) (−)	DEPOSIT/CREDIT (+)	BALANCE $1000 00
1001	9/3/89	Department Store Credit	51 03			948 97
1002	9/13/89	Electric	95 12			853 85
1003	9/14/89	Grocery	74 25			779 60
1004	9/15/89	Class Supplies	354 57			425 03
	9/16/89	Deposit			250 00	675 03
1005	9/21/89	Telephone	49 43			625 60

A manual checkbook register.

What happens when you make an invalid entry in your checkbook register or when you have to void an entry? Such procedures are messy because you have to erase or cross out entries, rewrite them, and recalculate everything. The limitations of manual spreadsheets are apparent even with this simple example of a checkbook register.

For complex business applications, the dynamic quality of an electronic spreadsheet such as 1-2-3 is indispensable. You can change one number and recalculate the entire spreadsheet in an instant. Entering new values is nearly effortless. Performing calculations on a column or row of numbers is accomplished with formulas—usually the same type of formulas that calculators use.

Compare the manual checkbook register to the following electronic one. Notice that the electronic checkbook register, which is displayed with the Wysiwyg spreadsheet publishing add-in of Release 3.1, is set up with columns and rows.

1

Columns are marked by letters across the top of the spreadsheet; rows are numbered along the side. Each transaction is recorded in a row, the same way you record data in a manual checkbook.

An "electronic" checkbook register

```
A:F8: (,2) [W11] +F7-D8+E8                                      READY

 A      A          B            C                   D        E         F
 1   CHECK #     DATE        DESCRIPTION           PAYMENT  DEPOSIT   BALANCE
 2   ----------------------------------------------------------------------
 3               01-Apr-90   Beginning balance              $1,000.00 $1,000.00
 4   1001        03-Apr-90   Department store credit  51.03            948.97
 5   1002        13-Apr-90   Electric                 95.12            853.85
 6   1003        14-Apr-90   Grocery                  74.25            779.60
 7   1004        15-Apr-90   Class supplies          354.57            425.03
 8               16-Apr-90   Deposit                          250.00   675.03
 9   1005        21-Apr-90   Telephone                49.43            625.60
10   1006        23-Apr-90   Clothing store           62.35            563.25
11   *********************** APRIL TOTALS            $686.75 $1,250.00 ***************
12   1007        02-May-90   Grocery                  65.83            497.42
13               07-May-90   Deposit                          275.00   772.42
14   1009        10-May-90   Department store credit  50.00            722.42
15   1009        10-May-90   Electric                 75.34            647.08
16   1010        15-May-90   Bookstore                95.24            551.84
17   1011        21-May-90   Hardware store           31.24            520.60
18               21-May-90   Deposit                          250.00   770.60
19   1012        24-May-90   Grocery                  85.21            685.39
20   *********************** MAY TOTALS              $402.86  $525.00  ***************
```

Assigning column letters, row numbers, and worksheet letters lends itself well to creating formulas. The formula +F7–D8+E8 in the upper left corner of the electronic checkbook translates to:

Previous BALANCE minus PAYMENT plus DEPOSIT

As you can see from this simple example, formulas enable you to establish mathematical relationships between values stored in certain places on your spreadsheet. You can make changes to a spreadsheet and quickly see the results. In the electronic checkbook, if you delete an entire transaction (row), the spreadsheet automatically recalculates itself. You can also change an amount and not worry about recalculating your figures, because the electronic spreadsheet updates all balances.

If you forget to record a check or deposit, using 1-2-3 you can insert a new row at the location of the omitted transaction and enter the information. Subsequent entries are moved down one row, and the new balance is automatically calculated. Inserting new columns is just as easy. Indicate where you want the new column to go, and 1-2-3 inserts a blank column at that point, moving existing information to the right of that column.

What if you want to know how much you have spent at the local department store since the beginning of the year? With a manual checkbook, you have to look for each check written to the store and total the amounts. Not only does this task take considerable time, but you may overlook some of the checks. An electronic checkbook can sort your checks by description so that all similar transactions are together. You then create a formula that totals all the checks written to the department store.

This simple checkbook example demonstrates how valuable an electronic spreadsheet is for maintaining financial data. Although you may choose not to use 1-2-3 to balance your personal checkbook, an electronic spreadsheet is an indispensable tool in today's modern office.

The 1-2-3 Electronic Spreadsheet

1-2-3 has a number of capabilities, but the foundation of the program is the electronic spreadsheet. The framework of this spreadsheet contains the graphics and data-management elements of the program. You can produce graphics quickly through the use of simple menu commands. Some graphs can even be displayed automatically by pressing a single key. Data management and macro programming occur in the standard row and column spreadsheet layout.

In addition to the multiple worksheet and file-linking capabilities provided with 1-2-3 Releases 3 and 3.1, two more dynamic features are offered in Release 3.1: Wysiwyg (an acronym for "what-you-see-is-what-you-get") and mouse control. Wysiwyg is an add-in program providing state-of-the-art desktop publishing features for enhancing on-screen and printed 1-2-3 worksheets and graphics. With Wysiwyg you can create presentation-style reports and graphics in minutes. When Wysiwyg is active in Release 3.1, you can use a mouse to quickly move around one or more worksheets, select commands and files, and specify ranges.

The importance of the worksheet as the basis for 1-2-3 cannot be overemphasized. The commands for the related features of 1-2-3 are initiated from the same 1-2-3 main menu as the spreadsheet commands, and all the commands have the same format. For example, all the commands for graphics display refer to data in the spreadsheet, and they use this data to draw graphs on the screen. For easy data management, the database is composed of records that are actually rows of cell entries in a spreadsheet. Similarly, macros and advanced macro commands are statements placed in adjacent cells in out-of-the-way sections of a worksheet or in their own files. When Wysiwyg is active in Release 3.1, you have access to an additional menu—the Wysiwyg menu—which enables you to enhance the on-screen image and the printed output.

1

1-2-3's integrated electronic spreadsheet replaces traditional financial modeling tools, reducing the time and effort needed to perform even sophisticated accounting tasks.

```
A:F7: (C2) [W11] @PMT(F4,F6/12,F5)                          READY
```

A	A	B	C	D	E	F	G
1	TERMS OF LOAN						
2							
3		First Payment Date				31–Jul–90	
4		Principal Borrowed				$10,000	
5		Term in Months				48	
6		Beginning Interest Rate				10.50%	
7		Payment				$256.03	
8							
9	==						
10	AMORTIZATION SCHEDULE						
11	==						
12							
13	Payment	Payment		Current	Interest	Principal	Principal
14	Number	Date	Rate	Payment	Portion	Portion	Balance
15	1	31–Jul–90	10.50%	$256.03	$87.50	$168.53	$9,831.47
16	2	31–Aug–90	10.50%	$256.03	$86.03	$170.01	$9,661.46
17	3	30–Sep–90	10.50%	$256.03	$84.54	$171.50	$9,489.96
18	4	31–Oct–90	10.50%	$256.03	$83.04	$173.00	$9,316.97
19	5	30–Nov–90	10.50%	$256.03	$81.52	$174.51	$9,142.45
20	6	31–Dec–90	10.50%	$256.03	$80.00	$176.04	$8,966.42

```
                                                            CALC
```

1-2-3's three-dimensional worksheet capability allows a single file to contain up to 256 worksheets for better organization of worksheet information.

```
A:B5: (C0) [W11] +B:B5+C:B5                                 READY
```

C	A	B	C	D	E
1					
2	PRODUCT 2	Jan	Feb	Mar	Apr
3	===				
4	Sales				
5	Northeast	$9,336	$10,300	$10,207	$9,177
6	Southeast	5,272	7,300	8,490	9,381

B	A	B	C	D	E
1					
2	PRODUCT 1	Jan	Feb	Mar	Apr
3	===				
4	Sales				
5	Northeast	$21,000	$23,070	$26,500	$31,200
6	Southeast	15,300	15,329	17,402	18,000

A	A	B	C	D	E
1					
2	REGIONAL INCOME REPORT	Jan	Feb	Mar	Apr
3	===				
4	Sales				
5	Northeast	$30,336	$33,370	$36,707	$40,377
6	Southeast	20,572	22,629	25,892	27,381

The Size of 1-2-3's Worksheet

With 256 columns and 8,192 rows, a single 1-2-3 worksheet contains more than 2,000,000 cells. The rows are sequentially numbered from 1 to 8192. The columns are lettered from A to Z, AA to AZ, BA to BZ, and so on, to IV for the last column. In addition, each file you create can contain up to 256 separate worksheets—each lettered from A to IV.

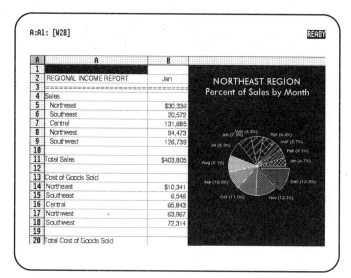

A:A1: [W28]   READY

A	A	B	NORTHEAST REGION
1			
2	REGIONAL INCOME REPORT	Jan	
3	==========================		
4	Sales		
5	Northeast	$30,336	
6	Southeast	20,572	
7	Central	131,685	
8	Northwest	94,473	
9	Southwest	126,739	
10			
11	Total Sales	$403,805	
12			
13	Cost of Goods Sold		
14	Northeast	$10,341	
15	Southeast	6,546	
16	Central	65,843	
17	Northwest	63,967	
18	Southwest	72,314	
19			
20	Total Cost of Goods Sold		

With 1-2-3's graphics capabilities, you can create seven different graph types, and see worksheets and graphics together on-screen.

A:A1: [W25] 'Physical Inventory: Hand tool stores #3   READY

A	A	B	C	D	E	F
1	Physical Inventory: Hand tool stores #3					
2						
3		ON HAND	UNIT OF	UNIT	INVENTORY	P.O.
4	DESCRIPTION	QUANTITY	ISSUE	COST	VALUE	DATE
5	Hammer, claw	2	EA	6.75	13.50	02-Aug-89
6	Screwdriver, flat tip set	17	EA	9.95	169.15	
7	Tack hammer, 3/8 drive	24	EA	4.30	103.20	
8	Air hammer, magnetized	1	KT	67.32	67.32	24-Aug-89
9	Phillips screwdriver set	8	EA	8.73	69.84	
10	Hack saw	3	EA	11.89	35.67	08-Sep-89
11	Counter sink set, 10 pc	3	KT	13.44	40.32	15-Sep-89
12	Drop light, 100 foot	4	EA	17.99	71.96	
13	Square	0	EA	37.50	0.00	15-Sep-89
14	Hex wrench	2	KT	14.50	29.00	
15	Wrench, box/open	0	ST	46.70	0.00	31-Oct-89
16	Pipe wrench, 14 inch	4	EA	56.70	226.80	
17						
18						
19						
20						

1-2-3's database commands and statistical functions help to manage and manipulate data.

Although the 1-2-3 worksheet contains so many columns and rows, there are some limitations to using the entire sheet. If you imagine storing just one character in each of the 2,097,152 available cells, you end up with a worksheet that is far larger than the 640K maximum random-access memory (RAM) of an IBM PC.

1

A good way to visualize the default 1-2-3 worksheet is as a giant sheet of grid paper that is about 21 feet wide and 171 feet high.

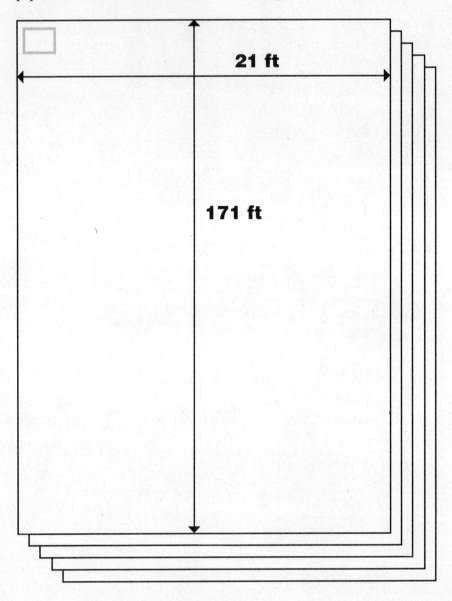

21 ft

171 ft

For 1-2-3 Releases 3 and 3.1, the program alone requires at least 1M of RAM. 1-2-3 needs this amount of RAM because the program keeps in its memory all cell formats, worksheet and command ranges, print options, and graph settings.

The Worksheet Window

Because the 1-2-3 grid is so large, you cannot view the entire worksheet on the screen at one time. The screen thus serves as a window onto a small section of the worksheet. To view other parts of the worksheet, use the direction keys (Tab, PgUp, PgDn, Home, End, and arrow keys) to move the cell pointer around the worksheet. When you reach the edge of the current window, the window shifts to display different parts of the worksheet.

To illustrate the window concept, imagine cutting a one-inch square hole in a piece of cardboard. If you place the cardboard over this page, you will be able to see only a one-inch square piece of text. The rest of the text is still on the page; the data is simply hidden from view. When you move the cardboard around the page (the same way that the window moves when the direction keys are used), different parts of the page become visible.

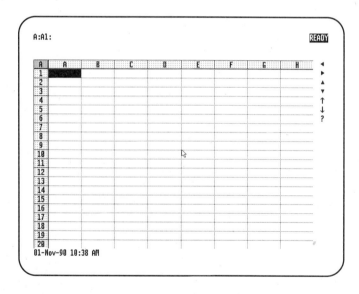

The default 1-2-3 worksheet displays 8 columns (each 9 characters wide) and 20 rows.

You can change the default number of columns that are displayed by narrowing or widening one or more of the columns. In Release 3.1, Wysiwyg allows you to change the height of individual rows, as well as change the width of columns.

In Releases 3 and 3.1, when you create multiple worksheets, one behind another, you can easily page through the worksheets using special combinations of the keys on your keyboard. In addition, you can view portions of three consecutive worksheets on-screen at one time.

Cells

Each row in a 1-2-3 worksheet is assigned a number; each column is assigned a letter. The intersections of the rows and columns are called cells. Cells are identified by their row and column coordinates. The cell located at the intersection of column A and row 15, for example, is called A15. The cell at the intersection of column X and row 55 is named X55. If you decide to open two or more worksheets, a cell is further identified by a letter prefix indicating which worksheet the cell is on, for example, A:K12, B:K12, and C:K12. The letter A represents the first worksheet in the stack; B, the second; C, the third, and so on. Cells can be filled with two types of information: labels, which are text entries; or values, which consist of numbers and/or formulas.

A cell pointer allows you to enter information into the current cell. In 1-2-3, as in most spreadsheets, the cell pointer looks like a highlighted rectangle on the computer's screen. The cell pointer typically is one row high and one column wide.

In this example, the cell pointer highlights a numeric value in cell D7.

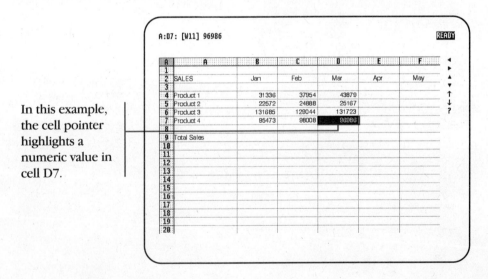

18

The direction keys on your keyboard move the cell pointer around the worksheet. Release 3.1, however, offers you another way to move the cell pointer: by moving a mouse and clicking a mouse button. These methods of navigating the 1-2-3 worksheet are discussed in detail in Chapter 2.

Formulas

1-2-3 enables mathematical relationships to be created between cells. Suppose, for example, that the cell named C1 contains the following formula:

    +A1+B1

Cell C1 then displays the sum of the contents of cells A1 and B1. (The + sign before A1 tells 1-2-3 that what you have entered into this cell is a formula, not text.) The cell references serve as variables in the equation. Each time you modify the contents of cell A1 and/or B1, the sum in cell C1 automatically reflects these changes. For example, if A1 originally contains the value 4 and B1 the value 3, the formula computes to 7. If you change the value in A1 to 5, the formula automatically recalculates to 8.

You now know that only a portion of the entire 1-2-3 worksheet is visible at one time. Although you see only values in the cells, 1-2-3 stores all the data, formulas, and formats in memory. A simple 1-2-3 worksheet displays values, not the formulas "behind" them.

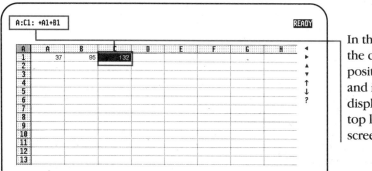

In this example, the cell pointer is positioned on C1, and its formula is displayed at the top left of the screen.

1

"What If" Analysis

1-2-3 enables you to play "what if" with your model. After you have built a set of formulas into 1-2-3's worksheet, you can modify and recalculate the worksheet with amazing speed, using several sets of assumptions. If you use only paper, a pencil, and a calculator to build your model, every change requires recalculation of each correlation. If the model has 100 formulas and you change the first one, you must make 100 manual calculations so that the change flows through the entire model. If you use a 1-2-3 worksheet, however, the same change requires pressing only a few keys—the program does the rest. This capability permits you to perform extensive "what if" analyses.

Suppose, for example, that you want to forecast sales for two products over the next six months and to recalculate the revenue totals for different discounts.

If you enter 50% into B1 as the discount rate, 1-2-3 calculates the sales price figures.

	A:B1: (P8) [W9] 0.5								READY
	A	**B**	**C**	**D**	**E**	**F**	**G**	**H**	
1	Discount	50%							
2									
3									
4			Jan	Feb	Mar	Apr	May	Jun	
5									
6	Product 1								
7	Unit Price	14.95							
8									
9	Unit Sales		104	120	115	133	142	135	
10	Sales price		$777	$897	$860	$994	$1,061	$1,009	
11									
12									
13	Product 2								
14	Unit Price	17.95							
15									
16	Unit Sales		95	87	105	94	102	113	
17	Sales Price		$853	$781	$942	$844	$915	$1,014	
18									
19									
20									

With 1-2-3's Undo feature, you have even greater flexibility in playing the "what if" game with your worksheet. By inserting a new value, you can see the implications throughout the worksheet. If the results are unsatisfactory, simply use the Undo feature (press Alt-F4), and the worksheet returns to its previous condition. (The Undo feature is explained in greater detail in Chapter 3.)

Functions

You can create simple formulas, involving only a few cells, when you refer to the cell addresses and use the appropriate operators (+, –, /, and *). Each formula is stored in memory, and only its value appears in the cell.

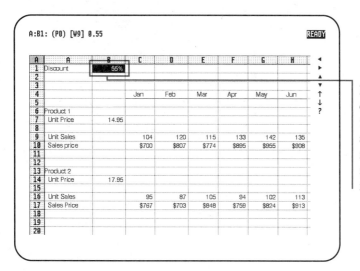

| A:B1: (P0) [W9] 0.55 | | | | | | | READY |

	A	B	C	D	E	F	G	H
1	Discount	55%						
2								
3								
4			Jan	Feb	Mar	Apr	May	Jun
5								
6	Product 1							
7	Unit Price	14.95						
8								
9	Unit Sales		104	120	115	133	142	135
10	Sales price		$700	$807	$774	$895	$955	$908
11								
12								
13	Product 2							
14	Unit Price	17.95						
15								
16	Unit Sales		95	87	105	94	102	113
17	Sales Price		$767	$703	$848	$759	$824	$913
18								
19								
20								

If you change the discount rate from 50% to 55%, 1-2-3 automatically recalculates the new sales price figures.

You can create complex formulas by using 1-2-3's functions. These shortcuts help you make common mathematical computations with a minimum of typing. Functions act as abbreviations for long and cumbersome formulas. The @ symbol signals 1-2-3 that an expression is a function. For instance, you can use the shorter @SUM function @SUM(A1..E1) instead of typing the formula +A1+B1+C1+D1+E1. Building applications would be difficult without 1-2-3's capability for calculating mathematical, statistical, logical, financial, and other types of formulas. 1-2-3 comes with many functions that help you create complex formulas for a wide range of applications, including business, scientific, and engineering applications. (You learn more about 1-2-3's functions in Chapter 7.)

Commands

1-2-3 has many commands that help you perform a number of tasks in the worksheet. You use these commands at every phase of building, using, and enhancing a worksheet application. In worksheet cells, you enter data in the form of text, numbers, and formulas. You perform operations on this data with Release 3.1's two command menus: the 1-2-3 main menu and the Wysiwyg menu. Commands from the 1-2-3 menu are activated by pressing the slash (/) key, and commands from the Wysiwyg menu are executed by pressing the colon (:) key. Each of these actions displays a separate menu of commands from which you choose the command you want. Although some of the options appearing on the main 1-2-3 and Wysiwyg menus are identical, they are used for different purposes. (Chapter 3 tells you how commands are selected, and Chapter 4 begins a discussion of specific commands.)

1

The 1-2-3 main menu enables you to format the worksheet; name ranges; erase, copy, and move data; perform calculations; store files; protect worksheet cells; protect files with passwords; use add-in programs; print the worksheets; and do much more, such as create graphs and retrieve files. The Wysiwyg menu lets you enhance the appearance of text and numbers you enter, as well as enhance the look of reports and graphs you print.

A 1-2-3 worksheet enhanced with lines, shadows, and fonts selected with Wysiwyg commands.

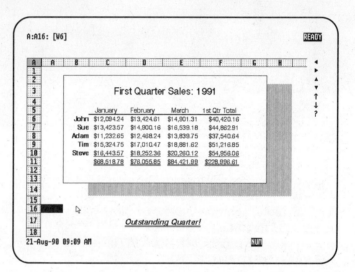

1-2-3 Graphics

The spreadsheet alone makes 1-2-3 a powerful program with all the functions many users need. The addition of graphics features, which accompany the spreadsheet, makes 1-2-3 an even more valuable tool that you can use to present data visually and to conduct graphic "what if" analyses. You can quickly design and alter graphs as worksheet data changes—without using commands to redefine a modified graph. This means that you can change graphs almost as fast as 1-2-3 recalculates data.

1-2-3 Releases 3 and 3.1 have seven basic graph types: bar, stacked bar, line, pie, XY (scatter), HLCO (high-low-close-open), and mixed (bar and line). You can represent up to six ranges of data on a single graph (except for pie graphs and scatter diagrams). You also have great flexibility in your choices of graph formats, colors, shading, grids, scaling, labels, titles, and subtitles. In Release 3.1, Wysiwyg allows you to choose colors from a palette of 224 colors, and also enables you to add symbols and other graphic elements to your graphs. (The process of creating and printing graphs is covered in Chapter 11; using Wysiwyg to enhance the appearance of graphs is the subject of Chapter 12.)

The line graph is the default graph type for 1-2-3. That is, if you do not specify a particular type, 1-2-3 displays the data as a line graph.

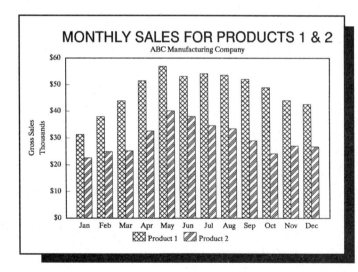

The bar graph, typically used to show the trend of numeric data across time, often compares two or more data items.

1

The XY (scatter) graph compares one numeric data series to another, determining whether one set of values appears to depend on the other.

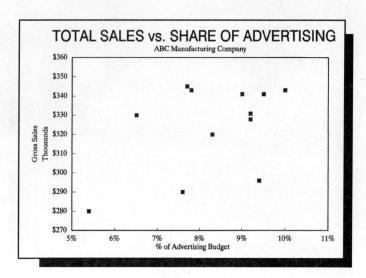

The stacked-bar graph includes two or more data series that total 100 percent of a specific category.

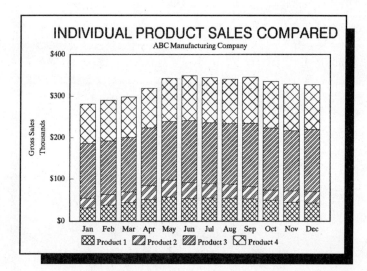

1

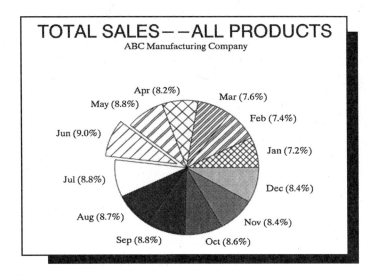

The pie graph shows only one data series, in which the parts total 100 percent of a specific numeric category.

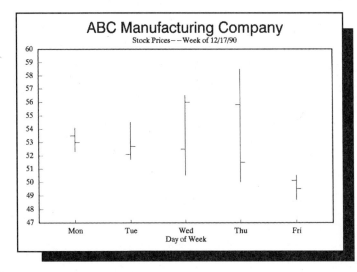

The HLCO (high-low-close-open) graph is used to track stock performance over time.

25

1

The mixed graph shows a combination bar-and-line graph to track two different types of data, such as sales performance against advertising expenses.

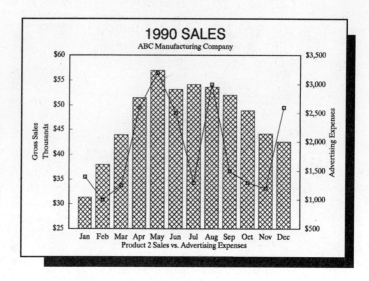

1-2-3 Database Management

The row and column structure that stores data in a spreadsheet program is similar to the structure of a relational database. When you use 1-2-3's true database management commands and functions, you can sort, query, extract, and perform statistical analyses on data in up to 8,191 records (with up to 256 fields of information). In Releases 3 and 3.1 you can also access and easily manipulate data from an external database, such as dBASE. 1-2-3 can access these external databases whether they are located on disks, CD-ROMs, or mainframe computers.

One important advantage of a 1-2-3 database over independent database programs (like dBASE) is that its database commands are similar to others used in the 1-2-3 program. For example, you can add database records and fields with commands that are available in the worksheet part of 1-2-3. This similarity allows you to learn the use of the 1-2-3 database manager along with the rest of the 1-2-3 program.

A row in 1-2-3 is equal to a record in a conventional database. In that record, you might store a client's name, address, and phone number.

1-2-3 has sophisticated facilities for performing sort and search operations. You can sort the database on any number of items and by numerous criteria, and you can find a particular record with a few simple keystrokes. These and other 1-2-3 database operations are explained further in Chapter 13.

1

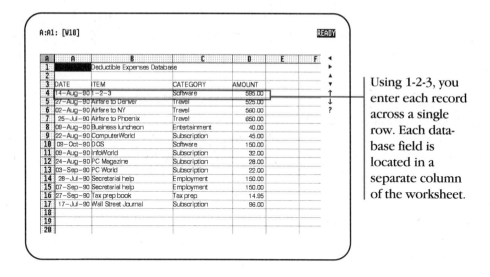

Using 1-2-3, you enter each record across a single row. Each database field is located in a separate column of the worksheet.

Printing Reports and Graphs

By using 1-2-3's commands for printing, you can print worksheet data and graphs for either draft review or more formal presentations. You can send data and graphs directly from 1-2-3 to the printer or save worksheet data in a text file so that the data can be incorporated in another program, such as a word processing program. You also can save data and graphs to a file format that retains your selected report enhancements (such as boldface type, underlining, and italic) so that you can print later with an operating system command.

With the printing commands from the Wysiwyg menu, you can combine text and graphics anywhere on a page for sophisticated, publishing-quality output; you can preview all pages, including text and graphics, before printing; you can print in portrait or landscape mode on laser printers; and you can automatically compress a worksheet print range to fit a single page.

Releases 3 and 3.1 enable you to print a single worksheet range, as well as a range that spans multiple worksheets or 1-2-3 main menu files. You can also print a series of noncontiguous ranges from the same worksheet or from different worksheets or files.

For greater printer control, 1-2-3 lets you stop your printer to change the paper, ribbon, or toner cartridge and then resume printing at the point where the printer stopped. Also, you can cancel printing from the main printing menu. One of the major benefits of printing with Releases 3 and 3.1 is that as soon as you

1

start printing, you can return to work within the worksheet on-screen while the printing job runs in the background. (Chapters 8 and 9 discuss printing in greater detail.)

Macros and the Advanced Macro Commands

Two other features help to make 1-2-3 the most powerful and popular integrated spreadsheet, graphics, and database program. When you use 1-2-3's macros and advanced macro commands, you can automate and customize 1-2-3 for your particular applications.

By using 1-2-3 macros, you can reduce multiple keystrokes to a two-keystroke operation. Simply press two keys, and 1-2-3 does the rest—whether you're formatting a range, creating a graph, or printing a worksheet.

You can create a macro, for example, to format a cell to display currency. Suppose that you place numbers requiring currency and other different formats in several adjacent cells. Because 1-2-3 formats cells in range groups (contiguous cells) you have to use quite a few keystrokes to format several adjacent cells with different formats. You can create a macro that will, in effect, "record" your actions as you specify the keystrokes to format a cell to display currency. Then, after you assign a name and save the macro, you can format a cell with currency by simply typing a single keystroke combination instead of seven keystrokes.

Think of simple keystroke macros as the building blocks for advanced macro command programs. When you begin to add advanced macro commands to simple keystroke macros, you control and automate many of the actions required to build, modify, and update 1-2-3 models. At the most sophisticated level, 1-2-3's advanced macro commands are used as a full-fledged programming language for developing custom business applications.

When you use 1-2-3's advanced macro commands, you see what kind of power is available for your 1-2-3 applications. For the applications developer, the set of advanced macro commands is much like a programming language (such as BASIC), but the programming process is significantly simplified by all the powerful features of 1-2-3's spreadsheet, database, and graphics commands. Macros and the advanced macro commands are discussed in Chapter 14.

28

Summary

In this overview chapter, you saw how one of the simplest examples of a spreadsheet—a checkbook register—becomes easier to use in electronic form. You were introduced to the features of 1-2-3's spreadsheet, such as its size, the worksheet window, cells, and the concept of multiple worksheets within a single file. The enhancement features available with the Wysiwyg add-in in Release 3.1 were discussed. You learned how 1-2-3 worksheets are designed and can be recalculated for "what if" analyses. And you learned about 1-2-3's powerful commands and functions, with which you can build formulas for a wide variety of applications.

The chapter gave you a glimpse of 1-2-3's flexible graphics capabilities. You had a quick view of 1-2-3's database and its power for managing and reporting on stored data. The chapter touched on macros and the advanced macro commands, which allow you to automate and customize your use of 1-2-3 and its graphics and database capabilities.

Specifically, you learned the following key information about 1-2-3:

- The 1-2-3 worksheet contains 8,192 rows and 256 columns. All rows on the 1-2-3 worksheet are assigned numbers. All columns on the 1-2-3 worksheet are assigned letters from A to IV. A file can contain up to 256 worksheets. Each worksheet is lettered from A to IV.

- Wysiwyg, an add-in program provided with Release 3.1, enables you to enhance 1-2-3 worksheets and graphics through commands available in a separate Wysiwyg menu.

- A cell is the intersection of a column and a row. Cells are identified by their column and row coordinates (A2, B4, and G10, for example). When multiple worksheets are used, cells are identified by preceding the column and row coordinates with the worksheet letter (B:A2, C:B4, and D:G10, for example).

- The cell pointer is the highlighted rectangle that enables you to enter data into the worksheet.

- Formulas can be used in 1-2-3 to create mathematical relationships between cells. 1-2-3's functions are built-in formulas that automatically perform complex operations.

- 1-2-3 commands are initiated by pressing the slash (/) key to display a menu. In Release 3.1, Wysiwyg commands can be initiated by pressing the colon :. You can also use a mouse to access the 1-2-3 and Wysiwyg menus in Release 3.1.

1

■ 1-2-3's graphics capability enables you to create seven types of graphs from worksheet data. These graphs can be displayed and printed with worksheet data. Many options are available for enhancing the appearance of these graphs.

■ Each row of a 1-2-3 database corresponds to a database record. With the database features available in 1-2-3, you can perform complex operations, such as sorting and searching records. You can also access information from external databases, such as dBASE.

■ Macros and the advanced macro commands deliver exceptional power to 1-2-3 by automating both simple and complex tasks into two-keystroke operations.

The power of 1-2-3 is best realized by actually using the program. The next chapter shows you how to get started.

Getting Started

2

This chapter helps you get started using 1-2-3 and Wysiwyg. Before you begin, be sure that 1-2-3 is installed on your computer system. Follow the instructions in your Lotus documentation or the Appendix of this book to complete the installation. Even if you have already installed 1-2-3, you may want to check the appendix to make sure you haven't overlooked any important details.

The information in this chapter will be useful if you are new to computers or 1-2-3. If you find this introductory material too basic and want to begin using the 1-2-3 worksheet immediately, you can skip to Chapter 3. However, if you want to begin using Wysiwyg, you should first read the sections of this chapter that relate to Wysiwyg.

Starting 1-2-3 and Wysiwyg

Exiting 1-2-3

Learning the keyboard

Understanding mouse terminology

The 1-2-3 and Wysiwyg screens

Introducing multiple worksheets

The 1-2-3 help system and tutorial

2

Key Terms in This Chapter

1-2-3 Access System	The 1-2-3 menu system that links all of 1-2-3's different programs. It includes options for accessing the main 1-2-3 program, modifying installation settings, and translating files between 1-2-3 and other software programs.
Alphanumeric keys	The keys in the center section of the computer keyboard. Most of these keys resemble those on a typewriter keyboard.
Numeric keypad	The keys on the right side of the Personal Computer AT and enhanced keyboards. This keypad is used for entering and calculating numbers, for moving the cell pointer in the worksheet area, or for moving the cursor and menu pointer in the control panel.
Function keys	The 10 keys on the left side of the Personal Computer AT keyboard or the 12 keys at the top of the enhanced keyboard. These keys are used for special 1-2-3 functions, such as accessing help, editing cells, and recalculating the worksheet.
Control panel	The area above the reverse-video border of the 1-2-3 worksheet. The control panel contains three lines that display important information about the contents of a cell, command options and explanations, special prompts or messages, and mode indicators.
Worksheet area	The largest part of the 1-2-3 screen, where data that has been entered into the worksheet is displayed.
Status line	A single line located at the bottom of the 1-2-3 screen that displays information such as the file-and-clock indicator, error messages, and status and key indicators.
Icon panel	The area on the right side of the screen containing seven icons for use with a mouse. The icon panel appears only when Wysiwyg is loaded and a mouse driver is installed.
Perspective view	The screen display (resulting from the /Worksheet Window Perspective command) that shows parts of three worksheets or files on-screen at one time.

Starting 1-2-3

Getting into 1-2-3 is quite easy. Starting from DOS, you can go directly to a fresh worksheet or you can enter 1-2-3 by way of the 1-2-3 Access System, which provides several menu options. The following discussion shows you both ways to begin.

Starting 1-2-3 from DOS

Starting 1-2-3 directly from DOS is a shortcut and requires less memory than using the 1-2-3 Access System. In the following instructions, the assumption is that the 1-2-3 program is on drive C of your hard disk, in a subdirectory named \123R3. To start 1-2-3, follow these steps:

1. With the C> system prompt displayed on your screen, change to the \123R3 directory by typing **cd\123R3** and pressing ⏎Enter.
2. Start 1-2-3 by typing **123** and pressing ⏎Enter.

After a few seconds, the 1-2-3 logo appears. The logo remains on-screen for a few seconds. Then the worksheet is displayed, and you're ready to use 1-2-3.

Starting 1-2-3 from the 1-2-3 Access System

Lotus devised the 1-2-3 Access System as a way to move quickly between the programs in the 1-2-3 package. For example, the 1-2-3 Access System has a series of menus that enable you to translate between 1-2-3 and other programs, such as dBASE, Symphony, and Multiplan.

To start the 1-2-3 Access System, follow these steps:

1. With the C> system prompt displayed on your screen, change to the \123R3 directory by typing **cd\123R3** and pressing ⏎Enter.
2. Start the 1-2-3 Access System by typing **lotus** and pressing ⏎Enter.

The 1-2-3 Access System screen appears.

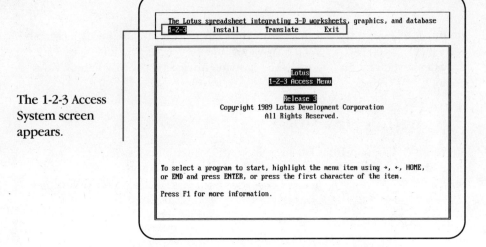

The **1**-2-3 option of the Access System screen starts the main 1-2-3 program.

The **I**nstall option accesses the 1-2-3 Install program, which changes the options set during installation.

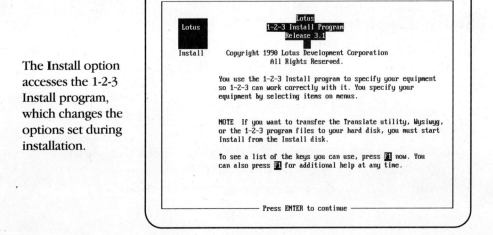

See the Lotus documentation for specific installation instructions.

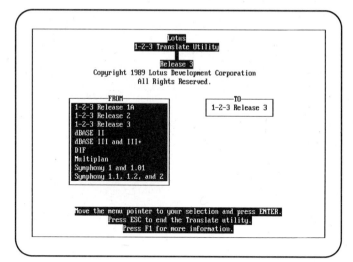

The **Translate** option accesses the 1-2-3 Translate utility, which allows you to translate files between 1-2-3 and other software programs.

The Translate utility provides links among different versions of 1-2-3, and also between 1-2-3 and other software programs, such as dBASE, Symphony, and Multiplan. An example of using the Translate utility is included in Chapter 10 of this book. For further information, refer to the Lotus documentation or Que's *Using 1-2-3 Release 3.1,* 2nd Edition.

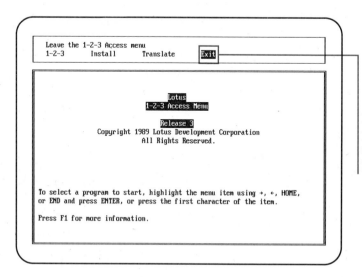

Exit quits the 1-2-3 program and returns you to DOS.

Starting Wysiwyg

2

To take advantage of the new Wysiwyg features of 1-2-3 Release 3.1, you have to load the Wysiwyg add-in into memory. This multistep procedure must be performed each time you start 1-2-3 unless you set 1-2-3 to load and invoke Wysiwyg automatically. You can save time by configuring your system to load and invoke Wysiwyg automatically. The automatic and manual methods of loading Wysiwyg are presented in the following sections.

Starting Wysiwyg Automatically

If you choose the automatic method of loading and invoking Wysiwyg, you need to complete the following procedure only once. Wysiwyg will then load and invoke each time you access 1-2-3. This automatic method is the recommended procedure for accessing Wysiwyg.

To configure your system to load and invoke Wysiwyg automatically, follow these steps:

1. From within 1-2-3, access the Add-in menu by pressing and holding the `Alt` key and pressing `F10`.

2. Select **Settings System Set**.

   Note: To select commands from menus, press the first letter of the command (`S` `S` `S` in this example) or highlight the command and press `Enter`. If you use a mouse and Wysiwyg is loaded, point to a command and click the left mouse button. Chapter 3 discusses command selection in detail.

3. From the list of files that appears, type or highlight **WYSIWYG.PLC** and press `Enter`.

4. Select **Yes**.

5. Select **No-key**.

   Note: Although you can choose to attach Wysiwyg with a function key, it is recommended that you select the **No-key** option.

   Once you make your selection, the Wysiwyg copyright screen appears, and then the worksheet appears.

6. To save this setting, select **Update**.

7. To return to the 1-2-3 worksheet, select **Quit**.

The next time you start 1-2-3, and each time thereafter, the 1-2-3 worksheet loads, and then Wysiwyg loads automatically.

Starting Wysiwyg Manually

If you choose the manual method of loading Wysiwyg, you must complete the entire procedure that follows each time you access 1-2-3. This option is preferable if you will seldom need the spreadsheet publishing features offered with Wysiwyg (requiring additional memory and processing time).

To load Wysiwyg manually, follow these steps:

1. From within 1-2-3, access the Add-in menu by pressing and holding the [Alt] key and pressing [F10].

2. Select **Load**.

   Note: To select commands from menus, press the first letter of the command or highlight the command and then press [↵Enter]. If you use a mouse and Wysiwyg is loaded, point to a command and click the left mouse button.

3. From the list of files that appears, type or highlight **WYSIWYG.PLC** and press [↵Enter].

4. Select **No-key**.

   Note: Although you can choose to attach Wysiwyg to a function key, it is recommended that you select the **No-key** option.

   Once you make your selection, the Wysiwyg copyright screen appears, and then the Wysiwyg worksheet appears.

5. To return to the 1-2-3 worksheet, select **Quit**.

Exiting 1-2-3

There are two ways to leave the 1-2-3 program to return to DOS: by using the **/System** command or the **/Quit** command. Both commands are accessible from the 1-2-3 main menu. To access the main menu, press the slash (/) key. The **System** and **Quit** commands are listed among the options on this menu.

Using /System To Leave 1-2-3 Temporarily

The **/System** command returns you to the DOS system prompt, but you do not exit the 1-2-3 program—your departure is only temporary.

2

To leave 1-2-3 temporarily, follow these steps:

1. Call up the 1-2-3 menu by pressing ⌙/⌐.

   Note: Mouse users can access a menu by moving the mouse pointer to the area above the worksheet frame. This action automatically generates the 1-2-3 or Wysiwyg menu (depending on which menu was used most recently). Click the right mouse button to toggle between the two menus.

The 1-2-3 main menu is displayed.

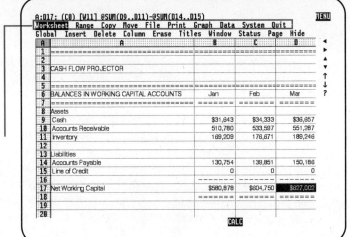

2. Select **System**.

   Note: To select commands from menus, press the first letter of the command or highlight the command and press ⌐Enter⌐. If you use a mouse and Wysiwyg is loaded, point to a command and click the left mouse button.

3. While at the DOS level, perform the desired system operation (such as changing drives or directories, copying files, or accessing other programs).

4. To return to the 1-2-3 worksheet, type **exit** and press ⌐Enter⌐. You return to the current worksheet, in the exact place where you issued the **/System** command.

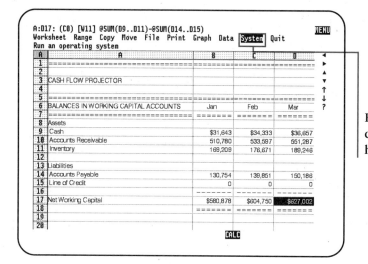

Here, the **System** command is highlighted.

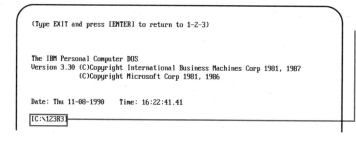

After you select the **System** command, the DOS prompt is displayed.

The Advantages of Using /System

/System is a useful command when you need to check the amount of space remaining on a disk before you copy a file to it, or when you want to see how large a particular worksheet is before you load the worksheet. /System saves you the trouble of quitting the 1-2-3 program, issuing the appropriate DOS commands, and then getting back into the worksheet.

The /System command is particularly useful for giving you access to your system's file-handling commands. For example, if you want to save your worksheet but your data diskette is full, you can use the /System command to suspend 1-2-3 processing while you prepare a new diskette using the DOS FORMAT command. After you return to 1-2-3 by typing **exit** and pressing Enter, you can save your worksheet to the new diskette with /**File S**ave.

2

The Limitations of Using /System

You should be aware of two potential problems in using the /System command. First, if you have a large worksheet that takes up most of memory, the /System command may fail because there is not enough memory to run another program. If the /System command fails, 1-2-3 displays the error message `Cannot Invoke DOS`, and the ERROR indicator appears in the upper right corner of the screen.

The second problem is that certain programs you run from 1-2-3 by using the /System command may cause 1-2-3 to abort when you try to return by typing **exit** and pressing Enter. You can safely invoke from 1-2-3 DOS file-management commands such as FORMAT, COPY, DELETE, DIRECTORY, and DISKCOPY, and most business-application programs. Starting one of the many memory-resident utility programs, however, causes 1-2-3 to abort when you type **exit** and press Enter. Before trying to use the /System command during an important 1-2-3 session, take a few minutes to experiment with the programs you want to use.

Using /Quit To Exit 1-2-3

The /Quit command from the 1-2-3 main menu allows you to exit both the worksheet and the 1-2-3 program. You are asked to verify this choice before you exit 1-2-3, because your data will be lost if you quit 1-2-3 without saving your file. To exit 1-2-3, follow these steps:

1. Call up the 1-2-3 menu by pressing ⌐/⌐ or moving the mouse pointer to the top of the screen (and clicking the right mouse button to switch to the 1-2-3 menu, if necessary).

   Note: If you haven't saved your file, do so now by selecting File **S**ave. Next, enter the file name. If the file name already exists, select **R**eplace to update the current file. Then press ⌐/⌐ again before proceeding with the next step. The process of saving files is explained in the next chapter.

2. Select **Q**uit.

   Note: To select commands from menus, press the first letter of the command or highlight the command and then press ⌐↵Enter⌐. If you use a mouse and Wysiwyg is loaded, point to a command and click the left mouse button.

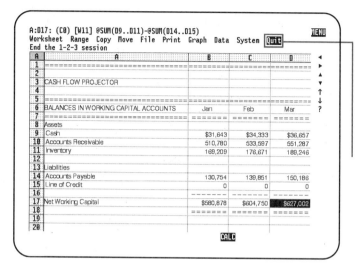

Here, the **Quit** command is highlighted.

3. If you have already made changes to the file since it was last saved and you want to abandon these changes, select **Yes**.

   Otherwise, if you need to save the file before exiting 1-2-3, select **No**. Then use /**File S**ave to save your file before you exit 1-2-3.

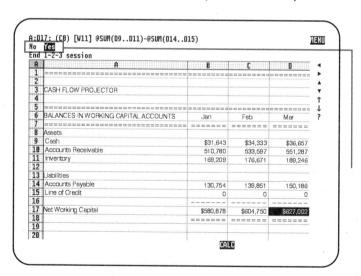

You are asked to verify that you want to exit.

Note: If you started 1-2-3 from the 1-2-3 Access System, you return to the Access System when you select /**Quit**. To exit the 1-2-3 Access System and return to the operating system, select **Exit**.

2

If you have made changes in your current worksheet but have not saved them with /File Save, 1-2-3 beeps and displays a reminder when you try to exit.

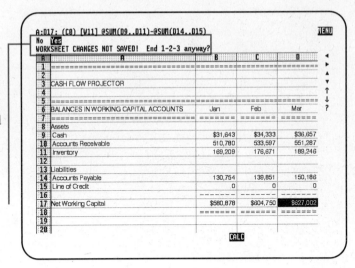

Learning the Keyboard

Before you begin learning 1-2-3, you need to get to know your keyboard. Each of the two most popular keyboards consists of these sections: the alphanumeric keys in the center, the numeric keypad with direction keys on the right, and the function-key section on the left or across the top. The enhanced keyboard, the standard keyboard for all new IBM personal computers and most compatibles, also has a separate grouping of direction keys.

The original IBM Personal Computer AT keyboard

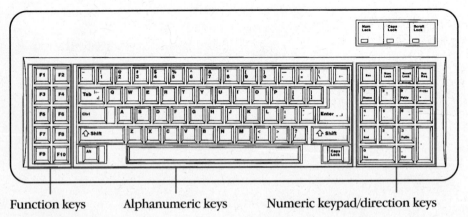

Function keys   Alphanumeric keys   Numeric keypad/direction keys

The enhanced keyboard Function keys

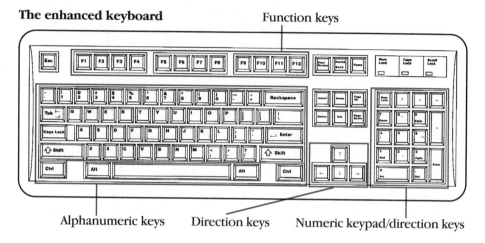

Alphanumeric keys   Direction keys   Numeric keypad/direction keys

The Alphanumeric Keys

Most of the alphanumeric keys on the computer keyboard perform the same actions as those on a typewriter. In 1-2-3 several of the keys have special functions. For example, the slash (/) key accesses the 1-2-3 menu, the colon (:) key accesses the Wysiwyg menu, and the period (.) key defines a range of cells. Table 2.1 highlights each of these important keys.

Table 2.1
The Special Keys

Key	Action
Esc	Returns to the previous menu; erases the current entry during editing, or the range or command specification; returns from a help screen; clears error messages from the screen.
Tab	Moves the cell pointer one screen to the right.
Shift Tab	Moves the cell pointer one screen to the left.
Caps Lock	Activates capitalization of all alphabetic characters when keys for those characters are pressed. Displays the CAP indicator in the status line when active. Remains in effect until you press this key again (acts as a toggle).
Shift	Changes lowercase letters and characters to uppercase. When not in Num Lock mode, enables typing of numbers on the numeric keypad.

43

2

Table 2.1 (continued)

Key	Action
Ctrl	When used with the left- or right-arrow key, moves the cell pointer one screen to the left or right in READY mode or moves the cursor five characters to the left or right in EDIT mode; when used with Break, returns 1-2-3 to READY mode or halts execution of a macro.
Alt	When used with other keys, invokes macros, activates Record mode, performs an Undo, or executes other commands.
Space bar	Inserts a space within a cell entry; moves the menu pointer one item to the right when selecting commands from a menu.
Backspace	Erases the previous character in a cell during cell definition; erases the character to the left of the cursor during editing.
Enter	Accepts an entry into a cell or selects a highlighted menu command.
.	Defines a range of cells or anchors one corner when defining a range. Also used as a decimal point.
:	Calls up the Wysiwyg menu; also used to anchor one corner when defining a range.
/	Calls up the 1-2-3 main menu; also functions as a division sign in formulas.
<	Used as an alternative to the slash (/) for calling up the 1-2-3 main menu; also used in logical formulas.
Scroll Lock	Scrolls the entire window one row or column when the cell pointer is moved. Displays the SCROLL indicator in the status line when active. Acts as a toggle.
Pause	Pauses a macro, a recalculation, and some commands until you press any key. On AT keyboards, Pause is Ctrl Num Lock.
Num Lock	Activates the numeric representation of keys in the numeric keypad. Displays the NUM indicator in the status line when active. Acts as a toggle.

2

Table 2.1 (continued)

Key	Action
[Ins]	Changes 1-2-3 from insert mode to overtype mode during editing. When pressed, causes the OVR indicator to be displayed in the status line and enables new characters to overwrite existing text. Acts as a toggle.
[Del]	Deletes the character above the cursor during the editing process.

The Numeric Keypad and Direction Keys

The keys in the numeric keypad are used mainly for data entry and for moving the cell pointer or cursor. The enhanced keyboard has separate direction keys for this movement function.

To use the numeric keypad to enter numbers rather than to position the cell pointer or cursor, you can either press Num Lock before and after you enter the numbers and then move to the next cell, or hold down Shift only when you press the number keys.

Neither way is ideal, because you have to switch between functions. If you have an enhanced keyboard, you don't have this problem because your keyboard has a special set of direction keys that have no other purpose. If you don't have an enhanced keyboard, you can create a simple macro that lets you enter numbers and move to the next cell without having to press Shift or Num Lock.

The Function Keys

You use the function keys F1 through F10 for special tasks, such as accessing Help, editing cells, and recalculating the worksheet. Although the enhanced keyboard has 12 function keys (F1 through F12), 1-2-3 uses only the first 10 of these. A plastic function-key template that describes each key's function on the enhanced keyboard is provided with the Lotus software. Another version of the template is provided for users with AT or compatible keyboards. Table 2.2 explains the operations of the function keys.

2

Table 2.2
The Function Keys

Key	Action
F1	(**Help**) Accesses 1-2-3's on-line help facility.
F2	(**Edit**) Shifts 1-2-3 to EDIT mode.
F3	(**Name**) Displays a list of names in the control panel any time a command or formula can accept a range name or file name. Pressing F3 a second time switches to a full-screen display. After @ is entered in a formula, displays a list of functions.
F4	(**Abs**) Changes a relative cell address into an absolute or a mixed cell address during cell definition (in POINT or EDIT mode). In Wysiwyg, also predefines a range—allowing multiple 1-2-3 and Wysiwyg commands to then be executed on that range.
F5	(**GoTo**) Moves the cell pointer to the specified cell coordinates (or range name).
F6	(**Window**) Moves the cell pointer to the other side of a split screen.
F7	(**Query**) Repeats the most recent /**Data Query** operation.
F8	(**Table**) Repeats the most recent /**Data Table** operation.
F9	(**Calc**) Recalculates all worksheets in memory. If entering or editing a formula, converts the formula to its current value.
F10	(**Graph**) Displays the current graph on-screen.

Understanding Mouse Terminology

In Release 3.1, to use a mouse with Wysiwyg, you have to load a mouse driver before starting 1-2-3. 1-2-3 does not provide the mouse driver; the company that manufactures the mouse provides the driver. Directions for adding a mouse driver are in the documentation you received with your mouse.

When you load Wysiwyg into memory, your mouse can replace some of the activities normally done from the keyboard. The mouse pointer, a small arrow appearing on-screen, points to the center of the screen when 1-2-3 is loaded with Wysiwyg. Pressing either the right or left mouse button enables you to use the mouse and mouse pointer to select commands, switch between the 1-2-3 and

2

Wysiwyg menus, move the cell and menu pointers, and select ranges. Before using the mouse, you should become familiar with additional terms such as point, click, click-and-drag, icon, and icon panel.

To *point* means to move the mouse until the tip of the arrow is pointing on something. For example, if you are instructed to point to (or highlight) cell B5, then you must move the mouse until the tip of the arrow is over cell B5.

When you *click* the mouse, you press and immediately release one of the two buttons on the mouse. (If your mouse has three buttons, only the two outside buttons are active. The center button is not used in 1-2-3.) Normally, you only click a mouse button after you point with the mouse. The left button on the mouse usually acts as the Enter key. The right button has two functions. The right button usually acts as the Esc key; if you are typing text into a cell, for example, pressing the right button erases the text from the edit line and returns 1-2-3 to READY mode. The second function of the right mouse button is to switch between the 1-2-3 menu and the Wysiwyg menu.

When installing 1-2-3, you can reverse the operations of the mouse buttons. That is, you can make the right button the Enter button and the left button the Esc/Switch menu button. This is helpful if you are left-handed because reversing the buttons enables you to use your index finger on the primary button and your middle finger on the secondary button.

Click-and-drag is a combination of pointing, clicking, and moving the mouse. You normally use this method to highlight a range of items at the same time. To click-and-drag, follow these steps:

1. Move the mouse pointer to the desired beginning location, such as the upper left corner of a range.
2. Press and hold the left mouse button; do not release the button at this time (this anchors the cell pointer).
3. Move the mouse to the desired ending location, such as the lower right corner of a range, and release the mouse button. The desired range is highlighted.
4. Click the left mouse button again to finish specifying the range.

For example, to select a range from B5 through D10, point to cell B5, press and hold the left mouse button and point to cell D10; then release the left mouse button and press the left button again.

Chapter 4 discusses how to use the mouse to specify a three-dimensional range in multiple-worksheet applications.

2

An *icon* is a character that represents an action. These characters are displayed on the right side on the screen—within the *icon panel*. There are four triangles, two arrows, and one question mark. When you point and click on one of the icons, you invoke an action.

Clicking any of the triangles has the same action as pressing one of the arrow keys; the cell pointer moves one cell in the direction indicated by the triangle. Clicking the arrows is the same as pressing Ctrl-PgUp or Ctrl-PgDn to access another worksheet in a multiple-worksheet application. The up arrow represents the Ctrl-PgUp key combination and the down arrow represents the Ctrl-PgDn key combination. Finally, clicking the question mark selects Help, just as if you pressed the Help (F1) function key.

When Wysiwyg and a mouse are installed, the seven mouse icons appear within the icon panel—on the right side of the screen.

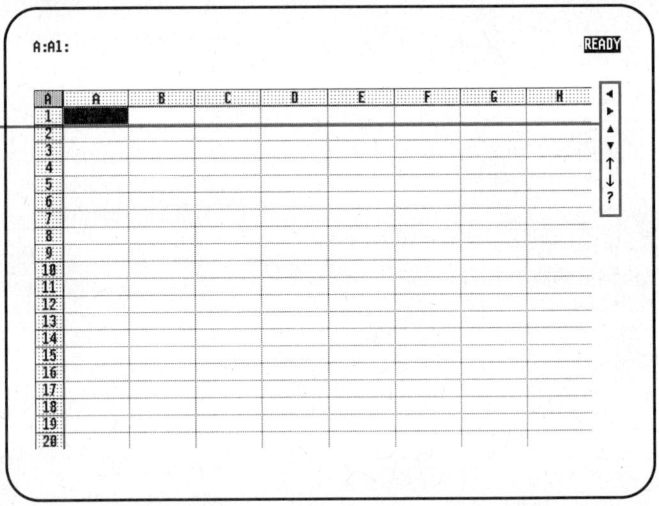

Understanding the 1-2-3 Screen

The main 1-2-3 display is divided into three parts: the control panel at the top of the screen, the worksheet area, and the status line at the bottom of the screen. (As discussed in the previous section, the Wysiwyg screen also includes an icon panel with seven icons, located on the right side of the screen). A reverse-video border separates the control panel from the worksheet area. This border contains the letters and numbers that mark the columns and rows of the worksheet area. The sections that follow describe each of these areas in more detail.

The Control Panel

The *control panel*, the area above the reverse-video border, can show three lines of information. The control panel contains data about the current cell as well as the menu commands.

```
A:F7: (C2) [W11] @PMT(F4,F6/12,F5)                           EDIT
@PMT(F4,F6/12,F5)_
```

	A	B	C	D	E	F	G
1	TERMS OF LOAN						
2	===						
3		First Payment Date				30−Nov−90	
4		Principal Borrowed				$10,000	
5		Term in Months				48	
6		Beginning Interest Rate				10.50%	
7		Payment				$256.03	
8							
9	===						
10	AMORTIZATION SCHEDULE						
11	===						
12							
13	Payment	Payment	Current		Interest	Principal	Principal
14	Number	Date	Rate	Payment	Portion	Portion	Balance
15	1	30−Nov−90	10.50%	$256.03	$87.50	$168.53	$9,831.47
16	2	30−Dec−90	10.50%	$256.03	$86.03	$170.01	$9,661.46
17	3	30−Jan−91	10.50%	$256.03	$84.54	$171.50	$9,489.96
18	4	28−Feb−91	10.50%	$256.03	$83.04	$173.00	$9,316.97
19	5	30−Mar−91	10.50%	$256.03	$81.52	$174.51	$9,142.45
20	6	30−Apr−91	10.50%	$256.03	$80.00	$176.04	$8,966.42

The first line of the control panel shows information about the current cell (the cell highlighted by the cell pointer).

In this example, the control panel includes the following cell information:

```
A:F7: (C2) [W11] @PMT(F4,F6/12,F5)
```

This line displays the address of the cell (A:F 7), followed by the display format chosen (C2 for *Currency, 2* decimal places), the column width (11 characters), and the content of the cell (in this case, a formula). When applicable, this line also shows the protection status of the cell (U if unprotected or PR if protected). The upper right corner of the first line always displays the mode indicator (EDIT in this example). Mode indicators are explained in detail later in this chapter. When Wysiwyg is active, information applicable to Wysiwyg, such as row height, graph, and text format, also appears on this line.

The second line of the control panel contains any characters that are being entered or edited or displays the options in a menu. The preceding example shows a formula to be edited.

The third line of the control panel provides explanations of the current menu item or the next hierarchical menu. As you move the menu pointer from one item to the next in a command menu, the explanation on the third line of the control panel changes to correspond with the highlighted option.

2

This example
shows the 1-2-3
main menu with
the Worksheet
menu option
highlighted. The
third line of the
control panel
displays the
/Worksheet
commands.

```
A:F7: (C2) [W11] @PMT(F4.F6/12.F5)                              MENU
Worksheet  Range  Copy  Move  File  Print  Graph  Data  System  Quit
Global  Insert  Delete  Column  Erase  Titles  Window  Status  Page  Hide
   A         B          C         D         E         F         G
 1  TERMS OF LOAN
 2 ================================================================
 3            First Payment Date                           30-Nov-90
 4            Principal Borrowed                             $10,000
 5            Term in Months                                      48
 6            Beginning Interest Rate                         10.50%
 7            Payment                                        $256.03
 8
 9 ================================================================
10  AMORTIZATION SCHEDULE
11 ================================================================
12
13  Payment   Payment    Current              Interest  Principal  Principal
14  Number    Date       Rate      Payment    Portion   Portion    Balance
15       1    30-Nov-90  10.50%    $256.03    $87.50    $168.53    $9,831.47
16       2    30-Dec-90  10.50%    $256.03    $86.03    $170.01    $9,661.46
17       3    30-Jan-91  10.50%    $256.03    $84.54    $171.50    $9,489.96
18       4    28-Feb-91  10.50%    $256.03    $83.04    $173.00    $9,316.97
19       5    30-Mar-91  10.50%    $256.03    $81.52    $174.51    $9,142.45
20       6    30-Apr-91  10.50%    $256.03    $80.00    $176.04    $8,966.42
```

The Worksheet Area

The largest part of the 1-2-3 screen is composed of the *worksheet area*. As
described in Chapter 1, the 1-2-3 worksheet consists of 256 lettered columns and
8,192 numbered rows, yet only a portion of the worksheet is displayed on the
screen at any time. All information entered into the worksheet is stored in a
cell—the intersection of a column and a row.

The Status Line

The status line is the bottom line of the 1-2-3 screen. This line normally displays
the current date and time, but you can change it to reflect the current file name
or to display neither date and time nor file name. The current date and time can
be displayed in the status line in two different formats. When certain types of
errors occur, the status line displays the appropriate error messages. This line
also contains any status or key indicators, described in the following sections.

The 1-2-3 Indicators

The 1-2-3 screen may display three different types of *indicators*. The mode
indicators appear in the upper right corner of the control panel. The status
indicators appear within the status line along the bottom of the screen, and the
key indicators appear within the status line in the lower right corner. The 1-2-3
indicators are summarized in table 2.3. The next few sections explain each of
these types of indicators.

Table 2.3
The 1-2-3 Indicators

Indicator	Description

The Mode Indicators

EDIT	F2 has been pressed, and a cell entry is ready to be edited.
ERROR	An error has occurred, or you used Ctrl Break to cancel a macro. 1-2-3 is waiting for you to press Esc or ↵Enter to clear the error message or to press F1 (Help) to discover information about the cause and possible correction.
FILES	1-2-3 is waiting for you to select a file name from the list of file names.
FIND	1-2-3 is in the middle of a /**Data Query F**ind operation and cannot respond to commands.
HELP	F1 (Help) has been pressed, and 1-2-3 is displaying a help screen.
LABEL	A label is being entered.
MENU	A list of command choices is displayed.
NAMES	1-2-3 is waiting for you to select from a list of range names, graph names, print-settings names, database drivers, external databases, or external table names.
POINT	Either 1-2-3 prompted you to select a range or you used the direction keys to specify a range while entering a formula.
READY	1-2-3 is waiting for a command or cell entry.
STAT	1-2-3 is displaying the status of the current worksheet.
VALUE	A number or formula is being entered.
WAIT	1-2-3 is in the middle of a command or process and cannot respond to other commands until the indicator disappears.

The Status Indicators

CALC	If the CALC indicator is in blue (or white reverse video on monochrome monitors), the file is set to manual recalculation and there has been a change since the last calculation. Press F9 (Calc) to recalculate the worksheet and clear the indicator.

51

2

Table 2.3 (continued)

Indicator	Description
	If the CALC indicator is in red (or white and flashing on monochrome monitors), the file is set to automatic recalculation and is in the middle of a background formula recalculation. You can continue to work, but the values of some formulas may change during the recalculation.
CIRC	A circular reference (a formula that refers to itself) has been found. The /**W**orksheet **S**tatus command displays the location of the circular reference.
CMD	A 1-2-3 macro is executing.
FILE	You pressed [Ctrl][End], the File key. When combined with an arrow key, the File key moves across multiple files in memory.
GROUP	The current file is in GROUP mode—you selected /**W**orksheet **G**lobal **G**roup **E**nable to modify multiple worksheets in a file at the same time.
MEM	Random-access memory is almost exhausted. If you continue to enter data, you can receive a `Memory full` error message.
PRT	Indicates a background print is in progress. Disappears when the print job is complete.
RO	The current file is read-only. The file can only be saved with a different name. Applies to files used on a network or multiuser system. Sometimes occurs if you run out of memory while reading a file.
SST	A macro is in single-step execution (STEP mode).
STEP	[Alt][F2] (Record) has been pressed, and you selected **S**tep to "step through" a macro one character or command at a time. When you start a macro, this indicator changes to SST.
ZOOM	You used /**W**orksheet **W**indow to split the screen into multiple windows, and then pressed [Alt][F6] to enlarge the current window to fill the entire screen. To return the display to multiple windows, press [Alt][F6] again.

The Key Indicators

CAP	[Caps Lock] has been pressed and is active—all letters are entered as uppercase. Acts as a toggle.

Table 2.3 (continued)

Indicator	*Description*
END	The ⌊End⌋ key has been pressed and is active, waiting for you to press a direction key. Acts as a toggle.
NUM	⌊Num Lock⌋ has been pressed and is active. You can use the numeric keypad to enter numbers without using ⌊⇧Shift⌋. Acts as a toggle.
OVR	The ⌊Ins⌋ key has been pressed while in EDIT mode—1-2-3 replaces any keystrokes above the cursor with the typed characters. Acts as a toggle.
SCROLL	⌊Scroll Lock⌋ has been pressed and is active. Whenever you use an arrow key, the entire window moves in the direction of the arrow. Acts as a toggle.

The Mode Indicators

One of 1-2-3's modes is always in effect, depending on what you are doing. The mode indicator is shown in reverse video in the upper right corner of the screen, within the control panel. For example, READY appears whenever data can be entered into the worksheet or whenever the menu can be invoked. VALUE is displayed as the mode indicator when you enter numbers or formulas; and LABEL appears when you enter letters, as in a title or label. You see the EDIT indicator after you press Edit (F2) in order to edit a formula or label in the control panel.

The Status Indicators

Other indicators report the status of the worksheet. They include general message indicators, such as CALC and GROUP, and warnings, such as CIRC and MEM. These indicators appear in reverse video along the bottom line of the screen. Note that when an error occurs, 1-2-3 displays a message in the lower left corner. To clear the error and get back to READY mode, press Esc or Enter.

The Key Indicators

The key indicators NUM, CAP, and SCROLL represent the keyboard's Num Lock, Caps Lock, and Scroll Lock keys, respectively. These keys are "lock" keys because they can temporarily lock the keyboard into a certain function. When a lock key is active, 1-2-3 displays the key's indicator in reverse video in the lower right corner of the screen. Many keyboards also use different lights that show when a particular lock key is active. Each lock key is a toggle, which means that pressing the key repeatedly turns its function alternately on and off. Therefore, to turn off a lock key that is on, you simply press it again.

Two other key indicators used within 1-2-3 are OVR for the Ins key and END for the End key. When OVR appears in reverse video at the bottom of the screen, you know that 1-2-3 is in overtype mode. That is, whatever you type while in EDIT mode replaces existing characters, numerals, or symbols.

Understanding the Wysiwyg Screen

The 1-2-3 and Wysiwyg screens are similar in structure. Both screens display the worksheet frame (column letters and row numbers), the mode indicator in the upper right corner, the clock (or file name) at the bottom left corner of the screen, and status and key indicators along the bottom of the screen. As with the 1-2-3 screen, the top three lines of the Wysiwyg screen comprise the control panel. The only differences in the Wysiwyg screen are the Wysiwyg format abbreviations that are displayed between the current cell address and the cell contents.

For example, {Bold} indicates boldface type.

A:A7:	{Bold}	[W14]	'Variable Margin			READY

	A	B	C	D	E	F
1	VARIABLE MARGIN WORKSHEET					
2						
3		QTR 1	QTR 2	QTR 3	QTR 4	TOTAL
4	Sales	130,855.00	170,382.38	179,583.80	243,683.90	724,505.08
5	Variable Costs	81,762.64	114,483.00	120,796.70	125,584.00	442,626.34
6						
7	Variable Margin	49,092.36	55,899.38	58,787.10	118,099.90	281,878.74
8						
9						
10						
11						
12						
13						
14						
15						
16						
17						
18						
19						
20						

As explained earlier, the right side of the Wysiwyg screen displays an icon panel for use with the mouse. Table 2.4 describes the function of each of these symbols. To select an icon, place the mouse pointer on the icon and click the left mouse button. Click and hold down the button to scroll continuously.

Table 2.4
The Wysiwyg Screen's Icon Panel

Symbol	Function
◄	Moves the cell pointer one cell to the left
►	Moves the cell pointer one cell to the right
▲	Moves the cell pointer up one cell
▼	Moves the cell pointer down one cell
↑	Moves the cell pointer to the next worksheet or file in memory
↓	Moves the cell pointer to the previous worksheet or file in memory
?	Activates a help screen

Introducing Multiple Worksheets

You use multiple-worksheet files in two basic situations. First, multiple-worksheet files are ideal for consolidations. If you need a worksheet for many departments, you can build a separate, identical worksheet for each department. Each worksheet is smaller and easier to understand and use than a large single worksheet that contains all the data for each department. One of the worksheets can be a consolidation that combines the data from the individual departments.

For example, you can put a formula in a cell in one worksheet that refers to cells in other worksheets. An example of this technique is found in the next chapter. Use multiple-worksheet files for any consolidations that contain separate parts, such as products, countries, or projects.

Second, you can use multiple-worksheet files to put separate sections of an application into separate worksheets. You can put input areas, reports, formulas, notes, assumptions and constants, and macros in separate worksheets. Each worksheet, which is therefore smaller and more manageable, can be customized for its particular purpose.

In effect, using multiple worksheets creates a set of separate worksheets for a large file. One important advantage this technique provides is that you can make changes to one worksheet without risking accidental changes to the other worksheets. When the entire file is comprised of one worksheet, you can insert or delete a row or column in one area and accidentally destroy part of another

2

area that shares the same row or column. With multiple-worksheet files, you can design each worksheet so that you can insert and delete rows and columns anywhere and not affect any other part of the file.

Another common error is to accidentally write over formulas that are part of input areas. With multiple worksheets, you can separate input areas and formulas so that this error is less likely.

Understanding the Display with Multiple Worksheets

You can change the screen to view one worksheet or multiple worksheets in different ways. The default screen display is a single window that shows part of one worksheet. You can issue the /Worksheet Window Perspective command to display parts of three worksheets or files at one time. This is called perspective view.

A file with three worksheets in perspective view.

When you display worksheets in perspective view, the current worksheet or file is the one that displays the cell pointer (worksheet A in this example). To return to a single-worksheet display, select the command /Worksheet Window Clear.

Accessing the 1-2-3 Help System and Tutorial

2

One of the biggest selling points of 1-2-3 is its user-friendliness. Lotus tries to ensure that the spreadsheet program is easy to learn and use. The program offers you two basic kinds of assistance: a context-sensitive help system available at the touch of a key, and the 1-2-3 Tutorial—printed documentation and actual worksheets that are provided with the 1-2-3 software.

The 1-2-3 Help System

1-2-3 has a context-sensitive help system. In other words, when you need clarification on a particular topic, you can press Help (F1) at any time and read the displayed information or select the topic you need from the list that appears. If you press Help (F1) while in READY mode, the Help Index appears. Choose any of the topics in the Help Index to get to the other help screens.

By pressing Backspace, you can again look at the preceding screen. The repeated use of Backspace takes you back to previous help screens. Press Esc at any time to return to your worksheet.

If you are working from the Wysiwyg command menu, pressing Help (F1) brings up the Wysiwyg help screen. This help facility is completely separate from the 1-2-3 help screens. Therefore, if you want help on a Wysiwyg feature, you should display the Wysiwyg menu first.

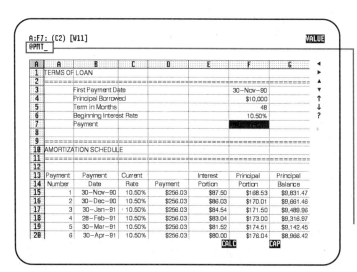

To access the help screen for a specific financial function, you can type the @ sign and function name—for example, @PMT. Then press F1 (Help).

2

A context-sensitive
screen about how
to use the @PMT
function appears.
To access the Help
Index, highlight
Help Index at the
bottom of the
screen and press
⏎Enter.

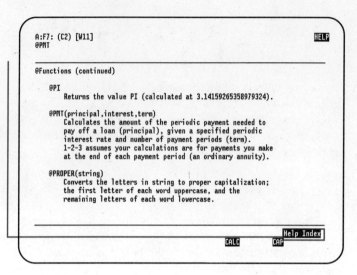

From the Help
Index, you can
choose many
different topics.

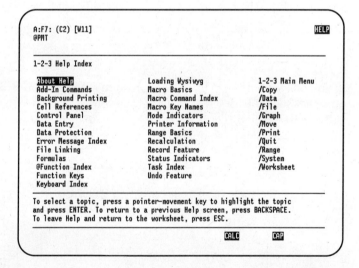

The 1-2-3 Tutorial

Lotus offers a self-paced series of lessons in a Tutorial manual, a book that comes
with the 1-2-3 documentation. The lessons are arranged in order of increasing
difficulty and build on each other. The Tutorial does not cover all of 1-2-3's
functions and commands, but it includes enough information to give you a basic
understanding of the program. The tutorial, however, does not provide any
assistance for users who want to use Wysiwyg or the mouse. Before you use the
Tutorial, you must successfully install 1-2-3 on your hard disk.

```
A:F7: (C2) [W11] @PMT(F4,F6/12,F5)                      HELP
Worksheet  Format  Graph  Print  Display  Special  Text  Named-Style  Quit
Column  Row  Page

Wysiwyg Help Index

About Wysiwyg Help     Macros in Wysiwyg        Wysiwyg Main Menu
Automatic Wysiwyg      Mouse Basics             :Display
Copying Formats        Moving Formats           :Format
Default Settings       Menus in Wysiwyg         :Graph
Display Modes          Printer Information      :Named-Style
Error Message Index    Ranges in Wysiwyg        :Print
Format File (.FM3)     Saving Wysiwyg Formats   :Special
Formatting Descriptions Text Editing Keys       :Text
Formatting Sequences   Text Formatting Options  :Worksheet
Graphics Editing Window Text Ranges
Icon Panel             Undo in Wysiwyg

To select a topic, click the topic with the left mouse button or use the
pointer-movement keys to highlight the topic and press ENTER. To return to
a previous Help screen, press BACKSPACE. To leave Help and return to the
worksheet, press ESC or press the right mouse button.
```

The Wysiwyg Help Index screen displays many topics to help you use Wysiwyg.

The best approach to using the Tutorial is to complete one or two lessons at a time. Then work with 1-2-3 for a while before you tackle the more advanced topics in subsequent lessons. After you feel comfortable with all the material in Chapter 1 (Lessons 1 through 6) of the Tutorial, you can try the other chapters. If necessary, you can learn about the more specialized topics, such as the database or macros, without going through all the preceding lessons.

Summary

This chapter presented the information you need to use 1-2-3 for the first time. You learned how to start and exit 1-2-3 from either DOS or the 1-2-3 Access System, and how to start and exit Wysiwyg. You also learned how to access the Install and Translate programs. The parts of the 1-2-3 screen and how 1-2-3 uses the keyboard and mouse also were presented. In addition, you learned how to use the on-line help facility and the 1-2-3 Tutorial.

Specifically, you learned the following key information about 1-2-3:

■ You can start 1-2-3 directly from DOS by typing **123** and pressing Enter from the \123R3 directory.

■ To start 1-2-3 from the 1-2-3 Access System (allowing entry into other 1-2-3 programs such as Install and Translate) type **lotus** (instead of **123**) and press Enter from the appropriate drive and directory.

2

- To take advantage of the new Wysiwyg features of 1-2-3 Release 3.1, you have to load the Wysiwyg add-in into memory. This procedure must be performed each time you start 1-2-3—unless you set 1-2-3 to load and invoke Wysiwyg automatically.

- The /System command enables you to leave 1-2-3 temporarily so that you can perform DOS commands. To return to the current 1-2-3 worksheet, type **exit** and press Enter from DOS.

- Use the /Quit command to exit the worksheet and the 1-2-3 program. 1-2-3 allows you the option of canceling this choice when changes are made to the worksheet since it was last saved.

- Most keyboards contain alphanumeric keys in the center of the keyboard, a numeric keypad and direction keys on the right side, and function keys on the left side or across the top.

- When you load Wysiwyg into memory, a mouse (if one is installed) can replace some of the activities normally done from the keyboard. Pressing either the left or right mouse button enables you to use the mouse to select commands, switch between the 1-2-3 and Wysiwyg menus, move the cell and menu pointers, and select ranges.

- The 1-2-3 screen consists of three different areas: the control panel (three lines at the top of the screen), the worksheet area (the major portion of the screen), and the status line (one line at the bottom of the screen). When Wysiwyg and a mouse are installed, the screen contains an icon panel with seven icons for use with the mouse (located on the right side of the screen).

- The mode indicator is always displayed in the top right corner of the screen. The status and key indicators are displayed at different times in the status line at the bottom of the screen.

- 1-2-3 provides a context-sensitive help system that you can access by pressing Help (F1). You can also access an index for both 1-2-3 and Wysiwyg with several options from which you can choose a particular topic.

- A 1-2-3 tutorial that teaches basic concepts and skills for using 1-2-3 is provided with the Lotus documentation. This tutorial—which does not cover using Wysiwyg or the mouse—is accompanied by sample worksheet files (located in your 1-2-3 program subdirectory).

Now that you are familiar with the 1-2-3 environment, you are ready to begin using 1-2-3 by entering data and formulas. The next chapter presents information on entering and editing data and formulas and moving around worksheets and files. Chapter 3 also presents the concept of multiple worksheets and information about using Wysiwyg.

Introducing Worksheet Basics

3

In Chapter 1, you learned that 1-2-3 is an integrated program that can do much more than make spreadsheet calculations. Depending on your business needs or assigned tasks, you can use 1-2-3 to create worksheets, generate presentation-quality reports, develop simple or complex databases, and produce graphics that illustrate worksheet data.

This chapter explores some of the simpler operations in 1-2-3: moving around the worksheet; selecting commands from menus; entering and editing data; using formulas and functions; and naming, saving, and retrieving files. This chapter also shows you how to use the mouse in Release 3.1 to navigate one or more worksheets and select commands and files from menus.

The screen display can expand from a single 1-2-3 worksheet to an array of worksheet files on-screen at the same time. In this chapter and later chapters, you learn how to build multiple-worksheet files. The multiple-worksheet file approach is useful for consolidating information quickly and efficiently.

If you have used other spreadsheet programs, you are familiar with some of the concepts discussed in this chapter. If this is your first experience with spreadsheets, however, the basics discussed in this chapter are informative and helpful.

Key Terms in This Chapter

Cursor	The underscore that appears inside the cell pointer or within the control panel in EDIT mode.
Range name	An alphanumeric name given to a cell or a rectangular group of cells.
Menu pointer	The rectangular bar that highlights menu commands.
Data	Labels or values entered into a worksheet cell.
Label	A text entry entered in the worksheet.
Value	A number or formula entered in the worksheet.
Label prefix	A single aligning character typed before a label.
Operator	A mathematical or logical symbol that specifies an action to be performed on data.
Order of preference	The order in which an equation or formula is executed; determines which operators act first.
Wild card	A character, such as a question mark (?) or asterisk (*) that represents any other single or multiple character(s).

Moving around the Worksheet

After you start entering data in your worksheet, you need some easy ways to move the cell pointer quickly and accurately. Remember that the 1-2-3 worksheet is immense—it contains 8,192 rows, 256 columns, and more than 2,000,000 cells. A multiple-worksheet file can contain up to 256 worksheets. You may have many blocks of data of various sizes in widely separated parts of one or more worksheets. 1-2-3 provides several ways to quickly move the cell pointer to any location in the worksheet.

Remember that the cell pointer and the cursor are not the same. The cell pointer is the bright rectangle that highlights an entire cell in the worksheet area. The cursor is the underscore that is sometimes in the cell pointer and sometimes in the control panel. The cursor indicates on-screen where keyboard activity takes effect; the cell pointer indicates the cell that is affected. Whenever you move the cell pointer, the cursor—inside the cell pointer—moves with it.

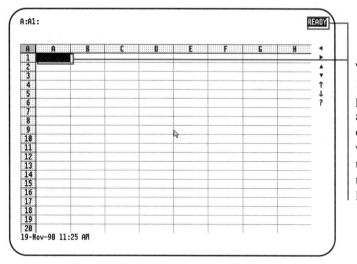

When you start
1-2-3, the cell
pointer appears
automatically in
cell A1 of the
worksheet, and
the mode indica-
tor displays
READY.

You control the cell pointer either with keyboard keys or with a mouse. (To use a mouse, you must have a mouse driver loaded, a mouse attached to the computer, and Wysiwyg in memory.) The following section shows you how to use your keyboard to move the cell pointer around the worksheet. In subsequent sections, you learn how to move around multiple worksheets, as well as how to use a mouse to navigate both single and multiple worksheets.

Keyboard Control of the Cell Pointer

When 1-2-3 is in READY mode, the program is ready for you to enter data into the highlighted cell. To enter data in another cell, use the direction keys to move the cell pointer to the new location. See the tables in this chapter for explanations of the direction keys.

When you begin to enter data, the READY mode indicator changes to LABEL or VALUE, depending on whether you are entering text or numbers. The cursor disappears from the cell pointer and appears in the control panel, where the action is taking place.

The POINT mode indicator signifies that you can position the cell pointer or highlight a range in your worksheet.

To edit a label or value in EDIT mode, move the cursor in the control panel with the Home, End, and left- and right-arrow keys. The actions of direction keys are described in table 3.1. To see direction keys and their actions in multiple worksheets and files, look for a separate table in a later section of this chapter.

3

When you enter text, the READY mode indicator automatically changes to LABEL.

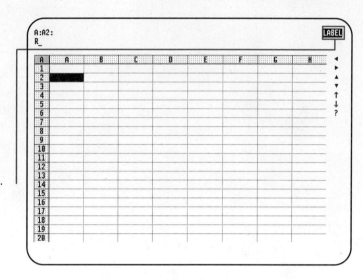

When 1-2-3 is in POINT mode, you can point out a range with the direction keys.

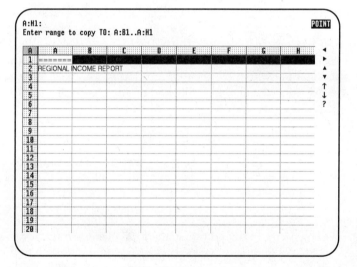

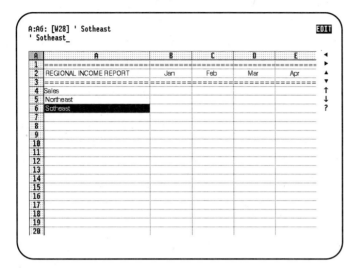

The direction keys have different actions when you are editing in EDIT mode, making a cell entry, or entering a command.

3

Table 3.1
Direction Keys

Key	Action
←	Moves the cell pointer one column to the left in the worksheet. In the control panel, moves the cursor one character to the left in EDIT mode or the menu pointer one item to the left in MENU mode.
→	Moves the cell pointer one column to the right in the worksheet. In the control panel, moves the cursor one character to the right in EDIT mode or the menu pointer one item to the right in MENU mode.
↑	Moves the cell pointer up one row.
↓	Moves the cell pointer down one row.
Tab⇆ or Ctrl→	Moves the cell pointer one screen to the right in the worksheet. In the control panel, moves the cursor five characters to the right in EDIT mode.

3

Table 3.1 (continued)

Key	Action
⇧Shift Tab⇆ or Ctrl ←	Moves the cell pointer one screen to the left in the worksheet. In the control panel, moves the cursor five characters to the left in EDIT mode.
PgUp	Moves the cell pointer up one screen.
PgDn	Moves the cell pointer down one screen.
Home	Returns the cell pointer to cell A1 from any location in the current worksheet. When used after the End key, positions the pointer at the lower-right corner of the current worksheet.
End	When used before any arrow key, moves the cell pointer (in the direction of the arrow key) to the next boundary between a blank cell and a cell containing data.
F5 (GoTo)	Moves the cell pointer to the cell coordinates (or range name) you specify.

Using the Basic Direction Keys

The arrow keys on the numeric keypad (or on the separate pad of the enhanced keyboard) are the basic keys for moving the cell pointer with the keyboard. The cell pointer moves in the direction of the arrow on the key as long as you hold down the key. When you reach the edge of the screen, the worksheet continues scrolling in the direction of the arrow.

Scrolling the Worksheet

You can scroll the worksheet—one screen at a time—to the right by pressing the Tab key and to the left with Shift-Tab (hold down the Shift key while pressing Tab). You can also scroll the worksheet by holding down the Ctrl key and pressing the right- or left-arrow key. To get the same effect up or down, use the PgUp and PgDn keys to move up or down one screen at a time. Scrolling provides quick ways of paging through the worksheet.

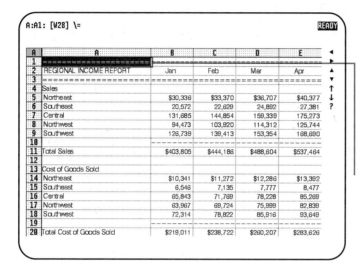

A:A1: [W28] \=   READY

A	A	B	C	D	E
1	============================				
2	REGIONAL INCOME REPORT	Jan	Feb	Mar	Apr
3	==				
4	Sales				
5	Northeast	$30,336	$33,370	$36,707	$40,377
6	Southeast	20,572	22,629	24,892	27,381
7	Central	131,685	144,854	159,339	175,273
8	Northwest	94,473	103,920	114,312	125,744
9	Southwest	126,739	139,413	153,354	168,690
10					
11	Total Sales	$403,805	$444,186	$488,604	$537,464
12					
13	Cost of Goods Sold				
14	Northeast	$10,341	$11,272	$12,286	$13,392
15	Southeast	6,546	7,135	7,777	8,477
16	Central	65,843	71,769	78,228	85,269
17	Northwest	63,967	69,724	75,999	82,839
18	Southwest	72,314	78,822	85,916	93,649
19					
20	Total Cost of Goods Sold	$219,011	$238,722	$260,207	$283,626

In this income worksheet, the cell pointer is positioned at cell A1.

3

A:F1: [W11] \=   READY

A	F	G	H	I	J	K	L
1	=======						
2	May	Jun	Jul	Aug	Sep	Oct	No
3	===						
4							
5	$44,415	$48,856	$53,742	$59,116	$65,028	$71,531	$7
6	30,119	33,131	36,445	40,089	44,098	48,508	$
7	192,800	212,080	233,288	256,617	282,278	310,506	34
8	138,318	152,150	167,365	184,101	202,511	222,762	24
9	185,559	204,114	224,526	246,978	271,676	298,844	32
10							
11	$591,211	$650,332	$715,365	$786,902	$865,592	$952,151	$1,04
12							
13							
14	$14,597	$15,911	$17,343	$18,904	$20,605	$22,460	$2
15	9,240	10,072	10,978	11,966	13,043	14,217	1
16	92,943	101,308	110,425	120,364	131,196	143,004	15
17	90,295	98,421	107,279	116,934	127,458	138,929	15
18	102,077	111,264	121,278	132,193	144,090	157,058	17
19							
20	$309,152	$336,976	$367,303	$400,361	$436,393	$475,669	$5

When you press Tab↹, the worksheet scrolls one screen to the right. The cell pointer now appears in cell F1 and columns F through K appear on-screen.

If you then press Shift-Tab, the worksheet scrolls one screen to the left. In this example, the cell pointer returns to its original location at cell A1.

3

When you press
PgDn , the
worksheet scrolls
down one screen.
The cell pointer
now appears in
cell A21 and rows
21 through 40
display on-screen.

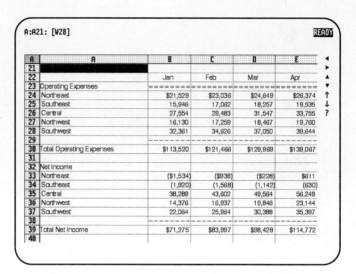

If you then press PgUp, the worksheet scrolls up one screen, and the cell pointer returns to its original location at cell A1. Pressing the Scroll Lock key to activate the scroll function makes the worksheet appear to move in the opposite direction of the arrow key you press—no matter where the cell pointer is positioned on the screen. For example, if the cell pointer is positioned in cell A1 and you press the Scroll Lock key followed by the right-arrow key, the entire worksheet (not just the cell pointer) moves one column to the right. Learning and using 1-2-3 is usually easier without activating the scroll function with the Scroll Lock key.

Using the Home and End Keys

The Home key provides a quick way to return to the beginning of the current worksheet when 1-2-3 is in READY or POINT mode. Pressing Home makes the cell pointer return to cell A1 from anywhere in the worksheet.

Pressing the Home key in POINT mode is a handy way to quickly highlight a range of data you plan to move or copy.

The Home and End keys have different actions in EDIT mode. For example, in EDIT mode, the Home key moves the cursor in the control panel.

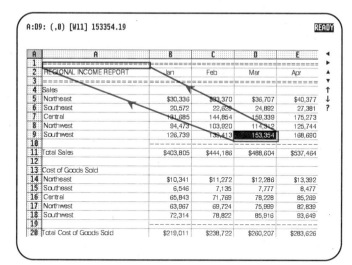

When you press Home in READY mode, the cell pointer moves to cell A1.

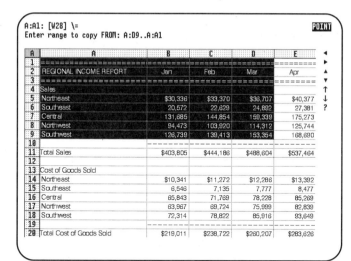

When you press Home in POINT mode, the cell pointer highlights a rectangle. One corner appears at A1, with the opposite corner at the original position of the cell pointer.

3

When you press F2 (Edit), the cursor appears in the control panel after the last character of your cell entry.

```
A:D9: (,0) [W11] 153354.19                                    EDIT
153354.19
```

	A	B	C	D	E
1					
2	REGIONAL INCOME REPORT	Jan	Feb	Mar	Apr
3					
4	Sales				
5	Northeast	$30,336	$33,370	$36,707	$40,377
6	Southeast	20,572	22,629	24,892	27,381
7	Central	131,685	144,854	159,339	175,273
8	Northwest	94,473	103,920	114,312	125,744
9	Southwest	126,739	139,413	153,354	168,690
10					
11	Total Sales	$403,805	$444,186	$488,604	$537,464
12					
13	Cost of Goods Sold				
14	Northeast	$10,341	$11,272	$12,286	$13,392
15	Southeast	6,546	7,135	7,777	8,477
16	Central	65,843	71,769	78,228	85,269
17	Northwest	63,967	69,724	75,999	82,839
18	Southwest	72,314	78,822	85,916	93,649
19					
20	Total Cost of Goods Sold	$219,011	$238,722	$260,207	$283,626

When you press Home in EDIT mode, the cursor moves to the first character in the cell entry.

```
A:D9: (,0) [W11] 153354.19                                    EDIT
153354.19
```

	A	B	C	D	E
1					
2	REGIONAL INCOME REPORT	Jan	Feb	Mar	Apr
3					
4	Sales				
5	Northeast	$30,336	$33,370	$36,707	$40,377
6	Southeast	20,572	22,629	24,892	27,381
7	Central	131,685	144,854	159,339	175,273
8	Northwest	94,473	103,920	114,312	125,744
9	Southwest	126,739	139,413	153,354	168,690
10					
11	Total Sales	$403,805	$444,186	$488,604	$537,464
12					
13	Cost of Goods Sold				
14	Northeast	$10,341	$11,272	$12,286	$13,392
15	Southeast	6,546	7,135	7,777	8,477
16	Central	65,843	71,769	78,228	85,269
17	Northwest	63,967	69,724	75,999	82,839
18	Southwest	72,314	78,822	85,916	93,649
19					
20	Total Cost of Goods Sold	$219,011	$238,722	$260,207	$283,626

1-2-3 uses the End key in a unique way. When you press an arrow key after you have pressed and released the End key, the cell pointer moves in the direction of the arrow key to the next boundary between a blank cell and a cell containing data. Because the cell pointer moves only to the next boundary, any gaps (blank lines) in your blocks of data will slow this procedure.

As the following example illustrates, you can use the End key with the arrow keys to quickly reach the borders of the worksheet area in a new (blank) worksheet. To learn how the End key works with the arrow keys, start with a blank worksheet and follow these steps:

1. If the cell pointer is not in cell A1 of a new worksheet, press Home .

3

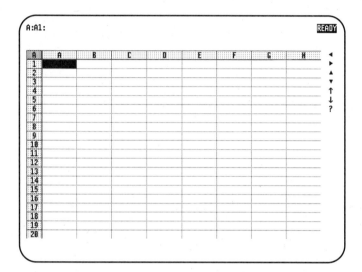

A blank worksheet with the cell pointer in cell A1.

2. Press End , and then press → .

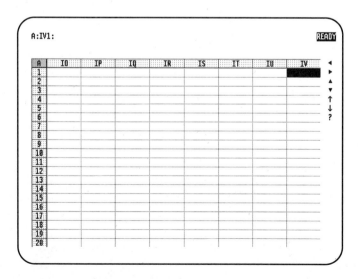

The cell pointer jumps to the upper right boundary of the worksheet, to cell IV1.

3. Press ⌨End, and then press ⌨↓.

The cell pointer jumps to the bottom right boundary of the worksheet, to cell IV8192.

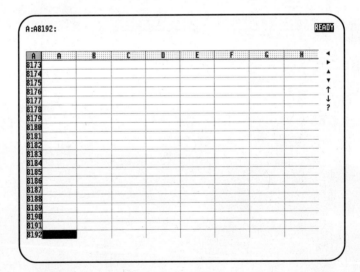

4. Press ⌨End, and then press ⌨←.

The cell pointer jumps to the bottom left boundary of the worksheet, to cell A8192.

From cell A8192, if you press the End key followed by the up-arrow key, the cell pointer returns to cell A1. In this case, using the Home key would perform the same operation.

You can use the End key followed by the Home key to move the cell pointer from any position on the worksheet to the lower right corner of the worksheet. (In a blank worksheet, however, the cell pointer remains in cell A1.) The End Home key combination has the opposite effect from that of the Home key used alone.

Using the GoTo (F5) Key

The GoTo (F5) key gives you a way to jump directly to any cell location.

	A	B	C	D	E
2	REGIONAL INCOME REPORT	Jan	Feb	Mar	Apr
4	Sales				
5	Northeast	$30,336	$33,370	$36,707	$40,377
6	Southeast	20,572	22,629	24,892	27,381
7	Central	131,685	144,854	159,339	175,273
8	Northwest	94,473	103,920	114,312	125,744
9	Southwest	126,739	139,413	153,354	168,690
11	Total Sales	$403,805	$444,186	$488,604	$537,464
13	Cost of Goods Sold				
14	Northeast	$10,341	$11,272	$12,286	$13,392
15	Southeast	6,546	7,135	7,777	8,477
16	Central	65,843	71,769	78,228	85,269
17	Northwest	63,967	69,724	75,999	82,839
18	Southwest	72,314	78,822	85,916	93,649
20	Total Cost of Goods Sold	$219,011	$238,722	$260,207	$283,626

A:A1: [W28] \=

Enter address to go to: A:A1

POINT

When you press F5 (GoTo), 1-2-3 prompts you for the new cell address.

In response to the prompt, type the desired cell address. When you work on a large worksheet, you might forget the cell addresses for specific parts of the worksheet and then have difficulty using the GoTo (F5) key. You can, however, create and use range names with the GoTo (F5) key so that you don't have to remember cell addresses.

You can assign a range name to a cell or a rectangular group of cells. Then you can press the GoTo (F5) key and type the range name instead of the cell address. When the range name refers to more than one cell, the cell pointer moves to the upper left corner of the range. (Ranges and range names appear in detail in Chapter 4.)

In this example, JANSALES (a range that begins in cell B5) is specified as the location to go to.

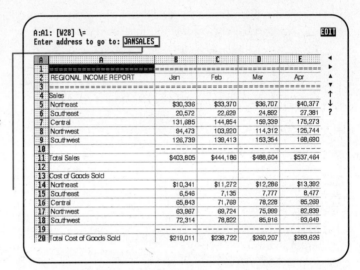

Moving around Multiple Worksheets

The additional direction keys that are available when you use multiple worksheets or files are shown in Table 3.2. The most important key combinations to remember for moving around multiple worksheets are Ctrl-PgUp (to move to the next worksheet—from worksheet A to worksheet B, for example) and Ctrl-PgDn (to move to the previous worksheet—such as from worksheet B to worksheet A). Don't worry about the other direction keys for multiple worksheets and files at this point. You can learn them when you begin building large multiple-worksheet files.

Table 3.2
Direction Keys for Multiple Worksheets

Key	Action
Ctrl PgUp	Moves the cell pointer to the next worksheet.
Ctrl PgDn	Moves the cell pointer to the previous worksheet.

Table 3.2 (continued)

Key	Action
Ctrl Home	Moves the cell pointer to cell A:A1 in the first worksheet of the file.
End, Ctrl Home	Moves the cell pointer to the end of the active area in the last worksheet in the file.
End, Ctrl PgUp	Moves the cell pointer back through the worksheets to the next cell that contains data (the intersection between a blank cell and a cell that contains data).
End, Ctrl PgDn	Moves the cell pointer forward through the worksheets to the next cell that contains data (the intersection between a blank cell and a cell that contains data).
Ctrl End, Ctrl PgUp	Moves the cell pointer to the next file.
Ctrl End, Ctrl PgDn	Moves the cell pointer to the previous file.
Ctrl End, Home	Moves the cell pointer to the first file in memory.
Ctrl End, End	Moves the cell pointer to the last file in memory.

Mouse Control of the Cell Pointer

You can use the left mouse button to move the cell pointer when 1-2-3 is in READY or POINT mode. There are several ways to move the cell pointer with the mouse. The simplest way is to point to a cell on screen and click the left mouse button. Another way is to use the icons on the right side of the worksheet. The seven icons in the icon panel include four solid triangles, each pointing in a different direction. Pointing to one of the triangles and clicking the left mouse button moves the cell pointer one cell in the direction of the triangle.

If you hold down the left mouse button while pointing to a triangle icon, the cell pointer keeps moving in the direction of the triangle. If you want to move the cell pointer to a cell not shown on the display, point to the appropriate triangle and hold down the left mouse button until the worksheet starts to scroll. When you reach the row or column you want, release the mouse button.

If you click the
triangle that points
to the right, the
cell pointer moves
from cell A1 to B1
in this example.

3

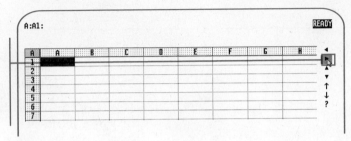

You can drag the cell pointer around the worksheet by positioning the mouse
pointer on the cell pointer, pressing and holding the left mouse button and
moving the cell pointer to the desired location. This method also allows you to
move the cell pointer to a cell not shown on the display—when the mouse
pointer moves past the edge of the worksheet, the screen begins scrolling. When
you release the mouse button, the scrolling stops.

For example, suppose the cell pointer is in cell A5. To move to a cell not currently shown on the screen, such as Z5, hold the left mouse button and move—
or drag—the mouse pointer to the right beyond the rightmost column displayed
on the screen. When you move the mouse beyond the last displayed column, the
entire worksheet scrolls to the left and the column letter shown in the first line of
the control panel changes. When you get to column Z, release the mouse button.
This method works similarly if you want to move to a cell above, below, to the
left, or to the right of the cells displayed on-screen.

You can use the End key with the triangles in the icon panel to move the cell
pointer to the next boundary between a blank cell and a cell containing data in
the current worksheet. Simply press and release the End key on the keyboard,
then click the triangle representing the direction you want the cell pointer to
move. This procedure provides the same results as using the End key with the
arrow keys on the keyboard (described in a previous section).

A quick way to move the cell pointer to cell A1 with the mouse is to move the
mouse pointer to the worksheet letter in the upper left corner of the worksheet
area, and click the left mouse button. This is the same as pressing the Home key
from the keyboard. Using the mouse to navigate multiple-worksheet files is
simple—you can click the left mouse button on the up or down arrow in the icon
panel to move the cell pointer to the next or previous worksheet, respectively. If
you are using perspective view to display multiple worksheets or files (three on a
screen at one time), simply point to a displayed cell in any worksheet or file and
click the left mouse button. The cell pointer will then move directly to the
specified cell in that worksheet or file.

Also, when working with multiple worksheets or files that appear in perspective view, you can move the mouse pointer to the Home position of a different worksheet or file by clicking the left mouse button on the desired worksheet letter.

Selecting Commands from Menus

3

The 1-2-3 main menu is always available whenever you start 1-2-3. Release 3.1 offers an additional menu system with the Wysiwyg spreadsheet publishing add-in program. If you want to use the Wysiwyg menu and the mouse, however, you must first load the Wysiwyg feature into memory. As you learned in Chapter 2, you can install the Wysiwyg program so that it loads automatically whenever you start 1-2-3.

The 1-2-3 and Wysiwyg menus offer several hundred command options, but you will probably use only a small portion of these on a frequent basis. Although some of the command options appearing in both the 1-2-3 and Wysiwyg main menus are the same (such as the Worksheet, Print, and Graph options), they are used to perform different types of tasks.

A helpful aspect of menus is the ease of starting commands. From the keyboard, you can either point to the option you want and press Enter, or you can just type the first letter of the command name. (A later section of this chapter discusses how to select menu commands if you are using a mouse.) To point to a command on the menu, use the left- and right-arrow keys on the keyboard. You can use the space bar interchangeably with the right-arrow key to move the menu pointer. After you highlight the desired command, press Enter.

If you move the menu pointer to the last command of a menu and press the right-arrow key again, the menu pointer reappears on the first command of the menu. Similarly, if the menu pointer is on the first command of a menu, press the left-arrow key to move to the last command. Note that you can also move the menu pointer to the end of the command line by pressing the End key or to the beginning of the line by pressing the Home key.

The other way to select a command from the keyboard is to enter its first letter. When you become familiar with the commands in 1-2-3's various menus, you will learn that typing is much faster than pointing. To select a menu command from the keyboard, you can either point or type.

3

Pointing To Commands

1. Call up the 1-2-3 menu by pressing ⌷ or call up the Wysiwyg menu by pressing ⦂.

2. Use ← or → to move the menu pointer until the desired command is highlighted.

The menu pointer, the rectangular bar that highlights menu selections, is positioned on the Copy option of the 1-2-3 menu.

```
A:B2: [W11] ^Jan                                              MENU
Worksheet  Range  Copy  Move  File  Print  Graph  Data  System  Quit
Copy a cell or range of cells
  A              A                  B           C           D           E         ◄
  1  ===========================================================================   ►
  2  REGIONAL INCOME REPORT        Jan         Feb         Mar         Apr         ▲
  3  ===========================================================================   ▼
  4  Sales                                                                         ↑
  5  Northeast                     $30,336     $33,370     $36,707     $40,377     ↓
  6  Southeast                      20,572      22,629      24,892      27,381     ?
  7  Central                       131,685     144,854     159,339     175,273
  8  Northwest                      94,473     103,920     114,312     125,744
  9  Southwest                     126,739     139,413     153,354     168,690
 10  ------------------------------------------------------------------------
 11  Total Sales                  $403,805    $444,186    $488,604    $537,464
 12
 13  Cost of Goods Sold
 14  Northeast                     $10,341     $11,272     $12,286     $13,392
 15  Southeast                       6,546       7,135       7,777       8,477
 16  Central                        65,843      71,769      78,228      85,269
 17  Northwest                      63,967      69,724      75,999      82,839
 18  Southwest                      72,314      78,822      85,916      93,649
 19  ------------------------------------------------------------------------
 20  Total Cost of Goods Sold     $219,011    $238,722    $260,207    $283,626
```

3. Press ↵Enter.

4. Continue this process, selecting the desired commands from the 1-2-3 or Wysiwyg menu and responding to any resulting prompts until the task is complete.

Typing Commands

1. Call up the 1-2-3 menu by pressing ⌷ or call up the Wysiwyg menu by pressing ⦂.

2. Select the desired command by typing the first letter of the command.

3. Continue selecting the desired commands from the 1-2-3 or Wysiwyg menu and responding to any prompts until the task is complete.

If you make the wrong command selection, you can press Esc at any time to return to the previous menu. For instance, if you realize that you should have selected Insert, not Delete, from the 1-2-3 /Worksheet menu, press Esc once to return to the /Worksheet menu. You can press Esc as many times as necessary to return to any location in the series of menus or to leave MENU mode completely.

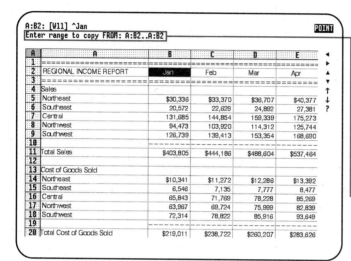

In this example, pressing [C] selects the Copy command from 1-2-3's main menu and takes you directly to a prompt.

Using the 1-2-3 Menu

As discussed in the previous section, the procedure for selecting commands from the 1-2-3 menu is simple. To select a command from the 1-2-3 main menu, make certain that 1-2-3 is in READY mode, and press the slash (/) key.

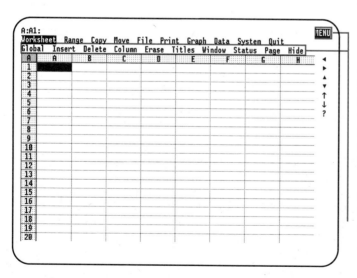

As soon as you press [/], the mode indicator in the upper right corner of the screen changes to MENU and the 1-2-3 main menu appears on the second line of the control panel.

The third line of the control panel contains either a brief explanation of the highlighted command or the menu that results from choosing the highlighted command (as shown in the previous screen). As you point to different commands by moving the menu pointer across the menu, a new explanation (or menu) appears as each command is highlighted. This assistance is displayed at all levels of menus.

Here, the third line of the control panel displays an explanation of the command that is highlighted.

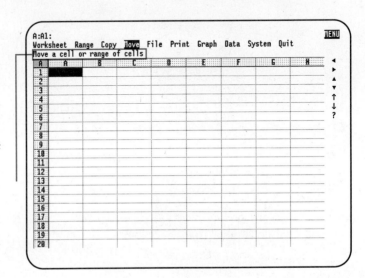

The 1-2-3 main menu provides the command options for building and modifying your worksheet and graphics applications. Table 3.3 summarizes the selections on the 1-2-3 main menu.

Table 3.3
Selections on the 1-2-3 Main Menu

Selection	Description
Worksheet	Changes global worksheet settings; inserts and deletes columns, rows, and worksheets; sets column widths, windows, and titles; hides worksheets.
Range	Formats, erases, justifies, names, transposes, protects, and searches ranges of data.
Copy	Copies ranges of data and formats.
Move	Moves ranges of data and formats.

Table 3.3 (continued)

Selection	Description
File	Accesses, saves, lists, combines, and imports files.
Print	Enables you to print worksheets and graphs to a printer or file.
Graph	Creates, names, saves, and adds enhancements to graphs.
Data	Performs sorts, queries, and regressions on 1-2-3 data-bases; imports databases from other programs.
System	Returns you to DOS while 1-2-3 and the current worksheet remain in memory.
Quit	Returns to READY mode.

Using the Wysiwyg Menu

In addition to the 1-2-3 menu, Release 3.1 includes a Wysiwyg menu to enhance your 1-2-3 worksheets. The Wysiwyg menu is not available for use until you load and invoke the program, just like other add-in programs available for 1-2-3. After Wysiwyg loads in memory, you can use a mouse with both 1-2-3 and Wysiwyg. However, to use a mouse you must also have mouse software, a graphics display monitor, and a graphics display card. To select a command from the Wysiwyg menu, make certain that 1-2-3 is in READY mode, and press the colon (:) key.

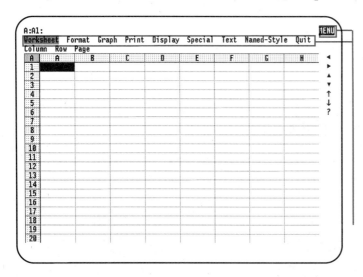

As soon as you press 🔳, the mode indicator in the upper right corner of the screen changes to MENU and the Wysiwyg main menu appears on the second line of the control panel.

The format of the Wysiwyg menu is similar to that of the 1-2-3 menu, because the third line of the control panel also contains either a brief explanation of the highlighted command or the menu that results from choosing the highlighted command (as shown in the previous screen). As you point to different commands by moving the menu pointer across the Wysiwyg menu, a new explanation (or menu) appears as each command is highlighted. Table 3.4 summarizes the selections on the Wysiwyg main menu.

3

Table 3.4
Selections on the Wysiwyg Main Menu

Selection	Description
Worksheet	Sets column widths, row heights, and page breaks.
Format	Adds boldface, italics, lines, shading, colors, and fonts.
Graph	Inserts a graph into a worksheet range, enhances and sizes the graph.
Print	Prints the formatted worksheet or graph, specifies page layout and enhancement options.
Display	Alters screen characteristics such as colors, size of cells, grid lines, and intensity.
Special	Copies, moves, imports, and exports formats.
Text	Edits, aligns, and reformats a range of text.
Named-Style	Assigns names to commonly-used format combinations.
Quit	Returns to READY mode.

The next section discusses how to use a mouse to select commands from both the 1-2-3 and Wysiwyg menus.

Using the Mouse to Select Menu Commands

When you move the mouse pointer into the control-panel area at the top of the screen, a menu automatically appears as if you pressed the slash (/) or colon (:) key from the keyboard.

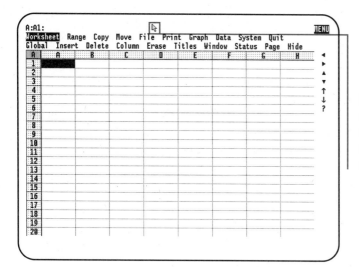

If you move the mouse pointer to the control panel, a menu automatically appears.

The menu that results (1-2-3 or Wysiwyg) is the last menu used in the current 1-2-3 session. If a menu has not yet been used in the current session, the 1-2-3 menu will appear first. Pressing the right mouse button while the mouse pointer is in the control-panel area switches between the 1-2-3 and Wysiwyg menus.

Using a mouse to select an option from a menu is easy. To select a 1-2-3 or Wysiwyg command with the mouse, follow these steps:

1. Move the mouse pointer to the control panel to automatically generate a 1-2-3 or Wysiwyg menu. If necessary, press the right mouse button to switch between menus.

2. Highlight the desired menu option with the mouse pointer and click the left mouse button. You select all options from resulting menus in the same way.

Continue clicking the left mouse button on the desired commands from the 1-2-3 or Wysiwyg menu. Respond to any resulting prompts by typing on the keyboard and pressing Enter to accept the entry.

You can scan the different menu items and view their descriptions on the third line of the control panel by pressing and holding the left mouse button while you move across the menu. When you release the mouse button, you select the command that was last highlighted.

3

While the mouse pointer is in the control panel and a menu is displayed, you can press the right button one or more times to return to previous menus. Moving the mouse pointer back to the worksheet area removes the menu from the screen and returns 1-2-3 to READY mode.

Using the mouse can greatly increase your speed and productivity. Experiment with using the mouse, the keyboard, or a combination of both to find which method works best for you.

Entering Data into the Worksheet

You can enter data into a cell by highlighting the cell with the cell pointer and typing the entry. To complete the entry, press Enter or any of the direction keys discussed in this chapter. If you press a direction key to complete the entry, the cell pointer also moves one cell in the selected direction. Using this method eliminates one step in data entry operations because you do not need to press the Enter key and a direction key after every entry.

If you are using a mouse, you can complete an entry by clicking one of the triangle keys in the icon panel. Note that this action has the same effect as pressing an arrow key on the keyboard to complete the entry—the cell pointer moves one cell in the specified direction.

If you enter data into a cell that already contains information, the new data replaces the earlier information. This is one way to change data in a cell; other methods involve using the Edit (F2) key and using the Wysiwyg **:Text Edit** command to edit data directly in a cell. Explanations of each of these procedures appear later in this chapter.

There are two types of cell entries: labels and values. Labels are text entries, and values can be either numbers or formulas (including functions, which 1-2-3 treats as built-in formulas). The type of entry can be determined from the first character you enter. Your entry is treated as a value (a number or a formula) when you start with one of the following characters:

> 0 1 2 3 4 5 6 7 8 9 + − . (@ # $

When you begin your entry with a character other than one of the preceding ones, 1-2-3 treats your entry as a label.

A value—whether a number, formula, or function—can be used for computing purposes. A label is a collection of characters and is not logically used in a calculation.

Entering Labels

Labels are commonly used in 1-2-3 for row and column headings, titles, explanation, and notes, and they play an important role in worksheet development. Without labels on a worksheet, you might know that column H is January data and row 11 is Inventory Assets, but how would someone else who is not familiar with the worksheet know?

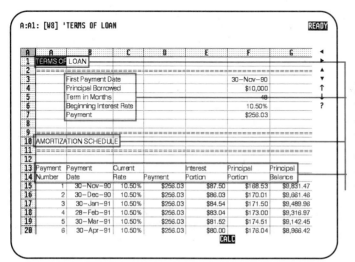

Labels make values more evident in a worksheet and help you find information quickly.

A label can be up to 512 characters long and can contain any string of characters and numbers. A label that is too long for the width of a cell continues (for display purposes) across the cells to the right, as long as the neighboring cells contain no other entries.

When you make an entry into a cell and the first character does not indicate a value entry, the assumption is that you are entering a label. After you type the first character, 1-2-3 shifts to LABEL mode.

You can control how labels are displayed in the cell. By preceding a text entry with a label prefix, you can tell 1-2-3 to left-justify ('), center (^), right-justify (") or repeat (\) a label when it is displayed. The following sections cover each of these options.

Aligning Labels

Because the default position for displaying labels is left-justified, you don't have to type the label prefix when entering most labels—1-2-3 automatically supplies it

3

for you. When your labels consist of numbers followed by text (as in addresses), you must use a label prefix before 1-2-3 will accept the entry into a cell.

When you enter only a number as a label—for example, the year **1991**—the assumption is that you are entering a value. You need some way to signal that you intend this numeric entry to be treated as text. You can indicate this by using one of the label prefixes. In this case, you can enter 1991 as a centered label by typing ^**1991**.

To align labels as you enter them into the worksheet, you must first type a label prefix. Use the following label prefixes for label alignment:

'   Left-justifies

"   Right-justifies

^   Centers

You can use label prefixes to align labels three different ways.

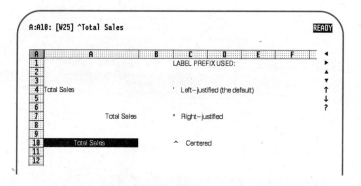

1-2-3 alone does not correctly center or right-align text that overflows a cell. However, if you have Wysiwyg in memory, you can correct this problem by preceding a label entry with a double caret (^ ^) to center, or a double quotation mark (" ") to right-justify the entry.

Repeating Label Characters

An additional label prefix is available for repeating one or more characters in a single cell. For example, you can use the repeat character—a backslash (\)—to create a separator line that fills an entire cell.

To repeat characters within a single cell, follow these steps:

1. Highlight the cell that will contain the repeating label.

   For example, highlight cell A2 to use the repeat character that creates a separator line.

2. Press ⌐\⌐, the repeat character, and then type the character(s) to be repeated within the highlighted cell.

   In this example, type \= to fill cell A2 with equal signs.

3. Press ⌐↵Enter⌐ to enter the label into the highlighted cell.

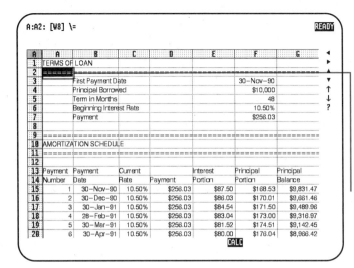

Cell A2 is now filled with equal signs. Repeat these steps in adjoining cells to form the remainder of the separator line.

Controlling Label Prefixes

You can control label prefixes in several different ways. If you want to change the alignment of a range of labels after the labels are entered, use the 1-2-3 /Range Label command. You can also use the Wysiwyg :Text Edit command or the Edit key (F2) (explained later in this chapter) to edit individual cells.

For example, suppose that you enter two rows of labels and then decide that you want the labels to be centered. You can change the alignment of a range of existing labels by using the /Range Label command. (You learn more about ranges in Chapter 4.)

To align a range of labels, follow these steps:

1. Select /Range Label.

2. Select one of the following alignment choices: **Left**, **Right**, or **Center**.

```
A:A13: [W8] 'Payment                                              MENU
Left  Right  Center
Center labels in cells
   A        B          C          D         E          F          G      ◄
 1 TERMS OF LOAN                                                          ►
 2 ==================================================================== ▲
 3        First Payment Date                          30-Nov-90          ▼
 4        Principal Borrowed                          $10,000            ↑
 5        Term in Months                              48                 ↓
 6        Beginning Interest Rate                     10.50%             ?
 7        Payment                                     $256.03
 8
 9 ====================================================================
10 AMORTIZATION SCHEDULE
11 ====================================================================
12
13 Payment  Payment    Current              Interest   Principal  Principal
14 Number   Date       Rate     Payment     Portion    Portion    Balance
15      1   30-Nov-90  10.50%   $256.03     $87.50     $168.53    $9,831.47
16      2   30-Dec-90  10.50%   $256.03     $86.03     $170.01    $9,661.46
17      3   30-Jan-91  10.50%   $256.03     $84.54     $171.50    $9,489.96
18      4   28-Feb-91  10.50%   $256.03     $83.04     $173.00    $9,316.97
19      5   30-Mar-91  10.50%   $256.03     $81.52     $174.51    $9,142.45
20      6   30-Apr-91  10.50%   $256.03     $80.00     $176.04    $8,966.42
                                                    CALC
```

In this example, select Center.

3. Specify the range of cells to be aligned.

   In this example, highlight the range A13..G14; then press ↵Enter.

```
A:A13: [W8] ^Payment                                             READY

   A        B          C          D         E          F          G      ◄
 1 TERMS OF LOAN                                                          ►
 2 ==================================================================== ▲
 3        First Payment Date                          30-Nov-90          ▼
 4        Principal Borrowed                          $10,000            ↑
 5        Term in Months                              48                 ↓
 6        Beginning Interest Rate                     10.50%             ?
 7        Payment                                     $256.03
 8
 9 ====================================================================
10 AMORTIZATION SCHEDULE
11 ====================================================================
12
13 Payment  Payment    Current              Interest   Principal  Principal
14 Number   Date       Rate     Payment     Portion    Portion    Balance
15      1   30-Nov-90  10.50%   $256.03     $87.50     $168.53    $9,831.47
16      2   30-Dec-90  10.50%   $256.03     $86.03     $170.01    $9,661.46
17      3   30-Jan-91  10.50%   $256.03     $84.54     $171.50    $9,489.96
18      4   28-Feb-91  10.50%   $256.03     $83.04     $173.00    $9,316.97
19      5   30-Mar-91  10.50%   $256.03     $81.52     $174.51    $9,142.45
20      6   30-Apr-91  10.50%   $256.03     $80.00     $176.04    $8,966.42
                                                    CALC
```

The cells are now centered, with each label in the range preceded by a caret (^).

If you want to set the alignment of an entire worksheet to the left, right, or center before you enter labels, you can use the /Worksheet Global Label command. This command will not change the alignment of existing labels, however. The alignment of existing labels can be changed by using the /Range Label command, the :Text Edit command, or Edit (F2).

To set the alignment of labels for the entire worksheet, follow these steps:

1. Select /**W**orksheet **G**lobal **L**abel.
2. Select one of the following alignment choices: **Left**, **Right**, or **Center**.

You can use the /**W**orksheet **S**tatus command to check the current alignment settings for the worksheet. This information appears near the bottom of the resulting screen.

Entering Numbers

As you know, values in 1-2-3 consist of numbers and formulas. 1-2-3 worksheets use numbers for many different types of applications—especially those that involve data entry.

The rules for entering numbers are the following:

- A number must begin with the numerals 0 through 9, a decimal point, a minus sign (–), or a dollar sign ($). If you type a plus sign (+) before a number you enter or you enter a number in parentheses, the + and the ( ) will not appear in the cell.
- You can end a number with a percent sign (%), which causes 1-2-3 to divide the number preceding the sign by 100.
- A number cannot have more than one decimal point.
- You can enter a number in scientific notation, which is called Scientific format in 1-2-3 (for example, $1.234E+06$).
- You cannot enter spaces after numbers.
- Do not start a number entry with a space(s). If you do, 1-2-3 treats the entry as a label. This does not cause an immediate error, but 1-2-3 treats the cell contents as zero the next time the number appears in a formula.

If you do not follow these rules, 1-2-3 beeps when you press Enter and automatically shifts to EDIT mode as if Edit (F2) were pressed.

Entering Formulas

In addition to simple values, you can enter formulas into cells. Enter formulas either by typing the formula into the cell or by pointing with the keyboard or the mouse, which entails moving the cell pointer so that 1-2-3 enters the cell addresses for you.

3

Suppose that you want to create a formula which adds a row of numbers. For example, you want to add the amounts in cells B4, B5, B6, and B7, and place the result in cell B9. To do this by typing, enter **+B4+B5+B6+B7** into cell B9. The + sign at the beginning of the formula indicates that a formula, not a label, is to be entered. 1-2-3 then switches to VALUE mode, the appropriate mode for entering numbers and formulas.

To enter a formula with cell addresses by pointing, follow these steps:

1. Begin with the cell pointer highlighting the cell that will hold the formula, and then press +.

In this example, highlight cell B9 and press +.

```
A:B9: (C0) [W11]                                            VALUE
+_
   A        A           B         C         D         E         F      ◄
   1   ==============================================================  ►
   2  SALES        Jan       Feb       Mar       Apr       May         ▲
   3   ==============================================================  ▼
   4  Product 1    $31,336   $37,954   $43,879   $51,471   $56,953     ↑
   5  Product 2     22,572    24,888    25,167    32,588    40,140     ↓
   6  Product 3    131,685   129,044   131,723   139,221   141,879     ?
   7  Product 4     95,473    98,008    96,986    95,318   103,538
   8             --------- --------- --------- --------- ---------
   9  Total Sales ███████
  10
```

2. Highlight the first cell address of the formula and press +.

In this example, highlight cell B4 and press +.

```
A:B4: (C0) [W11] 31336                                      POINT
+A:B4
   A        A           B         C         D         E         F      ◄
   1   ==============================================================  ►
   2  SALES        Jan       Feb       Mar       Apr       May         ▲
   3   ==============================================================  ▼
   4  Product 1    $31,336   $37,954   $43,879   $51,471   $56,953     ↑
   5  Product 2     22,572    24,888    25,167    32,588    40,140     ↓
   6  Product 3    131,685   129,044   131,723   139,221   141,879     ?
   7  Product 4     95,473    98,008    96,986    95,318   103,538
   8             --------- --------- --------- --------- ---------
   9  Total Sales
  10
```

The mode indicator in the upper right corner of the screen shifts from VALUE to POINT as you move the cell pointer to cell B4. Notice that the address for the cell appears after the plus sign in the second line of the control panel—in this case, +A:B4.

When you press + again, the cell pointer moves immediately from cell B4 back to the previous cell—in this example, to cell B9. The mode indicator also shifts back to VALUE.

3. Highlight the next cell address of the formula and press ⊞.

```
A:B5: (,0) [W11] 22572                                    POINT
+A:B4+A:B5
```

A	A	B	C	D	E	F
1	==					
2	SALES	Jan	Feb	Mar	Apr	May
3	==					
4	Product 1	$31,336	$37,954	$43,879	$51,471	$56,953
5	Product 2	22,572	24,888	25,167	32,588	40,140
6	Product 3	131,685	129,044	131,723	139,221	141,879
7	Product 4	95,473	98,008	96,986	95,318	103,538
8						
9	Total Sales					
10						

In this example, highlight cell B5 and press ⊞.

4. Continue pointing and entering plus signs until the formula is complete.

```
A:B9: (C0) [W11] +B4+B5+B6+B7                             READY
```

A	A	B	C	D	E	F
1	==					
2	SALES	Jan	Feb	Mar	Apr	May
3	==					
4	Product 1	$31,336	$37,954	$43,879	$51,471	$56,953
5	Product 2	22,572	24,888	25,167	32,588	40,140
6	Product 3	131,685	129,044	131,723	139,221	141,879
7	Product 4	95,473	98,008	96,986	95,318	103,538
8						
9	Total Sales	$281,066				
10						

In this example, highlight cell B6 and press ⊞; then highlight cell B7.

5. Press ↵Enter to complete the operation.

Remember that you can use a combination of typing and pointing (with or without a mouse) to enter a formula that contains one or more cell addresses. Use the method that works best for you. The easiest method is to point when cells are close to the one you are defining and to type references to distant cells. You get the same results with either method, and you can mix and match the two techniques within the same formula.

Using Mathematical Operators in Formulas

Operators are symbols that indicate arithmetic operations in formulas, and they are either logical or mathematical. Logical operators are discussed in Chapter 13, "Managing Data." The mathematical operators are the following:

3

Operator	Meaning
^	Exponentiation
+ , –	Positive, negative
* , /	Multiplication, division
+ , –	Addition, subtraction

This list indicates, from the top down, the order of precedence—that is, the order in which these operators are evaluated. For example, exponentiation takes place before multiplication, and division occurs before subtraction. Operations inside a set of parentheses are always evaluated first, and operators at the same level of precedence are evaluated in order from left to right.

Consider the following formula:

+F4*C6–G2^C7

The plus sign (+) indicates the beginning of a formula (rather than a label). The asterisk (*) tells 1-2-3 to multiply the values stored in cells F4 and C6. The minus sign (–) subtracts the result of the second element (G2^C7) from the first (+F4*C6). The caret (^) indicates exponentiation.

The first operator to be evaluated in a formula is exponentiation—the power of a number. In the formula 8+2^3, for example, 2^3 (2 to the power of 3) is evaluated before the addition. The answer is 16 (8+8), not 1000 (10 to the power of 3).

The next set of operators to be evaluated indicates the sign of a value (whether it is positive or negative). Notice the difference between a + or – sign that indicates a positive or negative value and a + or – sign that indicates addition or subtraction. When used as signs, these operators are evaluated before multiplication and division; when used as indicators of addition and subtraction, they are evaluated after multiplication and division. For example, 5+4/–2 is evaluated as 5+(–2), with 3 as the answer. The – sign indicates that 2 is negative, then 4 is divided by –2, and finally 5 is added to –2, resulting in the answer of 3.

You can use parentheses to override the order of precedence. Consider the order of precedence in the following formulas, in which cell B3 contains the value 2, cell C3 contains the value 3, and cell D3 contains the value 4. Notice how parentheses affect the order of precedence and the results in the first two formulas.

Formula	Evaluation	Result
+C3–D3/B3	3–(4/2)	1
(C3–D3)/B3	(3–4)/2	–0.5
+D3*C3–B3^C3	(4*3)–(2^3)	4
+D3*C3*B3/B3^C3–25/5	((4*3*2)/(2^3)–(25/5))	–2

Correcting Errors in Formulas

It is easy to make errors when you enter formulas—especially when you enter formulas that are complex. 1-2-3 provides ways to help you discover and correct these sometimes inevitable errors.

If you try to enter a formula that contains a logical or mathematical error, the program will beep, change to EDIT mode, and move the cursor to the section of the formula where the problem most likely exists. You can then correct the error and continue.

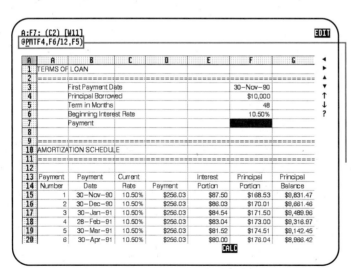

The formula shown in the control panel contains an error.

If you don't know what the problem is, give yourself time to think by converting the formula to a label. To do this, follow these steps (while in EDIT mode):

1. To convert a formula to a label from EDIT mode, press Home, ' , and then press ↵Enter.

The formula shown in the control panel has been converted to a label.

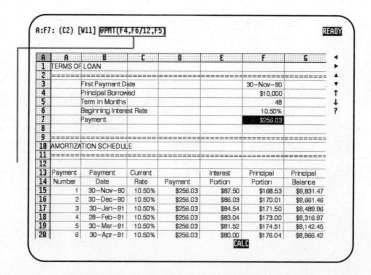

2. After you correct the formula, delete the apostrophe by pressing F2 to switch to EDIT mode. Next, press Home, followed by Del; then press ↵Enter.

The corrected formula is shown in the control panel.

If your formula is long and complex, break it down into logical segments and test each segment separately. Using smaller segments helps to debug the formula. Also, because 1-2-3 limits individual cell entries to 512 characters, the reduced size may be necessary for the program to accept the formula.

Common errors include open parentheses and commas that are missing from built-in formulas (functions). What appears to be a logical error may be only a missing punctuation mark. When 1-2-3 beeps to indicate a formula error, check the formula for a missing parenthesis or comma near the cursor.

Formulas that contain embedded or trailing spaces result in errors. To find a trailing space, press the End key while in EDIT mode. If the cursor is more than one character beyond the end of a formula, you can delete the trailing spaces with the Backspace key.

1-2-3 provides two commands to help you examine and analyze your formulas. The /**P**rint **P**rinter **O**ptions **O**ther **C**ell-Formulas command (discussed in Chapter 8) prints a list of all the formulas in your worksheet. The /**R**ange **F**ormat **T**ext command (discussed in Chapter 4) displays existing formulas in their worksheet locations.

Using Functions in Formulas

Like most electronic spreadsheets, 1-2-3 includes built-in functions. These functions fall into eight basic categories: (1) mathematical and trigonometric, (2) date and time, (3) financial, (4) statistical, (5) database, (6) logical, (7) string, and (8) special. Some of 1-2-3's functions are described in the text that follows. You can learn more about 1-2-3's functions in Chapter 7.

The mathematical and trigonometric functions perform standard arithmetic operations such as computing absolute value (@ABS) or square root (@SQRT), rounding numbers (@ROUND), and computing the sine (@SIN), cosine (@COS), and tangent (@TAN).

The date and time functions, such as @DATE and @TIME, convert dates and times to serial numbers. The serial numbers allow you to perform date and time arithmetic or to document your worksheets and reports.

The financial functions calculate returns on investments (@IRR and @RATE), loan payments (@PMT), present values (@NPV and @PV), future values (@FV), and compound growth periods (@TERM and @CTERM).

The statistical functions perform standard calculations on lists, such as summing values (@SUM), calculating averages (@AVG), finding minimum and maximum values (@MIN and @MAX), and computing standard deviations and variances (@STD and @VAR).

The database functions perform statistical calculations on a field of a database, based on certain criteria. These functions, such as @DSUM and @DAVG, have names and uses similar to the statistical functions.

The logical functions, such as @IF, @TRUE, and @FALSE, let you perform conditional tests. You can use these functions to test whether a condition is true or false.

The string functions help you manipulate text. You can use string functions to repeat text characters (@REPEAT), to convert letters to uppercase or lowercase (@UPPER or @LOWER), and to change strings to numbers and numbers to strings (@VALUE and @STRING).

The special functions perform a variety of tasks. For example, @CELL and @CELLPOINTER can return up to 10 different characteristics of a cell, including its width, format, type of address, and prefix.

Entering a 1-2-3 Function

As noted earlier, 1-2-3 has a variety of functions that perform many different tasks—from simple arithmetic to complex statistical analysis and depreciation calculations. Functions consist of three parts: the @ sign, a function name, and an argument or range. Note that range refers to the range of the cells that the function will use.

Consider the following function:

> @SUM(B1..E1)

This formula uses the @SUM function to compute the total of the range of four cells from B1 through E1. The @ sign signals that the entry is a function. SUM is the name of the function being used. You can enter function names with upper- or lowercase letters; this book uses uppercase letters to denote 1-2-3 functions. The statement (B1..E1) is the argument (in this case, a range). A function's arguments, always enclosed in parentheses, specify the cell or range of cells on which the function will act. This function tells 1-2-3 to compute the sum of the numbers in cells B1, C1, D1, and E1, and to display the result in the cell containing the formula.

Some functions can be quite complex. For example, you can combine several functions in a single cell by having one function use other functions as its arguments. The length of an argument, however, is limited—functions, like formulas, can contain only 512 characters per cell.

When you enter a function that requires a cell address, you can enter the address by typing or pointing.

3

To enter the formula @SUM(B7..B4) by pointing, follow these steps:

1. Move the cell pointer to the cell that will contain the formula, and type @ S U M (.

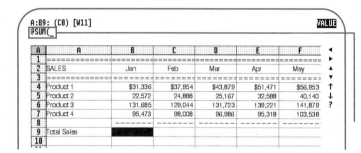

The @ sign, function name, and opening parenthesis are typed.

2. Move the cell pointer to a corner of the range and press .

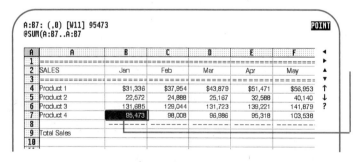

The cell pointer is anchored at B7.

3. Press ↑ three times.

```
A:B4: (C0) [W11] 31336                              POINT
@SUM(A:B7..A:B4)
```

A	A	B	C	D	E	F
1						
2	SALES	Jan	Feb	Mar	Apr	May
3						
4	Product 1	$31,336	$37,954	$43,879	$51,471	$56,953
5	Product 2	22,572	24,888	25,167	32,588	40,140
6	Product 3	131,685	129,044	131,723	139,221	141,879
7	Product 4	95,473	98,008	96,986	95,318	103,538
8						
9	Total Sales					
10						

The range of cells between B7 and B4 is highlighted.

4. Type the closing) and press ↵Enter.

```
A:B9: (C0) [W11] @SUM(B7..B4)                       READY
```

A	A	B	C	D	E	F
1						
2	SALES	Jan	Feb	Mar	Apr	May
3						
4	Product 1	$31,336	$37,954	$43,879	$51,471	$56,953
5	Product 2	22,572	24,888	25,167	32,588	40,140
6	Product 3	131,685	129,044	131,723	139,221	141,879
7	Product 4	95,473	98,008	96,986	95,318	103,538
8						
9	Total Sales	$281,066				
10						

1-2-3 enters the sum of B7..B4 into cell B9.

Note: You can also use a mouse to specify ranges used in functions. Specifying ranges with a mouse is covered in detail in Chapter 4.

Entering Formulas with Multiple Worksheets

Formulas can add values from other worksheets within the same file by including the other worksheets' letters as part of the cell address. For example, you can add the value in cell C4 from worksheet B to the value in cell C4 from worksheet C, and place the result in cell C4 of worksheet A. To do this, enter the following formula into cell C4 of worksheet A:

    +B:C4+C:C4

To use pointing to see other worksheets as you construct formulas, access 1-2-3's /Worksheet Window Perspective command to view three worksheets together. In

the following example, worksheet A is the consolidation worksheet, and
worksheets B and C are the detailed worksheets to be combined in worksheet A.
Note that these worksheets are structured in the same manner. Making
worksheets the same is not necessary, but creating formulas is much easier in
similar formats.

3

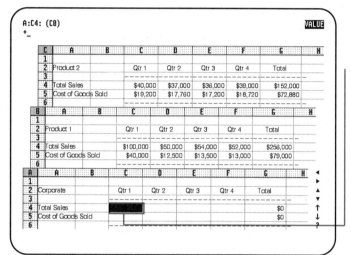

To enter a
multiple-
worksheet formula
by pointing,
highlight the cell
where you want to
place the formula
and type +.

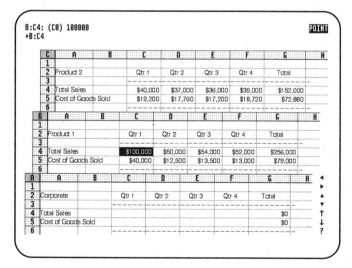

Move to the first
cell address in the
formula by
pressing F6
(Window) or
Ctrl PgUp, or by
clicking the up
arrow with the left
mouse button;
then type +.

3

Press [F6] (Window) twice, press [Ctrl][PgUp] twice, or click the up arrow twice with the left mouse button to reach the second worksheet to be summed, worksheet C.

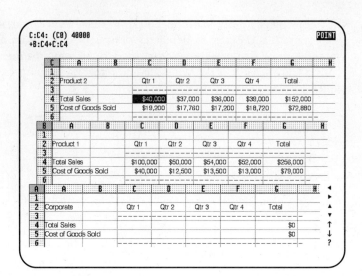

After you finish pointing to cells in each of the worksheets to be summed in the consolidation worksheet, press [↵Enter] to complete the formula.

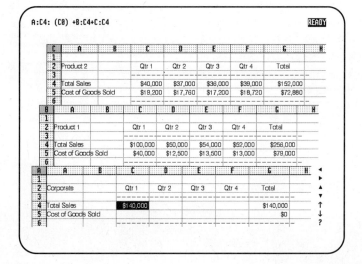

Adding Notes to Numbers and Formulas

You can add a descriptive note to a cell that contains a value; this technique helps explain a number or a formula. Type a semicolon (;) immediately after the number or formula, and then type the note. Do not type a space between the semicolon and the first character of the note. Your notes appear in the control panel but not in the worksheet. Using notes to annotate values does not affect the results of any other formulas that refer to these values.

100

```
A:C7: (C0) +C4-C5; Includes Products 1 and 2 only          READY
```

	A	B	C	D	E	F	G	H
1								
2	Corporate		Qtr 1	Qtr 2	Qtr 3	Qtr 4	Total	
3								
4	Total Sales		$140,000	$87,000	$90,000	$91,000	$408,000	
5	Cost of Goods Sold		$59,200	$30,260	$30,700	$31,720	$151,880	
6								
7	Gross Margin		$80,800	$56,740	$59,300	$59,280	$256,120	
8								
9								
10	G & A Expenses		$25,000	$35,000	$45,000	$55,000	$160,000	
11	Interest Expense		$3,000	$3,000	$3,000	$3,000	$12,000	
12								
13	Profit Before Tax		$52,800	$18,740	$11,300	$1,280	$84,120	
14								
15								

Add notes to cell entries to explain numbers and formulas in the worksheet.

3

Editing Data in the Worksheet

One of the first things you need to be able to do when entering data into a 1-2-3 worksheet is to modify the contents of cells without retyping the complete entry. You can easily change an existing cell entry by using the Edit (F2) key from the keyboard or by using the Wysiwyg :Text Edit command that allows you to use a mouse.

Using the Edit (F2) Key

To edit data with the Edit (F2) key, begin by moving the cell pointer to the appropriate cell and pressing Edit (F2). After you press Edit (F2), the mode indicator in the upper right corner of the screen changes to EDIT. The contents of the cell are duplicated in the second line of the control panel (the edit line), the cursor appears at the end of the entry, and you are ready for editing.

When you first press Edit (F2), 1-2-3 is in insert mode. Any new characters you type are inserted at the cursor, and any characters on the right side of the cursor are pushed one position to the right. If you activate overtype mode by pressing the Ins key on the numeric keypad, any new character you type replaces the character directly above the cursor, and the cursor moves one position to the right. When 1-2-3 is in overtype mode, the indicator OVR appears at the bottom of the screen. Pressing the Ins key again switches 1-2-3 back to insert mode.

To edit the contents of a cell with the keyboard, follow these steps:

1. Highlight the appropriate cell and press F2 (Edit).

   Notice that the mode indicator changes to EDIT. (If the entry contains more than one line of characters, the control panel expands to display the entire cell entry.)

In this example, highlight cell A12 and press F2 (Edit).

```
A:A12: [W17] 'Adverrtising Expense                                    EDIT
'Adverrtising Expense_
```

	A	B	C	D	E	F
2	SALES	Jan	Feb	Mar	Apr	May
4	Product 1	$31,336	$37,954	$43,879	$51,471	$56,953
5	Product 2	22,572	24,888	25,167	32,588	40,140
6	Product 3	131,685	129,044	131,723	139,221	141,879
7	Product 4	95,473	98,008	96,986	95,318	103,538
9	Total Sales	$281,066	$289,894	$297,755	$318,598	$342,510
12	Adverrtising Expense					

2. With the contents of the cell displayed in the second line of the control panel, move the cursor to the part of the entry you want to edit (by pressing ← or →).

   In this example, use ← to move the cursor to the second "r."

3. Use one or more of the editing keys, described in table 3.3, to modify the cell's contents.

   In this example, press Del to delete the character above the cursor.

4. Press ↵Enter (or type any new characters and then press ↵Enter) to complete the edit and return the worksheet to READY mode.

You can also use Edit (F2) when you enter data into a cell for the first time. If you make a mistake while you enter the data, you can correct the error without retyping the entire entry. Table 3.5 provides a listing of the key actions available with the Edit (F2) key.

Table 3.5
Key Actions Available with Edit (F2)

Key	Action
←	Moves the cursor one position to the left.
→	Moves the cursor one position to the right.

Table 3.5 (continued)

Key	Action
Tab⇥ or Ctrl→	Moves the cursor five characters to the right.
⇧Shift Tab⇥ or Ctrl←	Moves the cursor five characters to the left.
Home	Moves the cursor to the first character in the entry.
End	Moves the cursor one position to the right of the last character in the entry.
←Backspace	Deletes the character to the left of the cursor.
Del	Deletes the character above the cursor.
Ins	Toggles between insert and overtype modes.
Esc	Clears the edit line. When pressed again, abandons changes and leaves EDIT mode.

Wysiwyg Editing

The **:Text Edit** command on the Wysiwyg menu provides you with additional editing features. With this command, you can enter and edit a range of labels right in the worksheet (instead of the control panel). The process is similar to that of editing a paragraph within a word processing program, because Wysiwyg treats the range that you specify for editing as a "paragraph."

A:A12	row: 1 col: 5 Left-Aligned					LABEL

	A	B	C	D	E	F
1	===					
2	SALES	Jan	Feb	Mar	Apr	May
3	===					
4	Product 1	$31,336	$37,954	$43,879	$51,471	$56,953
5	Product 2	22,572	24,888	25,167	32,588	40,140
6	Product 3	131,685	129,044	131,723	139,221	141,879
7	Product 4	95,473	98,008	96,986	95,318	103,538
8		--------	--------	--------	--------	--------
9	Total Sales	$281,066	$289,894	$297,755	$318,598	$342,510
10		=======	=======	=======	=======	=======
11						
12	Advertising Expense					
13						
14						

The **:Text Edit** command allows you to edit a range of data within the worksheet area.

103

When you choose **:Text Edit** and specify a cell or range of cells, a vertical-line cursor appears in front of the first character in the label. Move the cursor by using the arrow keys on the keyboard, or clicking the triangle icons with the mouse. Delete characters using Del and Backspace; insert characters by typing them from the keyboard. Complete the edit by pressing Esc or clicking the right mouse button.

Table 3.6 lists the editing keys available when you use the **:Text Edit** command in Wysiwyg. Notice that more editing keys are available this way than by using the Edit (F2) key; some of the same keys used with both methods have different meanings.

Table 3.6
Key Actions Available with :Text Edit

Key	Action
←	Moves the cursor one position to the left in the range.
→	Moves the cursor one position to the right in the range.
↑	Moves the cursor up one row in the range.
↓	Moves the cursor down one row in the range.
Tab⇆ or Ctrl→	Moves the cursor to the end of the next word.
⇧Shift Tab⇆ or Ctrl←	Moves the cursor to the beginning of the previous word.
PgUp	Moves the cursor up one screen.
PgDn	Moves the cursor down one screen.
Home	Moves the cursor to the first character in the line. When pressed a second time, moves the cursor to the first character of the paragraph (range).
End	Moves the cursor to the last character in the line. When pressed a second time, moves the cursor to the last character of the paragraph (range).
↵Enter	Starts a new line.

Table 3.6 (continued)

Key	Action
◆Backspace	Deletes the character to the left of the cursor.
Del	Deletes the character to the right of the cursor.
Ins	Toggles between insert and overtype modes.
Esc	Completes the edit and returns 1-2-3 to READY mode.
Ctrl ↵Enter	Creates an end-of-paragraph symbol and begins a new line.
F3	Displays a menu of different formats that can be applied to the text in the range.

Using the Undo Feature

When you use electronic spreadsheet packages, you can destroy hours of work by using the wrong commands or typing over existing entries. For example, if you type over a complicated formula, you can undo the new entry and restore the old one. It is easy to confuse the command to delete rows or columns (/**W**orksheet **D**elete) with the command to erase a range (/**R**ange Erase) and delete a row or column while intending merely to erase data. The results can be difficult to recover from—particularly when formulas depend on those deleted rows or columns.

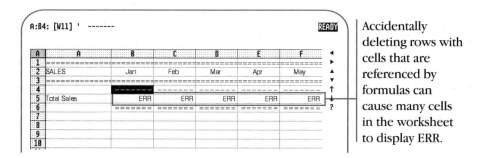

Accidentally deleting rows with cells that are referenced by formulas can cause many cells in the worksheet to display ERR.

The Undo feature, which is activated by pressing the key combination Alt-F4 (hold down the Alt key and press F4), in most cases returns the worksheet to its previous appearance and condition before the most recent command or entry. You can undo only the last command or entry, and once you press Undo (Alt-F4), 1-2-3 provides you with a No/Yes menu that allows you to change your mind before Undo acts. If you select **Yes** from this menu, Undo performs and cannot be reversed.

Press Alt F4 (Undo) to undo the last command. 1-2-3 prompts you with a menu to verify your selection.

```
A:B4: [W11] '  -------                                    MENU
No Yes
Undo most recent modifications to worksheet data
A           A          B         C        D        E        F      ◄
 1     ==================================================================
 2    SALES          Jan        Feb       Mar      Apr      May    ▲
 3     ==================================================================
 4                                                                 ↑
 5    Total Sales    ERR        ERR       ERR      ERR      ERR    ↓
 6                                                                 ?
 7
 8
 9
10
```

In this example, selecting **Yes** returns the original contents to the deleted rows.

```
A:B4: (C0) [W11] 31336                                    READY

A          A          B          C          D          E          F      ◄
 1    ==================================================================
 2   SALES          Jan        Feb        Mar        Apr        May    ▲
 3    ==================================================================
 4   Product 1     $31,336    $37,954    $43,879    $51,471    $56,953  ↑
 5   Product 2      22,572     24,888     25,167     32,588     40,140  ↓
 6   Product 3     131,685    129,044    131,723    139,221    141,879  ?
 7   Product 4      95,473     98,008     96,986     95,318    103,538
 8
 9   Total Sales  $281,066   $289,894   $297,755   $318,598   $342,510
10    ==================================================================
11
12
```

Using the command that resets (clears) all range names (/**Range Name Reset**), instead of the command that deletes individual range names (/**Range Name Delete**), is another common mistake that can create frustration—especially when many range names are used in a worksheet. Undo is a quick solution for recovering the lost range names. You must, however, catch errors immediately because the only command you can reverse is the last one you entered.

The Undo feature also has other uses. Every user is sometimes apprehensive about using certain commands because of the possibility of unexpected results or potential disasters. With Undo you can proceed with a command, having confidence that if you don't like the results you can reverse them. However, note that some commands cannot be reversed—especially those that involve changes to a file on disk, such as /**File Erase**.

Activating and Deactivating Undo

Initially, the Undo feature is disabled, so you must use commands to enable Undo. To turn on the Undo feature, select the command /**Worksheet Global Default Other Undo Enable**.

To make this change permanent—so that the Undo feature is active each time you access 1-2-3—you must also select the command /**Worksheet Global Default Update** before exiting 1-2-3. You can use the /**Worksheet Global Default Status** command to check whether or not the Undo feature is active.

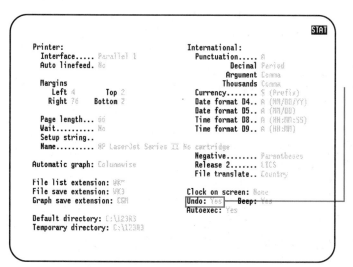

When the Undo feature is active, the Undo: line of the /**Worksheet Global Default Status** screen displays Yes.

In order for the Undo feature to work, 1-2-3 creates a temporary backup copy of the entire worksheet whenever you start a command or cell entry. This information is stored in your computer's temporary memory (RAM). Storing this data takes up space and limits the worksheet size you can build with 1-2-3.

As a worksheet grows in size, the amount of memory reserved for holding a backup copy of the last worksheet image becomes exhausted, and you may not be able to use the Undo feature. Under these circumstances, you can deactivate the Undo feature temporarily with the /**Worksheet Global Default Other Undo Disable** command.

107

This command makes the Undo feature unavailable, but it creates more room for your worksheet to grow. If you later start to work on another worksheet (before exiting 1-2-3), you can reactivate the Undo feature with the command /Worksheet Global Default Other Undo Enable.

If you become accustomed to the Undo feature and rely on it heavily for security, avoid building worksheets so large that they prevent your use of Undo.

What Can't Be Undone?

There is no way to undo some commands. You cannot "unerase," "unsave," or "unextract" a disk file; neither can you "unprint" your last printed output.

You can undo most other commands, however, including the entire sequence of commands associated with creating graphs, setting up ranges for data query commands, and all "undo-able" steps embedded within a macro.

Naming, Saving, and Retrieving Files

The sections that follow explain file operations that beginning 1-2-3 users need most often—naming, saving, and retrieving files. For more information about other file operations, including deleting and listing files; specialized operations such as protecting files with passwords; combining, linking, and transferring files; and using the Translate Utility, see Chapter 10.

Naming Files

1-2-3 file names are up to eight characters long with a three-character extension. Note that in Release 3.1, you can create file names with more than eight characters. However, to maintain compatibility with DOS and earlier versions of 1-2-3, it is highly recommended that you use no more than eight characters in your file names.

The basic rules for naming files are the following:

- File names may include the characters A through Z, the numbers 0 through 9, the hyphen (–), and the underscore (_). Depending on your system, you may be able to use other special characters, but 1-2-3 will not accept the characters <, >, or *. Although 1-2-3 separates the file name from the three-letter extension with a period (.), the program does not accept the period within the file name. Therefore, the following file names are illegal:

CH<15>.WK1

TOM*BBS.PRN

SALES.89.WK1

- File names should not contain blank spaces. For example, SALES RPT.WK1 is not a valid file name. Note that Release 3.1 supports the use of spaces in file names, but for compatibility reasons, it is not recommended that they be used.

- 1-2-3 automatically converts lowercase letters to uppercase letters in file names.

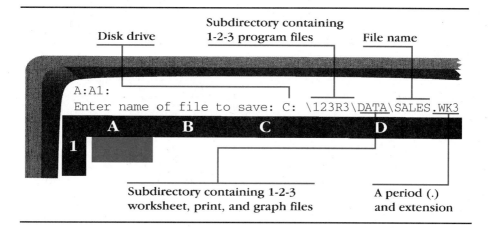

Although you determine the eight-character file name, 1-2-3 automatically creates the extension based on its type of file format. The basic file extensions are the following:

- WK3 is the extension automatically added to names of worksheet files saved with the /**File S**ave command. If you choose to back up an existing file while saving, the BAK extension is assigned to the previous version of the file.

- PRN is the extension automatically added to names of 1-2-3 files that you save in text (ASCII) format with the /**Print F**ile command. PRN files can be printed or imported into 1-2-3 and other programs.

- CGM or PIC (depending on the current /**Worksheet G**lobal **D**efault **Graph** setting) is the extension automatically added to names of graph files saved with the /**Graph S**ave command.

Note: The different versions of Release 3 can read older 1-2-3 worksheets with WK1 and WK3 extensions, but if you want to use WK3 files with earlier versions of 1-2-3, you need to use the Translate Utility (discussed in Chapter 10) or save your worksheet files with WK1 extensions from within Release 3 or 3.1.

In addition to creating files with the WK3, BAK, PRN, and CGM or PIC extensions, 1-2-3 enables you to supply your own extension. Simply enter the file name according to the previously listed rules, enter a period, and add an extension of one to three characters. Note that 1-2-3 does not display any file name with your special extension when the program lists worksheet, print, or graph files. The /**File** **R**etrieve command, for example, displays all worksheet (WK3, WK1, and WKS) files except for those with your special extensions. To retrieve your special file, type the file name, including the period and extension, after the `Name of file to retrieve:` prompt.

Remember to be descriptive when you think of a name for the new file. Choose a file name that relates something about the file's contents. This will prevent confusion once you have created several different files and need to access a particular file quickly. The following list provides some good examples of file names:

File name	Description
INV_JUN	Inventory worksheet for June
PRO_REST	*Pro forma* worksheet for a planned restaurant
EMPLSTDP	Employee list for the Data Processing Department

If you work with many different worksheets containing basically the same information, you should use similar names without, of course, using the same names. For example, if you use the name SALES91 for a sales worksheet for the year 1991, you can name the sales worksheets for 1992 and 1993 SALES92 and SALES93, respectively. This naming technique will help you recall file names later.

Saving Files

Computerized spreadsheets have one danger that is not as common in the paper-and-pencil world. If you keep track of your business accounts manually, you can simply get up from your desk and walk away when you decide to quit working. There's nothing to "exit," nothing to turn off (except, perhaps, a calculator), and usually nothing that might cause your work to vanish from your desk. Unless they are misplaced or accidentally thrown away, the materials you use in a manual accounting system remain safely on your desk until morning.

With electronic spreadsheets—and with computer files in general—the risks of power outages or human errors can be costly in terms of data and time loss. If you exit 1-2-3 without saving your file, any work that you have done since the last time you saved the file is lost. You can recover the data only by retyping it into the worksheet. You should make an effort, therefore, to save your files frequently—at least once every half hour to one hour (depending on how many changes are made).

To save a new or existing file with the keyboard, follow these steps:

1. Select /File Save.

```
A:B4: (C0) [W11] 31336                                          EDIT
Enter name of file to save: C:\123R3\DATA\FILE0001.WK3_
```

A	A	B	C	D	E	F	
1	=========	======	======	======	======	======	▶
2	SALES	Jan	Feb	Mar	Apr	May	▲
3	=========	======	======	======	======	======	▼
4	Product 1	$31,336	$37,954	$43,879	$51,471	$56,953	↑
5	Product 2	22,572	24,888	25,167	32,588	40,140	↓
6	Product 3	131,685	129,044	131,723	139,221	141,879	?
7	Product 4	95,473	98,008	96,986	95,318	103,538	
8		--------	--------	--------	--------	--------	
9	Total Sales	$281,066	$289,894	$297,755	$318,598	$342,510	
10		======	======	======	======	======	
11							
12							

When you save a new worksheet file, 1-2-3 automatically displays a default file name such as FILE0001.WK3.

You can press
Esc followed by
F3 (Name) to
view a full-screen
list of all
worksheet files on
the current drive
and directory.

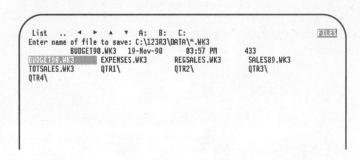

```
   List  ..  ◄  ►  ▲  ▼  A:  B:  C:                          FILES
   Enter name of file to save: C:\123R3\DATA\*.WK3
            BUDGET90.WK3   19-Nov-90    03:57 PM      433
   BUDGET90.WK3          EXPENSES.WK3       REGSALES.WK3      SALES89.WK3
   TOTSALES.WK3          QTR1\              QTR2\             QTR3\
   QTR4\
```

2. Highlight one of the displayed worksheet file names or type a new file
   name.

Remember to
choose descriptive
file names that
identify the files
for ease in locating
them later.

```
A:B4: (C0) [W11] 31336                                         EDIT
Enter name of file to save: C:\123R3\DATA\TOTSALES

   A        A          B         C         D         E         F      ◄
  1  ===================================================================  ►
  2  SALES         Jan        Feb       Mar       Apr       May         ▲
  3  -------------------------------------------------------------------  ▼
  4  Product 1    $31,336    $37,954   $43,879   $51,471   $56,953      ↑
  5  Product 2     22,572     24,888    25,167    32,588    40,140      ↓
  6  Product 3    131,685    129,044   131,723   139,221   141,879      ?
  7  Product 4     95,473     98,008    96,986    95,318   103,538
  8  -------------------------------------------------------------------
  9  Total Sales $281,066   $289,894  $297,755  $318,598  $342,510
 10  ===================================================================
 11
 12
```

3. Press Enter. 1-2-3 automatically supplies a WK3 extension for a new
   file and saves the file on disk.

   If you are saving an existing file, another menu appears with the options
   Cancel, **R**eplace, and **B**ackup. To update the current file on disk, select
   Replace.

Choose the
Backup option if
you want to save
the latest changes
made to an
existing file.

```
A:B4: (C0) [W11] 31336                                         MENU
Cancel  Replace  Backup
Create a backup file from a file on disk (with a .BAK extension)
   A        A          B         C         D         E         F      ◄
  1  ===================================================================  ►
  2  SALES         Jan        Feb       Mar       Apr       May         ▲
  3  -------------------------------------------------------------------  ▼
  4  Product 1    $31,336    $37,954   $43,879   $51,471   $56,953      ↑
  5  Product 2     22,572     24,888    25,167    32,588    40,140      ↓
  6  Product 3    131,685    129,044   131,723   139,221   141,879      ?
  7  Product 4     95,473     98,008    96,986    95,318   103,538
  8  -------------------------------------------------------------------
  9  Total Sales $281,066   $289,894  $297,755  $318,598  $342,510
 10  ===================================================================
 11
 12
```

112

3

Backup is an alternative to the **C**ancel and **R**eplace options of /**F**ile **S**ave. **B**ackup renames the older version of your file—using the same file name—and adds BAK as the file extension. The current version of your file is then saved with the WK3 extension. This process allows you always to have available your two most recent worksheet versions.

Saving on the Hard Disk and also on a Floppy Diskette

If you use a hard disk system, you may want to save your worksheets on the hard disk as well as on a floppy diskette. To do this, follow these steps:

1. To save your worksheet on the hard disk, select /**F**ile **S**ave, type the file name after the hard disk drive and directory prompt and press ⏎Enter.

   Note: If you are saving a file that has been previously saved, highlight (or type) the existing file name, press ⏎Enter, and select **R**eplace.

2. To save your worksheet on a floppy diskette, select /**F**ile **S**ave, and press the Esc key one or more times—until the prompt Enter name of file to save: is all that remains.

3. Type the disk drive designation (for example **A:**), followed by the file name and press ⏎Enter.

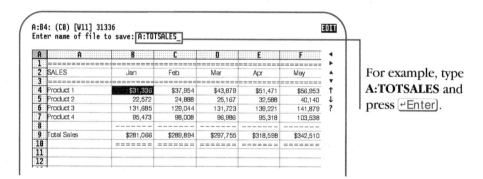

For example, type **A:TOTSALES** and press ⏎Enter.

Checking Disk Space before Saving

As you use 1-2-3, you soon have several worksheet files that take up significant disk space. Although hard disk users generally don't have to worry about running out of disk space when saving, floppy diskette users need to check the amount of disk space periodically. You need to monitor the amount of disk space your files

3

use, however, no matter what type of system you use. Nothing is worse than getting the message `Disk full` after you have worked on an important worksheet and are attempting to save it.

You can avoid this problem by using 1-2-3's /System command. Whenever you select /System, 1-2-3 steps aside and displays the DOS prompt. Even though the DOS prompt is displayed, 1-2-3 and your current worksheet are still in memory.

At the DOS prompt, type **CHKDSK** and press Enter to see how much space is available on your disk.

To check the space remaining on a floppy diskette, you must follow the CHKDSK command with the disk drive designation, such as **CHKDSK A:**.

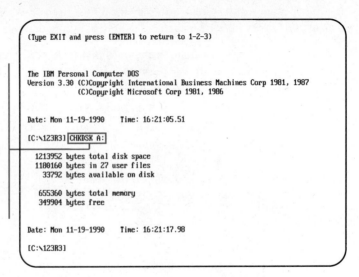

```
(Type EXIT and press [ENTER] to return to 1-2-3)


The IBM Personal Computer DOS
Version 3.30 (C)Copyright International Business Machines Corp 1981, 1987
                (C)Copyright Microsoft Corp 1981, 1986


Date: Mon 11-19-1990    Time: 16:21:05.51

[C:\123R3] CHKDSK A:

  1213952 bytes total disk space
  1180160 bytes in 27 user files
    33792 bytes available on disk

   655360 bytes total memory
   349904 bytes free


Date: Mon 11-19-1990    Time: 16:21:17.98

[C:\123R3]
```

You also can use the FORMAT command of DOS to format a new diskette if you need one (see your DOS manual).

If you are using a hard disk system, and your hard disk is almost full, you can erase some of the old files before saving the new files. (First make sure that you have a proper backup of the old files.)

When you finish the DOS operations, type **exit** and press Enter to return to the 1-2-3 worksheet. Now you can save the current worksheet.

One point to remember: When you use /System to exit to DOS, do not start any program from DOS that will alter memory, such as a memory-resident program. If you do, you won't be able to return to the 1-2-3 worksheet, and you will lose any work you have not saved.

114

Retrieving Files

To call a file back into memory from disk, use the /File Retrieve command. If you are just starting 1-2-3, this command brings a new file into memory. Otherwise, this command replaces the current file with the new file. Therefore, be sure you have saved the current file with /File Save before retrieving a new file.

To retrieve a file with the keyboard, follow these steps:

1. Select /File Retrieve.

   The files displayed have the WK3 extension. Any WK1 and WKS files from older versions of 1-2-3 are also listed.

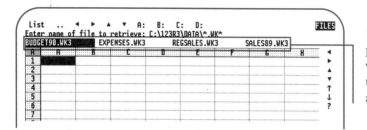

1-2-3 displays a partial list of worksheet files in the current drive and directory.

2. If you don't see the file name you want, press ⎡F3⎤ (Name).

   When you highlight a file name, you also see the date and time the file was created, as well as its size.

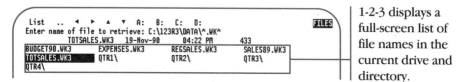

1-2-3 displays a full-screen list of file names in the current drive and directory.

3. Select the desired file name by highlighting or typing it; then press ⎡↵Enter⎤.

Using Wild Cards for File Retrieval

When you retrieve files, you can use wild cards with 1-2-3. Wild cards—the asterisk (*) and the question mark (?)—are helpful when you need to limit the

3

number of files that are displayed on-screen, or when you are unsure of the exact spelling of a file you wnt to retrieve.

If you want to display only those file names that begin or end with a certain character or characters, use the asterisk (*). For example, you can type **S*** and then press ⏎Enter at the `Name of file to retrieve:` prompt.

All the file names that begin with the letter S are displayed.

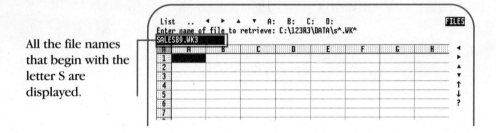

You can use the asterisk (*) wild card in place of any combination of characters; the question mark (?) wild card stands for any one character. The asterisk can be used by itself or following other characters. According to these rules, SALES*.WK1 is acceptable, but *89.WK1 is not. The question mark wild card, on the other hand, can be used in any character position. Therefore, instead of the incorrect retrieval name *89.WK1, you can enter **?????89.WK1**.

Retrieving Files from Subdirectories

1-2-3 keeps track of subdirectory names as well as file names. When you issue the /**F**ile **R**etrieve command, for example, subdirectories of the current directory are displayed with the file names.

The backslash (\) symbol following a name (within a list of file names) indicates a subdirectory name.

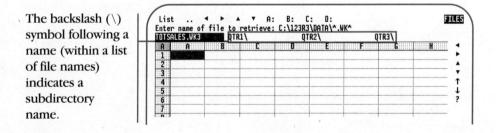

When you select a subdirectory name, 1-2-3 displays the list of files in that subdirectory.

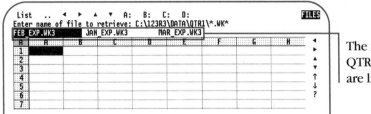

The files in the QTR1 subdirectory are listed.

3

When you need to access a file that is on a different drive—or one that is in a directory that is not a subdirectory of the current directory—use the Esc key or the Backspace key after selecting /File Retrieve. When you press Esc while the default path name shows on the control panel, 1-2-3 changes to EDIT mode. You can then edit the file specification just as you would any label entry. When you press Esc a second time, 1-2-3 erases the current drive and directory specification. You can then enter the specification for the drive and directory you want.

You can use the Backspace key to erase the path name, one entire subdirectory at a time. To reverse the process, select a subdirectory name from the list of files and press Enter.

Some valid file names, with their drive and directory specifications, are the following:

File name	Description
B:\SAMPLE1.WK3	Worksheet file on drive B
C:\123R3\SAMPLE1.WK3	Worksheet file in subdirectory \123R3 on drive C
C:\123R3\DATA*.PIC	List of all PIC files in subdirectory DATA of subdirectory \123R3 on drive C. 1-2-3 displays the list and waits for you to select a specific file name.
A:*.*	List of all files on drive A. 1-2-3 displays all file names and waits for you to select a specific file name.

3

Summary

This chapter on 1-2-3 basics covered many important concepts that are essential for beginning 1-2-3 users. You learned about moving the cell pointer around the worksheet using the keyboard and the mouse; selecting commands from the 1-2-3 and Wysiwyg menus; entering and editing data, formulas, and labels; using the Undo feature; and naming, saving, and retrieving 1-2-3 files.

Specifically, you learned the following key information about 1-2-3:

■ The arrow keys move the cell pointer horizontally and vertically, one cell at a time. When used with the End key, however, they can move the cell pointer quickly—even to the remote borders of 1-2-3's large worksheet.

■ The PgUp, PgDn, Tab, and Shift-Tab keys help you move around the worksheet one screen at a time (up, down, right, and left, respectively).

■ The Home key moves the cell pointer to the upper left corner of a worksheet—to cell A1. When you specify a cell address for the GoTo (F5) function key, you make the cell pointer jump almost instantly to any cell in the worksheet.

■ Commands are selected with the keyboard from 1-2-3's menu system by pressing slash (/) and from Wysiwyg's menu system by pressing colon (:). Next, either point to the desired command and press Enter or directly select the command by typing the first letter of the menu command.

■ To select 1-2-3 or Wysiwyg commands with a mouse, move the mouse pointer to the control-panel area to generate a menu. Press the right mouse button to toggle between menus. Commands are selected by clicking the left mouse button on the desired command.

■ Two types of data can be entered into a 1-2-3 worksheet: labels and values. Labels are text entries, and values include numbers, formulas, and functions.

■ Label prefixes are used to affect how text data is displayed in individual cells. The label prefixes include ' (left-justify), "(right-justify), ^ (center), and \ (repeat label). The /Range Label command aligns labels in a range of cells, and the /Worksheet Global Label command changes the alignment of labels for the entire worksheet.

■ A strength of 1-2-3 is its capability to accept and compute complex numerical data, formulas, and functions. 1-2-3's functions, always identified by the @ symbol preceding the function's name, are used within formulas to provide exceptional power in your worksheets.

- The Edit (F2) key is used to modify any data that has been entered (or is currently being entered) into the worksheet. The direction keys are used to move the cursor in the control panel while editing a cell entry. In Wysiwyg, you can use **:T**ext Edit to edit a range of data within the worksheet itself.

- The Undo feature, activated by pressing Alt-F4, enables you to "undo" the previous command before the next command is executed. To use Undo, you must first select the command **/**Worksheet Global Default Other Undo Enable. To release the extra memory required by Undo, you can temporarily deactivate the Undo feature with the **/**Worksheet Global Default Other Undo Disable command.

- File names used in 1-2-3 should be no more than eight characters in length, followed by a period (.) and a three-character extension. File extensions used in 1-2-3 include WK3 for worksheet files (WK1 and WKS for older versions of 1-2-3), BAK for backup worksheet files, PRN for ASCII print files, and CGM or PIC for graph files.

- The **/F**ile **S**ave command is used to save the current worksheet file. If the file name already exists, 1-2-3 prompts you to **R**eplace the existing file or **C**ancel the command. The **B**ackup option ensures that the previous two versions of the worksheet will always be available.

- The **/F**ile **R**etrieve command is used to call an existing file into memory. 1-2-3 provides a list of worksheet files (and subdirectories) located in the current directory. The wild-card characters, * and ?, are used to limit the files displayed with the **/F**ile **R**etrieve command.

The 1-2-3 basics provided in this chapter will enable you to begin working with ranges, which are discussed in the next chapter.

3

Working with Ranges

This chapter (with the next two chapters) teaches you the principles of using commands and shows you how to use some of the fundamental 1-2-3 commands needed to build worksheets. Although most of the commands discussed in this chapter are from the /Range menu, some options from the /Worksheet menu are also included. Chapters 4, 5, and 6 discuss the commands you use to create a worksheet.

To make sense of the command structure, you first need to understand the concept of ranges. While some commands affect the entire worksheet, others affect only certain cells or groups of cells. 1-2-3 uses the term *range* for a rectangular block of cells, and many useful 1-2-3 actions are built around the range concept. Multiple-worksheet applications allow for the definition of three-dimensional ranges. This chapter explains the concept of ranges and shows you how to use them with specific commands.

Ranges offer many advantages that make your work less tedious and more efficient. When you use *ranges*, you can execute commands that affect all the cells in a group rather than one individual cell. For example, you can format a block of cells to be displayed as currency by executing a single command on the specified range of cells.

4

Key Terms in This Chapter

Range	A rectangular group of cells used in a worksheet operation. For example, the rectangular area A5..D10 is a range. Ranges can be three-dimensional in multiple-worksheet applications.
Range commands	Commands used to manipulate cells in ranges. You can access the /Range commands through the **R**ange option on the 1-2-3 main menu.
Range name	An alphanumeric name of up to 15 characters given to a rectangular group of cells.
GROUP mode	In a multiple-worksheet file, the /**W**orksheet **G**lobal **G**roup **E**nable command enables you to perform certain commands on all worksheets at once.
Preselecting a range	Selecting the range to be affected by a command with the F4 key before the command is issued.
Range name table	A list of all range names and their corresponding cell addresses. This list is produced with the /**R**ange **N**ame **T**able command.
Formatting	The process of changing the way data is displayed in the worksheet. Formatting is accomplished with the /**R**ange **F**ormat or /**W**orksheet **G**lobal **F**ormat commands.

When you use range names instead of cell addresses, you can quickly process blocks of cells in commands and formulas. A descriptive range name will help you and others recognize the nature of the data that the range contains. You can use the range name with the GoTo (F5) key to move the cell pointer quickly to that range in the worksheet.

Using the Mouse

To use a mouse with 1-2-3 Release 3.1, you need a mouse, mouse software, and a graphics monitor and graphics card that support a mouse. Also, Wysiwyg must be loaded in memory. You can use a mouse to select commands and files, specify ranges, and move the cell pointer within a worksheet or between multiple worksheets and files. In the examples throughout this chapter, notice that 1-2-3 commands always begin with a slash (/), and Wysiwyg commands always begin with a colon (:). Refer to the following sections of the specified chapters for further information on using the mouse:

- Chapter 2—"Understanding Mouse Terminology"
- Chapter 3—"Mouse Control of the Cell Pointer"
      "Using the Mouse To Select Menu Commands"
- Chapter 4—"Using the Mouse To Specify Ranges"

What Is a Range?

1-2-3's definition of a range is a rectangular block of adjacent cells. The smallest possible range is one cell, and the largest is the entire worksheet. Remember that ranges are specified by the cells in the upper-left and lower-right corners of the range.

This large range is made up of cells C4..E9.

This range is the smallest possible range: one cell. The range's address is A9.

This range is one column in width. The address for the range is F4..F9.

A:A1: [W13] \=					READY
	A	B	C	D	E	F
1						
2 SALES			Jan	Feb	Mar	1st Qtr
3						
4 Product 1			$31,336	$37,954	$43,879	$113,169
5 Product 2			22,572	24,888	25,167	$72,627
6 Product 3			131,685	129,044	131,723	$392,452
7 Product 4			95,473	98,008	96,986	$290,467
8						
9 Total Sales			$281,066	$289,894	$297,755	$868,715
10						

Access the /Range commands by selecting **Range** from the 1-2-3 main menu. You then see the following menu of commands:

Format Label Erase Name Justify Prot Unprot Input Value Trans Search

Table 4.1 provides a brief description of the actions of each of these commands.

Table 4.1
Selections on the /Range Menu

Selection	Description
Format	Changes the display of values or formula results in a cell or range of cells.
Label	Aligns text labels in a cell or range of cells.
Erase	Deletes the contents of a cell or range of cells.
Name	Assigns, modifies, or deletes a name associated with a cell or range of cells.
Justify	Fits text within a desired range by wrapping words to form complete paragraphs with lines of approximately the same length.
Prot (Protect)	Prevents changes to cell ranges when /Worksheet Global Protection is enabled.
Unprot (Unprotect)	With /Worksheet Global Protection active, enables changes to a range of cells and identifies (through increases in intensity or changes of color) which cells' contents can be changed.
Input	With /Worksheet Global Protection active, restricts movement of the cell pointer to unprotected cells in a range.
Value	Copies formulas in a range to their values in another specified range (or the same range).
Trans (Transpose)	Reorders columns of data into rows or rows of data into columns.
Search	Finds or replaces a string of data within a specified range.

Designating a Range

Many commands act on ranges. For example, the /Range Erase command prompts you for the range to erase. You can respond to a prompt for a range in the following three ways:

- Type the addresses of the upper-left and lower-right cells in the range.
- Use the direction keys or the mouse to highlight the cells in the range.
- Type the range name or press Name (F3) to display a list of range names and select the range name you want.

Each method is covered in the following sections. You also learn how to preselect a range so that you can execute multiple commands on a single range more quickly.

Typing Range Addresses

Using the typing method, you specify a range by typing the address of the upper-left and lower-right corners. Be sure to separate the two addresses with one or two periods. 1-2-3 always stores a range with two periods, but you have to type only one period.

To specify the range C4..F9, you can type **C4..F9** or **C4.F9**. 1-2-3 stores the range containing C4, F4, C9, and F9 as the four range corners.

You can type cell addresses to specify a range in several situations: when the range does not have a range name, when the range you want to specify is far from the current cell, or when you know the addresses of the range. Experienced 1-2-3 users rarely type cell addresses; they highlight a range in POINT mode or use range names instead.

125

Highlighting a Range

The second method, that of highlighting the cells in the range in POINT mode, is used most often. You can point to and highlight a range in commands and functions just as you can point to a single cell in a formula.

Following the prompt to enter a range, 1-2-3 displays the address of the cell pointer in the control panel. This single cell, shown as a one-cell range, is anchored. The default range with most /Range commands is an anchored one-cell range. When the cell is anchored, you highlight a range as you move the cell pointer.

When a range is highlighted, the cells of the range appear in reverse video. Reverse video allows ranges to be specified easily, with little chance for error. As you move the cell pointer, the reverse-video rectangle expands until you finish specifying the range.

Suppose, for example, that you select the /Range Erase command. 1-2-3 displays the prompt Enter range to erase:.

The location of the cell pointer marks the beginning of the anchored range.

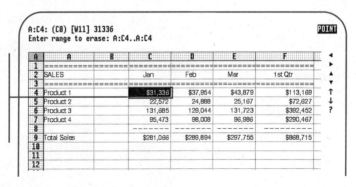

To clear an incorrectly highlighted range, press Esc or Backspace. The highlight collapses to the anchored cell only, and the anchor is removed—allowing you to move the cell pointer to the correct location at the beginning of the range.

You can use the End key with the direction keys to quickly highlight large ranges. Use the End key to move the cell pointer to the boundaries of contiguous data ranges.

Pointing (or highlighting) is faster and easier than typing the range addresses. You also make fewer errors by pointing than by typing, because you can see the range as you specify it. A later section of this chapter shows you how to highlight a range with a mouse.

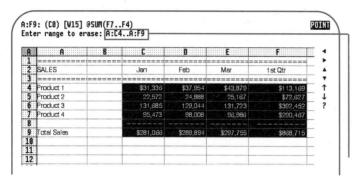

After you press
End ↓ and
End →, the range
A:C4..A:F9 is
highlighted and
the address
appears in the
control panel.

4

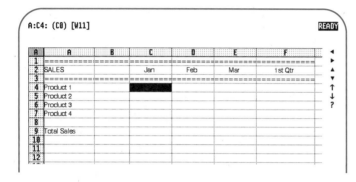

When you press
⤶Enter, 1-2-3
executes the
command using
the highlighted
range, and the cell
pointer returns to
the originating
cell.

Typing a Range Name

Another way to specify a range is to type an existing range name at the prompt. Range names, which should be descriptive, can contain as many as 15 characters and can be used in formulas and commands.

The use of range names is advantageous for several reasons. Range names are easier to remember than cell addresses and it may be faster to use a name than to point to a range in another part of the worksheet. Range names also make formulas easier to understand. For example, when you see the range name NOV_SALES_R1 (rather than the cell address) in a formula, you have a better chance of remembering that the entry represents "November Sales for Region 1." The process of assigning names to ranges is described in a later section of this chapter.

Specifying Three-Dimensional Ranges

If your file has more than one worksheet, you can specify three-dimensional ranges that span two or more worksheets. You can specify three-dimensional ranges with the keyboard or mouse. The next section of this chapter demonstrates how to use a mouse to specify ranges.

To specify a three-dimensional range with the keyboard, follow these steps:

1. Highlight the range in the first (or last) worksheet to be included in the three-dimensional range.

   If you are specifying a single-cell range across multiple worksheets, be sure to press ⌷ (period) to anchor the range.

2. Press Ctrl PgUp one or more times to move forward through worksheets or press Ctrl PgDn one or more times to move backward through worksheets.

In this example, a three-dimensional range that includes a rectangular range across three worksheets is specified.

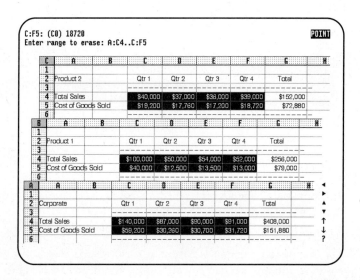

3. Press ↵Enter to complete the operation.

Using GROUP Mode

The /Worksheet Global Group command offers an alternative to using three-dimensional ranges by having certain commands affect the same range on all worksheets in the current file. The /Worksheet commands controlled by GROUP mode include: Insert, Delete, Column, Titles, and Page; /Worksheet Global commands affected include Format, Label, Col-Width, Prot, and Zero; /Range commands affected include: Format, Label, Prot, and Unprot. When the /Worksheet Global Group Enable command is issued, all worksheets acquire the settings of the current worksheet. To disable GROUP mode, use the /Worksheet Global Group Disable command.

GROUP mode is useful when you work with multiple worksheets with identical settings and structure—for example, consolidating financial reports from different regions.

Using the Mouse To Specify Ranges

You can use a mouse to quickly specify ranges in single worksheets and multiple-worksheet files. Click-and-drag the mouse to designate ranges.

To specify a single-worksheet range with a mouse, follow these steps:

1. Click the left mouse button on the upper-left corner of the range, and hold the button down.
2. Drag the mouse to the lower-right corner of the range.
3. Release the mouse button. The desired range is highlighted.
4. Click the left mouse button again to finish specifying the range.

   Note: You can cancel the highlighted range by clicking the right mouse button.

To specify a three-dimensional range with a mouse, follow these steps:

1. Highlight the range in the first (or last) worksheet to be included in the three-dimensional range. (Follow steps 1 through 3 in the preceding example.)

   If you are specifying a single-cell range across multiple worksheets, press ⌴ (period) to anchor the range.
2. Click the left mouse button on the up arrow icon (↑) one or more times to move forward through worksheets, or click the down arrow icon (↓) one or more times to move backward through worksheets.
3. Click the left mouse button again to finish specifying the range.

   Note: You can cancel the highlighted range by clicking the right mouse button.

Preselecting a Range with Wysiwyg

Before issuing a command, you can select the range to be affected by the command. This technique is called *preselecting* a range. When you preselect a range, you can issue several Wysiwyg formatting commands that affect the same range. The range that you preselect remains selected. For example, if you want to change the font of some numbers and then outline the cells that contain the numbers, preselect the range and perform both commands. You can preselect a range only when Wysiwyg is active. Ranges can be preselected either from the keyboard or with a mouse. To preselect a range from the keyboard, follow these steps:

1. Move the cell pointer to the upper-left corner of the range.

2. Press the F4 key.

The mode indicator changes from READY to POINT and an anchored range address appears in the control panel.

```
A:C4: (C0) [W11] 31336                                    POINT
A:C4..A:C4
   A       A        B        C         D         E          F       ◄
  1                                                                 ►
  2   SALES                   Jan       Feb       Mar      1st Qtr  ▲
  3                                                                 ▼
  4   Product 1            $31,336    $37,954   $43,879   $113,169  ↑
  5   Product 2             22,572     24,888    25,167    $72,627  ↓
  6   Product 3            131,685    129,044   131,723   $392,452  ?
  7   Product 4             95,473     98,008    96,986   $290,467
  8
  9   Total Sales         $281,066   $289,894  $297,755   $868,715
 10
 11
 12
```

3. Highlight the range using the direction keys.

   Note: Do not press ↵Enter after highlighting the range.

In this example, the range A:C4..A:E7 has been preselected.

```
A:E7: (,0) [W11] 96986                                    POINT
A:C4..A:E7
   A       A        B        C         D         E          F       ◄
  1                                                                 ►
  2   SALES                   Jan       Feb       Mar      1st Qtr  ▲
  3                                                                 ▼
  4   Product 1            $31,336    $37,954   $43,879   $113,169  ↑
  5   Product 2             22,572     24,888    25,167    $72,627  ↓
  6   Product 3            131,685    129,044   131,723   $392,452  ?
  7   Product 4             95,473     98,008    96,986   $290,467
  8
  9   Total Sales         $281,066   $289,894  $297,755   $868,715
 10
 11
 12
```

130

4. Select one or more Wysiwyg (or 1-2-3) commands to be performed on the range (such as **:Format Italics Set**).

5. When you finish working with the preselected range, simply move the cell pointer (using a direction key) or press `Esc`.

To preselect a range with the mouse, follow these steps:

1. Move the cell pointer to the upper-left corner of the range.

2. Press and hold the `Ctrl` key and click the left mouse button.

   The mode indicator changes from READY to POINT and an anchored range address appears in the control panel. You can now release the `Ctrl` key (but not the mouse button).

3. Highlight the range by dragging the mouse pointer to the lower right corner of the range, then release the mouse button.

   Note: Do not press `⏎Enter` after highlighting the range.

4. Select one or more Wysiwyg (or 1-2-3) commands to be performed on the range (such as **:Format Italics Set**).

5. When you finish working with the preselected range, simply move the cell pointer or click the left mouse button.

Dealing with Remembered Ranges

1-2-3 remembers ranges previously specified with certain commands by highlighting the range when the command is reissued. These commands include **/D**ata, **/G**raph, **/P**rint, and **/R**ange Search from the 1-2-3 menu, and **:Graph** and **:Print** from the Wysiwyg menu. If the previous range is what you need, press Enter to select the highlighted range. If you want to specify a new range, first press Backspace to cancel the old range (the cell pointer moves to the current worksheet cell). Then specify the range with the keyboard or mouse.

In addition to using Backspace to cancel a previous range, you can also use Esc or the right mouse button. When you use this method, the cell pointer moves to the upper-left corner of the old range, not to the current worksheet cell. For example, suppose the cell pointer is in cell M1, and you want to print this part of the worksheet. The range previously printed was A2..G18. When you choose the **/P**rint **P**rinter **R**ange command, 1-2-3 remembers the old range. If you press Backspace now, 1-2-3 cancels the old range and returns the cell pointer to cell M1. If you press Esc or the right mouse button, 1-2-3 cancels the old range but moves the cell pointer to cell A2, the upper-left corner of the old range.

Using Range Names

Range names can contain as many as 15 characters and should describe the range's contents. The advantage of naming ranges is that they are easier to understand than cell addresses. For example, the phrase SALES_MODEL25 is a more understandable way of describing the sales for Model #25 than its cell coordinates. (Note that the underscore is part of the range name.)

Range names can be useful tools for processing commands and generating formulas. Whenever you must designate a range that has been named, you can respond with the range name instead of entering cell addresses or pointing to cell locations. 1-2-3's /Range Name command lets you tag a specific range of the worksheet with any name you choose. After naming the range, you can type the name and press Enter instead of typing the cell addresses that indicate the range's boundaries.

The /Range Name command lets you give the name SALES1 to the cells in the range A:C4..A:E4.

```
A:E4: (C0) [W11] 43879                                              POINT
Enter name to create: SALES]          Enter range: A:C4..A:E4

     A           A           B        C         D         E         F        ◄
 1  ===========================================================================  ►
 2  SALES                             Jan       Feb       Mar      1st Qtr     ▲
 3  ===========================================================================  ▼
 4  Product 1                       $31,336   $37,954   $43,879   $113,169     ↑
 5  Product 2                        22,572    24,888    25,167    $72,627     ↓
 6  Product 3                       131,685   129,044   131,723   $392,452     ?
 7  Product 4                        95,473    98,008    96,986   $290,467
 8                                  --------  --------  --------  --------
 9  Total Sales                    $281,066  $289,894  $297,755  $868,715
10
11
12
```

The simplest way to compute the sum of this range is to use the function @SUM(SALES1). In a similar way, you can use the function @MAX(SALES1) to determine the maximum value in the range. In functions and formulas, you can always use range names in place of cell addresses.

You can also use a range name to jump from one part of the worksheet to another.

Once you establish a range name, 1-2-3 automatically uses that name, instead of cell addresses, throughout the worksheet. For example, any formulas in the worksheet that refer to a named range include that name within the formula (rather than the cell addresses of the range).

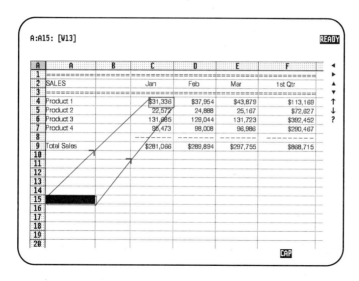

A:F4: (C0) [W15] @SUM(SALES1)   READY

A	A	B	C	D	E	F
1	=======	=======	=======	=======	=======	=======
2	SALES		Jan	Feb	Mar	1st Qtr
3	=======	=======	=======	=======	=======	=======
4	Product 1		$31,336	$37,954	$43,879	$113,169
5	Product 2		22,572	24,888	25,167	$72,627
6	Product 3		131,685	129,044	131,723	$392,452
7	Product 4		95,473	98,008	96,986	$290,467
8			-------	-------	-------	-------
9	Total Sales		$281,066	$289,894	$297,755	$868,715
10						
11						
12						

When you name the range, you can use it in a formula or in response to a command prompt that asks for a range.

A:A15: [W13]   READY

A	A	B	C	D	E	F
1	=======	=======	=======	=======	=======	=======
2	SALES		Jan	Feb	Mar	1st Qtr
3	=======	=======	=======	=======	=======	=======
4	Product 1		$31,336	$37,954	$43,879	$113,169
5	Product 2		22,572	24,888	25,167	$72,627
6	Product 3		131,685	129,044	131,723	$392,452
7	Product 4		95,473	98,008	96,986	$290,467
8			-------	-------	-------	-------
9	Total Sales		$281,066	$289,894	$297,755	$868,715
10						
11						
12						
13						
14						
15						
16						
17						
18						
19						
20						

CAP

Type **SALES1** after pressing F5 (GoTo) and the cell pointer moves to cell C4—the first cell (upper-left corner) of the range named SALES1.

You can also designate the ranges of cells to be printed or to be extracted and saved to another worksheet. If you set up special names corresponding to different areas and you want to print or extract and save these areas to another worksheet, you can enter a predefined range name rather than actual cell addresses. For example, if you want to print a portion of a worksheet, you can use the command /**P**rint **P**rinter **R**ange. Then you can type an existing range name, such as PART_1 or PART–5, in response to the prompt for entering a print range.

You can name ranges in one of two ways. You can either issue the /**R**ange **N**ame **C**reate command to create a new range name or you can select /**R**ange **N**ame **L**abels to use a label already on the worksheet as a name for a range.

When you create a name, you assign a name to one or more cells. When you use the **Labels** option, you pick up a label from the worksheet and make it the range name of a one-cell range above, below, to the left, or to the right of the label. You can assign more than one label at a time, but each label applies only to one adjacent cell.

Naming a Group of Cells

The **/Range Name Create** command is ideal when you need to give a name to a multicell range. To use **/Range Name Create** to specify a name for any range, even one cell, follow these steps:

1. Select **/Range**.

Range is the second option on the 1-2-3 main menu.

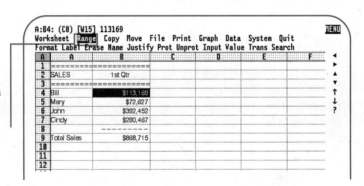

2. Select **Name Create**.

3. At the prompt `Enter name:`, type the range name you want, and then press `Enter`. Do not use a name that can be confused with a cell address, such as Q1.

   For this example, type **QTR1** and press `Enter`.

4. At the prompt `Enter range:`, select the range you want to name by typing the cell addresses, highlighting the range, or typing an existing range name; then press `Enter`.

134

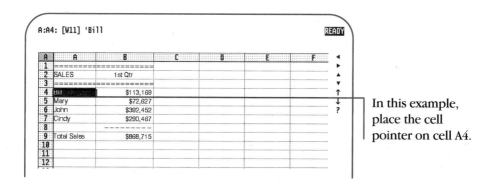

```
A:B9: (C0) [W15] 868715                                      POINT
Enter name to create: QTR1          Enter range: A:B4..A:B9

 A        A            B         C        D        E        F      ◄
 1  ==============================                                 ►
 2  SALES        1st Qtr                                           ▲
 3  ==============================                                 ▼
 4  Bill             $113,169                                      ↑
 5  Mary             $72,627                                       ↓
 6  John             $392,452                                      ?
 7  Cindy            $290,467
 8                 ---------
 9  Total Sales      $868,715
10
11
12
```

For this example, select A:B4..A:B9 as the range to name and press ↵Enter.

Naming a Single Cell

If you need to assign names to a series of one-cell entries with adjacent labels or to a series of columns or rows with headings, use the **/R**ange Name **L**abels command. This command is similar to **/R**ange Name Create except that the names for ranges are taken directly from adjacent cells. These names must be text entries (labels); you cannot use numeric entries and blank cells to name adjacent cells with the **/R**ange Name **L**abels command.

To assign names to single-cell entries, follow these steps:

1. Position the cell pointer on the first label you want to use as a range name. Remember that you can use this command only on adjacent cells.

```
A:A4: [W11] 'Bill                                           READY

 A        A            B         C        D        E        F      ◄
 1  ==============================                                 ►
 2  SALES        1st Qtr                                           ▲
 3  ==============================                                 ▼
 4  Bill             $113,169                                      ↑
 5  Mary             $72,627                                       ↓
 6  John             $392,452                                      ?
 7  Cindy            $290,467
 8                 ---------
 9  Total Sales      $868,715
10
11
12
```

In this example, place the cell pointer on cell A4.

2. Select **/R**ange Name **L**abels.

3. Select the appropriate option: **Right**, **Down**, **Left**, or **Up**, depending on the location of the cells to be named.

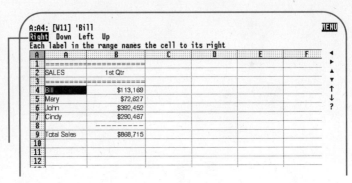

In this example, select **Right** because the range you want to name is to the right of the current cell.

4. At the prompt `Enter label range:`, select the cells containing the labels you want to use as range names; then press ⏎Enter.

In this example, select the range A4..A7; then press ⏎Enter.

Deleting Range Names

You can delete range names individually or all at once. The /**R**ange Name **D**elete command allows you to delete a single range name, and the /**R**ange Name **R**eset command causes all range names to be deleted. The second command is powerful; use it with caution.

To delete a single range name, follow these steps:

1. Select /**R**ange Name **D**elete.
2. When 1-2-3 displays a list of range names, select the range name you want to delete, and then press ⏎Enter.

In this example, the range name `QTR1` is highlighted. Press ⏎Enter to delete the highlighted range name.

A:A1: [W13] \=

Enter name to delete:

FEB		JAN		MAR		QTR1	

A	A	B	C	D	E	F
1						
2	SALES		Jan	Feb	Mar	1st Qtr
3						
4	Product 1		$31,336	$37,954	$43,879	$113,169
5	Product 2		22,572	24,888	25,167	$72,627
6	Product 3		131,685	129,044	131,723	$392,452
7	Product 4		95,473	98,008	96,986	$290,467
8			-------	-------	-------	-------
9	Total Sales		$281,066	$289,894	$297,755	$868,715
10						
11						
12						

To delete all the range names in a worksheet, select /**R**ange **N**ame **R**eset.

Note: Use this command with caution. 1-2-3 deletes all range names as soon as you enter the command, without giving you a chance to verify your selection. Of course, if the Undo feature is active, you can use Alt-F4 to reverse this command.

If you delete a range name, 1-2-3 no longer uses that name and reverts to using the range's cell address. For example, @SUM(SALES1) returns to @SUM(C4..E4). The contents of the cells within the range, however, remain intact. To erase the contents of ranges, use the /**R**ange **E**rase command, which is explained in the next section.

You can use the /**R**ange **N**ame **U**ndefine command to dissociate a range name from a particular worksheet range. The range name would continue to exist within formulas, but a formula would evaluate to ERR because no range is associated with the range name. This command is useful when you want to redefine a range name used in a formula without causing the range name to evaluate to ERR.

Listing Range Names

Suppose that you select the /**R**ange **E**rase command and then you can't remember the name of the range you want to erase. You can use the Name (F3) function key to produce a list of the range names in the current worksheet.

To display a list of the range names in the current worksheet, follow these steps:

1. Make sure that the worksheet is in POINT mode, and then press F3 (Name).

In this example, F3 (Name) was pressed in POINT mode.

137

2. If the range names extend beyond the right edge of the control panel, use the arrow keys to display the additional names.

3. To display a full-screen list of range names, press F3 a second time.

1-2-3 displays the entire list (or as much of it as the screen can hold).

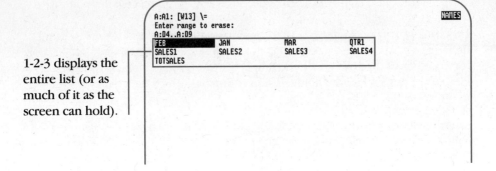

4. Move the cell pointer to the name you want to use and press ↵Enter. 1-2-3 then returns you to the worksheet.

You can use the spacebar, the arrow keys, and the Home and End keys to select the name of the range you want to use. You can also press Tab or Shift-Tab to move right or left one screen (or line) at a time.

Note: If you want to print the displayed list of range names, hold down Shift and press PrtSc. (If you have an enhanced keyboard, press Print Screen.) Using Shift-PrtSc or Print Screen while your printer is turned on prints whatever appears on the screen.

To move the cell pointer to a certain range, use the Name (F3) key with the GoTo (F5) key to select the range name. When you press GoTo (F5) and then Name (F3), 1-2-3 displays an alphabetical list of your worksheet's range names in the control panel. To designate the range you want to go to, select a name from the list by using the space bar, arrow keys, Home and End keys, and Tab or Shift-Tab. When you press Enter, the list disappears, and the cell pointer is positioned at the beginning of the selected range.

Documenting Range Names

You can document each range name with the /**Range Name Note** command. After you create a range name, 1-2-3 enables you to attach a note containing up to 52 characters. This feature is useful for describing the contents of the range name. For example, you can use a range note to describe a complex formula that refers to multiple worksheets. The **/R**ange **N**ame **N**ote command results in a menu with five options. These options are described in table 4.2.

Table 4.2
Selections on the /Range Name Note Menu

Selection	Description
Create	Allows you to attach a new range name note or edit an existing one.
Delete	Erases a single range name note.
Reset	Erases all range name notes.
Table	Copies a list of all range names and their corresponding cell addresses and range name notes to any location on the worksheet.
Quit	Returns the worksheet to READY mode.

Creating a Table of Range Names

If you have created several range names in your worksheet, you can document them in a table in the worksheet. 1-2-3 provides the **/R**ange **N**ame **T**able command to perform this task.

To create a range name table, follow these steps:

1. Move the cell pointer to the location where you want the upper-left corner of the table to appear.

   For example, move the cell pointer to a cell located a few rows below the data in the worksheet.

2. Select **/R**ange **N**ame **T**able.

3. Press ⏎Enter to select the current location of the cell pointer.

Note: Creating a table of range names is simple, but you must be careful where you place the table. Make certain that the table will not write over an important part of the worksheet. The range-name table includes range names and addresses at the time the table is created. This list is not automatically updated when you create, delete, or move ranges. For an up-to-date table, you must re-create the table with the **/R**ange **N**ame **T**able command.

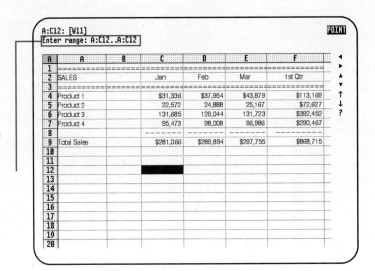

1-2-3 asks for the location of the table.

1-2-3 produces a table with all the range names in a column and with the referenced ranges to the immediate right.

Erasing Ranges

With the /Range Erase command, you can erase sections of the worksheet. You can use this command on ranges as small as a single cell or as large as the entire worksheet.

To erase a range, follow these steps:

1. Select /**R**ange **E**rase.

2. When 1-2-3 prompts you to supply a range, select the range you want to erase and press ⏎Enter.

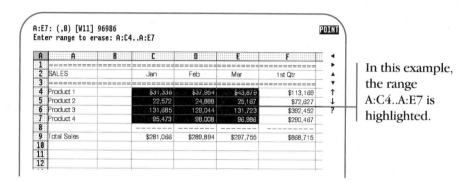

In this example, the range A:C4..A:E7 is highlighted.

Note: Although you can indicate a range to be erased by typing the cell addresses of the range or by entering a range name, highlighting the range lets you see the boundaries of the range you want to erase before 1-2-3 erases the range. Highlighting helps to prevent accidental erasure of important data.

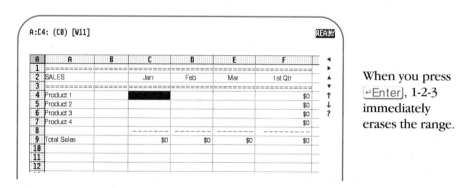

When you press ⏎Enter, 1-2-3 immediately erases the range.

After you erase a range, you can recover it with the Undo feature if it is enabled (immediately press Alt-F4 to "undo" the /**R**ange **E**rase command). Otherwise, if the Undo feature is not active, you have to reenter all the data in order to restore the range (or if the file has been saved since the data was entered, you can retrieve the file using /**F**ile **R**etrieve).

Formatting Cell Contents

You now know that 1-2-3 expects you to enter data in a certain way. If, for example, you try to enter **1,234**, the program beeps, switches to EDIT mode, and waits for you to remove the comma. You get the same result if you try to enter **10:08 AM**—in this case, the colon and the AM are the offenders. If you try to enter **$9.23**, the program accepts the entry, but removes the **$**.

1-2-3 would have limited usefulness if you could not change the way data is displayed on-screen. You can, however, control not only the display of data with commas, time, and currency, but also with a variety of other formats. You determine formats with one of the options of the **/Range Format** or **/Worksheet Global Format** commands. The **/Worksheet** commands are discussed in the next chapter.

Table 4.3 provides examples of the formats that are available in 1-2-3. These formats primarily affect the way numeric values are displayed in a worksheet. Notice that **Text** format causes a formula to appear in a cell as a formula rather than a value and **Hidden** format affects the display of every kind of entry.

Cell formats specified with **/Range Format** are automatically displayed within parentheses in the first line of the control panel. The worksheet's default cell format, however, does not appear in the control panel. You can use the **/Worksheet Status** command to view the current default worksheet format.

Table 4.3
1-2-3 Format Options

Format	Description	Examples Data entered	* Data displayed
Fixed	Controls the number of decimal places displayed.	15.56	16
Sci	Displays large or small numbers, using scientific (exponential) notation.	–21	–2E+01
Currency	Displays currency symbols and commas.	234567.75	$234,568
, (Comma)	Inserts commas to mark thousands and multiples of thousands.	1234567	1,234,567

Table 4.3 (continued)

Format	Description	Examples Data entered	* Data displayed
General	Displays values with up to 10 decimal points or uses scientific notation; the default format in a new worksheet.	26.003	26.003
+/−	Creates horizontal bar graphs or time-duration graphs; useful for omputers that cannot display graphs.	4.1 −3	++++ − − −
Percent	Displays a decimal number as a whole number with a % sign.	0.25	5%
Date	Displays serial-date numbers. **/Range Format Date Time** sets time formats.	@DATE(89,8,1) @NOW	01-Aug-89 07:48 AM
Text	Displays formulas as text, not the compute values that 1-2-3 normally displays.	+B5+B6 @SUM(C4..C8)	+B5+B6 @SUM(C4..C8)
Hidden	Hides contents from the display and does not print them; hidden contents are still evaluated.	289	
Other	Generates a menu with additional formatting options: **Automatic, Color, Label,** and **Parentheses.**		
Reset	Returns the format to the current **/Worksheet Global** format.		

formatted with no decimal places

Setting Range and Worksheet Global Formats

Although you frequently use the /Range Format command to format individual ranges in your worksheet, you can also change the default format for the entire worksheet. The /Worksheet Global Format command controls the format of all cells in the worksheet and the /Range Format command controls specific ranges.

Generally, you use the /Worksheet Global Format command when you are just starting to enter data in a worksheet. Be sure to choose a format that the majority of cells will use. After you set all the cells to that format, you can use the /Range Format command to override the Global format setting for specific cell ranges.

The /Range Format command takes precedence over the /Worksheet Global Format command. This means that whenever you change the global format, all the affected numbers and formulas will change automatically unless they were previously formatted with the /Range Format command. In turn, when you format a range, the format for that range will override any already set by /Worksheet Global Format.

Although the /Range Format command is generally used on cells that contain data, you can choose to select a format for cells that are now blank but will eventually contain data. Any information put in these cells later will be displayed according to the format you chose with /Range Format.

To change the format of a cell or range of cells, follow these steps:

1. Select /Range Format.
2. From the resulting menu, select the desired type of format.

In this example, select **Currency**.

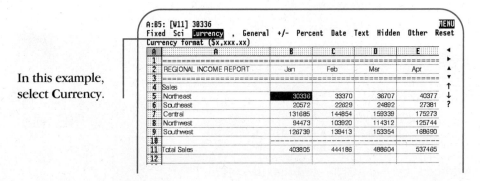

3. If you are prompted to enter the number of decimal places, type a new number and press ⏎Enter or simply press ⏎Enter to accept the displayed default number.

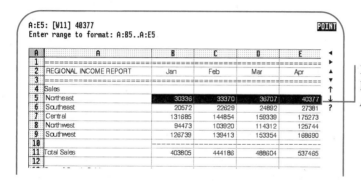

```
A:B5: [W11] 30336                                        EDIT
Enter number of decimal places (0..15): 0
```

In this example,
type [0] for zero
decimal places and
press [←Enter].

4. Highlight the range you want to format.

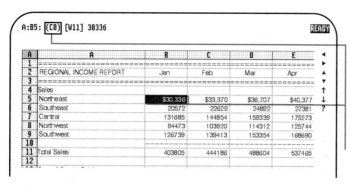

```
A:E5: [W11] 40377                                        POINT
Enter range to format: A:B5..A:E5
```

In this example,
highlight the range
A:B5.. A:E5.

5. Press [←Enter] to complete the command.

```
A:B5: (C0) [W11] 30336                                   READY
```

The cell pointer
appears on the
first cell of the
formatted range;
the control panel
indicates the
designated format.

General Format

General format is the default format for all new worksheets. When numbers appear in General format, commas that separate thousands and multiples of thousands are not displayed. Trailing zeros to the right of the decimal point are also suppressed. General format uses scientific notation for numbers too large or too small to be displayed normally.

Fixed Format

4

1-2-3's Fixed format is similar to General format because it does not display commas or dollar signs. Fixed format, however, lets you choose the number of decimal places to be displayed (up to 15).

Scientific (Sci) Format

Sci (Scientific) format causes 1-2-3 to display numbers in exponential form (scientific notation). Unlike General format, Sci format lets you control the number of decimal places and therefore the amount of precision to be displayed.

Currency Format

Currency format displays numbers in cells with a dollar sign ($) before each entry, and with commas to separate thousands and multiples of thousands. Negative values appear in parentheses ( ). Although the dollar sign is the default, other symbols can be used as currency indicators. Currency format also gives you the option of controlling the number of decimal places (up to 15 may be used).

Comma (,) Format

The , (Comma) format is similar to Currency format, except that no dollar signs appear in the number display. Commas separate hundreds from thousands, hundreds of thousands from millions, and so on. Parentheses ( ) identify negative numbers. After you choose the , (Comma) format, you can specify the number of decimal places you want. Only in Currency and , (Comma) formats are negative values displayed within parentheses. In other formats, negative values are preceded by a minus sign.

By using the /Worksheet Global Default Other International Negative command, you can choose either parentheses or minus signs to indicate negative values; for example, (12,300) or –12,300, ($12,300) or –$12,300. This command applies only to Currency and , (Comma) formats.

146

The +/– Format

The +/–format creates a horizontal bar "graph" of plus or minus signs within the cell, depending on the value of the number you enter in the cell. Asterisks appear if the size of the bar graph exceeds the column width. If you enter zero in a cell, a period (.) appears on the graph and displays left-justified in the cell.

You can use this format to mark a value in a long column of numbers. As you scan the column, the +'s and –'s stand out and are easy to locate.

Percent Format

The **P**ercent format is used to display percentages. When you select this format, you also select the number of decimal places. The values displayed in the worksheet are the values you enter, multiplied by 100 and followed by a percent sign. When you use the **P**ercent format, remember to enter numbers with the correct decimal point. To display 12%, for example, you must enter **.12**, not **12**.

Date and Time Formats

1-2-3 represents any given date internally as an integer equal to the number of days from December 31, 1899, to the given date. For example, January 1, 1900, is represented by the number 1; December 31, 2099 (the last date in 1-2-3's calendar), is represented by 73050. To enter a date into the worksheet, you can use one of the three date functions: @DATE, @DATEVALUE, or @NOW.

1-2-3 calculates a period of hours as a fraction expressed in decimals. The calculations are based on a 24-hour clock (military time). You can use one of the time functions (@TIME, @TIMEVALUE, or @NOW) to enter a time into the worksheet. You can specify nine date and time formats with the /**R**ange Format **D**ate and /**W**orksheet **G**lobal Format **D**ate commands.

Text Format

Text format displays formulas as they are entered in the command line, not the computed values that 1-2-3 normally displays. Numbers that are entered with this format are displayed as in **G**eneral format.

The two most important applications of this format are setting up table ranges for /**D**ata Table commands and debugging. Because you can display all the formulas on-screen with the **T**ext format, finding and correcting problems is a relatively easy task. You usually have to widen the cell width to see your complete formulas when you use this technique.

4

Hidden Format

The /Range Format Hidden command suppresses the cell contents for any given range. If you want to hide all the cells in a column or range of columns, instead use the /Worksheet Column Hide command, discussed in the next chapter.

Although a cell with Hidden format appears as a blank cell on-screen, its contents appear in the control panel when you highlight the cell, and the contents are still available for calculations or formulas. All the formulas and values can be calculated and readjusted when values are changed. The contents of hidden cells within a range to be printed do not appear on your printed copy.

Other Automatic Format

Cells formatted with /Range Format Other Automatic automatically change to the cell format that 1-2-3 interprets from the appearance of the cell's initial entry. For example, a cell format changes to Currency with two decimal places when you make the entry $1,200.00. This setting is only an initial format setting. After an entry is made, cells are no longer formatted with Other Automatic format, but with the new format determined by the first cell entry.

Other Color Format

Cells formatted with /Range Format Other Color display negative values in a separate color on a color monitor and in high intensity on a monochrome monitor. The color format works with any other format that may be in effect, and it may be turned on or off without affecting the other format.

Other Label Format

Any existing values appear in General format when you use /Range Format Other Label. When you type a number in a cell formatted with this command, the number changes to a label with a label prefix.

Other Parentheses Format

Cells formatted with /Range Format Other Parentheses display parentheses around any value entry. This format works with any other format that may be in effect, and it can be turned on or off without affecting the other format.

Reset Format

The /Range Format Reset command resets the format of the indicated range to the global default setting. When the format of a range is reset, the format indicator for any cell within the range disappears from the control panel. The Reset option does not appear on the /Worksheet Global Format menu.

Controlling the International Formats

1-2-3 enables you to control the punctuation and currency sign displayed by , (Comma) and Currency formats, and to control the way the date and time are displayed when you use the special international Date and Time formats. To control these settings globally for the worksheet, use the /Worksheet Global Default Other International command. This command allows you to choose the format 1-2-3 uses for displaying the date and time, currency symbols, negative values (with a minus sign or parentheses), and punctuation.

Summary

This chapter showed you how to create worksheets with many of the /Range commands. You learned how to use the /Range commands to create and name ranges, delete range names and erase ranges, move quickly to a named range, and display existing range names in the control panel or on the full screen. You also learned how to format a cell or a range of cells to determine how values and formula results appear on-screen.

Specifically, you learned the following key information about 1-2-3:

- A range in 1-2-3 is defined as a rectangular block of adjacent cells. Ranges can be three-dimensional in multiple-worksheet applications. Ranges are identified by the cell addresses of their upper-left and lower-right corners, separated by one or two periods. Examples of ranges include C4..G17 and A:D20..C:H41.

- A range can be designated by: typing the cell addresses; highlighting the range with the direction keys or the click-and-drag technique of the mouse; or typing an existing range name.

- Three-dimensional ranges can be specified by using the Ctrl-PgUp and Ctrl-PgDn key combinations to move through the worksheets forward or backward, respectively. Clicking the up- and down-arrow icons with the left mouse button produces the same results.

4

■ When Wysiwyg is in memory, you can use the F4 key to preselect a command. This enables you to perform many commands on a single range without having to respecify the range after each command.

■ You use /Range Name Create and /Range Name Labels commands to name ranges of cells within the worksheet. The Create option is commonly used to name new multicell ranges. The Labels option is useful for naming a series of one-cell entries with adjacent labels, or a series of columns or rows with headings.

■ The /Range Name Delete and /Range Name Reset commands can delete one or all range names, respectively. Use the Reset option with caution; all range names are deleted immediately with its selection, and 1-2-3 does not require verification of this command. The /Range Name Undefine command dissociates a range name from a specific cell address.

■ To list all ranges named in the current worksheet, press Name (F3) in POINT mode (when 1-2-3 prompts for a range with the /Range commands).

■ You can use the Name (F3) key with the GoTo (F5) key to select the name of a range where you want to move the cell pointer. If you press GoTo (F5) and then press Name (F3), 1-2-3 displays an alphabetical list of your worksheet's range names in the control panel.

■ The /Range Name Note command enables you to document a range name by attaching a note of up to 52 characters to the range name.

■ The /Range Name Table command lists all range names and their corresponding locations within the worksheet. You should execute this command in a remote portion of the worksheet to avoid overwriting your worksheet data.

■ The /Range Erase command erases single-cell or multicell ranges. You can denote a range to be erased by typing the cell addresses of the range, entering a range name, or pointing to the range. Pointing is the preferred method because it allows you to see the boundaries of the range you want to erase before 1-2-3 erases the range.

■ The /Range Format command changes the way data is displayed in the worksheet. Available formatting options within 1-2-3 include Currency, Fixed, Percent, Text, Hidden, and , (Comma).

The next chapter discusses the various tasks that can be performed with the /Worksheet and :Worksheet commands, such as setting column widths, creating windows, freezing titles, inserting and deleting rows and columns, and protecting the worksheet.

Building a Worksheet

5

After you enter and format some data, you can use commands from 1-2-3's /Worksheet menu and Wysiwyg's **:**Worksheet menu to control the way your data is displayed and organized. In the last chapter, you learned how to manipulate data in specified ranges. This chapter shows you how to use commands that affect the entire worksheet at once.

In this chapter, you learn how to establish global settings for your worksheet; change column widths and row heights; insert and delete columns, rows, and worksheets; recalculate formulas; protect certain areas of your worksheet; and perform other tasks. The next chapter shows you how to modify your worksheet by making more substantial changes.

5

Key Terms in This Chapter

/Worksheet commands	1-2-3 commands that affect the entire worksheet or certain defined areas of the worksheet. The /Worksheet command is found on the 1-2-3 main menu.
:Worksheet	Wysiwyg commands that adjust column widths and row heights, and add or remove horizontal and vertical page breaks. The :Worksheet command is found on the Wysiwyg main menu.
Windows	Two separate screens that appear, either horizontally or vertically, after you execute the /Worksheet Window command. Windows allow you to view different parts of the worksheet at the same time.
Automatic recalculation	A default 1-2-3 setting indicating that the worksheet is calculated each time a cell's content changes.

Using the Mouse

To use a mouse with 1-2-3 Release 3.1, you need a mouse, mouse software, and a graphics monitor and graphics card that support a mouse. Also, Wysiwyg must be loaded into memory. You can use a mouse to select commands and files, specify ranges, and move the cell pointer within a worksheet or between multiple worksheets and files. In the examples throughout this chapter, notice that the 1-2-3 commands always begin with a slash (/) and the Wysiwyg commands always begin with a colon (:). Refer to the following sections of the specified chapters for further information on using the mouse:

- Chapter 2—"Understanding Mouse Terminology"
- Chapter 3—"Mouse Control of the Cell Pointer"
        "Using the Mouse To Select Menu Commands"
- Chapter 4—"Using the Mouse To Specify Ranges"

Using Worksheet Commands

1-2-3 offers a group of commands that perform some tasks similar to the /Range commands, but affect one or more worksheets or preset segments of one or more worksheets. With /Range commands, you define the range of cells affected by the commands. You do not have the same freedom with the /Worksheet and :Worksheet commands; they affect entire worksheets, columns, or rows.

/Worksheet is the first command option on the 1-2-3 main menu. When you select /Worksheet, 1-2-3 offers the following group of commands:

Global Insert Delete Column Erase Titles Window Status Page Hide

Table 5.1 provides a brief description of the actions of each of these commands.

5

Table 5.1
Selections on the /Worksheet Menu

Selection	Description
Global	Sets formats that affect the entire worksheet, and enables and disables GROUP mode.
Insert	Inserts blank columns, rows, and worksheets.
Delete	Deletes entire columns, rows, worksheets, and active files.
Column	Sets column widths, hides and redisplays columns.
Erase	Removes all worksheets and files from memory.
Titles	Freezes or unfreezes the display of titles.
Window	Splits the screen into two windows, displays multiple worksheets or files in perspective view, displays the current graph in the right window, and restores the original screen.
Status	Displays the current status of global worksheet settings and hardware configuration.
Page	Inserts a character that controls page breaks in printed worksheets.
Hide	Hides and redisplays selected worksheets in a multiple-worksheet file.

Erasing the Worksheet

The /Worksheet Erase command clears all current worksheets and files from the screen and memory. The effect is the same as if you quit 1-2-3 and restarted it from the operating system. You can use this command to create a new worksheet—with no data and the default worksheet settings. This command does not erase the worksheet file stored on disk.

Be sure that you understand the difference between the /Worksheet Erase command and the /Range Erase command. The /Range Erase command can remove the contents of every cell in the worksheet, except those that are protected. The /Range Erase command does not, however, alter any of the global settings, such as column widths, cell formats, and print settings. After you issue the /Worksheet Erase command, the worksheet is exactly as it was when you loaded 1-2-3.

To erase all current worksheets and files from the screen and the computer's memory, follow these steps:

1. Select /Worksheet.

1-2-3 displays the menu of Worksheet commands.

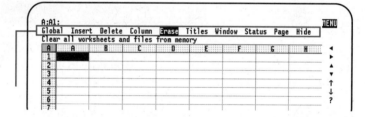

2. Select Erase.

Because this command is potentially destructive, 1-2-3 prompts you for verification.

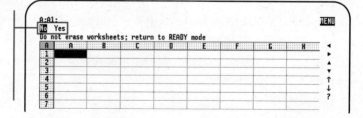

3. To erase the worksheet, select Yes.

154

If you change your mind or need to save your file before erasing the worksheet, select **No**.

Note: After a worksheet has been erased with /**Worksheet Erase**, you cannot recover it—unless the Undo feature is active, and Alt-F4 is pressed before you issue the next command. You should always save worksheets you want to keep before you clear the worksheet with this command.

Setting Column Widths

You can control the worksheet's column widths to accommodate data entries that are too wide for the default column width. You can also reduce column widths to give the worksheet a better appearance when a column contains narrow entries. With 1-2-3, you have several options for setting column widths: one column at a time with the keyboard, one column at a time with the mouse, all the columns in the worksheet at once, or a range of contiguous columns. Suppose that you are setting up a worksheet of cash flow projections and want to display long labels in the first column. You can set the width of the first column of your worksheet individually, and then set the other columns to any smaller width you choose. The sections that follow provide the necessary steps to carry out the commands for changing column widths.

As a reminder, you can use GROUP mode (issue the /**Worksheet Global Group Enable** command) to set the column widths of multiple worksheets at the same time. When GROUP mode is enabled, you can modify the widths of a single column, contiguous columns, or all columns in a multiple-worksheet application. This is particularly useful for consolidation applications, when all worksheets in a file normally use the same structure.

Setting the Width of a Single Column

To change the width of a single column, you can use the /**Worksheet Column Set-Width** command. (**Note:** The Wysiwyg **:Worksheet Column Set-Width** command also performs the same operation.) You can also use the mouse to quickly change the width of a single column. The following examples describe each of these methods.

To change the width of a single column from the keyboard, follow these steps:

1. Position the cell pointer within the column whose width you want to change.
2. Select /**Worksheet Column**.

155

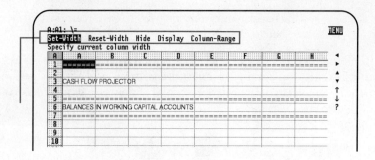

The options for
changing widths
appear.

3. Select Set-Width.

4. At the prompt `Enter column width:`, either type a width between 1
   and 240, or press ← or → until the desired column width is displayed.

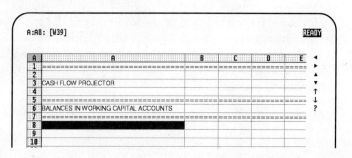

In this example,
type 39.

The advantage of using the left- and right-arrow keys is that the column width
expands and contracts each time you press a key. To get a good idea of what the
width requirements are, experiment when you enter the command.

5. Press ↵Enter to complete the command.

After changing
column widths,
continue entering
data into your
worksheet.

To return the width of a single column to the default width of nine characters, use the /**Worksheet Column R**eset-Width command. (You can also use the Wysiwyg **:Worksheet Column R**eset-Width command to perform the same task.)

To change the width of a single column with the mouse, follow these steps:

1. Position the mouse pointer within the top border of the worksheet and point to the vertical line that marks the right side of the column to be sized.

2. Press and hold the left mouse button. A double-headed arrow pointing left and right appears in the top border.

3. To increase the width of the column, move the mouse to the right. To decrease the width of the column, move the mouse to the left.

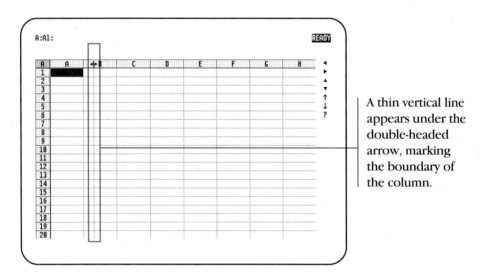

A thin vertical line appears under the double-headed arrow, marking the boundary of the column.

4. Release the left mouse button when the desired column width is marked.

To use a mouse to return a column to the default width of nine characters, press and hold Shift and click the left mouse button.

Setting the Widths of All Columns at Once

You can set all the column widths in the worksheet at one time with the command /**Worksheet G**lobal **C**olumn-Width. This command is normally used in the early stages of worksheet creation. Many of the /**Worksheet G**lobal commands have corresponding /**Range** commands that affect only certain areas of the worksheet; in this case, the corresponding commands that affect parts of the worksheet are the /**Worksheet Column Set-Width** and /**Worksheet Column Column-Range Set-Width** commands.

To change the widths of all columns in the worksheet at one time, follow these steps:

1. Select /**Worksheet Global Column-Width**.

2. At the prompt `Enter global column width:`, either type a width between 1 and 240, or press ← or → until the desired column width is displayed.

In this example, type **12**.

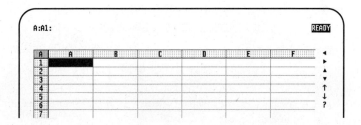

3. Press ↵**Enter** to complete the command. Each column in the worksheet now has a width of 12 characters instead of the original default of 9 characters.

In this example, fewer columns now appear on-screen.

Note: The /**Worksheet Global Column-Width** command does not alter the width of columns already set with either the /**Worksheet Column Set-Width** or /**Worksheet Column Column-Range** commands.

Setting the Width of Contiguous Columns

If you want to set a group of adjacent columns to the same width, use the /**Worksheet Column Column-Range Set-Width** command. This command keeps you from having to set each adjacent column individually.

To change the widths of contiguous columns, follow these steps:

1. Position the cell pointer on the first or last column in the range of columns whose widths you want to change.

2. Select /**Worksheet Column Column-Range Set-Width**.

3. At the prompt `Enter range for column-width change:`, highlight cells in the range of columns you want to change; then press ⏎Enter.

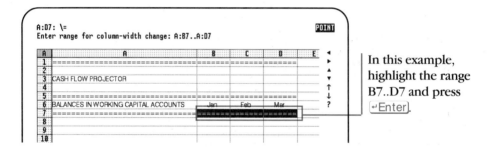

In this example, highlight the range B7..D7 and press ⏎Enter.

4. At the prompt `Enter column width:`, either type a width between 1 and 240, or press ← or → until the desired column width is displayed; then press ⏎Enter.

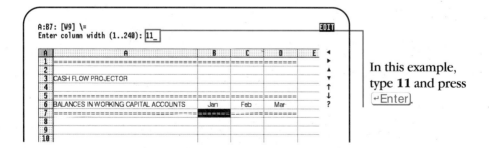

In this example, type **11** and press ⏎Enter.

Note: The **Reset-Width** option, on the same menu as **Set-Width**, does not prompt you for a specific width, but returns the widths of all selected columns to the default column-width setting.

To verify the global column-width setting, use the command /Worksheet Status. Refer to the section "Checking the Status of Global Settings" later in this chapter.

Setting Row Heights

The Wysiwyg features of 1-2-3 Release 3.1 make it possible to view a variety of type fonts on screen. However, many fonts are too large to fit in a normal size cell (with a default height of 14 points). When you format a cell to display a large font, 1-2-3 automatically adjusts the height of the row to compensate for the size of the font. 1-2-3 also lets you adjust the row height manually. You can use the mouse to quickly set the height of a single row. To adjust the height of a range of rows (as well as a single row), use the Wysiwyg command **:Worksheet Row Set-Height**. The following procedures describe each of these methods.

To adjust the height of a single row with the mouse, follow these steps:

1. Position the mouse pointer within the left border of the worksheet and point to the horizontal line that marks the bottom of the row to be sized.

2. Press and hold the left mouse button. A double-headed arrow pointing up and down appears in the left border.

3. To increase the height of the row, move the mouse down. To decrease the height of the row, move the mouse up.

A thin horizontal line appears to the right of the double-headed arrow, marking the boundary of the row.

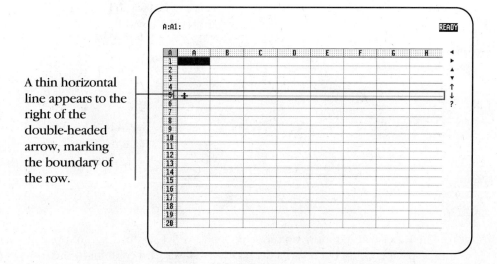

4. Release the left mouse button when the desired row height is marked.

To adjust the height of a range of rows (or a single row) with the keyboard, follow these steps:

1. Select **:Worksheet R**ow Set-Height.

2. At the prompt `Select the rows to set height to:`, highlight the range of rows to set; then press ⏎Enter.

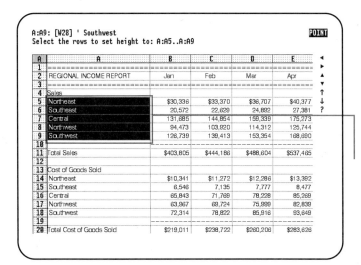

In this example, rows 5 through 9 are highlighted.

3. At the prompt `Enter row height:`, either type a point size between 1 and 255, or press ↑ or ↓ until the desired row height is displayed; then press ⏎Enter.

In this example, specify 18 as the point size and press ⏎Enter.

Note: Once you set the height of a row or rows by using **:Worksheet R**ow Set-Height, the height does not automatically adjust when you change the font size for that row. To make the row sizes automatically adjust again, select the command **:Worksheet R**ow Auto, and select the rows you want to reset.

You can use GROUP mode (issue the /**Worksheet G**lobal **G**roup **E**nable command) to set the row heights of one or more worksheets in a multiple-worksheet application at the same time.

5

```
A:A5: {H18} [W28] ' Northeast                                    READY

  A              A              B        C        D        E      ◀
  1  ==================================================================  ▶
  2  REGIONAL INCOME REPORT    Jan      Feb      Mar      Apr        ▲
  3  ==================================================================  ▼
  4  Sales                                                            ↑
  5  Northeast                $30,336  $33,370  $36,707  $40,377     ↓
  6  Southeast                 20,572   22,629   24,892   27,381     ?
  7  Central                  131,685  144,854  159,339  175,273
  8  Northwest                 94,473  103,920  114,312  125,744
  9  Southwest                126,739  139,413  153,354  168,690
  10
  11 Total Sales             $403,805 $444,186 $488,604 $537,465
  12
  13 Cost of Goods Sold
  14 Northeast                $10,341  $11,272  $12,286  $13,392
  15 Southeast                  6,546    7,135    7,777    8,477
  16 Central                   65,843   71,769   78,228   85,269
  17 Northwest                 63,967   69,724   75,999   82,839
  18 Southwest                 72,314   78,822   85,916   93,649
  19
```

Rows 5 through 9 display an increased row height of 18 points.

Splitting the Screen

Sometimes the size of a 1-2-3 worksheet can be unwieldy. For example, if you want to compare data in column A with data in column N, you need to be able to "fold" the worksheet so that you can see both parts at the same time. To do this, you can split the 1-2-3 screen display into two windows, either horizontally or vertically. This feature helps you to overcome some of the inconvenience of not being able to see the entire worksheet at one time. By splitting the screen with the /Worksheet Window command or with the mouse, you can make the changes in one area and immediately see their effects in the other.

The Horizontal and Vertical options of the /Worksheet Window menu split the screen in the manner indicated by their names. The screen splits at the point at which the cell pointer is positioned when you select the command Horizontal or Vertical. In other words, you don't have to split the screen exactly in half. Remember that the dividing line requires specifying either one row or one column, depending on whether you split the screen horizontally or vertically.

To split the screen into two horizontal or two vertical windows with the keyboard, follow these steps:

1. Position the cell pointer at the location where you want to split the screen.
2. Select /Worksheet Window.
3. Select either Horizontal or Vertical to split the screen.

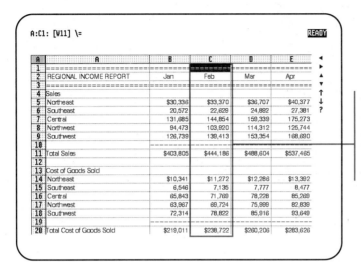

In this example, position the cell pointer in any row of column C to split the screen vertically.

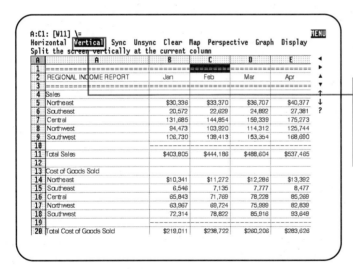

To compare two columns that cannot be seen together on the 1-2-3 screen, select Vertical.

5

5

The screen is split vertically into two windows.

```
A:B1: [W11] \=                                    READY

A       A                B      A   C       D       E
1  ================================  1  ===========================
2  REGIONAL INCOME REPORT    Jan    2  Feb      Mar     Apr
3  ================================  3  ===========================
4  Sales                            4
5  Northeast          $30,336       5  $33,370  $36,707  $40,377
6  Southeast           20,572       6  22,629   24,892   27,381
7  Central            131,685       7  144,854  159,339  175,273
8  Northwest           94,473       8  103,920  114,312  125,744
9  Southwest          126,739       9  139,413  153,354  168,690
10                                 10
11 Total Sales       $403,805      11  $444,186 $488,604 $537,465
12                                 12
13 Cost of Goods Sold             13
14 Northeast          $10,341      14  $11,272  $12,286  $13,392
15 Southeast            6,546      15  7,135    7,777    8,477
16 Central             65,843      16  71,769   78,228   85,269
17 Northwest           63,987      17  69,724   75,999   82,839
18 Southwest           72,314      18  78,822   85,916   93,649
19                                 19
20 Total Cost of Goods Sold $219,011 20 $238,722 $260,206 $283,626
```

To split the screen into two horizontal or two vertical windows with the mouse, follow these steps:

1. Position the mouse pointer at the worksheet letter in the upper left corner of the worksheet border.

2. Press and hold the left mouse button.

3. To create two horizontal windows, move the mouse down. A double-headed arrow pointing up and down appears in the left border.

   To create two vertical windows, move the mouse to the right. A double-headed arrow pointing left and right appears in the top border.

In this example, moving the mouse down displays a horizontal line—indicating the position of the horizontal window to be added.

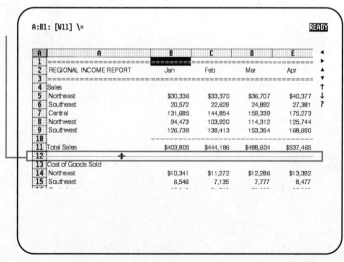

4. Release the left mouse button when the desired position of the window is marked.

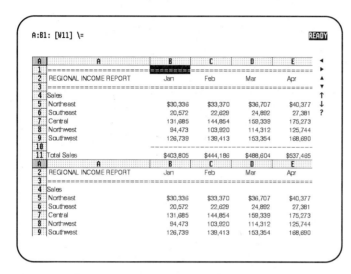

In this example, the screen is split horizontally into two windows.

5

After you use the **Horizontal** option to split the screen, the cell pointer appears in the top window. When you specify a **Vertical** division, the cell pointer appears in the left window. To jump the division between the windows, use the Window (F6) function key, or click the left mouse button on a cell in the opposite window.

After the screen is split, you can change the screen display so that the windows scroll independently rather than together (the default mode). To scroll the windows independently, select /Worksheet Window Unsync. This command can be reversed by selecting the command /Worksheet Window **S**ync.

You can display the current graph on-screen, to the right of worksheet data, by selecting the /Worksheet Window **G**raph command. Any changes made to the graph data or graph settings are reflected within the displayed graph automatically. 1-2-3 graphs are covered in detail in Chapters 11 and 12.

As you learned in Chapter 3, the /Worksheet Window **P**erspective command can be used to display up to three worksheets (or files) on screen at a time. You cannot add horizontal or vertical windows when perspective view is in use.

To return to the single-window screen after selecting the **H**orizontal, **V**ertical, **G**raph, or **P**erspective options, select /Worksheet Window **C**lear. When you use the **C**lear option, the single window takes on the settings of the top or left window, depending on how the screen was split.

Freezing Titles on the Screen

If you need to freeze rows and/or columns along the top and left edges of the worksheet so that they remain in view as you scroll to different parts of the worksheet, use the /Worksheet Titles command. The /Worksheet Titles command is similar to the /Worksheet Window command. With both commands, you can see one area of a worksheet while you work on another area. The unique function of the /Worksheet Titles command, however, is that it freezes all the cells to the left or above (or both to the left and above) the cell pointer's position so that those cells cannot move off the screen.

Because the default screen shows 20 rows by 8 columns (with the original column widths and row heights), you have to shift the screen if your data is outside of this screen area. In fact, you may have to scroll the screen several times in order to enter or view all the information.

Suppose that you want to keep on-screen the headings in rows 1-14, and the payment numbers and dates in columns A and B.

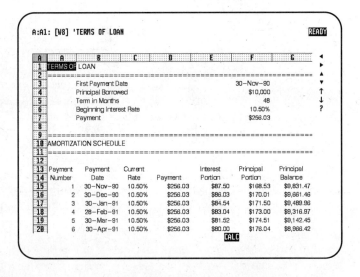

To freeze worksheet titles on the screen, follow these steps:

1. Position the cell pointer one cell below and to the right of the rows and/or columns you want to freeze.

   In this example, position the cell pointer in cell C15 to freeze columns A and B, and rows 1-14.

2. Select /Worksheet Titles.

166

3. Select **Both**, **Horizontal**, or **Vertical**. The **Both** option allows you to freeze rows and columns above and to the left of the cell pointer.

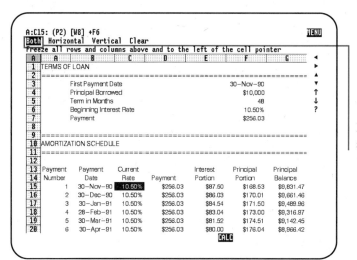

In this example, select **Both**.

5

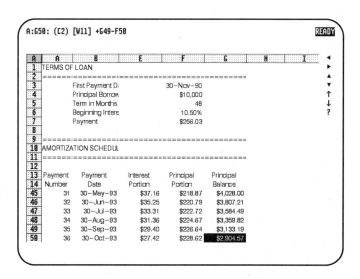

Now, no matter where you move the cell pointer, rows 1-14 and columns A and B are always displayed.

When you freeze columns and/or rows, you cannot move the cell pointer into the frozen area while 1-2-3 is in READY mode. If you try to move the cell pointer into the frozen area, 1-2-3 beeps. Similarly, the Home key moves the cell pointer only

167

to the upper left cell in the unfrozen area. (Normally, the Home key moves the cell pointer to cell A1.) You can avoid this restriction, however, by using the GoTo (F5) key to move the cell pointer to the frozen titles area.

5

Here, /Worksheet Titles Horizontal was used to freeze the row(s) above the cell pointer. Rows 9-14 remain at the top of the screen when you scroll up and down.

```
A:A29: [W8] +A28+1                                        READY
```

	A	B	C	D	E	F	G
9							
10	AMORTIZATION SCHEDULE						
11							
12							
13	Payment	Payment	Current		Interest	Principal	Principal
14	Number	Date	Rate	Payment	Portion	Portion	Balance
29	15	30–Jan–92	10.50%	$256.03	$65.64	$190.40	$7,311.12
30	16	29–Feb–92	10.50%	$256.03	$63.97	$192.06	$7,119.06
31	17	30–Mar–92	10.50%	$256.03	$62.29	$193.74	$6,925.32
32	18	30–Apr–92	10.50%	$256.03	$60.60	$195.44	$6,729.88
33	19	30–May–92	10.50%	$256.03	$58.89	$197.15	$6,532.74
34	20	30–Jun–92	10.50%	$256.03	$57.16	$198.87	$6,333.86
35	21	30–Jul–92	10.50%	$256.03	$55.42	$200.61	$6,133.25
36	22	30–Aug–92	10.50%	$256.03	$53.67	$202.37	$5,930.88
37	23	30–Sep–92	10.50%	$256.03	$51.90	$204.14	$5,726.75
38	24	30–Oct–92	10.50%	$256.03	$50.11	$205.92	$5,520.82
39	25	30–Nov–92	10.50%	$256.03	$48.31	$207.73	$5,313.09
40	26	30–Dec–92	10.50%	$256.03	$46.49	$209.54	$5,103.55
41	27	30–Jan–93	10.50%	$256.03	$44.66	$211.38	$4,892.17
42	28	28–Feb–93	10.50%	$256.03	$42.81	$213.23	$4,678.94

```
                                                          CALC
```

Here, /Worksheet Titles Vertical was used to freeze column(s) to the left of the cell pointer. Columns A and B remain on the left side of the screen when you scroll left and right.

```
A:E1: [W11]                                               READY
```

	A	B	E	F	G	H	I
1	TERMS OF LOAN						
2							
3		First Payment Da		30–Nov–90			
4		Principal Borrow		$10,000			
5		Term in Months		48			
6		Beginning Intere		10.50%			
7		Payment		$256.03			
8							
9							
10	AMORTIZATION SCHEDUL						
11							
12							
13	Payment	Payment	Interest	Principal	Principal		
14	Number	Date	Portion	Portion	Balance		
15	1	30–Nov–90	$87.50	$168.53	$9,831.47		
16	2	30–Dec–90	$86.03	$170.01	$9,661.46		
17	3	30–Jan–91	$84.54	$171.50	$9,489.96		
18	4	28–Feb–91	$83.04	$173.00	$9,316.97		
19	5	30–Mar–91	$81.52	$174.51	$9,142.45		
20	6	30–Apr–91	$80.00	$176.04	$8,966.42		

```
                                                          CALC
```

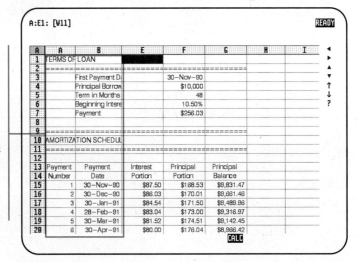

To unlock the frozen worksheet titles, use the /**Worksheet Titles Clear** command. Now you can move the cell pointer freely throughout the worksheet.

Inserting Columns, Rows, and Worksheets

Suppose that you are finished creating a worksheet, but you want to enhance its general appearance. You can improve it by inserting blank columns and rows in strategic places to highlight headings and other important items. Whether you want to insert additional data or add blank rows or columns to separate sections of your worksheet, you can use the /**Worksheet Insert** command to insert columns or rows. You can insert multiple adjacent columns and rows each time you invoke this command. Later in this section, you learn how to use /**Worksheet Insert** to add worksheets to a multiple-worksheet application.

To insert a new column or row into the worksheet, follow these steps:

1. Position the cell pointer at the location of the new column or row to be inserted.

   For example, position the cell pointer in column D to add a new column of data.

2. Select /**Worksheet Insert**.

3. Select **Column** or **Row**.

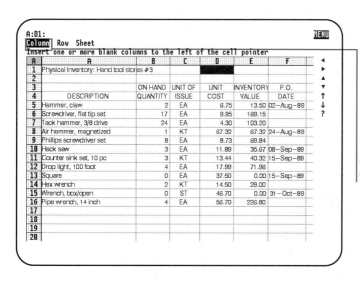

In this example, select **Column** to insert a new column in the worksheet.

4. In response to the prompt, designate the range where you want the new column(s) or row(s) to be inserted. If you want to insert more than one column or row, use the arrow keys or the mouse to highlight multiple columns or rows.

In this example, be sure that the cell pointer is positioned in column D to insert a single column.

A:D1:						POINT
Enter column insert range: A:D1..A:D1						

	A	B	C	D	E	F
1	Physical Inventory: Hand tool stores #3					
2						
3		ON HAND	UNIT OF	UNIT	INVENTORY	P.O.
4	DESCRIPTION	QUANTITY	ISSUE	COST	VALUE	DATE
5	Hammer, claw	2	EA	6.75	13.50	02–Aug–89
6	Screwdriver, flat tip set	17	EA	9.95	169.15	
7	Tack hammer, 3/8 drive	24	EA	4.30	103.20	
8	Air hammer, magnetized	1	KT	67.32	67.32	24–Aug–89
9	Phillips screwdriver set	8	EA	8.73	69.84	
10	Hack saw	3	EA	11.89	35.67	08–Sep–89
11	Counter sink set, 10 pc	3	KT	13.44	40.32	15–Sep–89
12	Drop light, 100 foot	4	EA	17.99	71.96	
13	Square	0	EA	37.50	0.00	15–Sep–89
14	Hex wrench	2	KT	14.50	29.00	
15	Wrench, box/open	0	ST	46.70	0.00	31–Oct–89
16	Pipe wrench, 14 inch	4	EA	56.70	226.80	
17						
18						
19						
20						

5. Press ↵Enter to complete the command. Existing worksheet data is moved to the right of the cell pointer if you are inserting a column, or below the cell pointer if you are inserting a row.

In this example, when you press ↵Enter, a blank column is displayed, ready for you to enter new data to the database.

A:D1:						READY

	A	B	C	D	E	F
1	Physical Inventory: Hand tool stores #3					
2						
3		ON HAND	UNIT OF		UNIT	INVENTORY
4	DESCRIPTION	QUANTITY	ISSUE		COST	VALUE
5	Hammer, claw	2	EA		6.75	13.50 02–
6	Screwdriver, flat tip set	17	EA		9.95	169.15
7	Tack hammer, 3/8 drive	24	EA		4.30	103.20
8	Air hammer, magnetized	1	KT		67.32	67.32 24–
9	Phillips screwdriver set	8	EA		8.73	69.84
10	Hack saw	3	EA		11.89	35.67 08–
11	Counter sink set, 10 pc	3	KT		13.44	40.32 15–
12	Drop light, 100 foot	4	EA		17.99	71.96
13	Square	0	EA		37.50	0.00 15–
14	Hex wrench	2	KT		14.50	29.00
15	Wrench, box/open	0	ST		46.70	0.00 31–
16	Pipe wrench, 14 inch	4	EA		56.70	226.80
17						
18						
19						
20						

5

When you insert columns, 1-2-3 automatically shifts all data to the right of the new column, and modifies all the cell formulas for the change. If you insert rows, 1-2-3 inserts a blank row—all data located below the new row is automatically shifted down one row, and any formulas are modified. 1-2-3 does not have the capability of inserting or deleting partial columns and rows.

If you want to create a multiple-worksheet application, you can insert worksheets with the /Worksheet Insert Sheet command. This command lets you add up to 255 worksheets to the current file. To add one or more worksheets, follow these steps:

1. Select /Worksheet Insert Sheet.

2. Select **Before** or **After** to indicate whether you want the new worksheet(s) inserted before or after the current worksheet.

   In this example, select **After**.

3. At the prompt `Enter number of worksheets to insert:`, enter a number from 1 to 255 to indicate how many worksheets are to be inserted.

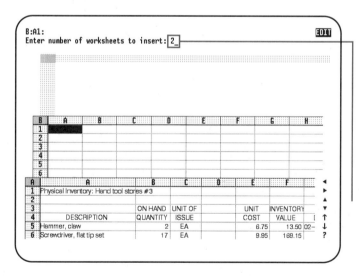

In this example, type **2** to add two new worksheets—creating a multiple-worksheet file with three worksheets.

4. Press ⏎Enter to complete the command.

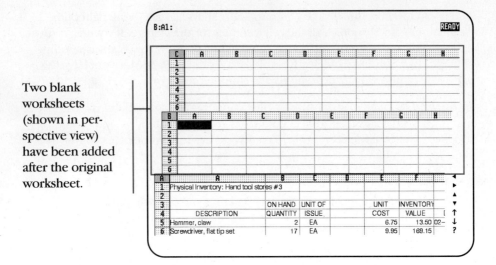

Two blank
worksheets
(shown in per-
spective view)
have been added
after the original
worksheet.

5

Deleting Columns and Rows

You can delete single (or multiple) columns or rows with the /**Worksheet Delete**
command. After you select this command, choose **Column** or **Row** from the
menu that appears on-screen. If you choose **Row**, 1-2-3 asks you to specify a
range of rows to be deleted; the range you specify needs to include only one cell
from each row to be deleted. In the next section, you learn how to use
/**Worksheet Delete Sheet** to delete one or more worksheets from a multiple-
worksheet application.

To delete existing columns or rows from the worksheet, follow these steps:

1. Position the cell pointer at the location of the first row or column to be
   deleted.

   For example, position the cell pointer in row 6.

2. Select /**Worksheet Delete**.

3. Select **Column** or **Row**.

   For example, select **Row** to delete rows from the worksheet.

4. In response to the prompt, designate the range where you want the
   column(s) or row(s) deleted.

172

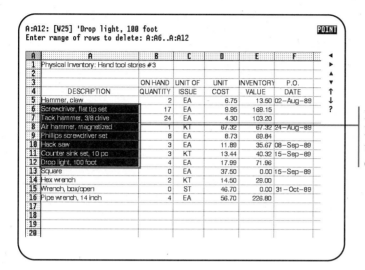

```
A:A12: [W25] 'Drop light, 100 foot                          POINT
Enter range of rows to delete: A:A6..A12
```

	A	B	C	D	E	F
1	Physical Inventory: Hand tool stores #3					
2						
3		ON HAND	UNIT OF	UNIT	INVENTORY	P.O.
4	DESCRIPTION	QUANTITY	ISSUE	COST	VALUE	DATE
5	Hammer, claw	2	EA	6.75	13.50	02–Aug–89
6	Screwdriver, flat tip set	17	EA	9.95	169.15	
7	Tack hammer, 3/8 drive	24	EA	4.30	103.20	
8	Air hammer, magnetized	1	KT	67.32	67.32	24–Aug–89
9	Phillips screwdriver set	8	EA	8.73	69.84	
10	Hack saw	3	EA	11.89	35.67	08–Sep–89
11	Counter sink set, 10 pc	3	KT	13.44	40.32	15–Sep–89
12	Drop light, 100 foot	4	EA	17.99	71.96	
13	Square	0	EA	37.50	0.00	15–Sep–89
14	Hex wrench	2	KT	14.50	29.00	
15	Wrench, box/open	0	ST	46.70	0.00	31–Oct–89
16	Pipe wrench, 14 inch	4	EA	56.70	226.80	
17						
18						
19						
20						

In this example, highlight rows 6 through 12 (in any column).

5. Press ↵Enter to complete the command.

```
A:A6: [W25] 'Square                                         READY
```

	A	B	C	D	E	F
1	Physical Inventory: Hand tool stores #3					
2						
3		ON HAND	UNIT OF	UNIT	INVENTORY	P.O.
4	DESCRIPTION	QUANTITY	ISSUE	COST	VALUE	DATE
5	Hammer, claw	2	EA	6.75	13.50	02–Aug–89
6	Square	0	EA	37.50	0.00	15–Sep–89
7	Hex wrench	2	KT	14.50	29.00	
8	Wrench, box/open	0	ST	46.70	0.00	31–Oct–89
9	Pipe wrench, 14 inch	4	EA	56.70	226.80	
10						
11						
12						
13						
14						
15						
16						
17						
18						
19						
20						

The original data in rows 6 through 12 is removed from the worksheet, and the data that appeared below these rows moves up.

5

Remember that /Worksheet Delete is different from /Range Erase. /Range Erase simply erases data from a cell or range of cells— not entire columns or rows of data.

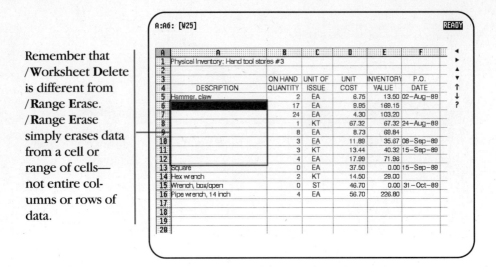

If you plan to use the command /Worksheet Delete to delete a column or row containing values, keep in mind that all formulas in the worksheet that still refer to these cells will then result in ERR. Also remember that when you use the /Worksheet Delete command, the columns or rows you delete may be gone forever. This command deletes entire columns or rows, not just the range of cells you specify in those columns or rows.

If the Undo feature is enabled, you can undo the deletion by pressing Undo (Alt-F4) before executing another command. Otherwise, the only remedies are to re-create the missing data or retrieve the worksheet file again. This latter approach works only if you have saved a copy of your worksheet that contains the missing data.

Deleting Worksheets and Files

If a file has multiple worksheets, you can delete an entire worksheet the same way you delete a row or a column. Use /Worksheet Delete Sheet to delete one or more worksheets from a file. You cannot delete all the worksheets from a file; at least one worksheet must remain after the deletion. To delete one or more worksheets in a multiple-worksheet file, follow these steps:

1. Select /Worksheet Delete Sheet.
2. At the prompt `Enter range of worksheets to delete:`, use Ctrl PgUp or Ctrl PgDn or the mouse to specify the worksheets to be deleted.

174

Note: You only need to specify a range with one cell from each worksheet to be deleted, not each entire worksheet.

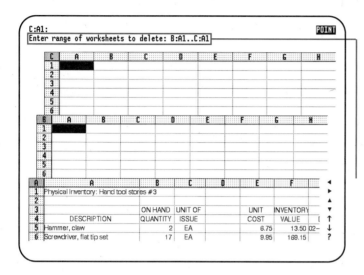

In this example, specify worksheets B and C as the worksheets to delete.

3. Press ⏎Enter to complete the command.

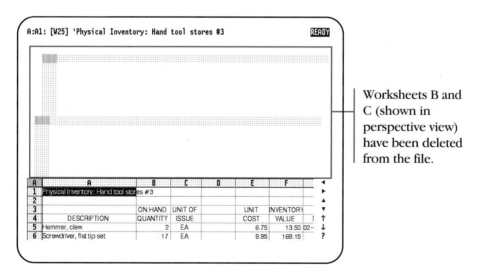

Worksheets B and C (shown in perspective view) have been deleted from the file.

Remember that when you delete worksheets containing data referenced by formulas in the remaining worksheet(s), these formulas will then result in ERR.

Also, the only way you can recover a deleted worksheet (besides reentering the data) is to press Undo (Alt-F4) before executing another command. Of course, the Undo feature must be active before you can use this method.

If you have multiple files in memory, you can remove a file from memory with **/Worksheet Delete File**. To complete this procedure, follow these steps:

1. Select **/Worksheet Delete File**.

5

A list of files currently in memory is presented.

```
A:A1: [W17]                                                      FILES
Enter name of file in memory to delete: C:\CP\QS31\QTR4TOT.WK3
QTR4TOT.WK3        DEPT1.WK3           DEPT2.WK3
         A      A       B       C       D       E       F       G       H
         1   Department 2 Sales
         2
         3           OCT     NOV     DEC     TOTAL
         4           $15,677 $13,760 $20,047 $49,484
         5
         6
         A      A       B       C       D       E       F       G       H
         1   Department 1 Sales
         2
         3           OCT     NOV     DEC     TOTAL
         4           $1,267  $2,854  $3,444  $7,565
         5
         6
         A      A           B       C       D       E       F       G
         1
         2                  Fourth Quarter Sales
         3
         4
         5                  Dept_1      $7,565
         6                  Dept_2      $49,484
```

2. At the prompt `Enter name of file in memory to delete:`, select the file name by typing or highlighting the name and pressing ↵Enter, or using the mouse.

After you delete a file from memory, more memory is available; you can add data to the existing file(s) in memory or open another file.

Hiding Columns and Worksheets

With the **/Worksheet Column Hide** and **/Worksheet Hide** commands, you can suppress the display of one or more columns or worksheets, respectively. One important use of this command is to suppress the display of unwanted columns when you are printing reports. When you hide intervening columns, a report can display data from two or more separated columns on a single page.

Other uses of these commands include suppressing the display of sensitive information (such as financial statements), hiding the display of cells that have a numeric value of zero, and fitting noncontiguous columns on-screen. The procedures that follow describe how to hide and redisplay columns, and how to hide and redisplay worksheets.

To hide one or more columns, follow these steps:

1. Select /**Worksheet Column Hide**.

2. Specify the columns to hide by either typing or highlighting the range.

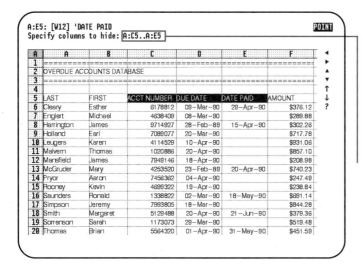

In this example, columns C through E are specified.

3. Press ⏎Enter), and the specified columns are hidden from view.

Although the hidden columns do not appear on the display, numbers and formulas in hidden columns are still present, and cell references to cells in hidden columns continue to work properly. You can tell which columns are missing only by noting the break in column letters at the top of the display. The hidden columns are temporarily redisplayed, however, when you use certain commands, such as /**Copy** or /**Move**; the hidden columns are marked with an asterisk (such as C*) during this temporary display.

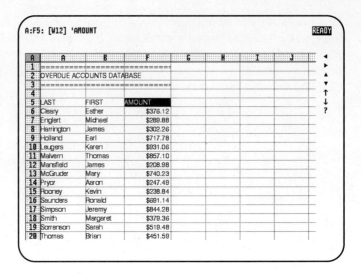

In this example, columns C through E are now hidden.

```
A:F5: [W12] 'AMOUNT                                              READY

  A       A          B          F          G      H      I      J
  1 =====================================
  2 OVERDUE ACCOUNTS DATABASE
  3 =====================================
  4
  5 LAST       FIRST      AMOUNT
  6 Cleary     Esther       $376.12
  7 Englert    Michael      $289.88
  8 Harrington James        $302.26
  9 Holland    Earl         $717.78
 10 Leugers    Karen        $931.06
 11 Malvern    Thomas       $857.10
 12 Mansfield  James        $208.98
 13 McGruder   Mary         $740.23
 14 Pryor      Aaron        $247.49
 15 Rooney     Kevin        $238.84
 16 Saunders   Ronald       $691.14
 17 Simpson    Jeremy       $844.28
 18 Smith      Margaret     $379.36
 19 Sorrenson  Sarah        $519.48
 20 Thomas     Brian        $451.59
```

This screen shows how hidden columns are temporarily displayed when using /Copy.

```
A:F5: [W12] 'AMOUNT                                              POINT
Enter range to copy FROM: A:F5..A:F5

  A       A          B          C*         D*        E*        F
  1 =====================================
  2 OVERDUE ACCOUNTS DATABASE
  3 =====================================
  4
  5 LAST       FIRST      ACCT NUMBER DUE DATE  DATE PAID  AMOUNT
  6 Cleary     Esther        6178812  09-Mar-90 29-Apr-90    $376.12
  7 Englert    Michael       4638409  08-Mar-90              $289.88
  8 Harrington James         9714927  28-Feb-89 15-Apr-90    $302.26
  9 Holland    Earl          7089077  20-Mar-90              $717.78
 10 Leugers    Karen         4114529  10-Apr-90              $931.06
 11 Malvern    Thomas        1020886  20-Apr-90              $857.10
 12 Mansfield  James         7949146  18-Apr-90              $208.98
 13 McGruder   Mary          4253520  23-Feb-89 20-Apr-90    $740.23
 14 Pryor      Aaron         7456362  04-Apr-90              $247.49
 15 Rooney     Kevin         4699322  19-Apr-90              $238.84
 16 Saunders   Ronald        1338822  02-Mar-90 18-May-90    $691.14
 17 Simpson    Jeremy        7993805  18-Mar-90              $844.28
 18 Smith      Margaret      5129488  20-Apr-90 21-Jun-90    $379.36
 19 Sorrenson  Sarah         1173073  29-Mar-90              $519.48
 20 Thomas     Brian         5564320  01-Apr-90 31-May-90    $451.59
```

To redisplay hidden columns, follow these steps:

1. Select **/Worksheet Column Display**.

2. At the prompt `Specify hidden columns to redisplay:`, enter the range of columns to redisplay.

```
A:E5: [W12] 'DATE PAID                                          POINT
Specify hidden columns to redisplay: A:C5..A:E5
```

A	A	B	C*	D*	E*	F	
1	================	=========	=========	=========	=========	=========	◄
2	OVERDUE ACCOUNTS DATABASE						►
3	================	=========	=========	=========	=========	=========	▲
4							▼
5	LAST	FIRST	ACCT NUMBER	DUE DATE	DATE PAID	AMOUNT	↑
6	Cleary	Esther	6178812	09–Mar–90	29–Apr–90	$376.12	↓
7	Englert	Michael	4638409	08–Mar–90		$289.88	?
8	Harrington	James	9714927	28–Feb–89	15–Apr–90	$302.26	
9	Holland	Earl	7089077	20–Mar–90		$717.78	
10	Leugers	Karen	4114529	10–Apr–90		$931.06	
11	Malvern	Thomas	1020886	20–Apr–90		$857.10	
12	Mansfield	James	7949146	18–Apr–90		$208.98	
13	McGruder	Mary	4253520	23–Feb–89	20–Apr–90	$740.23	
14	Pryor	Aaron	7456362	04–Apr–90		$247.49	
15	Rooney	Kevin	4699322	19–Apr–90		$238.84	
16	Saunders	Ronald	1338822	02–Mar–90	18–May–90	$691.14	
17	Simpson	Jeremy	7993805	18–Mar–90		$844.28	
18	Smith	Margaret	5129488	20–Apr–90	21–Jun–90	$379.36	
19	Sorrenson	Sarah	1173073	29–Mar–90		$519.48	
20	Thomas	Brian	5564320	01–Apr–90	31–May–90	$451.59	

In this example, specify columns C through E.

3. Press ↵Enter, and the hidden columns are redisplayed.

```
A:F1: [W12] \=                                                 READY
```

A	A	B	C	D	E	F	
1	================	=========	=========	=========	=========	=========	◄
2	OVERDUE ACCOUNTS DATABASE						►
3	================	=========	=========	=========	=========	=========	▲
4							▼
5	LAST	FIRST	ACCT NUMBER	DUE DATE	DATE PAID	AMOUNT	↑
6	Cleary	Esther	6178812	09–Mar–90	29–Apr–90	$376.12	↓
7	Englert	Michael	4638409	08–Mar–90		$289.88	?
8	Harrington	James	9714927	28–Feb–89	15–Apr–90	$302.26	
9	Holland	Earl	7089077	20–Mar–90		$717.78	
10	Leugers	Karen	4114529	10–Apr–90		$931.06	
11	Malvern	Thomas	1020886	20–Apr–90		$857.10	
12	Mansfield	James	7949146	18–Apr–90		$208.98	
13	McGruder	Mary	4253520	23–Feb–89	20–Apr–90	$740.23	
14	Pryor	Aaron	7456362	04–Apr–90		$247.49	
15	Rooney	Kevin	4699322	19–Apr–90		$238.84	
16	Saunders	Ronald	1338822	02–Mar–90	18–May–90	$691.14	
17	Simpson	Jeremy	7993805	18–Mar–90		$844.28	
18	Smith	Margaret	5129488	20–Apr–90	21–Jun–90	$379.36	
19	Sorrenson	Sarah	1173073	29–Mar–90		$519.48	
20	Thomas	Brian	5564320	01–Apr–90	31–May–90	$451.59	

Press ↵Enter to redisplay columns C through E.

In multiple-worksheet applications, you can hide entire worksheets with the **/Worksheet Hide** command. This command is especially helpful when used to hide worksheets containing formulas, macros, and sensitive data (such as sales information).

5

179

Building a Worksheet

To hide one or more worksheets in a multiple-worksheet file, follow these steps:

1. Select /Worksheet Hide Enable.
2. Specify the worksheet(s) to hide by either typing or using the direction keys or mouse to highlight the worksheet range.

In this example, worksheet B is specified.

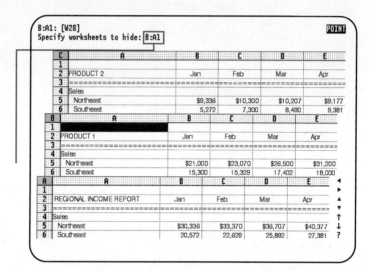

3. Press ⏎Enter to hide the specified worksheet(s) from view.

In this example, worksheet B is now hidden.

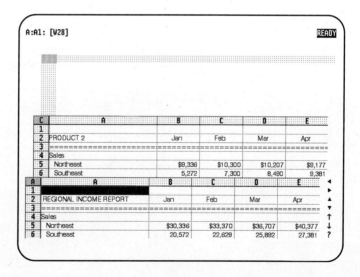

Although hidden worksheets do not appear on the display, numbers and formulas in hidden worksheets are still present, and cell references to cells in hidden worksheets continue to work properly. You can tell which worksheets are missing only by noting the break in worksheet letters on the left side of the screen. The hidden worksheets are temporarily redisplayed, however, when you use certain commands, such as /Copy or /Move; the hidden worksheet letters are marked with an asterisk (such as B*) during this temporary display.

To redisplay hidden worksheets in a multiple-worksheet application, follow these steps:

1. Select /**Worksheet Hide Disable**.

2. At the prompt `Specify worksheets to redisplay:`, enter the range of worksheets to redisplay.

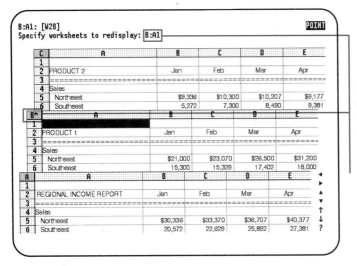

In this example, specify worksheet B. An asterisk appears next to the worksheet letter.

3. Press ⏎Enter to redisplay the hidden worksheet(s).

Suppressing the Display of Zeros

The /**Worksheet Global Zero** command enables you to suppress the display in the worksheet of all cells that have a numeric value of zero. For example, this technique is useful for preparing reports for a presentation where cells showing $0.00 would look odd. As an alternative, you may choose to have a label (such as No Charge), instead of a blank, displayed in zero-value cells.

You can enter formulas and values for all the items in the report, including the zero items, and then display the results with all the zeros removed or replaced by a label. The actual formula or value is displayed in the control panel when the cell pointer highlights a cell that contains a zero, or a formula that evaluates to zero.

Suppose that you have a worksheet that lists product codes and their associated costs. In some cases, the costs are $0.00, perhaps entered in error.

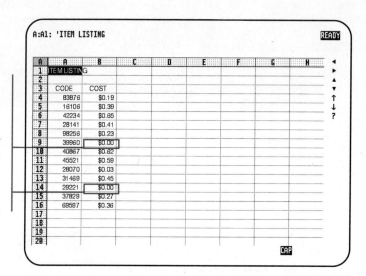

To suppress the display of zeros or to substitute a label for zero entries, follow these steps:

1. Select /Worksheet Global Zero.

2. If you want to suppress the display of zeros by substituting a blank, select **Yes** to complete this procedure.

   Or

   If you want to suppress the display of zeros by substituting a label, select **Label** and continue with the next step.

In this example, select **Label**.

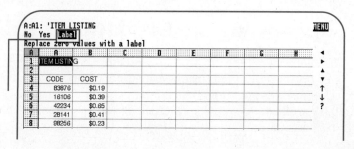

182

3. When 1-2-3 prompts you to enter the text for the label to appear in every zero-value cell, type the text and press ↵Enter.

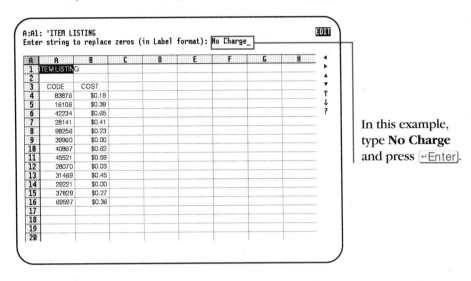

In this example, type **No Charge** and press ↵Enter.

If you want the zeros visible again, use the command /**Worksheet Global Zero No**. When you use the /**File Save** command to save your worksheet, the zero suppression or label substitution features of this command are not saved with the worksheet. Therefore, these features are not present when you retrieve a file.

Note: This command is not selective; all cells in the worksheet with a zero value are affected by the substitution. A cell with the value .004 would be displayed as 0.00 if a 2-decimal place format were used. Because the value is not truly zero, it would therefore not be changed by the /**Worksheet Global Zero** command.

183

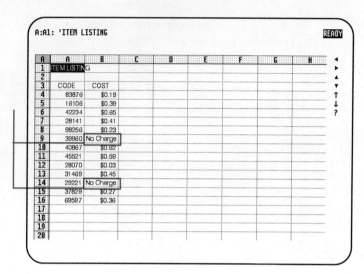

All zero values in the worksheet are replaced with the label No Charge.

Recalculating the Worksheet

One of the primary functions of a spreadsheet program is to recalculate cells with formulas when a value or formula in one of the cells changes. 1-2-3 provides two basic recalculation methods: automatic recalculation and manual recalculation. Using automatic recalculation, the default, 1-2-3 recalculates the formulas that are affected whenever a cell in the worksheet changes. In manual recalculation, the worksheet is recalculated only when the user requests it, either from the keyboard with the Calc (F9) key or from a macro.

1-2-3 also provides three orders of recalculation: the natural order and two linear orders, either columnwise or rowwise. Natural order is the default, but you can choose any of the three orders. You also can choose the number of times worksheets are recalculated. You select the recalculation options by using the /Worksheet Global Recalc command. Settings specified with this command affect all active worksheets and files. The recalculation options are described in Table 5.2.

Table 5.2
Selections on the /Worksheet Global Recalc Menu

Selection	Description
Order of Recalculation	
Natural	1-2-3 does not recalculate any cell until the cells that it depends on have been recalculated. This is the default setting.
Columnwise	Recalculation begins at cell A:A1 of the first active file and continues down column A, then goes to cell A:B1 and down column B, and so forth—through all worksheets of all active files.
Rowwise	Recalculation begins at cell A:A1 of the first active file and proceeds across row 1, then goes across row 2, and so forth—through all worksheets of all active files.
Method of Recalculation	
Automatic	The worksheet is recalculated whenever a cell changes. This is the default setting.
Manual	The worksheet is recalculated only when you press F9 (Calc).
Number of Recalculations	
Iteration	The worksheet is recalculated a specified number of times when you change cell contents in automatic recalculation, or press F9 (Calc) in manual recalculation. The default is one iteration per recalculation.

5

As a beginning 1-2-3 user, you may not need to change the recalculation settings at all. 1-2-3's default settings are **A**utomatic recalculation (meaning that each time a cell's content changes, the program automatically recalculates any formulas that are affected), and **N**atural order (meaning that 1-2-3 does not recalculate any given cell until after the cells that it depends on have been recalculated). To save processing time, you can switch to **M**anual recalculation so that 1-2-3 recalculates the worksheet only when you press Calc (F9).

For more specialized applications, the **Columnwise** or **Rowwise** recalculation method can be used. Be extremely careful when you use these orders of recalculation, however; if they are used improperly, they can produce erroneous values on the worksheet.

For more information on automatic, manual, and iterative recalculation, and natural, columnwise, and rowwise orders of recalculation, refer to Que's *Using 1-2-3 Release 3.1*, 2nd Edition. You'll find an in-depth discussion and step-by-step examples on using the recalculation options.

Protecting the Worksheet

1-2-3 has special features that protect areas of a worksheet from possible destruction. Using a series of commands, you can set up ranges of cells that cannot be changed without special effort. In fact, columns and rows that contain protected cells cannot be deleted from the worksheet. These commands are particularly beneficial when you are setting up worksheets in which data will be entered by people who are not familiar with 1-2-3.

Protecting the Entire Worksheet

When you first create a worksheet, the global protection feature is not active, enabling you to make changes and add data anywhere in the worksheet. The /**Worksheet G**lobal **P**rot **E**nable command turns on the worksheet's protection system.

This protection system may be thought of as a series of barriers set up around all the cells in the worksheet. The barriers go down when the worksheet is first loaded, and all the cells in the worksheet can be modified. This arrangement is appropriate because you want to have access to everything in the worksheet when you first begin entering data.

After you finish making all your entries in the worksheet, you may want to make sure that certain areas are not modified, or you may want to set up areas with forms for data input and not allow the cell pointer to move anywhere else. To accomplish either of these tasks, you must first enable the protection feature with the /**Worksheet G**lobal **P**rot **E**nable command. After this command is issued, all the cells in the worksheet are protected. In other words, this command restores all the barriers in the worksheet.

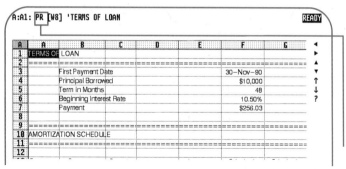

All cells in the worksheet are protected as indicated by the PR in the first line of the control panel.

Turning Off Protection in a Range

You can selectively unprotect certain cells or ranges with the /**R**ange Unprot command. In effect, you "tear down the barriers" that surround these individual cells or ranges of cells. You can reprotect these cells at any time by issuing the /**R**ange **P**rot command.

To turn off protection for a cell or range of cells in your worksheet, follow these steps:

1. Select /**R**ange Unprot.

2. Highlight the range of cells where you want to add or change data.

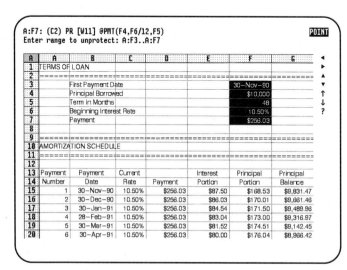

In this example, highlight the range F3..F7.

3. Press ⏎Enter to complete the command.

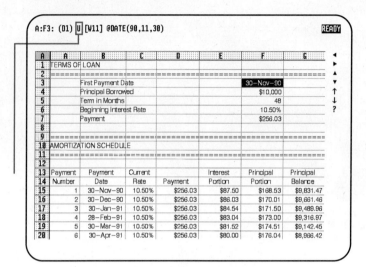

Unprotected cells are identified by a U in the control panel.

Suppose that you create a worksheet that includes a number of long and important formulas. You may want to protect these formulas against accidental deletion by using 1-2-3's protection capability. But what if you need to make a change in several of these formulas? You can move around the worksheet, unprotecting cells, changing the formulas, and then protecting the cells again. Or you can use the /Worksheet Global Prot Disable command to lower the barriers around all the cells. After making the necessary changes, you can restore protection to all the cells by using the /Worksheet Global Prot Enable command again.

Restricting Movement to a Particular Range

For even more protection, you can limit the movement of the cell pointer by using the /Range Input command. You must use this command, which allows movement to only cells unprotected with the /Range Unprot command, to set up special data input areas.

For example, suppose that you create a simple worksheet in which every cell is protected except for those in the range F3..F7, whose cells were unprotected with the /Range Unprot command.

To restrict input to unprotected cells in the worksheet, follow these steps:

1. Select /Range Input.

188

2. Highlight the range of cells that includes the unprotected cells in the data input area; then press ⏎Enter.

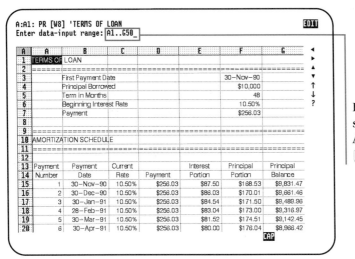

In this example, specify the range A1..G50 and press ⏎Enter.

Note: You should include the entire data input area (including protected areas) when specifying a range for the /**R**ange **I**nput command. This range should include all cells that are unprotected with /**R**ange **U**nprot.

3. After the range is entered, the first cell of the data input area moves to the upper left corner of the screen, and the cell pointer jumps immediately to the first unprotected cell in the range.

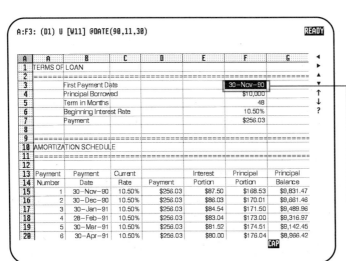

In this example, the cell pointer jumps to cell F3; only cells in the range F3..F7 can be accessed with the cell pointer.

You can now begin to enter or edit data in the unprotected cells. To move the cell pointer to the next unprotected cell after completing an entry, use the arrow keys.

The /Range Input command remains in effect until you press either the Enter key or the Esc key. The cell pointer then returns to the upper left corner of the data input range, and the worksheet returns to the same position on the screen as before the /Range Input command was issued.

Checking the Status of Global Settings

Use the /Worksheet Status command to check the status of all global settings for the worksheet. This command gives you an easy way to view the worksheet settings without having to experiment to find the settings.

To display the global settings of the current worksheet, select /Worksheet Status.

The current settings for the worksheet are displayed.

```
                                                            STAT

    Available memory: 372458 of 557268 Bytes (67%)

    Processor: 80386
    Math coprocessor: None

    Recalculation:
        Method.......... Automatic
        Order........... Natural
        Iterations....... 1

    Circular reference: (None)

    Cell display:
        Format.......... (G)
        Label prefix..... '
        Column width..... 9
        Zero setting..... No

    Global protection: Off
```

To return to the worksheet, press any key.

The information on the /Worksheet Status screen indicates the available memory as well as the global settings active in the current file. In this example, all settings shown are the original default settings. These settings indicate the following:

- The recalculation method is automatic, with natural order and one iteration per recalculation.

190

- No circular references currently exist.
- The cell display format is (G) for **General** (covered in Chapter 4).
- The label prefix is ' for left-justification (covered in Chapter 3).
- The column width is nine characters.
- Zero suppression is off.
- Global protection is disabled.

Entering a Page-Break Character

You can use a 1-2-3 command to enter a manual page break in the current worksheet (or in all worksheets of the current file if GROUP mode is enabled). The /**Worksheet** **P**age command inserts a blank row at the cell-pointer location.

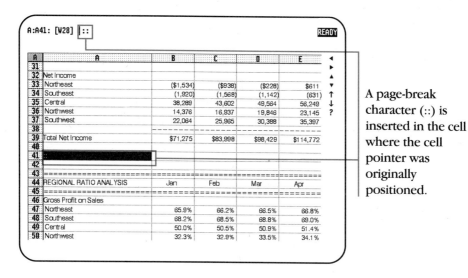

A page-break character (::) is inserted in the cell where the cell pointer was originally positioned.

The vertical bar (|) that precedes the page-break character (visible only in the control panel) tells 1-2-3 not to print the row. (This symbol is discussed in detail in Chapter 8.)

To enter a page-break character into a worksheet, follow these steps:

1. Position the cell pointer in the first column of the range to be printed, at the row location where you want a new page to begin.

2. Select /**Worksheet P**age.

Use a page-break character when printing a range from the worksheet. Although printing is not covered in detail until Chapter 8, the best time to insert page-break characters is while you are building the worksheet. As you become more experienced in building worksheets and printing reports, you will learn to think of printed pages as you build. Thinking ahead saves time and minimizes confusion when you're ready to print.

A page break is effective only when positioned at the left edge of the range being printed. If you add data to cells in the page-break row, the contents of those cells do not print when the page break is in effect.

You can remove a page break character by typing over it, deleting the row with /**Worksheet D**elete **R**ow, or erasing the cell with /**R**ange **E**rase.

Summary

This chapter showed you how the versatile /**W**orksheet commands can erase an entire worksheet, set column widths (individually or globally), split the screen into horizontal or vertical windows, and freeze titles for scrolling. The Wysiwyg :**W**orksheet commands can set column widths and row heights. You also learned how to insert and delete columns and rows, hide columns, suppress the display of zeros, recalculate and protect the worksheet, check the status of the global settings, and insert page breaks in a printed report.

Specifically, you learned the following key information about 1-2-3:

■ The /**W**orksheet **E**rase command erases all current worksheets and files from memory, but does not erase the file on disk.

■ The /**W**orksheet **C**olumn **S**et-Width command changes the width of a single column. To reset the column to its original default, use /**W**orksheet **C**olumn **R**eset-Width. You can use the :**W**orksheet **C**olumn **S**et-Width and :**W**orksheet **C**olumn **R**eset-Width commands in Wysiwyg to perform the same functions.

■ The /**W**orksheet **G**lobal **C**olumn-Width command changes the column width of all columns in the worksheet, except for those already changed.

- The /Worksheet Column Column-Range Set-Width command sets the width of contiguous columns. To reset these columns to the default, select /Worksheet Column Column-Range Reset-Width.

- The :Worksheet Row Set-Height command allows you to change the height of selected rows in Wysiwyg. The :Worksheet Row Auto command returns the height of selected rows to the current default.

- You can use the mouse to quickly set individual column widths and row heights. Position the mouse pointer on the right column boundary or the bottom row boundary in the worksheet border, press and hold the left mouse button and move the mouse pointer in the direction of the desired column width or row height. Then release the mouse button.

- The /Worksheet Window command splits the screen so that two different parts of the worksheet can be viewed at the same time. Worksheets can be split with the Horizontal or Vertical options. Use /Worksheet Window Clear to return to a single worksheet. You can also use a mouse to split the screen horizontally or vertically.

- The /Worksheet Window Graph command allows you to display the current graph on screen, to the right of worksheet data.

- The /Worksheet Titles command freezes titles along the top and left borders of the worksheet so that the titles remain in view when scrolling the worksheet. The /Worksheet Titles Clear command unfreezes the titles.

- The /Worksheet Insert command can insert one or more columns, rows, or worksheets into the current file. To delete one or more columns, rows, or worksheets, use /Worksheet Delete.

- The /Worksheet Column Hide command temporarily removes columns of data from the screen. Hidden columns also do not print when included in a print range. These columns can be restored with the /Worksheet Column Display command.

- The /Worksheet Hide Enable command temporarily suppresses the display of one or more worksheets in a multiple-worksheet file. Use the /Worksheet Hide Disable command to redisplay hidden worksheets.

- The /Worksheet Global Zero command suppresses the display of zeros in the worksheet. Blank cells or labels, instead of zeros, are displayed on-screen. The actual value (or formula) is displayed in the control panel when a zero-valued cell is highlighted.

- The /Worksheet Global Recalc command changes the method, order, and number of iterations used in worksheet recalculation.

5

- The /**W**orksheet **G**lobal **P**rot command allows you to turn protection on or off in a worksheet. /**R**ange **U**nprot can then unprotect individual cells or ranges in the worksheet, to allow entry only in those cells.

- The /**R**ange **I**nput command restricts input to only unprotected cells in a protected data-input range. The cell pointer moves only among the unprotected cells.

- The /**W**orksheet **S**tatus command displays a list of the worksheet's current global settings. These settings can be modified with the /**W**orksheet **G**lobal commands.

- The /**W**orksheet **P**age command inserts a blank row that contains a page-break character (::). This character indicates where a new page should begin when a worksheet is printed.

The next chapter shows you how to use the /**C**opy and /**M**ove commands to modify your worksheet data. You also learn how to use 1-2-3's search-and-replace feature.

5

Modifying a Worksheet

6

As you begin to create your own worksheets using the basic concepts and commands described in earlier chapters, you need to modify your worksheets by moving and copying data from one location to another. 1-2-3 provides the capability to move and copy data—saving you hours of work when building and modifying your worksheets.

This chapter shows you how to improve your worksheets by moving and copying data effectively. You also learn how to search for and replace a specific string of data in a range of cells in the worksheet.

Moving the contents of cells

Copying the contents of cells

Searching for and replacing cell contents

6

Key Terms in This Chapter

Relative cell address	A cell reference that adjusts for a new location when used in a formula copied to that location. This cell address is the default.
Absolute cell address	A cell reference that does not adjust for a new location when used in a formula copied to that location.
Mixed cell address	A cell reference that combines both relative and absolute cell addressing; used when copying a formula to a new location.
Search string	A set of characters used with the /Range Search command to find specified text in a range of cells.

Using the Mouse

To use a mouse with 1-2-3 Release 3.1, you need a mouse, mouse software, and a graphics monitor and graphics card that support a mouse. Also, Wysiwyg must be loaded into memory. You can use a mouse to select commands and files, specify ranges, and move the cell pointer within a worksheet or between multiple worksheets and files. In the examples throughout this chapter, notice that the 1-2-3 commands always begin with a slash (/), and the Wysiwyg commands always begin with a colon :. Refer to the following sections of the specified chapters for further information on using the mouse:

- Chapter 2—"Understanding Mouse Terminology"
- Chapter 3—"Mouse Control of the Cell Pointer"
        "Using the Mouse To Select Menu Commands"
- Chapter 4—"Using the Mouse To Specify Ranges"

Moving the Contents of Cells

In the days of manual spreadsheets, the process of moving data around on the page was called cutting and pasting because scissors and glue were used to move sections of the spreadsheet. 1-2-3 lets you cut and paste sections of the worksheet automatically.

With the /Move and /Copy commands, you can move and copy the contents of cells and ranges of cells from one part of the worksheet to another, as well as between multiple worksheets and files. The difference between moving and copying is that data that is moved from one location to another disappears from the first location; data that is copied appears in both locations.

Moving Data within a Single Worksheet

Suppose that you want to move the contents of the range C2..D3 to the range E2..F3 on your worksheet. To move a range within a single worksheet, follow these steps:

1. Select /Move.

2. At the prompt `Enter range to move FROM:`, specify the range you want to move; then press ⏎Enter .

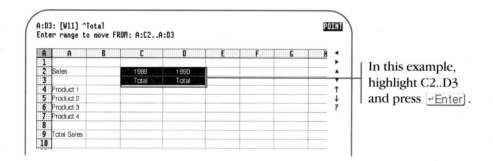

In this example, highlight C2..D3 and press ⏎Enter .

3. At the prompt `Enter range to move TO:`, highlight the upper left cell of the new location; then press ⏎Enter .

   Note: Highlighting the entire TO range is not necessary.

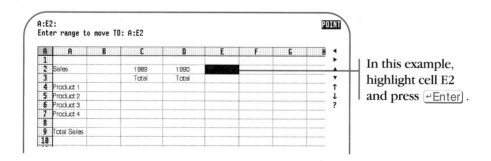

In this example, highlight cell E2 and press ⏎Enter .

197

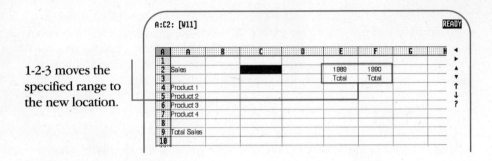

1-2-3 moves the specified range to the new location.

The cell pointer returns immediately to where it was when you initiated the /Move command. Remember that the cell pointer does not have to be positioned at the beginning of the FROM or TO range when you start the /Move command. You can always press Esc (or the right mouse button) to free the cell pointer and move it to the correct location.

Moving Data between Worksheets

You can move ranges of any size. You also can move them between worksheets. If you build a large application by starting with one worksheet, you can move parts of it into different worksheets (or files) as the application grows.

To move ranges between worksheets, follow these steps:

1. Select /Move.

2. At the prompt Enter range to move FROM:, specify the range you want to move. Then press ↵Enter.

In this multiple-worksheet ex-ample, the range to be moved from worksheet A to worksheet B is highlighted (A:C2..A:E6).

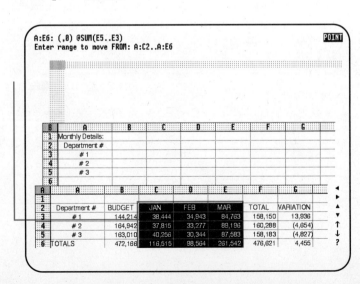

198

3. At the prompt `Enter range to move TO:`, highlight the upper left cell of the new location in another worksheet (using `Ctrl` `PgUp`, `Ctrl` `PgDn`, or the mouse). Then press `↵Enter`.

   Note: Highlighting the entire TO range is not necessary.

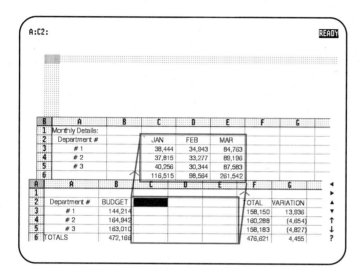

In this example, the TO range was specified as cell B:C2. The data moved from worksheet A to worksheet B.

Tips for Moving

Remember the following tips whenever you intend to move data in a single worksheet or between worksheets:

- When you move a range of cells, the TO range is completely overwritten by the FROM range that is moved. Any cell contents are lost. If there are cells with formulas that depend on the cell addresses in the TO range, the cells containing these formulas evaluate to ERR.

- If the Undo feature is enabled (with the /Worksheet **Global Default Other Undo Enable** command), you can reverse the effects of a /**Move** operation by pressing Alt-F4 before executing another command.

- Highlight ranges (rather than type ranges) to be moved to help avoid errors. Remember that you can also use the click-and-drag mouse technique to highlight the FROM and TO ranges when moving data.

- Use the End key for pointing to large ranges quickly. This method almost always reduces the number of required keystrokes for a move operation. If there are gaps (blank cells) within the blocks of data, however, the End key procedure is less useful because the cell pointer goes to the boundaries of each gap.

- If you are moving data from a multiple-worksheet file, ensure that there are as many worksheets in the TO range as specified in the FROM range that is being moved.
- Although you can move data between multiple worksheets within a single file, you cannot move data between separate files using the /**M**ove command.

Copying the Contents of Cells

You will often want to copy the contents of cells to other locations in a worksheet or between worksheets and files. When you copy data, you also copy with it cell formats and the protection status of the copied cell(s). In 1-2-3, you can copy data in the following ways:

- Copy the contents of one cell to another cell.
- Copy the contents of one cell to every cell in a range.
- Copy from one range to another range of equal size.
- Copy from one range to a larger range.
- Copy between worksheets or files.

The procedure used for each copy operation is basically the same. To copy a range, follow these steps:

1. Select /**C**opy.
2. At the prompt `Enter range to copy FROM:`, specify the FROM range.
3. At the prompt `Enter range to copy TO:`, specify the TO range.

The only elements that change are the dimensions and locations of the FROM and TO ranges. Remember that you can either type the coordinates of the FROM and TO ranges from the keyboard, or highlight (point to) the ranges in POINT mode (with the keyboard or a mouse).

Copying Data within a Single Worksheet

The basic methods of copying data within a single worksheet are described in the text that follows. The subsequent section explains how you also can copy data between multiple worksheets and files.

Method 1: Copying from one cell to another cell

1. Select /Copy.

2. At the prompt `Enter range to copy FROM:`, highlight the cell whose contents you want to copy; then press `↵Enter`. If the cell pointer is located on the cell to be copied, just press `↵Enter`.

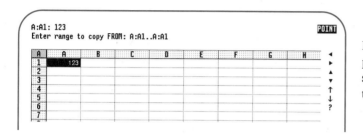

In this example, press `↵Enter` to select cell A1 as the FROM range.

3. At the prompt `Enter range to copy TO:`, highlight the cell where you want the data copied. Then press `↵Enter`.

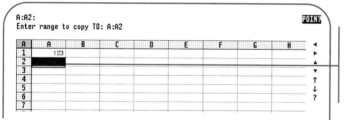

In this example, specify the TO range by highlighting cell A2 and pressing `↵Enter`.

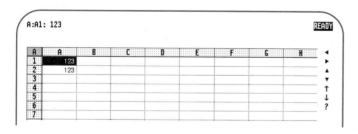

The contents of cell A1 have been copied to cell A2.

201

Method 2: Copying from one cell to a range of cells

1. Select /**Copy**.

2. At the prompt `Enter range to copy FROM:`, highlight the cell whose contents you want to copy; then press ⏎Enter. If the cell pointer is located on the cell to be copied, just press ⏎Enter.

In this example, press ⏎Enter to select cell A1 as the FROM range.

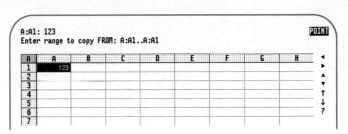

3. At the prompt `Enter range to copy TO:`, highlight the range of cells where you want the data copied; then press ⏎Enter.

In this example, specify the TO range by highlighting B2..H2 and pressing ⏎Enter.

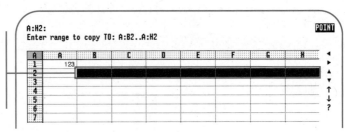

The contents of cell A1 have been copied to each cell in the range B2..H2.

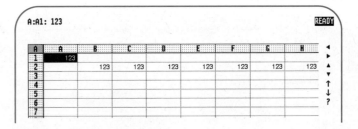

Method 3: Copying from one range to another range of equal size

1. Select /**Copy**.

2. At the prompt `Enter range to copy FROM:`, highlight the range of cells whose contents you want to copy; then press ⏎Enter.

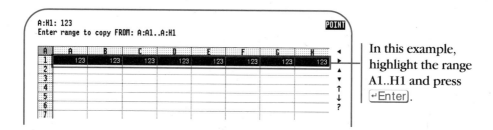

In this example, highlight the range A1..H1 and press ↵Enter.

3. At the prompt Enter range to copy TO:, highlight the first cell of the range where you want the data copied; then press ↵Enter.

   Note: With this method of copying, highlighting the entire TO range is not necessary.

6

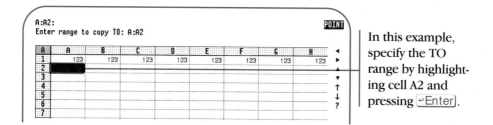

In this example, specify the TO range by highlighting cell A2 and pressing ↵Enter.

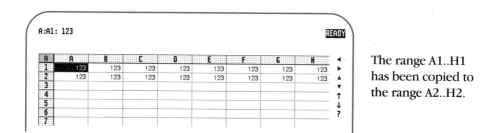

The range A1..H1 has been copied to the range A2..H2.

Method 4: Copying from one range of cells to a larger range of cells

1. Select /**Copy**.

2. At the prompt Enter range to copy FROM:, highlight the range of cells whose contents you want to copy; then press ↵Enter.

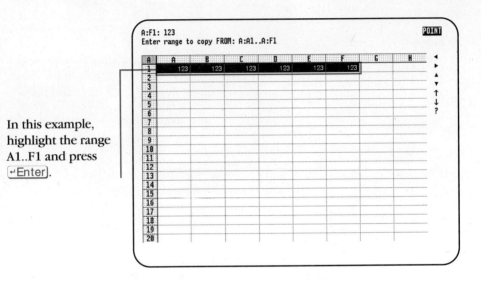

In this example, highlight the range A1..F1 and press ↵Enter.

3. At the prompt `Enter range to copy TO:`, highlight only the first cells in the rows or columns to which you want the data copied; then press ↵Enter.

In this example, to copy the data in row 1 (cells A1..F1) to rows 2 through 20 (cells A2..F20), specify the TO range by highlighting the first cells in rows 2 through 20—the range A2..A20; then press ↵Enter.

```
A:A1: 123                                                    READY
```

	A	B	C	D	E	F	G	H	
1	123	123	123	123	123	123			
2	123	123	123	123	123	123			
3	123	123	123	123	123	123			
4	123	123	123	123	123	123			
5	123	123	123	123	123	123			
6	123	123	123	123	123	123			
7	123	123	123	123	123	123			
8	123	123	123	123	123	123			
9	123	123	123	123	123	123			
10	123	123	123	123	123	123			
11	123	123	123	123	123	123			
12	123	123	123	123	123	123			
13	123	123	123	123	123	123			
14	123	123	123	123	123	123			
15	123	123	123	123	123	123			
16	123	123	123	123	123	123			
17	123	123	123	123	123	123			
18	123	123	123	123	123	123			
19	123	123	123	123	123	123			
20	123	123	123	123	123	123			

The range A1..F1 has been copied to the larger range A2..F20.

6

Think of this type of copying as an extension of the previous type. The results of this copy operation could have been reached by repeating the copy command 19 times and specifying 19 different single-row TO ranges. The first TO range would be A2, the second would be A3, the third A4, and so on. The results are the same for either method, but you can save a great deal of time by copying to the A2..A20 range, as shown.

The best way to learn how to use different FROM and TO ranges is to experiment on your own. After a while, the rules of copying become second nature to you.

Copying Data between Worksheets and Files

In addition to copying data within a single worksheet, you also can copy data between worksheets and files. You can use the same concepts from each of the methods described in the previous section; the example that follows uses the method of copying from one range to another range of equal size.

To copy ranges between worksheets, follow these steps:

1. Select /Copy.

2. At the prompt `Enter range to copy FROM:`, highlight the range of cells whose contents you want to copy; then press ⏎Enter.

205

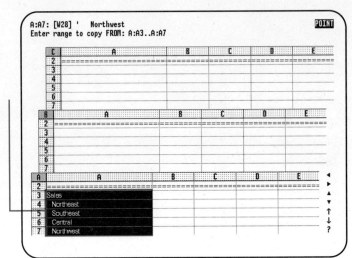

In this example, highlight the range A:A3..A:A7 and press ⏎Enter.

3. At the prompt Enter range to copy TO:, highlight the first cell of the range in each worksheet where you want the data copied (using Ctrl PgUp, Ctrl PgDn, or the mouse); then press ⏎Enter.

   Note: With this method of copying, highlighting the entire TO range is not necessary. However, you must highlight the first cell in each worksheet that will receive the copied data.

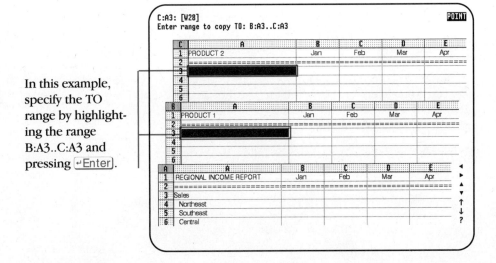

In this example, specify the TO range by highlighting the range B:A3..C:A3 and pressing ⏎Enter.

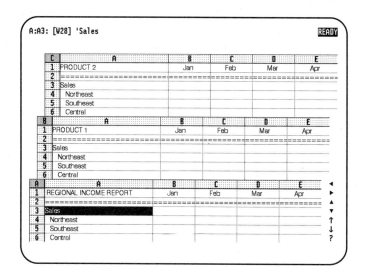

The range
A:A3. .A:A7 has
been copied
to the range
B:A3..C:A7.

Addressing Cells

Although the connection may not be obvious, the way you address cells is tied closely to copy operations. Two different methods of addressing cells can be used when copying: *relative* and *absolute*. These two methods of referencing cells are important for building formulas. The type of addressing you use when you reference cells in formulas can affect the results produced by these formulas when you copy them to different locations in the worksheet. The following sections cover relative and absolute addressing as well as the combination of both methods—known as *mixed addressing*.

Referencing Cells with Relative Addressing

Relative addressing, 1-2-3's default for referencing cells, means that when you copy a formula, unless you specify otherwise, the addresses of the cells in the formula are adjusted automatically to fit the new location. Suppose that you have summed the contents of one column, and you need to sum the contents of several adjacent columns, but you don't want to enter the @SUM function over and over again.

To copy a formula with a relative address, follow these steps:

1. Select /Copy.

2. At the prompt `Enter range to copy FROM:`, highlight the cell containing the formula to be copied; then press `⏎Enter`.

```
A:B11: (C0) [W13] @SUM(B5..B9)                              POINT
Enter range to copy FROM: A:B11..A:B11
```

A	A	B	C	D	E
1	============	=======	=======	=======	=======
2	INCOME REPORT	Jan	Feb	Mar	1st Quarter
3	============	=======	=======	=======	=======
4	Sales				
5	Northeast	$30,336	$33,370	$36,707	$100,413
6	Southeast	20,572	22,629	25,892	$69,093
7	Central	131,685	144,854	159,339	$435,877
8	Northwest	94,473	103,920	114,312	$312,706
9	Southwest	126,739	139,413	153,354	$419,506
10					
11	Total Sales	$403,805			
12					
13					
14					
15					

In this example, highlight cell B11 and press ⏎Enter.

3. At the prompt Enter range to copy TO:, highlight the range of cells where you want the formula copied; then press ⏎Enter.

```
A:E11: [W13]                                                POINT
Enter range to copy TO: A:C11..A:E11
```

A	A	B	C	D	E
1	============	=======	=======	=======	=======
2	INCOME REPORT	Jan	Feb	Mar	1st Quarter
3	============	=======	=======	=======	=======
4	Sales				
5	Northeast	$30,336	$33,370	$36,707	$100,413
6	Southeast	20,572	22,629	25,892	$69,093
7	Central	131,685	144,854	159,339	$435,877
8	Northwest	94,473	103,920	114,312	$312,706
9	Southwest	126,739	139,413	153,354	$419,506
10					
11	Total Sales	$403,805			
12					
13					
14					
15					

In this example, specify the TO range by highlighting C11..E11 and pressing ⏎Enter.

```
A:B11: (T) [W13] @SUM(B5..B9)                               READY
```

A	A	B	C	D	E
1	============	=======	=======	=======	=======
2	INCOME REPORT	Jan	Feb	Mar	1st Quarter
3	============	=======	=======	=======	=======
4	Sales				
5	Northeast	$30,336	$33,370	$36,707	$100,413
6	Southeast	20,572	22,629	25,892	$69,093
7	Central	131,685	144,854	159,339	$435,877
8	Northwest	94,473	103,920	114,312	$312,706
9	Southwest	126,739	139,413	153,354	$419,506
10					
11	Total Sales	@SUM(B5..B9)	@SUM(C5..C9)	@SUM(D5..D9)	@SUM(E5..E9)
12					
13					
14					
15					

1-2-3 copies the @SUM function to all the cells in the specified TO range, C11..E11.

Note: In the preceding example, the range of formulas appears in text format (rather than the resulting values) to show how each copied formula adjusts to its new location.

Referencing Cells with Absolute Addressing

In some cases, a formula has an important address that should not be changed when the formula is copied. To keep an address absolute, enter a $ before the cell's column letter and before the cell's row number. For example, $E$11 is an absolute address.

Now that you have summed the contents of several columns of sales, assume you want to calculate the percentage of sales represented by each month of the quarter. In the example, the best way to do this is to copy a formula that contains an absolute address. When you create the formula in cell B13, place a $ before the E and before the 11 in the second part of the formula.

To copy a formula with an absolute address, follow these steps:

1. Select /Copy.

2. At the prompt `Enter range to copy FROM:`, highlight the cell containing the formula with an absolute address to be copied. Then press `⏎Enter`.

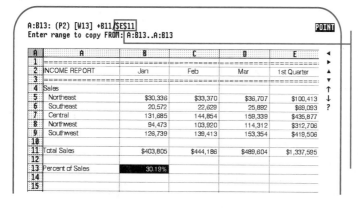

In this example, highlight cell B13 and press `⏎Enter`. Note that cell B13 contains an absolute address ($E$11) in the formula +B11/$E$11.

3. At the prompt `Enter range to copy TO:`, highlight the range of cells where you want the formula with the absolute address to be copied. Then press `⏎Enter`.

6

In this example, specify the TO range by highlighting C13..E13 and pressing ⏎Enter.

```
A:E13: [W13]                                            POINT
Enter range to copy TO: A:C13..A:E13
```

A	A	B	C	D	E
1	==========	==========	==========	==========	==========
2	INCOME REPORT	Jan	Feb	Mar	1st Quarter
3	==========	==========	==========	==========	==========
4	Sales				
5	Northeast	$30,336	$33,370	$36,707	$100,413
6	Southeast	20,572	22,629	25,892	$69,093
7	Central	131,685	144,854	159,339	$435,877
8	Northwest	94,473	103,920	114,312	$312,706
9	Southwest	126,739	139,413	153,354	$419,506
10					
11	Total Sales	$403,805	$444,186	$489,604	$1,337,595
12					
13	Percent of Sales	30.19%			
14					
15					

The range of formulas in row 13 is displayed in text format to show how each copied formula is adjusted to its new location.

```
A:B13: (T) [W13] +B11/$E$11                             READY
```

A	A	B	C	D	E
1	==========	==========	==========	==========	==========
2	INCOME REPORT	Jan	Feb	Mar	1st Quarter
3	==========	==========	==========	==========	==========
4	Sales				
5	Northeast	$30,336	$33,370	$36,707	$100,413
6	Southeast	20,572	22,629	25,892	$69,093
7	Central	131,685	144,854	159,339	$435,877
8	Northwest	94,473	103,920	114,312	$312,706
9	Southwest	126,739	139,413	153,354	$419,506
10					
11	Total Sales	$403,805	$444,186	$489,604	$1,337,595
12					
13	Percent of Sales	+B11/$E$11	+C11/$E$11	+D11/$E$11	+E11/$E$11
14					
15					

Note that the first address of each formula varies, but the second address remains absolute as $E$11 in all four formulas.

Mixing Relative and Absolute Addressing

In some cases, a formula has an important address that cannot be changed as the formula is copied. The last section discussed absolute addresses, which do not change at all when the address is copied. You also can create a mixed address, which can sometimes change, depending on the direction of the copy operation. Mixed addressing refers to a combination of relative and absolute addressing. Because a cell address has a column and a row, you can make either portion absolute, while leaving the other part relative.

If you plan to copy cells with absolute addresses, you must prepare the cells to be copied by preceding them with dollar signs ($) in both their column and row designations. The dollar signs tell 1-2-3 that the cells have been changed to absolute addresses.

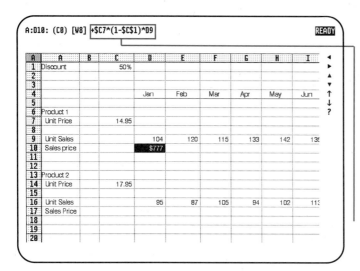

If you want to copy the formula from cell D10 to cell D17, the formula in D10 must contain one mixed address, one absolute address, and one relative address.

6

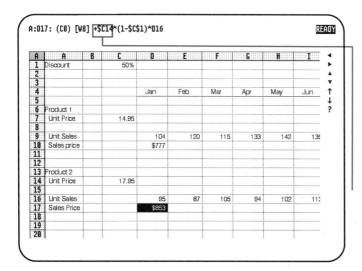

When the formula in D10 is copied to D17, a mixed address ($C14) is used at the beginning of the formula.

Each mixed address refers to the respective unit price of each product. In this example, column C is absolute and row 17 is relative. Also contained in the formula is an absolute address ($C$1) which refers to the discount percentage, and a relative address (D16), which refers to the monthly unit sales for each product.

Using the Abs (F4) Key To Change a Cell Address

There are two ways to enter dollar signs for absolute or mixed addresses in a formula. You can type the dollar signs as you create the formula, or you can later modify the formula by using the Abs (F4) key to have 1-2-3 enter the dollar signs for you. Use the Abs (F4) key in POINT or EDIT mode to make a cell address absolute, mixed, or relative. (Remember that in READY mode of Wysiwyg, you can use the F4 key to prespecify a range.) The Abs (F4) key is an eight-way toggle. Simply press the F4 key repeatedly (while in POINT or EDIT mode) until you get the kind of cell reference you want.

To change a cell address with the Abs (F4) key, follow these steps:

1. Highlight the cell containing the formula you want to change; then press F2 (Edit).

In this example, highlight cell B13 and press F2 (Edit).

A:B13: (P2) [W13] +B11/E11					EDIT
+B11/E11_					

A	A	B	C	D	E
1					
2	INCOME REPORT	Jan	Feb	Mar	1st Quarter
3					
4	Sales				
5	Northeast	$30,336	$33,370	$36,707	$100,413
6	Southeast	20,572	22,629	25,892	$69,093
7	Central	131,685	144,854	159,339	$435,877
8	Northwest	94,473	103,920	114,312	$312,706
9	Southwest	126,739	139,413	153,354	$419,506
10					
11	Total Sales	$403,805	$444,186	$489,604	$1,337,595
12					
13	Percent of Sales	30.19%			
14					
15					

2. With the cursor located beneath a cell address in the control panel, press F4 (Abs) five times to change the address to absolute.

   Note: The first four times you press F4 are for modifying the addressing of worksheet letters in multiple worksheet files (not used in this example).

212

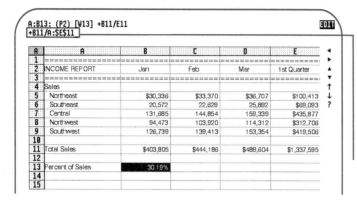

In this example, move the cursor under the second cell address, and then press [F4] (Abs) five times to change A:E11 to A:$E$11.

3. Press [F4] a sixth time and the address remains mixed—with the column relative and the row absolute.

6

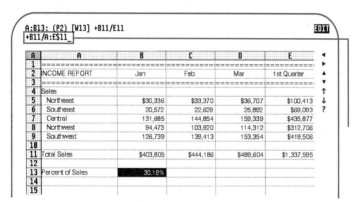

In this example, $E$11 changes to E$11.

4. Press [F4] a seventh time and the address remains mixed—with the column absolute and the row relative.

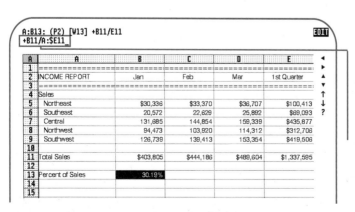

In this example, E$11 changes to $E11.

213

5. Press F4 an eighth time and the address changes from mixed back to relative (the default).

In this example, $E11 changes to E11.

```
A:B13: (P2) [W13] +B11/E11
+B11/A:E11_
```

A	A	B	C	D	E
1	=================	=========	=========	=========	=========
2	INCOME REPORT	Jan	Feb	Mar	1st Quarter
3	=================	=========	=========	=========	=========
4	Sales				
5	Northeast	$30,336	$33,370	$36,707	$100,413
6	Southeast	20,572	22,629	25,892	$69,093
7	Central	131,685	144,854	159,339	$435,877
8	Northwest	94,473	103,920	114,312	$312,706
9	Southwest	126,739	139,413	153,354	$419,506
10					
11	Total Sales	$403,805	$444,186	$489,604	$1,337,595
12					
13	Percent of Sales	30.19%			
14					
15					

Transposing Rows and Columns

For copy operations that are difficult to perform with 1-2-3's normal copy commands, 1-2-3 has two specialized copy commands: /**R**ange **T**rans and /**R**ange **V**alue. The /**R**ange **T**rans command copies columns into rows and rows into columns in single worksheet operations. When you use /**R**ange **T**rans to copy data to a multiple-worksheet range, 1-2-3 can perform three different types of transpositions—rows to columns, columns to worksheets, and worksheets to rows.

The /**R**ange **V**alue command, explained in the next section, copies the values (but not the formulas) from one range to another. In a single worksheet copy, the /**R**ange **T**rans command copies only values, but also copies each row of the FROM range into the corresponding column of the TO range, or each column of the FROM range into the corresponding row of the TO range. The result is a transposed copy of the FROM range. Suppose that you want to transpose the data in three rows to columnar format (in a single worksheet). To transpose the data, follow these steps:

1. Select /**R**ange **T**rans.

2. At the prompt `Enter FROM range for transpose:`, highlight the range of cells you want to transpose; then press `↵Enter`.

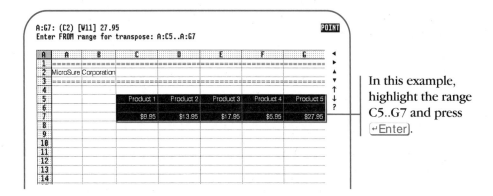

In this example, highlight the range C5..G7 and press ⏎Enter.

3. At the prompt `Enter TO range for transpose:`, highlight the columns to which you want the data copied.

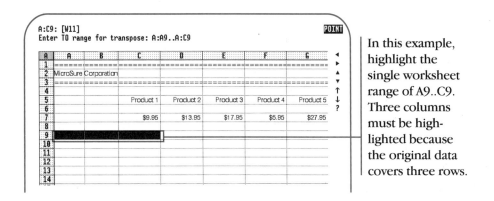

In this example, highlight the single worksheet range of A9..C9. Three columns must be highlighted because the original data covers three rows.

Note: If you specify a multiple-worksheet range, you must select the desired transposition option from the menu that results: **R**ows/Columns, **C**olumns/Worksheets, or **W**orksheets/Rows.

When copying formulas, the /**R**ange **T**rans command behaves just like the /**C**opy command. When a range is transposed, cell references in the transposed range are adjusted, just as references are adjusted in a normal /**C**opy command. This adjustment of cell references can lead to serious trouble when you use the /**R**ange **T**rans command to transpose a range containing formulas with relative and mixed call references. The transposed formulas will be incorrect; the values, however, will remain in the same order. Because the cell references are not transposed, the relative and mixed cell references in the transposed range will refer to incorrect locations after the transposition.

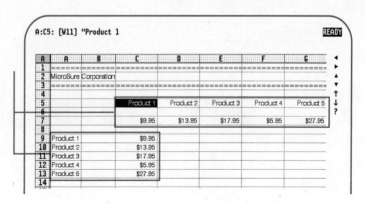

The data appears in its original location as well as transposed in the new location.

You can avoid the problem of incorrect cell references in transposed ranges by converting the formulas in the FROM range to values before transposing. Using the /**R**ange **V**alue command, discussed in the following section, is a convenient way to convert a range of formulas to values.

Converting Formulas to Values

The /**R**ange **V**alue command lets you copy only the values of the cells in one range to another range. This command is useful whenever you want to preserve the current formula values of a range of cells instead of having only the changed values after the worksheet has been updated. An important function of the /**R**ange **V**alue command is its capability for conversion of formulas to values. You don't have to worry, therefore, about formulas that depend on cell references (when using /**R**ange **T**rans, for example).

To convert formulas to values when copying, follow these steps:

1. Select /**R**ange **V**alue.
2. At the prompt `Enter range to copy FROM:`, highlight the range of formulas to be copied; then press ⏎Enter.
3. At the prompt `Enter range to copy TO:`, highlight the first cell in the range where you want the values copied; then press ⏎Enter.

216

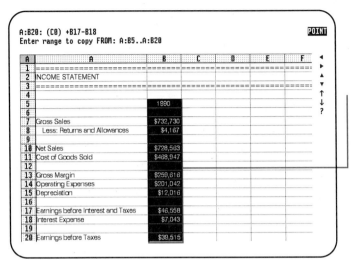

In this example, highlight the FROM range as B5..B20, and press ⏎Enter.

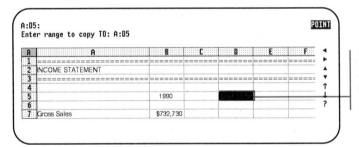

In this example, highlight cell D5 as the TO range, and press ⏎Enter.

Notice that the formula in cell B20 has become a value in cell D20.

6

Tips for Copying

Remember the following tips whenever you intend to copy data within the worksheet:

- When you copy a cell, 1-2-3 automatically copies the format of the cell with it. This automatic format-copying feature saves you from having to set the format for an entire range of cells before (or after) copying to them.

- Sometimes the FROM and TO ranges overlap when you copy. The general rule is to avoid overlapping the end points of the FROM and TO ranges to prevent problems with the copy operation. If you do overlap them, you may get mixed results. You can, however, overlap ranges without error when the FROM and TO ranges have the same upper left boundary (such as when using /**R**ange **V**alue to copy formulas onto themselves).

- Note particularly the finality of the /**C**opy command when you disable the Undo feature. If you copy over the contents of a cell, you have no way to retrieve the contents. Make sure that you have properly designated your ranges before you complete the command. You can retrieve the worksheet again if it has already been saved, but all changes made since the last save are lost.

Searching for and Replacing Cell Contents

Looking for a word or string of characters in a large worksheet can be time-consuming and tedious. 1-2-3 offers a feature that allows you to search for text easily. If necessary, you can replace a specified string of characters with other text everywhere the string occurs. Frequent users of word-processing software are familiar with this capability. It can be particularly useful for changing all occurrences of a particular misspelling to the correct spelling.

Whether you want to find the first occurrence of a string or you want to replace it with another string, you start with the same command, /**R**ange **S**earch. 1-2-3 performs the search column-by-column in the defined search range. The following section shows you how to search for a given string, and the subsequent section shows you how to search for a string and replace it with another string.

218

Searching for the Occurrence of a String

To search a specified range for a particular string in labels and/or formulas, follow these steps:

1. Select /**R**ange **S**earch.

2. Highlight the range you want to search; then press ⏎Enter.

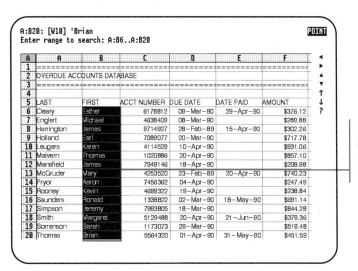

In this example, highlight the range B6..B20 and press ⏎Enter.

3. Define the string you want to search for and then press ⏎Enter. Note that the search string is not case sensitive; you can enter the string in upper- or lowercase characters.

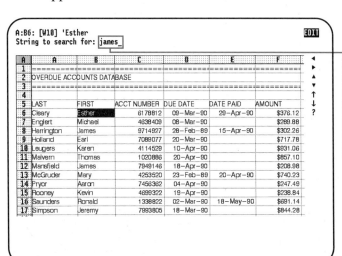

In this example, to search for all occurrences of James in the highlighted range, type **james**; then press ⏎Enter.

219

4. Indicate whether to search for formulas, labels, or both formulas and labels by selecting **Formulas**, **Labels**, or **Both**.

To check only cells that contain labels, select **Labels**.

```
A:B6: [W10] 'Esther                                          MENU
Formulas Labels Both
Search for string in labels only
```

	A	B	C	D	E	F
1	================	===	=======	=======	=======	=======
2	OVERDUE ACCOUNTS DATABASE					
3	================	===	=======	=======	=======	=======
4						
5	LAST	FIRST	ACCT NUMBER	DUE DATE	DATE PAID	AMOUNT
6	Cleary	Esther	6178812	09−Mar−90	29−Apr−90	$376.12
7	Englert	Michael	4638409	08−Mar−90		$289.88
8	Harrington	James	9714927	28−Feb−89	15−Apr−90	$302.26
9	Holland	Earl	7089077	20−Mar−90		$717.78
10	Leugers	Karen	4114529	10−Apr−90		$931.06
11	Malvern	Thomas	1020886	20−Apr−90		$857.10
12	Mansfield	James	7949146	18−Apr−90		$208.98
13	McGruder	Mary	4253520	23−Feb−89	20−Apr−90	$740.23
14	Pryor	Aaron	7456362	04−Apr−90		$247.49
15	Rooney	Kevin	4699322	19−Apr−90		$238.84
16	Saunders	Ronald	1338822	02−Mar−90	18−May−90	$691.14
17	Simpson	Jeremy	7993805	18−Mar−90		$844.28
18	Smith	Margaret	5129488	20−Apr−90	21−Jun−90	$379.36
19	Sorrenson	Sarah	1173073	29−Mar−90		$519.48
20	Thomas	Brian	5564320	01−Apr−90	31−May−90	$451.59

5. Select **Find** to find a particular string in the range of labels that are selected.

   1-2-3 highlights the first appearance of the string.

In this example, the first occurrence of James in the search range is highlighted by the cell pointer.

```
A:B8: [W10] James                                           MENU
Next Quit
Find next matching string without replacing current string
```

	A	B	C	D	E	F
1	================	===	=======	=======	=======	=======
2	OVERDUE ACCOUNTS DATABASE					
3	================	===	=======	=======	=======	=======
4						
5	LAST	FIRST	ACCT NUMBER	DUE DATE	DATE PAID	AMOUNT
6	Cleary	Esther	6178812	09−Mar−90	29−Apr−90	$376.12
7	Englert	Michael	4638409	08−Mar−90		$289.88
8	Harrington	James	9714927	28−Feb−89	15−Apr−90	$302.26
9	Holland	Earl	7089077	20−Mar−90		$717.78
10	Leugers	Karen	4114529	10−Apr−90		$931.06
11	Malvern	Thomas	1020886	20−Apr−90		$857.10
12	Mansfield	James	7949146	18−Apr−90		$208.98
13	McGruder	Mary	4253520	23−Feb−89	20−Apr−90	$740.23
14	Pryor	Aaron	7456362	04−Apr−90		$247.49
15	Rooney	Kevin	4699322	19−Apr−90		$238.84
16	Saunders	Ronald	1338822	02−Mar−90	18−May−90	$691.14
17	Simpson	Jeremy	7993805	18−Mar−90		$844.28
18	Smith	Margaret	5129488	20−Apr−90	21−Jun−90	$379.36
19	Sorrenson	Sarah	1173073	29−Mar−90		$519.48
20	Thomas	Brian	5564320	01−Apr−90	31−May−90	$451.59

6. To see the next appearance of the string, select **Next**.

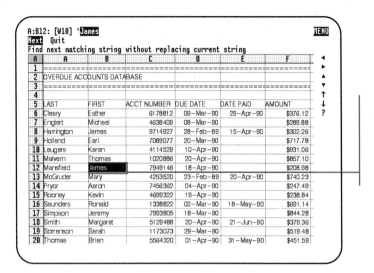

In this example, the next appearance of James in column B is highlighted.

7. At each of the successive prompts, select **Next** until 1-2-3 finds the last occurrence of your string in the range.

   Note: If you want to end the search before all occurrences of the string have been found, select **Quit**.

When 1-2-3 cannot locate another string, an error message is displayed.

8. Press ⏎Enter or Esc to return to READY mode.

Replacing One String with Another String

To replace a string in the worksheet with another specified string, you follow a procedure similar to that which finds a string within a range. You must, however, supply the string of characters that will replace the existing string.

To search a range for a particular string and replace that string with another string, follow these steps:

1. Select /**R**ange Search.
2. Highlight the range you want to search; then press ↵Enter.

In this example, highlight the range to search as C3..C20 and press ↵Enter.

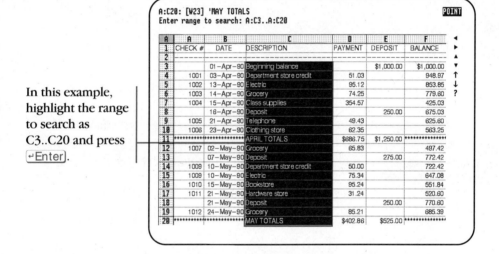

3. Define the string you want to search for; then press ↵Enter. Note that the search string is not case sensitive.

222

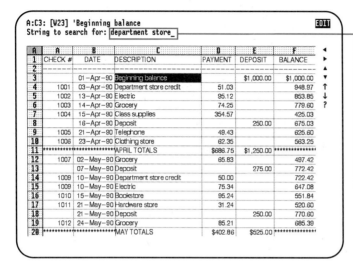

```
A:C3: [W23] 'Beginning balance                              EDIT
String to search for: department store_
```

	A	B	C	D	E	F
1	CHECK #	DATE	DESCRIPTION	PAYMENT	DEPOSIT	BALANCE
2						
3		01–Apr–90	Beginning balance		$1,000.00	$1,000.00
4	1001	03–Apr–90	Department store credit	51.03		948.97
5	1002	13–Apr–90	Electric	95.12		853.85
6	1003	14–Apr–90	Grocery	74.25		779.60
7	1004	15–Apr–90	Class supplies	354.57		425.03
8		16–Apr–90	Deposit		250.00	675.03
9	1005	21–Apr–90	Telephone	49.43		625.60
10	1006	23–Apr–90	Clothing store	62.35		563.25
11	***********************APRIL TOTALS			$686.75	$1,250.00	***************
12	1007	02–May–90	Grocery	65.83		497.42
13		07–May–90	Deposit		275.00	772.42
14	1009	10–May–90	Department store credit	50.00		722.42
15	1009	10–May–90	Electric	75.34		647.08
16	1010	15–May–90	Bookstore	95.24		551.84
17	1011	21–May–90	Hardware store	31.24		520.60
18		21–May–90	Deposit		250.00	770.60
19	1012	24–May–90	Grocery	85.21		685.39
20	***********************MAY TOTALS			$402.86	$525.00	***************

To search for Department store in the highlighted range, type **department store**; then press ⏎Enter

6

4. Indicate whether to search for formulas, labels, or both formulas and labels by selecting **F**ormulas, **L**abels, or **B**oth.

   If you need to correct a large range of formulas by changing a recurring cell reference, select **F**ormulas.

   For this example, select **L**abels.

5. Select **R**eplace to replace occurrences of the specified string with another string.

6. Define the string that will be used to replace occurrences of the specified search string; then press ⏎Enter. Note that this string is case sensitive; your use of uppercase and lowercase characters in your definition will be copied to the replacement string.

223

In this example, to replace the occurrences of `Department store` with `JCPenney`, type **JCPenney** and press ⏎Enter.

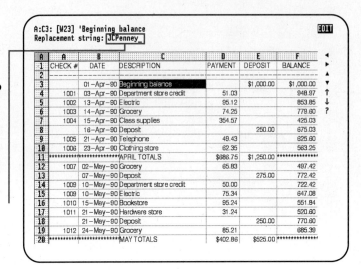

1-2-3 highlights the first occurrence of the search string and provides a menu with four options: **All**, **R**eplace, **N**ext, and **Q**uit.

7. Select one of the four options.

   All replaces every matching string with the new string.

   Replace completes the first instance of search and replace, and positions the cell pointer on the second occurrence—again offering you the same four menu options.

   Next lets you highlight the next occurrence of the search string without making the replacement—allowing you to use **R**eplace selectively.

   Quit ends the search and returns 1-2-3 to READY mode.

```
A:C4: [W23] 'Department store credit                              MENU
Replace  All  Next  Quit
Replace all remaining matching strings in range with replacement string
```

A	A	B	C	D	E	F
1	CHECK #	DATE	DESCRIPTION	PAYMENT	DEPOSIT	BALANCE
2						
3		01-Apr-90	Beginning balance		$1,000.00	$1,000.00
4	1001	03-Apr-90	Department store credit	51.03		948.97
5	1002	13-Apr-90	Electric	95.12		853.85
6	1003	14-Apr-90	Grocery	74.25		779.60
7	1004	15-Apr-90	Class supplies	354.57		425.03
8		16-Apr-90	Deposit		250.00	675.03
9	1005	21-Apr-90	Telephone	49.43		625.60
10	1006	23-Apr-90	Clothing store	62.35		563.25
11	**********	************	APRIL TOTALS	$686.75	$1,250.00	*************
12	1007	02-May-90	Grocery	65.83		497.42
13		07-May-90	Deposit		275.00	772.42
14	1009	10-May-90	Department store credit	50.00		722.42
15	1009	10-May-90	Electric	75.34		647.08
16	1010	15-May-90	Bookstore	95.24		551.84
17	1011	21-May-90	Hardware store	31.24		520.60
18		21-May-90	Deposit		250.00	770.60
19	1012	24-May-90	Grocery	85.21		685.39
20	**********	************	MAY TOTALS	$402.86	$525.00	*************

For this example, select **All**.

6

```
A:C14: [W23] 'JCPenney credit                                    READY
```

A	A	B	C	D	E	F
1	CHECK #	DATE	DESCRIPTION	PAYMENT	DEPOSIT	BALANCE
2						
3		01-Apr-90	Beginning balance		$1,000.00	$1,000.00
4	1001	03-Apr-90	JCPenney credit	51.03		948.97
5	1002	13-Apr-90	Electric	95.12		853.85
6	1003	14-Apr-90	Grocery	74.25		779.60
7	1004	15-Apr-90	Class supplies	354.57		425.03
8		16-Apr-90	Deposit		250.00	675.03
9	1005	21-Apr-90	Telephone	49.43		625.60
10	1006	23-Apr-90	Clothing store	62.35		563.25
11	**********	************	APRIL TOTALS	$686.75	$1,250.00	*************
12	1007	02-May-90	Grocery	65.83		497.42
13		07-May-90	Deposit		275.00	772.42
14	1009	10-May-90	JCPenney credit	50.00		722.42
15	1009	10-May-90	Electric	75.34		647.08
16	1010	15-May-90	Bookstore	95.24		551.84
17	1011	21-May-90	Hardware store	31.24		520.60
18		21-May-90	Deposit		250.00	770.60
19	1012	24-May-90	Grocery	85.21		685.39
20	**********	************	MAY TOTALS	$402.86	$525.00	*************

Note how all occurrences of the string `Department store` are replaced with the string `JCPenney`.

When 1-2-3 cannot locate another appearance of the string after you select **R**eplace or **N**ext, an error message is displayed. Press Enter or Esc to return to READY mode.

Tips for Using the Search-and-Replace Feature

Remember the following tips when using 1-2-3's search-and-replace feature:

- If you confine your search to a given range, you can accelerate the search, and you're less likely to accidentally replace strings you want to be left undisturbed.
- The search string can consist of more than a single word. In fact, the string can be as long as 512 characters and can contain many words.
- The string you are searching for is not case-sensitive. 1-2-3 will find any string that matches the characters you type, regardless of whether you type the string in uppercase, lowercase, or a combination of upper- and lowercase.
- Unlike the search string, the replacement string is case sensitive. The substitution will consist of precisely what you type, in keeping with your use of uppercase and lowercase.
- The /**R**ange **S**earch command will not search hidden columns. The command can be used, however, to search individual cells that have been formatted with the /**R**ange **F**ormat **H**idden command.

Summary

In this chapter, you learned that when building a worksheet, you can use the /**M**ove command to relocate cells and cell ranges, and the /**C**opy command to duplicate the contents of cells and cell ranges throughout a worksheet, or between multiple worksheets and files. By specifying relative, absolute, or mixed addressing, you can control cell references for formulas you use in your worksheets. You also learned that 1-2-3 provides a search-and-replace feature that allows you to find and/or replace specified strings of data in your worksheets.

Specifically, you learned the following key information about 1-2-3:

- The /**M**ove command enables you to move the contents of one or more cells to any location in a worksheet, or between multiple worksheets. The data that is moved appears only in the new location.
- The /**C**opy command enables you to copy information to other parts of a worksheet or between multiple worksheets and files. Once copied, the data appears in both locations.

■ The End key, in combination with the arrow keys, can be used with the /**M**ove and /**C**opy commands to quickly move or copy large ranges of data.

■ Two types of cell addresses that are helpful when copying formulas are relative and absolute cell addresses. Combinations of relative and absolute cell addresses are called mixed cell addresses. Dollar signs are used to indicate absolute and mixed cell addresses.

■ When creating or modifying relative, absolute, and mixed cell addresses, the Abs (F4) key can be used to toggle between the different types of cell references.

■ The /**R**ange **T**rans command copies data in a single worksheet from columns into rows, and rows into columns. In multiple-worksheet applications, you can transpose data from rows to columns, columns to worksheets, or worksheets to rows.

■ The /**R**ange **V**alue command copies a range of formulas to their equivalent values in another (or the same) range.

■ The /**R**ange **S**earch command finds a specified string of data in a range. This string can also be replaced with a new string.

The next chapter covers some of 1-2-3's built-in functions. Functions are used in formulas to perform complex calculations. A few of the categories of functions discussed include mathematical, financial and accounting, and string functions.

6

Using Functions

7

In addition to creating formulas, you can use a variety of ready-made formulas provided by 1-2-3. These built-in formulas—called functions—enable you to take advantage of 1-2-3's analytical capability. Functions are helpful when used with business, engineering, scientific, and statistical applications. You can use many of these powerful functions even in the simplest of worksheets. You can use functions by themselves, in your own formulas, or in macros and advanced macro-command programs to calculate results and solve problems.

1-2-3 provides the following types of functions:

- Mathematical and trigonometric
- Date and time
- Financial
- Statistical
- Database
- Logical
- String
- Special

Key Terms in This Chapter

Functions	1-2-3's built-in formulas that perform many different types of calculations.
Arguments	Inputs needed by most functions to perform their calculations.
Syntax	The format of a specific function.

This chapter first describes the basic steps for using 1-2-3 functions and then covers each of these groups in more detail. Several tables briefly describe all 1-2-3 functions. However, separate sections expand on the most commonly used functions. Refer to Que's *Using 1-2-3 Release 3.1*, 2nd Edition, for comprehensive coverage of each of 1-2-3's functions.

Using the Mouse

To use a mouse with 1-2-3 Release 3.1, you need a mouse, mouse software, and a graphics monitor and graphics card that support a mouse. Also, Wysiwyg must be loaded into memory. You can use a mouse to select commands and files, specify ranges, and move the cell pointer within a worksheet or between multiple worksheets and files. In the examples throughout this chapter, notice that the 1-2-3 commands always begin with a slash (/), and the Wysiwyg commands always begin with a colon (:). Refer to the following sections of the specified chapters for further information on using the mouse:

- Chapter 2—"Understanding Mouse Terminology"
- Chapter 3—"Mouse Control of the Cell Pointer"
        "Using the Mouse To Select Menu Commands"
- Chapter 4—"Using the Mouse To Specify Ranges"

Entering a 1-2-3 Function

If you have not yet reviewed Chapter 3, you should study the section of that chapter which introduces functions before you continue with this chapter. There you learn about the eight groups of functions that this chapter covers. Chapter 3 also describes the steps used to enter a specific function.

This chapter does not include numbered steps for entering each function, because you enter all functions with the same procedure. To enter a 1-2-3 function in a worksheet, follow this general four-step process:

1. Press @, the character that identifies a function.
2. Type the function name.
3. Type within parentheses any inputs or arguments that the function needs.
4. Press ⏎Enter.

An example of a function is @AVG. If you type the function **@AVG(1,2,3)**, 1-2-3 returns the calculated result 2, the average of the three arguments—the numbers 1, 2, and 3.

Some functions do not require arguments. For example, the mathematical function @PI returns the value of π; and the mathematical function @RAND produces a random number between 0 and 1.

Using Mathematical and Trigonometric Functions

1-2-3's mathematical and trigonometric functions are useful in engineering and scientific applications. These functions are also convenient tools and can be used to perform a variety of standard arithmetic operations, such as rounding values or calculating square roots.

Table 7.1 lists the 17 mathematical and trigonometric functions, their arguments, and the operations they perform. The sections that follow cover the @INT and @ROUND mathematical functions in detail.

Table 7.1
Mathematical and Trigonometric Functions

Function	Description
@ABS(*number or cell_reference*)	Computes the absolute value of the argument.
@ACOS(*angle*)	Calculates the arccosine, given an angle in radians.
@ASIN(*angle*)	Calculates the arcsine, given an angle in radians.

Table 7.1 (continued)

Function	Description
@ATAN(*angle*)	Calculates the arctangent, given an angle in radians.
@ATAN2(*number1, number2*)	Calculates the four-quadrant arctangent.
@COS(*angle*)	Calculates the cosine, given an angle in radians.
@EXP(*number or cell_reference*)	Computes the number e raised to the power of the argument.
@INT(*number or cell_reference*)	Returns the integer portion of a number.
@LN(*number or cell_reference*)	Calculates the natural logarithm of a number.
@LOG(*number or cell_reference*)	Calculates the common, or base 10, logarithm of a number.
@MOD(*number,divisor*)	Computes the remainder of a division operation.
@PI	Returns the value of π.
@RAND	Generates a random number between 0 and 1.
@ROUND(*number or cell_reference, precision*)	Rounds a number to a specified precision.
@SIN(*angle*)	Calculates the sine, given an angle in radians.
@SQRT(*number or cell_reference*)	Computes the positive square root of a number.
@TAN(*angle*)	Calculates the tangent, given an angle in radians.

Computing Integers with @INT

The @INT function converts a decimal number into an integer, or whole number. @INT creates an integer by truncating, or removing, the decimal portion of a number (without rounding). @INT uses the following syntax:

@INT(*number or cell_reference*)

@INT has one argument, which can be either a numeric value or a cell reference to a numeric value. The result of applying @INT to the values 3.1, 4.5, and 5.9 yields integer values of 3, 4, and 5, respectively.

@INT is useful for computations in which the decimal portion of a number is irrelevant or insignificant. Suppose, for example, that you have $1,000 to invest in XYZ company and that shares of XYZ sell for $17 each. You divide 1,000 by 17 to compute the total number of shares that you can buy. Because you cannot buy a fractional share, you can use @INT to truncate the decimal portion.

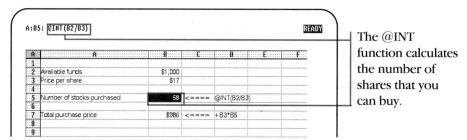

The @INT function calculates the number of shares that you can buy.

7

Rounding Numbers with @ROUND

The @ROUND function rounds values to the precision you specify. The function uses two arguments: the value you want to round, and the precision you want to use in the rounding. @ROUND uses the following syntax:

@ROUND(*number or cell_reference,precision*)

The first argument can be a numeric value or a cell reference to a numeric value. The *precision* argument determines the number of decimal places and can be an integer between –100 and +100. You use positive precision values to specify positions to the right of the decimal place. Negative values specify positions to the left of the decimal place. A precision value of 0 rounds decimal values to the nearest integer.

Note: The @ROUND function and the /Range Format command perform differently. @ROUND actually changes the contents of a cell; /Range Format alters only how 1-2-3 displays the cell's contents.

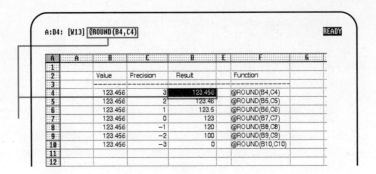

The @ROUND function rounds values to a specified precision.

Using Date and Time Functions

The 13 date and time functions enable you to convert dates, such as November 26, 1991, and times, such as 6:00 p.m., to serial numbers. You can then use the serial numbers to perform date and time arithmetic. These functions are valuable tools when dates and times affect calculations and logic in your worksheets.

1-2-3's internal calendar begins with the serial number 1, which represents January 1, 1900. The calendar ends with 73050, which represents December 31, 2099. 1-2-3 represents a single day with an increment of 1; therefore, 1-2-3 represents January 2, 1900, as 2. To display that serial number as a text date, format the cell with the /Range Format Date command.

Table 7.2 summarizes the date and time functions available. The sections that follow review examples of the @DATE, @DATEVALUE, and @NOW functions.

Table 7.2
Date and Time Functions

Function	Description
@DATE(*year,month,day*)	Calculates the serial number of the specified date.
@DATEVALUE(*date_string*)	Converts a date expressed as a string into a serial number.
@DAY(*date_number*)	Extracts the day number from a serial number.
@D360(*date1,date2*)	Calculates the number of days between two serial dates, based on a 360-day year.

234

Table 7.2 (continued)

Function	Description
@HOUR(*time_number*)	Extracts the hour number from a serial number.
@MINUTE(*time_number*)	Extracts the minute number from a serial number.
@MONTH(*date_number*)	Extracts the month number from a serial number.
@NOW	Calculates the serial date and time from the current system date and time.
@SECOND(*time_number*)	Extracts the seconds from a serial number.
@TIME(*hour,minutes,seconds*)	Calculates the serial number of the specified time.
@TIMEVALUE(*time_string*)	Converts a time expressed as a string into a serial number.
@TODAY	Calculates the serial number for the current system date.
@YEAR(*date_number*)	Extracts the year number from a serial number.

7

Converting Date Values to Serial Numbers with @DATE

To use dates in arithmetic operations, first convert the dates to serial numbers. You can then use those serial numbers in arithmetic operations and sorting. The most frequently used date function is @DATE, which converts any date into a serial number. You use the resulting number in calculations or display it as a date in 1-2-3. @DATE uses the following syntax:

@DATE(*year,month,day*)

You use numbers to identify a year, month, and day. For example, you enter the date November 26, 1989, into the @DATE function as @DATE(89,11,26). The serial number that results is 32838.

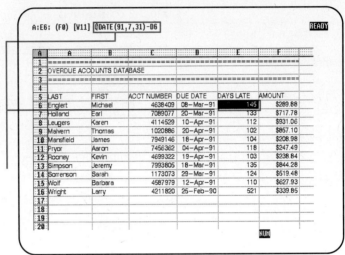

The @DATE function calculates the number of days a bill is overdue as of July 31, 1991.

Note: The numbers you enter to represent the year, month, and day must create a valid date. If the date is not valid, 1-2-3 returns ERR. For example, 1-2-3 allows you to specify February 29 only during leap years. You never can specify February 30.

Converting Date Strings to Serial Numbers with @DATEVALUE

@DATEVALUE computes the serial number for a date text string typed into a referenced cell. The text string must use one of the date formats recognized by 1-2-3. @DATEVALUE requires the following syntax:

@DATEVALUE(*date_string*)

If 1-2-3 cannot recognize the format used for the argument, the function results in ERR. After you enter the function, use the /**R**ange **F**ormat **D**ate command to display the serial date number as a text date.

Finding the Current Date and Time with @NOW

The @NOW function displays as a serial number both the current system date and the current system time. The numbers to the left of the decimal point specify the date. The numbers to the right of the decimal point define the time. This function, which requires no arguments, provides a convenient tool for adding dates to worksheets and reports.

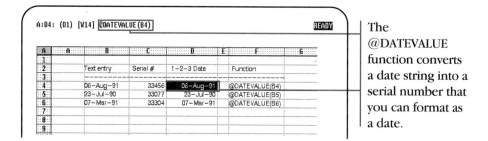

The @DATEVALUE function converts a date string into a serial number that you can format as a date.

After you enter the @NOW function, use the /**R**ange **F**ormat **D**ate command to display the serial date number as a text date or time.

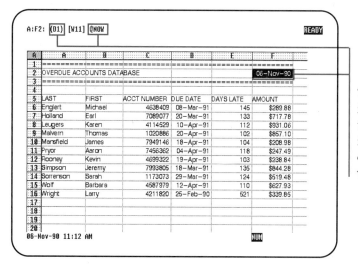

The @NOW function, formatted as a date, inserts the current date in a worksheet.

Using Financial Functions

The 12 financial functions enable you to perform a variety of business-related calculations. These calculations include discounting cash flows, computing loan amortization, calculating depreciation, and analyzing the return on investments. This set of functions helps you perform investment analysis and accounting, or budgeting for depreciable assets.

Table 7.3 summarizes the financial functions available in 1-2-3. The sections that follow describe the @PMT, @PV, and @FV functions in greater detail.

Table 7.3
Financial Functions

Function	Description
@CTERM (*interest, future_value, present_value*)	Calculates the number of periods required for a present value amount to grow to a future value amount given a periodic interest rate.
@DDB(*cost, salvage, life, period*)	Calculates depreciation using the double-declining-balance method.
@FV(*payments, interest, term*)	Calculates the future value of a series of equal payments compounded at the periodic interest rate.
@IRR(*estimate, range*)	Calculates the internal rate of return on an investment.
@NPV(*interest, range*)	Calculates the present value of a series of future cash flows at equal intervals when payments are discounted by the interest rate.
@PMT(*principal, interest, term*)	Calculates the loan payment amount.
@PV(*payments, interest, term*)	Calculates the present value of a series of future cash flows of equal payments discounted by the periodic interest rate.
@RATE(*future_value, present_value, term*)	Calculates the periodic rate required to increase the present value amount to the future value amount in a specified length of time.
@SLN(*cost, salvage, life*)	Calculates straight-line depreciation for one period.
@SYD(*cost, salvage, life, period*)	Calculates sum-of-the-years'-digits depreciation for a specified period.

7

Table 7.3 (continued)	
Function	*Description*
@TERM(*payments,interest, future_value*)	Calculates the number of payment periods necessary to accumulate the future value when payments compound at the periodic interest rate.
@VDB*(cost,salvage,life,start_period, end_period,depreciation,switch)*	Calculates the depreciation, using the variable-rate declining-balance method.

Calculating Loan Payment Amounts with @PMT

You use the @PMT function to calculate the periodic payments necessary to pay the principal on a loan with a given interest rate and time. Therefore, to use @PMT, you need to know the total loan amount (principal), periodic interest rate, and term, as shown in the following syntax:

@PMT(*principal,interest,term*)

Express the interest rate and the term in the same units of time. For example, if you make monthly payments, you should use the annual interest rate divided by 12. The term should be the number of months you will be making payments. @PMT operates on the assumption that payments are made at the end of each period.

To calculate the monthly car payment on a $12,000 car loan, you can use the @PMT function. The loan is repaid over 48 months, and the interest rate is 1%—12% divided by 12 periods per year.

Calculating Present and Future Values with @PV and @FV

@PV calculates the present value of a series of future cash flows of equal payments discounted by the periodic interest rate. Express the interest rate and the term in the same units of time. The @PV function uses the following syntax:

@PV(*payments,interest,term*)

One example of using @PV is to determine whether to receive contest winnings immediately in one lump sum or as a specified amount annually.

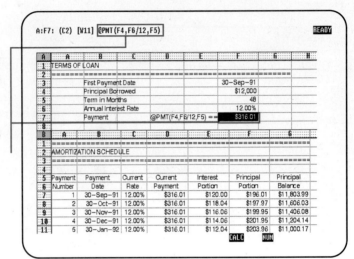

A:F7: (C2) [W11] @PMT(F4,F6/12,F5)   READY

	A	B	C	D	E	F	G	H
1	TERMS OF LOAN							
2	====	====	====	====	====	====	====	
3		First Payment Date				30−Sep−91		
4		Principal Borrowed				$12,000		
5		Term in Months				48		
6		Annual Interest Rate				12.00%		
7		Payment	@PMT(F4,F6/12,F5) ==			$316.01		
8								

	A	B	C	D	E	F	G
1	====	====	====	====	====	====	====
2	AMORTIZATION SCHEDULE						
3	====	====	====	====	====	====	====
4							
5	Payment	Payment	Current	Current	Interest	Principal	Principal
6	Number	Date	Rate	Payment	Portion	Portion	Balance
7	1	30−Sep−91	12.00%	$316.01	$120.00	$196.01	$11,803.99
8	2	30−Oct−91	12.00%	$316.01	$118.04	$197.97	$11,606.03
9	3	30−Nov−91	12.00%	$316.01	$116.06	$199.95	$11,406.08
10	4	30−Dec−91	12.00%	$316.01	$114.06	$201.95	$11,204.14
11	5	30−Jan−92	12.00%	$316.01	$112.04	$203.96	$11,000.17

CALC   NUM

The @PMT function calculates loan payments.

The @FV function calculates what a current amount will grow to, based on a specified interest rate and the number of years. Again, express the interest rate and the term in the same units of time. @FV uses the following syntax:

@FV(*payments,interest,term*)

You can use @FV to calculate the future value of a savings account that makes equal automatic deposits on a monthly basis. Simply specify the amount of deduction per month (payments), the monthly interest rate, and the specified number of months (term).

Using Statistical Functions

A set of 10 statistical functions enables you to perform all the standard statistical calculations on data in your worksheet or in a 1-2-3 database. You can find minimum and maximum values, calculate averages, and compute standard deviations and variances.

The attribute of all statistical functions is a list which can consist of value(s), cell reference(s), range(s), and formula(s). If the list contains more than one item, separate the items with commas, as in this example:

@SUM(B5..B20,B30..B40,B55,10%*B80,1000)

Table 7.4 lists the functions, their arguments, and the statistical operations they perform. The sections that follow cover the @AVG, @COUNT, @MAX, and @MIN statistical functions. Chapter 3 illustrates the @SUM function, the most commonly used 1-2-3 function.

Table 7.4
Statistical Functions

Function	Description
@AVG(*list*)	Calculates the arithmetic mean of a list of values.
@COUNT(*list*)	Counts the number of cells that contain entries.
@MAX(*list*)	Returns the maximum value in a list of values.
@MIN(*list*)	Returns the minimum value in a list of values.
@STD(*list*)	Calculates the population standard deviation of a list of values.
@STDS(*list*)	Calculates the sample population standard deviation of a list of values.
@SUM(*list*)	Sums a list of values.
@SUMPRODUCT(*range1,range2*)	Multiplies *range1* by *range2* and sums the values.
@VAR(*list*)	Calculates the population variance of a list of values.
@VARS(*list*)	Calculates the sample population variance of a list of values.

7

Note: The statistical functions perform differently when you specify cells as ranges instead of individually. When you specify a range of cells, 1-2-3 ignores empty cells within the specified range. When you specify cells individually, however, 1-2-3 takes empty cells into consideration for the particular functions mentioned. Also, when you specify cells, keep in mind that 1-2-3 treats cells containing labels as zeros. This is the case when the cell is part of a range or when you specify the cell individually. For this reason, do not erase cells by pressing the space bar and then pressing ⏎Enter.

Computing the Arithmetic Mean with @AVG

To calculate the average of a set of values, add all the values and then divide the sum by the number of values. Essentially, the @AVG function produces the same result as if you divided @SUM(*list*) by @COUNT(*list*). The @AVG function is a helpful tool for calculating the commonly used arithmetic mean, or average. Use the following syntax for this function:

> @AVG(*list*)

The *list* argument can contain any combination of values, cell addresses, single and multiple ranges, and range names.

The @AVG function can calculate the mean price-per-share of an imaginary company. The function's argument includes the list of stock prices. 1-2-3 ignores any empty cells in the list when calculating the average.

The @AVG function calculates the average price-per-share of stock.

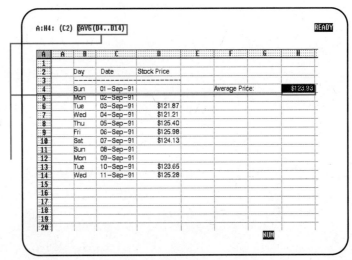

Counting Cell Entries with @COUNT

The @COUNT function totals the number of cells that contain entries of any kind, including labels, label-prefix characters, and the values ERR and NA. Use the following syntax for @COUNT:

> @COUNT(*list*)

The *list* argument can contain any combination of values, cell addresses, single and multiple ranges, and range names. For example, you can use @COUNT to show the number of share prices included in the @AVG calculation of the previous example.

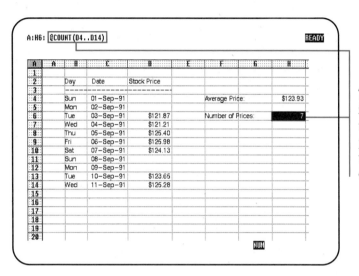

The @COUNT function calculates the number of prices per share used in the @AVG calculation.

Note: Be sure to include only ranges as the argument in the @COUNT function. If you specify an individual cell, 1-2-3 counts that cell as if it has an entry, even if the cell is empty.

Finding Maximum and Minimum Values with @MAX and @MIN

The @MAX function finds the largest value included in the *list* argument. The @MIN function finds the smallest value included in the *list* argument. These functions use the following syntax:

@MAX(*list*)

@MIN(*list*)

The @MAX and @MIN functions can help you find the highest and the lowest prices in the stock prices example. Although the example shows only seven values, the true power of these functions is clear when your list consists of several hundred items.

7

243

```
A:H8: (C2) @MAX(D4..D14)                                              READY
```

	A	B	C	D	E	F	G	H
1								
2		Day	Date	Stock Price				
3								
4		Sun	01–Sep–91			Average Price:		$123.93
5		Mon	02–Sep–91					
6		Tue	03–Sep–91	$121.87		Number of Prices:		7
7		Wed	04–Sep–91	$121.21				
8		Thu	05–Sep–91	$125.40		Maximum Price:		$125.98
9		Fri	06–Sep–91	$125.98		Minimum Price:		$121.21
10		Sat	07–Sep–91	$124.13				
11		Sun	08–Sep–91					
12		Mon	09–Sep–91					
13		Tue	10–Sep–91	$123.65				
14		Wed	11–Sep–91	$125.28				
15								
16								
17								
18								
19								
20								NUM

The highlighted @MAX function shows the highest price-per-share. The @MIN function shows the lowest stock price in the list.

7 Using Database Functions

1-2-3's 11 database functions are similar to the statistical functions, but they require different arguments to work with database ranges. Like other functions, the database functions perform—in one simple statement—calculations that otherwise require several statements. This efficiency and ease of application make these functions excellent tools for manipulating 1-2-3 databases. Table 7.5 describes the database functions.

The general syntax of each of these functions (except @DQUERY) is as follows:

@DSUM(*input_range,field,criteria_range*)

The input range and criteria range are the same as those used by the /Data Query command except that the input range for all database functions can include more than one range. The input range specifies the database to search. The criteria range specifies the records to select. Field indicates which field to select from the database records. Enclose the field name in quotes, as in this example:

@DSUM(REVENUE,"AMOUNT",CRITERIA)

Table 7.5
Database Functions

Function	Description
@DAVG	Calculates the arithmetic mean of items in a list.
@DCOUNT	Counts the number of entries in a list.
@DGET	Extracts a value or label from a field in a database that matches the selected criteria.
@DMAX	Returns the maximum value among items in a list.
@DMIN	Returns the minimum value among items in a list.
@DQUERY*(external_fn, arguments)*	Sends a command to an external data management program.
@DSTD	Calculates the standard deviation of items in a list.
@DSTDS	Calculates the sample standard deviation of items in a list.
@DSUM	Sums the values of items in a list.
@DVAR	Computes the variance of items in a list.
@DVARS	Computes the sample variance of items in a list.

Suppose that you want to compute database statistics of the average interest rates offered by money market funds for a given week. 1-2-3's database functions enable you to find the count, sum, mean (average), variance, standard deviation, maximum, and minimum rates of return.

As displayed in the control panel in the following example, the input range is A3..B10, the field name is "week 1", and the criteria range is D4..D5. In the lower part of the example, the database functions are in column B (shown in text format in column D).

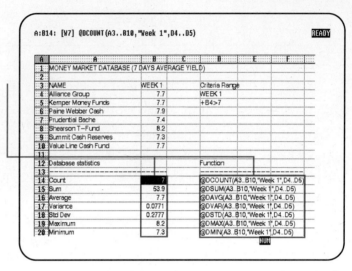

A:B14: [W7] @DCOUNT(A3..B10,"Week 1",D4..D5)   READY

	A	B	C	D	E	F
1	MONEY MARKET DATABASE (7 DAYS AVERAGE YIELD)					
2						
3	NAME	WEEK 1		Criteria Range		
4	Alliance Group	7.7		WEEK 1		
5	Kemper Money Funds	7.7		+B4>7		
6	Paine Webber Cash	7.9				
7	Prudential Bache	7.4				
8	Shearson T–Fund	8.2				
9	Summit Cash Reserves	7.3				
10	Value Line Cash Fund	7.7				
11						
12	Database statistics			Function		
13						
14	Count	7		@DCOUNT(A3..B10,"Week 1",D4..D5)		
15	Sum	53.9		@DSUM(A3..B10,"Week 1",D4..D5)		
16	Average	7.7		@DAVG(A3..B10,"Week 1",D4..D5)		
17	Variance	0.0771		@DVAR(A3..B10,"Week 1",D4..D5)		
18	Std Dev	0.2777		@DSTD(A3..B10,"Week 1",D4..D5)		
19	Maximum	8.2		@DMAX(A3..B10,"Week 1",D4..D5)		
20	Minimum	7.3		@DMIN(A3..B10,"Week 1",D4..D5)		

Examples of database functions used here with a money market database.

7 Using Logical Functions

Each of 1-2-3's nine logical functions enables you to test whether a condition is true or false. Many of these functions operate in a similar manner—by returning a 1 if the test is true or a 0 if the test is false. These logical tests are important for creating decision-making functions; the results of these functions depend on conditions elsewhere in the worksheet.

Table 7.6 summarizes the logical functions that 1-2-3 provides. The text that follows describes the @IF, @TRUE, and @FALSE logical functions in more detail.

Table 7.6
Logical Functions

Function	Description
@FALSE	Returns the logical value 0, for false.
@IF(*condition,true,false*)	Tests a condition and returns one result if the condition is true and another result if the condition is false.
@ISERR(*cell_reference*)	Tests whether the argument results in ERR.
@ISNA(*cell_reference*)	Tests whether the argument results in NA.
@ISNUMBER(*cell_reference*)	Tests whether the argument is a number.

246

Table 7.6 (continued)

Function	Description
@ISRANGE(*cell_reference*)	Tests whether the argument is a defined range.
@ISSTRING(*cell_reference*)	Tests whether the argument is a string.
@TRUE	Returns the logical value 1, for true.

Creating Conditional Tests with @IF

The @IF function represents a powerful tool—one you can use both to manipulate text within your worksheets and to affect calculations. For example, you can use an @IF statement to test the following condition: is the inventory on-hand below 1,000 units? You can return one value or label if the answer to the question is true, or another value or label if the answer is false. The @IF function uses the following syntax:

   @IF(*condition,true,false*)

The @IF function can use six operators when testing conditions. The following list shows the operators and their corresponding descriptions:

>   Greater than
<   Less than
=   Equal to
>=   Greater than or equal to
<=   Less than or equal to
<>   Not equal to

In addition, you can perform more complex conditional tests. Adding logical operators enables you to test multiple conditions in one @IF function. These operators and their descriptions are the following:

#AND#   Tests two conditions, both of which must be true in order for the entire test to be true.

#NOT#   Tests that a condition is not true.

#OR#   Tests two conditions; if either condition is true, the entire test condition is true.

7

```
A:D4:  [W14]  @IF(B4>4#AND#B4<10,"Valid","Not valid")                    READY
```

A	A	B	C	D	E	F	G	H
1								
2		Value		Result		Function		
3								
4		5		Valid		@IF(B4>4#AND#B4<10,"Valid","Not valid")		
5		3		Not valid		@IF(B5>4#AND#B5<10,"Valid","Not valid")		
6								
7		Wrench		OK		@IF(B7="Wrench","OK","Wrench only")		
8		Hammer		Wrench only		@IF(B8="Wrench","OK","Wrench only")		
9								
10		25-Jul-90		Past due		@IF(B10>@NOW,"Due date","Past due")		
11		15-Sep-90		Past due		@IF(B11>@NOW,"Due date","Past due")		
12								
13								
14								
15								

Examples of the @IF function test for specified values or labels.

The @IF function can check whether a specified cell's content is between 4 and 10, whether a cell contains a specified text string, and whether a 1-2-3 date falls before or after the current date. The results of these tests depend on whether the condition evaluates as true or false.

Checking for Errors with @TRUE and @FALSE

You use the @TRUE and @FALSE functions to check for errors. Neither function requires arguments, but each is useful for providing documentation for formulas and advanced macro commands. The @TRUE function always returns the value 1—the logical value for true. The @FALSE function always returns the value 0—the logical value for false. A common use for these functions is in combination with functions requiring a logical value, such as the following @IF formula:

@IF(B4>4#AND#B4<10,@TRUE,@FALSE)

This formula, similar to the formulas used in the previous example, returns the value of 1 (true) if cell B4 contains a value between 4 and 10; otherwise, returns a 0 (false).

Using String Functions

Another set of 1-2-3 functions includes the 19 string functions that manipulate text. You can use string functions to repeat text characters (a handy trick for creating worksheet and row boundaries and visual borders). You can also convert letters in a string to uppercase or lowercase, change strings into numbers, and change numbers into strings. String functions also are important when you prepare 1-2-3 data for use in other programs, such as word processing programs.

248

Included with the string functions are a few special functions for working with the Lotus Multibyte Character Set (LMBCS). The complete set of LMBCS characters, listed in the 1-2-3 documentation, includes everything from the copyright sign (©) to the lowercase *e* with the grave accent (è).

Table 7.7 summarizes the string functions available in 1-2-3. The sections that follow discuss the @LOWER, @UPPER, @PROPER, and @REPEAT string functions in more detail.

Table 7.7
String Functions

Function	Description
@CHAR(*number*)	Converts a code number into the corresponding LMBCS character.
@CLEAN(*string*)	Removes nonprintable characters from the specified string.
@CODE(*string*)	Returns the LMBCS code that corresponds to the first character of the specified string.
@EXACT(*string1,string2*)	Returns 1 (true) if arguments are exact matches; otherwise, returns 0 (false).
@FIND(*search_string, string,start_number*)	Locates the start position of one string within another string.
@LEFT(*string,number*)	Returns the specified number of characters from the left side of string.
@LENGTH(*string*)	Returns the number of characters in the string.
@LOWER(*string*)	Converts all characters in the string to lowercase.
@MID(*string,start_number, number*)	Returns a specified number of characters from the middle of another string, beginning at the specified starting position.
@N(*range*)	Returns as a value the contents of the cell in the upper left corner of a range.
@PROPER(*string*)	Converts the first character in each word of the string to uppercase, and the remaining characters in each word to lowercase.

7

249

Table 7.7 (continued)

Function	Description
@REPEAT(*string,number*)	Duplicates the string the specified number of times in a cell.
@REPLACE(*original_string, start_number,number, new_string*)	Replaces a number of characters in the original string with new string characters, starting at the character identified by the start position.
@RIGHT(*string,number*)	Returns the specified number of characters from right side of string.
@S(*range*)	Returns as a label the contents of the cell in the upper left corner of a range.
@STRING(*number, decimal_places*)	Converts a value to a string with the specified number of decimal places.
@TRIM(*string*)	Removes blank spaces from the string.
@UPPER(*string*)	Converts all characters in the string to uppercase.
@VALUE(*string*)	Converts the string to a value.

Strings are labels or portions of labels. Strings used within functions consist of characters enclosed in quotation marks, such as "Total." Some functions produce strings, but other functions produce numeric results. If a function's result is not of the data type you need, use @STRING to convert a numeric value to a string, or @VALUE to convert a string to a numeric value.

Converting the Case of Strings with @LOWER, @UPPER, and @PROPER

1-2-3 offers three different functions for converting the case of a string value. The @LOWER and @UPPER functions convert all characters in the referenced string to lowercase and uppercase. The @PROPER function converts characters in the string to proper capitalization—with the first letter in uppercase and all remaining letters in lowercase. The syntax of these functions is as follows:

@LOWER(*string*)
@UPPER(*string*)
@PROPER(*string*)

250

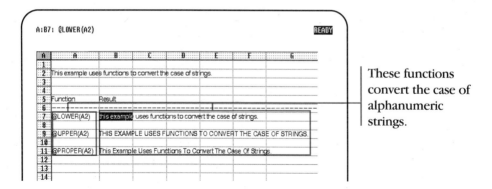

These functions convert the case of alphanumeric strings.

These three functions work with strings or references to strings. If a cell contains a number or is empty, 1-2-3 returns ERR for these functions.

The text versions of the formulas appear in column A, and the formulas and their results are in column B.

You can use @LOWER, @UPPER, or @PROPER to modify the contents of a database so all entries in a field appear with the same capitalization. This technique produces reports with a consistent appearance. To be sure that 1-2-3 sorts data with different capitalizations correctly, create a column using one of the functions that references the data and sort on this new column.

Repeating Strings with @REPEAT

The @REPEAT function repeats a string a specified number of times, much as the backslash (\) repeats strings to fill a single cell. However, @REPEAT has some distinct advantages over the backslash. With @REPEAT, you can repeat the string the precise number of times you want. If the result is wider than the cell width, the result displays in empty adjacent cells to the right. @REPEAT uses the following syntax:

@REPEAT(*string,number*)

The number argument indicates the number of times you want to repeat a string in a cell. For example, if you want to repeat the string -**- 4 times, you can enter the following function:

@REPEAT("-**-",4)

The resulting string will appear as: -**--**--**--**-.

7

Using Special Functions

1-2-3 provides a set of 14 special functions. You use these special tools to perform a variety of tasks. For example, two special functions return up to 10 different characteristics of a cell. Other special functions count the number of rows, columns, or sheets in a range. Special functions also enable you to trap worksheet errors and use specified keys in the functions' arguments to look up values in tables or lists.

Table 7.8 lists 1-2-3's special functions. The sections that follow discuss the @ERR, @NA, @HLOOKUP, and @VLOOKUP commands.

Table 7.8
Special Functions

Function	Description
@@(*location*)	Returns the contents of the cell referenced in the specified location.
@CELL(*attribute,range*)	Returns an attribute of the cell in the upper left corner of the range.
@CELLPOINTER(*attribute*)	Returns an attribute of the current cell.
@CHOOSE(*offset,list*)	Locates in a list the entry specified by the offset number.
@COLS(*range*)	Counts the number of columns in a range.
@COORD(*worksheet, column,row,cell_absolute*)	Constructs a cell address from values corresponding to rows, columns, and sheets.
@ERR	Displays ERR in the cell.
@HLOOKUP(*key,range, row_offset*)	Locates the number in a table and returns a value from that row of the range.
@INDEX(*range, column_offset,row_offset*)	Returns the contents of a cell specified by the intersection of a row and column within a range.
@INFO(*attribute*)	Retrieves system information.
@NA	Displays NA in the cell.
@ROWS(*range*)	Counts the number of rows in a range.
@SHEETS(*range*)	Computes the number of worksheets in a range.

7

Table 7.8 (continued)

Function	Description
@VLOOKUP(*key,range, column_offset*)	Locates the number in a lookup table and returns a value from that column of the range.

Trapping Errors with @ERR and @NA

When you create 1-2-3 applications, you may want to use @ERR or @NA to distinguish certain cell entries. Formulas that depend on cells with @NA or @ERR will return NA or ERR. Suppose, for example, that you are creating a checkbook-balancing worksheet in which checks with dollar amounts less than or equal to zero are unacceptable. One way to show that these checks are unacceptable is to use @ERR to signal that fact. You can use the following version of the @IF function:

@IF(B9<=0,@ERR,B9)

This statement says, "If the amount in cell B9 is less than or equal to zero, then display ERR in that cell; otherwise, display the amount."

In an inventory database, you can place the @NA function in cells to show uncounted inventory items. You can also use @IF and @NA together as in the following example:

@IF(C4=0,@NA,C4)

This statement says, "If the value in cell C4 is equal to zero, display NA in that cell, otherwise display the value."

Finding Table Entries with @HLOOKUP and @VLOOKUP

The @HLOOKUP and @VLOOKUP functions retrieve a string or value from a table, based on a specified key used to find the information. The operation and format of the two functions are essentially the same except that @HLOOKUP searches horizontal tables and @VLOOKUP searches vertical tables. These functions use the following syntax:

@HLOOKUP(*key,range,row_offset*)

@VLOOKUP(*key,range,column_offset*)

The key argument is the string or value that tells 1-2-3 which column (@HLOOKUP) or row (@VLOOKUP) to search. The key strings or values must be in the first column or row of the lookup table. (Numeric keys must be in ascending order for the functions to work properly.) The range argument is the area that makes up the entire lookup table. The offset argument specifies from which row (@HLOOKUP) or column (@VLOOKUP) to retrieve data. The number indicates how many rows or columns away from the key field 1-2-3 should look for the value. (The cell containing the key field is numbered 0.) If the offset specifies a number of columns or rows which is not within the table, 1-2-3 returns ERR.

The @HLOOKUP and @VLOOKUP functions are useful for finding any type of value you would have to look up manually in a table. Examples include tax amounts, shipping zones, and interest charges.

The @HLOOKUP function retrieves values from a table.

A:A14: [W7] @HLOOKUP(1988,$C$3..$G$9,3)   READY

	A	B	C	D	E	F	G	H	I
1									
2									
3			1986	1987	1988	1989	1990		
4	Item 1		344	774	884	256	145		
5	Item 2		442	777	158	919	252		
6	Item 3		106	827	953	572	368		
7	Item 4		605	320	124	904	535		
8	Item 5		277	787	200	745	52		
9	Item 6		437	150	832	471	150		
10									
11									
12	Result		Function						
13									
14	953		@HLOOKUP(1988,$C$3..$G$9,3)						
15	145		@HLOOKUP(1990,$C$3..$G$9,1)						
16	150		@HLOOKUP(1987,$C$3..$G$9,6)						
17	ERR		@HLOOKUP(1989,$C$3..$G$9,8)						
18									
19									
20									

NUM

Summary

This chapter described the functions that 1-2-3 provides to make formula and worksheet construction easier and more error-free. After you become accustomed to using these functions, you can use them regularly in your worksheets. Use the tables of this chapter as a reference for the available functions, their syntax, and the types of arguments they require.

Specifically, you learned the following key information about 1-2-3:

■ 1-2-3 includes built-in functions for use with eight different types of applications. These functions perform a variety of powerful calculations that save time when building worksheets.

■ Enter 1-2-3 functions by typing the @ symbol, followed by the function name and any required arguments within parentheses. Press Enter to complete the process.

■ The mathematical and trigonometric functions perform standard arithmetic operations, such as computing the integer with @INT and rounding numbers with @ROUND.

■ The date and time functions convert dates and times to serial numbers which can be used in sorting and arithmetic calculations. Examples include @NOW, @DATE, and @DATEVALUE. You can use @NOW to stamp the date on a worksheet or report.

■ The financial functions calculate cash flows, loans, annuities, and asset depreciation. The @PMT function calculates loan payments, while the @PV and @FV functions calculate present and future values, respectively.

■ The statistical functions perform standard statistical calculations on lists. For example, @AVG calculates the average of values in a list. @COUNT counts the total number of entries in a list. @MAX and @MIN find the maximum and minimum values in a list.

■ The database functions are similar to the statistical functions, but calculate and query databases.

■ The logical functions test whether a condition is true or false. The @IF function returns a different value or label depending on the outcome of a specified condition. You can use the @TRUE and @FALSE functions in conditional tests to display a 1 (true) or a 0 (false).

■ The string functions are used to manipulate text. For example, the @LOWER, @UPPER, and @PROPER functions convert the case of a specified label. The @REPEAT function repeats a string a specified number of times.

■ The special functions perform a variety of worksheet tasks. The @ERR and @NA functions trap errors or distinguish certain cell entries. The @HLOOKUP and @VLOOKUP functions return values from a specified row and column of a table.

In the next chapter, you learn how to print reports created in 1-2-3. This chapter also discusses the various options available for enhancing reports.

7

Printing Reports

1-2-3 is a powerful tool for developing information presented in a column-and-row format. You can enter and edit your worksheet and database files on-screen, as well as store the input on disk. To make good use of your data, however, you often need it in printed form. Examples include a target production schedule, a summary report to your supervisor, or a detailed reorder list to central stores.

Using 1-2-3's /**P**rint command, you can select from many options to meet your printing needs. You can choose to write directly from 1-2-3 to the printer by using the /**P**rint **P**rinter command sequence. You can use the /**P**rint **F**ile or **E**ncoded filename sequence to create a print file on disk. Later, you can produce a printout of the file from within 1-2-3 or from DOS. You can even merge the file into a word processing file.

You also can use the add-in program Wysiwyg to take advantage of presentation-quality printing features not found in the standard 1-2-3 /**P**rint commands. Wysiwyg is the subject of the next chapter.

Key Terms in This Chapter

Print defaults   Preset, standard specifications for a 1-2-3 print job.

Encoded file   File that you print to a disk. An encoded file has all the instructions necessary to output highlighted text and graphs to a specific printer.

Borders   One or more rows or columns of data or labels that 1-2-3 repeats on a multiple-page report.

Header   Information displayed on one line at the top of a page. A header may include a date and a page number.

Footer   Information displayed on one line at the bottom of a page. A footer may include a date and a page number.

8

Using the Mouse

To use a mouse with 1-2-3 Release 3.1, you will need a mouse, mouse software, and a graphics monitor and graphics card that support a mouse. Also, Wysiwyg must be loaded into memory. You can use a mouse to select commands and files, specify ranges, and move the cell pointer within a worksheet or between multiple worksheets and files. In the examples throughout this chapter, notice that the 1-2-3 commands always begin with a slash (/), and the Wysiwyg commands always begin with a colon (:). Refer to the following sections of the specified chapters for further information on using the mouse:

- Chapter 2—"Understanding Mouse Terminology"
- Chapter 3—"Mouse Control of the Cell Pointer"
            "Using the Mouse To Select Menu Commands"
- Chapter 4—"Using the Mouse To Specify Ranges"

To help you learn the basics of printing, this chapter assumes that:

- You have not changed 1-2-3's preset printing defaults.
- You produce reports on 8 1/2-by-11-inch paper.
- You send output to the printer in most cases.
- You want to use basic report-enhancement techniques such as hiding columns and rows, adding headers and footers, and repeating column and row headings.

If you want to change 1-2-3's default settings, consult Que's *Using 1-2-3 Release 3.1*, 2nd Edition.

Getting Started from the /Print Menu

Every print command in 1-2-3 starts from the /**Print** option of the main menu. After choosing /**Print**, you must select one of the first three options: **Printer**, **File**, or **Encoded**.

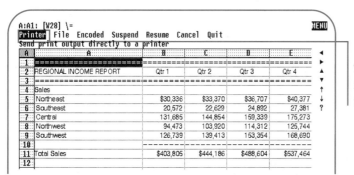

The /Print command options in the control panel.

You use the next three options, **Suspend**, **Resume**, and **Cancel**, only when a print job is in progress. These options are covered later in this chapter. The seventh option, **Quit**, returns you to READY mode.

To send your report directly to the current printer, choose **Printer**.

To create a text file on disk, select **File**. A text file can contain data but no graphs or special printer codes. Later, you can print the text file from the operating system prompt.

To create a disk file that includes instructions on printing, choose Encoded. An encoded file can contain data, graphs, and printer codes for 1-2-3 print options, such as fonts, colors, and line spacing. You can print an encoded file from the operating system prompt, but such a file is not suitable for transferring data to another program.

If you choose **File** or **Encoded**, you must respond to the prompt for a file name. Type a name that contains up to eight characters. You need not add a file extension because 1-2-3 automatically assigns the PRN (print file) or ENC (encoded file) extension. You can specify a different extension if you desire.

You use an encoded file for printing at another time or from another computer, while preserving all the special print options available in 1-2-3. When you create an encoded file, be sure that the selected printer is the same as the one you will use to print the file. An encoded file contains printer codes that control special printer features, such as fonts and line spacing. Because these codes are printer-specific, an encoded file created for one printer may not print correctly on another printer. The printer control codes embedded in the encoded file make sure that the final output looks the same as output printed directly from 1-2-3. To print an encoded file, you use the operating system COPY command with the /B option. Consider the following example:

    COPY C:\123R3\SALES.ENC/B LPT1:

This command prints the file SALES.ENC, located in directory C:\123R3, on the printer connected to the port LPT1 (usually the default printer port). Other printer ports are LPT2, COM1, and COM2.

After you select **Printer**, **File**, or **Encoded**, the second line of the control panel displays a menu with 11 options.

```
A:A1: [W28] \=                                               MENU
Range Line Page Options Clear Align Go Image Sample Hold Quit
Specify a range to print
A                A                 B         C         D         E
1 ==================================================================
2 REGIONAL INCOME REPORT          Qtr 1     Qtr 2     Qtr 3     Qtr 4
3 ==================================================================
4 Sales
5 Northeast                      $30,336   $33,370   $36,707   $40,377
6 Southeast                       20,572    22,629    24,892    27,381
7 Central                        131,685   144,854   159,339   175,273
8 Northwest                       94,473   103,920   114,312   125,744
9 Southwest                      126,739   139,413   153,354   168,690
10
11 Total Sales                   $403,805  $444,186  $488,604  $537,464
12
```

Table 8.1 outlines the various options on the main **Print** menu. Regardless of which option you select, you must choose **Range** and specify a range to print. Select **Go** and then **Quit** to return to the worksheet. All other selections are optional.

260

Table 8.1
Selections on the /Print Printer Menu

Selection	Description
Range	Shows the section of the worksheet to print or save to disk as a print file.
Line	Adjusts the paper line-by-line in the printer.
Page	Adjusts the paper page-by-page in the printer.
Options	Determines settings to enhance the appearance of the printout.
Clear	Erases previous settings.
Align	Signals the printer position at the top of the print page.
Go	Starts printing to the printer or a disk file.
Image	Selects a graph to print.
Sample	Prints a sample worksheet.
Hold	Returns to READY mode without closing the current print job.
Quit	Exits the **Print** menu and returns 1-2-3 to READY mode.

8

Printing Draft-Quality Reports

Printing does not have to be an arduous task. With 1-2-3, you can print quick reports by issuing a few simple commands. In this section, you learn a variety of printing techniques. Specifically, you learn to print a draft-quality report of one page or less. You also learn to print a multipage report with borders and to print multiple ranges with one print command.

Printing a One-Page Report

If you work with default print settings and haven't entered other print settings during the current worksheet session, printing one page or less involves only a few steps.

These steps include the following:

1. Choose to print to the printer or a file.
2. Highlight the range to print.
3. Choose the command to begin printing.

Two other steps may be necessary if you or someone else has changed the default settings or entered new print settings. First, you can check the default settings by selecting /**Worksheet Global Default Status**. A quick review of the top left section of the **Global Status** screen shows whether the printer and page layout settings are the ones you need. Second, you can clear any settings that another user entered by selecting /**Print Printer Clear All**. All settings return to the default settings (a later section of this chapter covers clearing print settings).

If you are certain that all default settings are correct and no other settings have been entered into the **Print** commands, you can print a draft-quality report of one page or less by completing the following steps:

1. Check that your printer is on-line and that you have positioned the paper properly.
2. Select /**Print Printer**.
3. Select **Range** to specify a range to print from the worksheet.
4. Indicate what part of the worksheet you want to print by highlighting the area. Then press ⏎Enter.

   You can use the PgUp, PgDn, and End keys to set ranges when you print. If you want to set a range that includes the entire active area of the worksheet, press Home to move to the top left corner. Then anchor the range (.), and move the cell pointer to the lower right corner of the active area with End Home.

In this example, highlight the range A1..E11 as the range to print, and press ⏎Enter.

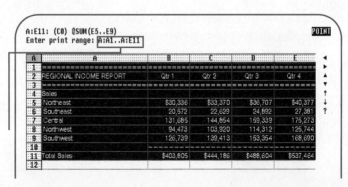

5. After you highlight the range you want to print, select **Align**.

   Choosing **Align** ensures that printing begins at the top of each page. Before printing, always make sure that you have correctly positioned your printer paper.

6. To begin printing, select **Go**.

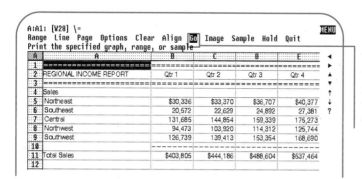

The **Go** option on the main **Print** menu sends your worksheet data to the printer.

7. After the printer finishes, select **Page** to advance to the top of the next page or eject the page from a laser printer.

8. Select **Quit**.

If you press Enter after selecting the **Go** option, the file prints a second time. If this accidently occurs, you can stop printing by pressing Esc and selecting **Cancel**. Even if the area of your worksheet to print is larger than one page, you can use the basic steps for printing one-page reports. However, setting the print range so a new page begins where you want can be tricky. Therefore, if you want to print a section of a large worksheet, you may need to use the **/Print Printer Options Borders** command, explained in the next section. This command allows you to repeat certain labels on each page.

8

This draft-quality report of less than one page is printed with 1-2-3's default settings.

```
========================================================================
REGIONAL INCOME REPORT          Qtr 1      Qtr 2      Qtr 3      Qtr 4
================================= ========== ========== ========== ==========
Sales
  Northeast                      $30,336    $33,370    $36,707    $40,377
  Southeast                       20,572     22,629     24,892     27,381
  Central                        131,685    144,854    159,339    175,273
  Northwest                       94,473    103,920    114,312    125,744
  Southwest                      126,739    139,413    153,354    168,690
                                ---------- ---------- ---------- ----------
Total Sales                     $403,805   $444,186   $488,604   $537,464
                                ---------- ---------- ---------- ----------
```

Printing Two or More Pages with Borders

If you want to print information correctly when splitting data between pages, remember that 1-2-3 treats numeric and text data differently. 1-2-3 prints numbers completely because they span only one cell. However, text—such as long labels that lie across several cells—may split awkwardly from one page to the next.

When printing two or more pages, you can repeat certain columns or rows on each printed page. 1-2-3 defines the repeated columns and rows as borders.

To repeat column or row borders on each page when printing, follow these steps:

1. Select /**P**rint Printer **O**ptions.

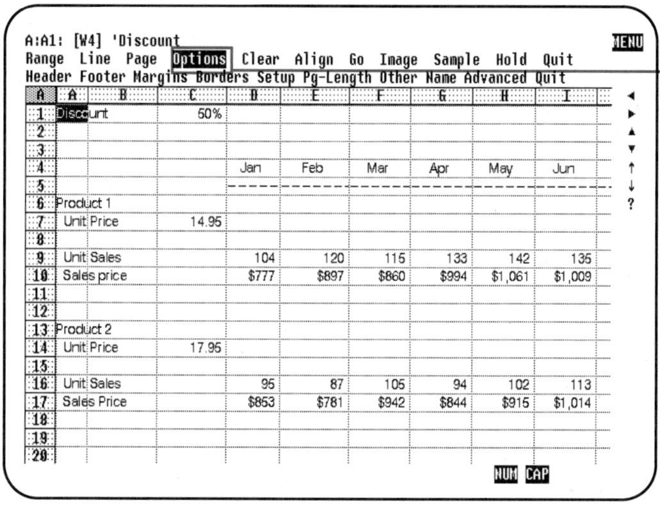

The **Options** command allows you to select different print settings to enhance your printouts.

2. Select **B**orders.

1-2-3 asks whether you want to locate the labels down one or more columns or across one or more rows. 1-2-3 also asks if you want the worksheet frame (sheet letter, row numbers, and column letters) printed.

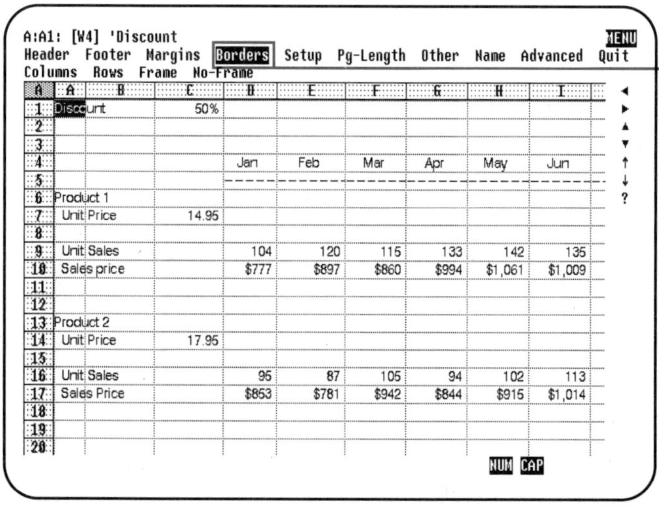

The **Borders** command enables you to select row or column borders to repeat on each page of the printout.

8

265

3. Select either **Columns** or **Rows**.

Suppose you want to print a report on two or more pages and repeat labels displayed in a column. To do this, select **Columns** after choosing **Options Borders**. To print a report on two or more pages and repeat labels displayed across a row, select **Rows** after choosing **Options Borders**.

In this example, select **Columns**.

After you choose **Columns**, the prompt `Enter border columns:` appears.

4. Show which rows or columns you want printed on each page by highlighting the rows or columns. Then press ⏎Enter.

5. To return to the main **Print** menu, select **Quit**.

6. To choose the range to print, select **Range**.

7. Highlight the desired print range and press ⏎Enter.

Note: Do not include in your print range the borders you want repeated on each page. 1-2-3 automatically prints the borders on every page of the printout. If you include the borders in the print range, 1-2-3 prints them twice on each page.

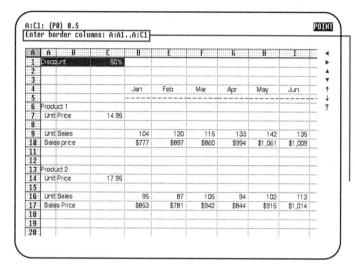

For columns A through C to appear as a border, highlight the range A1..C1 and press ⏎Enter.

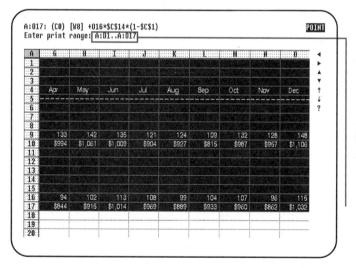

In this example, highlight the range to print as D1..O17 and press ⏎Enter. Note that this range does not include the columns specified as borders.

8

8. Select **Align G**o.

9. After the printer finishes printing, select **P**age to advance to the top of the next page or eject the page from a laser printer.

10. Select **Q**uit.

This is the first page of a two-page report that has column borders repeated on each page.

```
Discount           50%

                             Jan      Feb      Mar      Apr      May      Jun
                           -------  -------  -------  -------  -------  -------
Product 1
  Unit Price     14.95

  Unit Sales                  104      120      115      133      142      135
  Sales price                $777     $897     $860     $994   $1,061   $1,009


Product 2
  Unit Price     17.95

  Unit Sales                   95       87      105       94      102      113
  Sales Price                $853     $781     $942     $844     $915   $1,014
```

8

```
Discount          50%


                       Jul     Aug     Sep     Oct     Nov     Dec
                     ------- ------- ------- ------- ------- -------
Product 1
  Unit Price    14.95

  Unit Sales             121     124     109     132     128     148
  Sales price           $904    $927    $815    $987    $957  $1,106

Product 2
  Unit Price    17.95

  Unit Sales             108      99     104     107      96     115
  Sales Price           $969    $889    $933    $960    $862  $1,032
```

This is the second page of the report with borders.

8

Printing Multiple Ranges

For many reports, a single two-dimensional print range, like those used in the preceding examples, is all you need. You can, however, create a print job that includes more than one two-dimensional range in a worksheet. You also can print one or more three-dimensional ranges, or a combination of two- and three-dimensional ranges.

You specify a three-dimensional print range just as you specify a two-dimensional range—by entering cell addresses, by entering an assigned range name, or by pointing. When pointing, remember to use Ctrl-PgUp and Ctrl-PgDn to move up and down through active worksheets. With the mouse, you can click on the up- and down-arrows in the icon panel to move to the next or previous worksheet.

A printout of the selected three-dimensional range in landscape mode.

8

NATIONAL MICRO

	Jan	Feb	Mar	Apr	May	Jun	Jul	Aug	Sep	Oct	Nov	Dec	Total
SALES REPORT													
Northeast	$31,366	$34,503	$37,953	$41,748	$45,923	$50,515	$55,567	$61,123	$67,236	$73,959	$81,355	$89,491	$670,739
Southeast	30,572	33,629	36,992	40,691	44,760	49,237	54,160	59,576	65,534	72,087	79,296	87,225	653,760
Central	131,685	135,636	139,705	143,896	148,213	152,659	157,239	161,956	166,815	172,819	176,974	182,463	1,868,877
Northwest	94,473	96,362	98,290	100,256	102,261	106,306	106,722	108,520	110,690	112,904	115,162	112,463	1,265,080
Southwest	126,739	129,274	131,859	134,426	137,186	139,930	142,722	145,583	148,495	151,465	154,494	157,584	1,699,835
Total Sales	$414,835	$429,404	$444,799	$461,087	$478,343	$496,647	$516,086	$536,759	$558,769	$582,234	$607,281	$634,048	$6,160,292
COST OF GOODS													
Northeast	$10,341	$11,375	$12,513	$13,764	$15,140	$16,654	$18,320	$20,152	$22,167	$24,384	$26,822	$29,504	$221,135
Southeast	6,546	7,201	7,921	8,713	9,584	10,542	11,597	12,756	14,032	16,435	16,979	18,142	139,982
Central	65,843	67,818	69,853	71,948	74,107	76,330	78,620	80,779	83,408	85,435	88,487	98,142	934,446
Northwest	63,967	65,746	67,882	69,882	76,240	76,335	78,030	80,478	83,948	75,440	77,935	79,535	857,931
Southwest	72,314	73,746	75,235	76,740	78,275	79,840	81,437	83,066	84,727	86,422	88,150	89,913	969,882
Total Cost of Goods Sold	$219,011	$225,401	$232,073	$239,048	$246,346	$253,992	$262,011	$270,431	$279,282	$288,597	$298,414	$308,771	$3,123,375
OPERATING EXPENSES													
Northeast	$21,529	$23,682	$26,050	$28,655	$31,521	$34,673	$38,140	$41,954	$46,149	$50,764	$55,841	$61,425	$460,382
Southeast	15,946	17,541	19,295	21,224	23,347	25,681	28,249	31,074	34,182	35,600	41,360	45,494	340,994
Central	27,554	28,383	29,232	30,109	31,047	31,943	32,901	33,888	34,905	35,952	37,030	38,141	391,047
Northwest	16,130	16,453	16,782	17,117	17,460	17,809	18,165	18,528	18,899	19,277	19,662	20,056	216,337
Southwest	32,361	33,008	33,668	34,342	35,029	35,729	36,444	37,173	37,916	38,674	39,448	40,237	434,029
Total Operating Expenses	$113,520	$119,064	$125,027	$131,447	$138,368	$145,834	$153,899	$162,617	$172,051	$182,267	$193,341	$205,354	$1,842,789

To specify multiple print ranges, enter each range as you would enter a single print range, and enter an argument separator after each range. You can use the semicolon (;) or the comma (,).

To print multiple print ranges, follow these steps:

1. Select /**Print Printer R**ange.
2. Type or highlight the first range you want to print.
3. Type ⊡ or ⊡ to separate the ranges.
4. Type or highlight the second range you want to print.
5. Repeat steps 3 and 4 for each additional range you want to add.
6. Press ⏎Enter to select all ranges.
7. Select **Align Go P**age **Q**uit to print the ranges and finish printing.

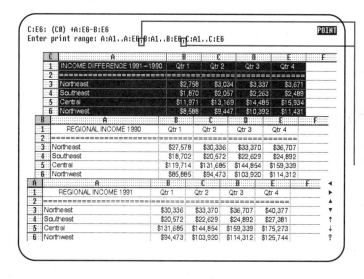

8

The three worksheet ranges are separated by commas.

You can specify any combination of two-and three-dimensional ranges. The following examples are valid multiple print ranges:

A:A1..A:H10, A:J55..A:P120

A:A1..A:H10;B:C5..B:E12;C:C1..C:D5

A:A1..C:D10;A:F10..D:H20;C:C1..C:H10

In a print job, each range prints below the last, in the order specified when you entered the ranges. If you prefer to have each range on a separate page, insert page breaks with /**Worksheet P**age at the bottom of each range.

Excluding Segments within a Designated Print Range

Because the /Print commands require that you specify a range to print, you can print only rectangular blocks from the worksheet. You can, however, suppress the display of cell contents within the range. You can hide entire rows or columns, or you can remove from view a segment that spans only part of a row or a column. You can hide a column (or range) of sensitive financial information. You can also compress the worksheet so that the most important data fits on a one-page report.

Excluding Columns

As you learned in Chapter 5, you can use /Worksheet Column Hide to mark columns you don't want to appear on-screen. If you include these marked columns in a print range, they do not appear on the printout.

To print a worksheet range and exclude one or more columns within that range, follow these steps:

1. Select /Worksheet Column Hide.

2. When the prompt Specify columns to hide: appears, highlight the column or columns you want to hide. Then press ⏎Enter.

Move the cell pointer to column E (the column to hide) and press ⏎Enter.

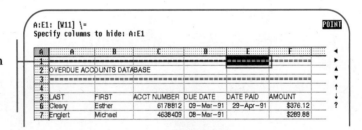

3. Select /Print Printer Range.

4. Highlight the range you want to print, and press ⏎Enter.

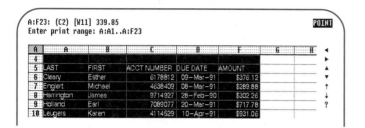

In this example,
highlight the range
to print as A1..F23,
and press ⏎Enter.

5. Select **Align G**o **P**age **Quit.**

```
================================================================
OVERDUE ACCOUNTS DATABASE
================================================================

LAST         FIRST      ACCT NUMBER  DUE DATE    AMOUNT
Cleary       Esther        6178812   09-Mar-90   $376.12
Englert      Michael       4638409   08-Mar-90   $289.88
Harrington   James         9714927   28-Feb-89   $302.26
Holland      Earl          7089077   20-Mar-90   $717.78
Leugers      Karen         4114529   10-Apr-90   $931.06
Malvern      Thomas        1020886   20-Apr-90   $857.10
Mansfield    James         7949146   18-Apr-90   $208.98
McGruder     Mary          4253520   23-Feb-89   $740.23
Pryor        Aaron         7456362   04-Apr-90   $247.49
Rooney       Kevin         4699322   19-Apr-90   $238.84
Saunders     Ronald        1338822   02-Mar-90   $691.14
Simpson      Jeremy        7993805   18-Mar-90   $844.28
Smith        Margaret      5129488   20-Apr-90   $379.36
Sorrenson    Sarah         1173073   29-Mar-90   $519.48
Thomas       Brian         5564320   01-Apr-90   $451.59
Tuke         Samuel        1020886   15-Feb-89   $236.63
Wolf         Barbara       4587979   12-Apr-90   $627.93
Wright       Larry         4211820   25-Feb-89   $339.85
```

The printed report
excludes the
information from
the hidden
column.

8

273

Note: To restore hidden columns, select /Worksheet Column Display. When the hidden columns (marked with an asterisk) reappear on-screen, you can specify which column or columns to display.

Excluding Rows

To prevent specific rows of the worksheet from printing, you must mark these rows with a symbol for nonprinting. You enter the symbol for nonprinting by typing two vertical bars (||) in the first column of the print range in each row you want to exclude.

After you type both vertical bars, only one appears on-screen, and neither vertical bar appears on the printout. If the row you want to exclude contains data in the first column of the print range, you must insert a new column for the vertical bars. Keep in mind that the column with the vertical bars must be the first column of the print range. To avoid alignment problems when inserting this new column, use /Worksheet Column Hide to suppress printing of the column.

To print a worksheet range and suppress one or more rows within that range, follow these steps:

1. Highlight the first column of the row you want to suppress from the printout.

   Note: If the first cells in the rows marked for omission already contain data, use /Worksheet Insert Column to insert a blank column to the left of the print range.

Highlight a cell in row 6, the first row to suppress from the printout.

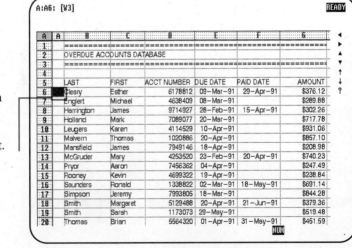

2. Press ⌶ (the symbol for nonprinting) twice, and then press ↵Enter.

```
A:A6: [W3] ||                                              READY
```

	A	B	C	D	E	F	G
1		===	========	=========	========	========	=======
2		OVERDUE ACCOUNTS DATABASE					
3		===	========	=========	========	========	=======
4							
5		LAST	FIRST	ACCT NUMBER	DUE DATE	DATE PAID	AMOUNT
6		Cleary	Esther	6178812	09-Mar-91	29-Apr-91	$376.12
7		Englert	Michael	4638409	08-Mar-91		$289.88
8		Harrington	James	9714927	28-Feb-90	15-Apr-91	$302.26
9		Holland	Earl	7089077	20-Mar-91		$717.78
10		Leugers	Karen	4114529	10-Apr-91		$931.06
11		Malvern	Thomas	1020886	20-Apr-91		$857.10
12		Mansfield	James	7949146	18-Apr-91		$208.98
13		McGruder	Mary	4253520	23-Feb-91	20-Apr-91	$740.23
14		Pryor	Aaron	7456362	04-Apr-91		$247.49
15		Rooney	Kevin	4699322	19-Apr-91		$238.84
16		Saunders	Ronald	1338822	02-Mar-91	18-May-91	$691.14
17		Simpson	Jeremy	7993805	18-Mar-91		$844.28
18		Smith	Margaret	5129488	20-Apr-91	21-Jun-91	$379.36
19		Sorrenson	Sarah	1173073	29-Mar-91		$519.48
20		Thomas	Brian	5564320	01-Apr-91	31-May-91	$451.59

The symbol for nonprinting appears as a single bar in the worksheet.

3. Repeat steps 1 and 2 until you have marked all rows to suppress from the printout with two vertical bars.

4. To define the range to print, select /Print Printer Range.

5. Highlight the range you want to print, and press ↵Enter. You must include the column with the vertical bars as the first column in the print range.

6. If you insert a new column for the vertical bars, hide the column to avoid alignment problems in your printout. To do this, select Quit from the Print menu. Then highlight the new column, select /Worksheet Column Hide, and press ↵Enter. Then select /Print Printer to access the Print menu again, and continue with the next step.

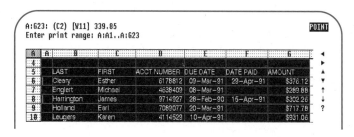

```
A:G23: (C2) [W11] 339.85                                   POINT
Enter print range: A:A1..A:G23
```

	A	B	C	D	E	F	G
4							
5		LAST	FIRST	ACCT NUMBER	DUE DATE	DATE PAID	AMOUNT
6		Cleary	Esther	6178812	09-Mar-91	29-Apr-91	$376.12
7		Englert	Michael	4638409	08-Mar-91		$289.88
8		Harrington	James	9714927	28-Feb-90	15-Apr-91	$302.26
9		Holland	Earl	7089077	20-Mar-91		$717.78
10		Leugers	Karen	4114529	10-Apr-91		$931.06

In this example, highlight the range to print as A1..G23 and press ↵Enter.

Note: You must hide column A before printing to avoid alignment problems. The marked rows are suppressed although the symbols for nonprinting are not visible on-screen.

    7. Select **Align Go Page Quit.**

Rows marked with two vertical bars in the first column of the print range do not appear in the printed output.

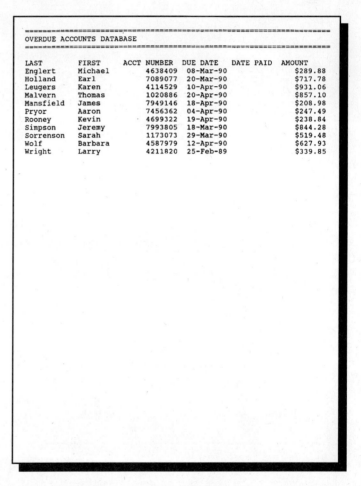

```
===================================================================
OVERDUE ACCOUNTS DATABASE
===================================================================

LAST        FIRST      ACCT NUMBER  DUE DATE   DATE PAID  AMOUNT
Englert     Michael      4638409    08-Mar-90             $289.88
Holland     Earl         7089077    20-Mar-90             $717.78
Leugers     Karen        4114529    10-Apr-90             $931.06
Malvern     Thomas       1020886    20-Apr-90             $857.10
Mansfield   James        7949146    18-Apr-90             $208.98
Pryor       Aaron        7456362    04-Apr-90             $247.49
Rooney      Kevin        4699322    19-Apr-90             $238.84
Simpson     Jeremy       7993805    18-Mar-90             $844.28
Sorrenson   Sarah        1173073    29-Mar-90             $519.48
Wolf        Barbara      4587979    12-Apr-90             $627.93
Wright      Larry        4211820    25-Feb-89             $339.85
```

To restore the worksheet after you finish printing, remove the vertical bars from the extreme leftmost cells of the marked rows. If you inserted a column for the vertical bars, display the column again, if necessary, with /Worksheet Column **Display.** Then delete the column with /Worksheet Column **Delete.**

Excluding Ranges

If you want to hide an area that partially spans one or more rows and columns, use /Range Format Hidden to mark the range. To exclude a worksheet range from a printout, follow these steps:

1. Specify the range you want to hide and press ⏎Enter.
2. To choose the range to print, select **/Print Printer Range**.
3. Highlight the range you want to print and press ⏎Enter. Be sure to include the hidden range within the range to print.
4. Select **Align Go Page Quit**.

```
==================================================================================
OVERDUE ACCOUNTS DATABASE
==================================================================================

LAST      FIRST    ACCT NUMBER  DUE DATE   DATE PAID   AMOUNT
                   6178812      09-Mar-90  29-Apr-90   $376.12
                   4638409      08-Mar-90              $289.88
                   9714927      28-Feb-89  15-Apr-90   $302.26
                   7089077      20-Mar-90              $717.78
                   4114529      10-Apr-90              $931.06
                   1020886      20-Apr-90              $857.10
                   7949146      18-Apr-90              $208.98
                   4253520      23-Feb-89  20-Apr-90   $740.23
                   7456362      04-Apr-90              $247.49
                   4699322      19-Apr-90              $238.84
                   1338822      02-Mar-90  18-May-90   $691.14
                   7993805      18-Mar-90              $844.28
                   5129488      20-Apr-90  21-Jun-90   $379.36
                   1173073      29-Mar-90              $519.48
                   5564320      01-Apr-90  31-May-90   $451.59
                   1020886      15-Feb-89  30-Mar-90   $236.63
                   4587979      12-Apr-90              $627.93
                   4211820      25-Feb-89              $339.85
```

1-2-3 suppresses the range hidden with /Range Format Hidden from the printout.

8

After you finish printing, restore the hidden range to the global format with the /**R**ange Format **R**eset command.

If you find yourself repeating print operations (hiding the same columns, setting and resetting ranges), you can save time and minimize frustration with print macros. Chapter 14 explains the basics about macros. For more detailed information, see Chapters 13 and 14 of Que's *Using 1-2-3, Release 3.1*, 2nd Edition.

Controlling Paper Movement

If you print a report shorter than full-page length, the printer does not automatically advance to the top of the next page. Instead, the next print operation begins where the preceding operation ended. Similarly, if you print a report with more than one page, 1-2-3 automatically inserts page breaks in the document between pages. But the paper does not advance to the top of the next page after 1-2-3 has printed the last page.

You can, however, control movement of the paper in your printer from within 1-2-3. You can specify the "top" of a page in any paper position, advance the paper by line or by page, and insert precise page breaks.

Using the Line, Page, and Align Options

If you are using continuous-feed paper, position the paper so the print head is at the top of the page. Then turn on the printer. If your printer is already on, turn it off and then on again. Do not advance the paper manually once the printer is on. 1-2-3 coordinates a line counter with the current page-length setting. Because 1-2-3 does not count any lines you advance manually, page breaks could crop up in strange places.

You control the movement of the paper in your printer with the Line, **P**age, and **A**lign options.

The **Line** option of the **Print** menu advances the paper one line at a time. The **Page** option advances paper one complete page at a time. You use the **Align** option to set the beginning of a page.

If you want to advance paper one line at a time, issue the /**Print Printer Line** command. This command sequence causes the printer to skip a line. An example of when you would use this is to separate several small printed ranges that fit on one page.

To advance paper one line at a time, follow these steps:

1. Select /**Print Printer**.
2. Select **Line** for each line you want to advance.

If you want to advance to a new page after printing less than a full page, select /**Print Printer Page**. When you issue this command, the printer skips to a new page. (The following section shows how you can embed in the print range a page-break symbol that instructs 1-2-3 to advance automatically.)

To advance to a new page after printing less than a full page, select /**Print Printer Page**.

Use /**Print Printer Align** to align the paper perforation with the print head and to set (or reset) correct page breaks. When you begin a print job at the top of a page, always select **Align** before printing. To align the printer and set the beginning of a page, select /**Print Printer Align**.

Setting Page Breaks within the Worksheet

As discussed in Chapter 5, you insert page breaks in the worksheet with the /**Worksheet Page** command. Execute this command with the cell pointer at the first column of the range to print. You should also be in the row that begins the new page. The command automatically inserts a new blank row at the location of the cell pointer. The left edge of the row displays a page-break symbol (::).

8

An alternative to using /Worksheet **Page** is to add page breaks to your document manually. To do this, insert a blank row into your worksheet where you want a page break. Then enter a page-break symbol into the blank cell in the first column of the print range in that row. To enter the page-break symbol, type |::. The vertical bar appears only in the control panel, not in the worksheet. The contents of cells in any row marked by the page-break symbol do not print.

When you print the range containing the page-break symbol, 1-2-3 automatically advances the paper at that point. 1-2-3 then begins to print the data after the page-break symbol on a new page. 1-2-3 does not print anything on the same line as the page-break symbol.

Note: Be careful when entering page breaks into the worksheet, either manually or with the /Worksheet **Page** command. You can accidentally delete the wrong row after you finish printing. Avoid accidents by typing the page-break symbol in the first column in the print range of a blank row. Check to be sure that the row is blank by using the End key and the arrow keys to scan across the row. You can also add a new row with /Worksheet **Insert R**ow.

Stopping the Printer

After starting to print, if you see an error in the worksheet data or print settings, you may decide to correct the error before the report finishes printing. By selecting /**P**rint Cancel, you can stop the current print job and remove any other print jobs from the queue. However, after you have canceled the current print jobs, you cannot restart them. This command cancels reports printed in 1-2-3 (/**P**rint **P**rinter) and Wysiwyg (**:P**rint).

To stop all printing, select /**P**rint Cancel.

When you select /**P**rint Cancel, printing may not stop immediately. This may be true if the printer has an internal print buffer or if your computer has a software print spooler. Turning the printer off for a few seconds clears the printer buffer. If printing resumes when you turn the printer back on, you probably have a print spooler (OS/2 automatically installs one). Refer to the documentation for your print spooler for instructions on how to clear it.

The /**P**rint Cancel command resets 1-2-3's page and line counters to 1. If the printer stops in the middle of a page, you need to take one of the following steps to realign the paper:

1. Turn the printer off. Advance the paper manually to the top of the page. Turn the printer back on, and select /**P**rint **Printer Align**.
2. With the printer on, use /**P**rint **Printer Line** to advance the paper, one line at a time, to the top of the next page. Then select **Align**.

You cannot cancel an individual print job. You must cancel all print jobs or none. In some cases, however, you may want to stop the printer temporarily. For instance, you may need to refill the paper bin or change the ribbon.

To stop the printer temporarily:

1. Select /**P**rint **Suspend**.
2. Select **Quit** to return to the READY mode. You can make changes on your worksheet while 1-2-3 has suspended printing.

Then, after you finish changing the paper or ribbon, start the printer again.

To restart the printer, select /**P**rint **Resume**. You also need to use /**P**rint **Resume** if you selected /**P**rint **Printer Options Advanced Wait Yes** or /**W**orksheet **Global Default Printer Wait Yes**. The printer is therefore at the end of a page, waiting for another sheet of paper.

Another time to use /**P**rint **Resume** is when a printer error has occurred. After correcting the error, invoke /**P**rint **Resume** to clear the error message and resume printing.

8

Changing Headers, Footers, and Margins

If you prepare a report for distribution, you can add some simple enhancements. For example, you can add headers and footers, or you can change the page layout by adjusting the margins and page length.

1-2-3 reserves three lines in a document for a header and an additional three lines for a footer. If specified, headers and footers appear at the top and bottom of each page of your printout. You can keep the six lines reserved for these options (regardless of whether you use them), or you can drop all six lines by selecting the /**Print P**rinter **O**ptions **O**ther Unformatted command (illustrated later in this chapter).

Access the **H**eader and **F**ooter options from the /**Print P**rinter **O**ptions menu. The header or footer can be up to 512 characters of text within one line of your printed output. You can also position the header and footer at the left, right, or center of the page. However, the size of both the paper and the printed characters limits the size of the header and footer lines. For example, when printing on 8 1/2-by-11-inch paper with 1/2-inch margins and 10-characters-per-inch type, you can only print 75 characters in the header or footer.

1-2-3 prints the header text on the first line after any blank top margin lines. The header is followed by two blank header lines for spacing. 1-2-3 prints the footer text line above any blank bottom margin lines and below two blank footer lines (for spacing).

You can manually enter all features of the text. However, 1-2-3 provides special characters for controlling page numbers, the current date, and the positioning of text within a header or footer. The following list shows the characters that you use to place page numbers and dates in headers, and to set the alignment of the header.

Character	Function
#	Automatically prints consecutive page numbers, starting with 1.
##n	Automatically prints consecutive page numbers starting with number n. For example, ##3 is used for a print job with 3 as the page number of the first page.

@   Automatically prints the current date.

| Automatically separates text. Absence of a | symbol left-justifies all text. The first | symbol centers the text that follows. The second | symbol right-justifies remaining text.

\   When followed by a cell address or range name, the backslash fills the header or footer with the contents of the indicated cell. After supplying the backslash, you can use POINT mode to indicate the desired cell. When you include a backslash, 1-2-3 left-aligns and places only the contents of the indicated cell in the header or footer.

To add a header or footer, follow these steps:

1. Select /**Print Printer Range**.

2. Highlight the desired print range and press ⏎Enter.

   For example, highlight the range A1..E11 and press ⏎Enter.

3. Select **Options**.

4. Select **Header** or **Footer**.

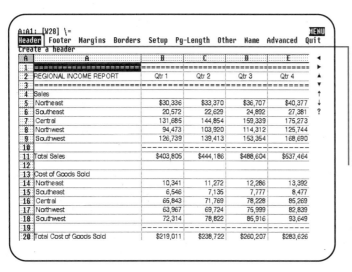

For example, select **Header** to add a header to the report.

5. When the prompt Enter header: or Enter footer: appears, type the text or codes for date and page number and press ⏎Enter.

   For example, type @|**NATIONAL MICRO**|# and press ⏎Enter

8

283

@ | NATIONAL MICRO |

@ tells 1-2-3 to include the date in your header (or footer). Make sure that your computer is set to the correct date.

| tells 1-2-3 how to align the different items in the header (or footer) line.

tells 1-2-3 to print a page number.

6. To return to the main **Print** menu, select **Quit**.

7. Select **Align Go Page Quit**.

To a limited extent, 1-2-3 can insert the contents of a cell into a header or footer. When the prompt to enter a header or footer appears, use the backslash character (\) followed by a cell address or existing range name. Your printed output contains that cell's contents in the header or footer. You cannot, however, use this capability effectively when you want to segment a header or footer into left, center, and right portions.

Note the effect of using an address in the following header lines. Each entry is after the prompt Enter header:.

Entry	Result
\A1	Prints the contents of cell A1 left-justified.
|\A1	Prints the string \A1 (not the contents of cell A1) centered within the header.
@|\A1	Prints the date left-justified and the string \A1 (not the contents of cell A1) centered.
\A3..A6	Prints the contents of cell A3 only, not the range A3..A6.
\SALES	Prints the contents of the range named SALES, if it exists. Otherwise, prints nothing in the header.

Whenever the print range exceeds one single page, 1-2-3 repeats the header on each succeeding page, and the page number increases by one. If you have used the special page-number character (#) and want to print your report a second time before you leave the Print menu, reset the page counter and set the top of the form by selecting **Align** before you choose **Go**.

284

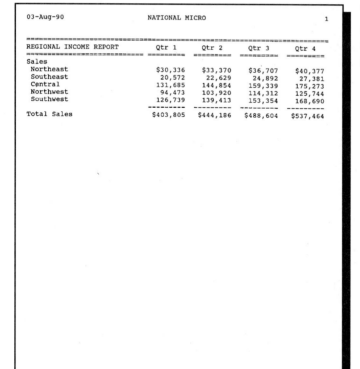

```
03-Aug-90              NATIONAL MICRO                    1

========================================================================
REGIONAL INCOME REPORT      Qtr 1     Qtr 2     Qtr 3     Qtr 4
========================= ========= ========= ========= =========
Sales
  Northeast               $30,336   $33,370   $36,707   $40,377
  Southeast                20,572    22,629    24,892    27,381
  Central                 131,685   144,854   159,339   175,273
  Northwest                94,473   103,920   114,312   125,744
  Southwest               126,739   139,413   153,354   168,690
                         --------- --------- --------- ---------
Total Sales              $403,805  $444,186  $488,604  $537,464
```

The header appears at the top of the printed report.

8

If the centered or right-justified text in your header or footer doesn't print, look at the right-margin setting (discussed in the next section). Make sure that the right margin is appropriate for the current type size and paper width. To change the header, repeat the sequence to establish the text, pressing Esc to remove the display of the existing header from the control panel. (You can delete a header or footer without removing other specified options.)

To print a footer on the last page of a report (or on a single-page report), you must use the **P**age command. If you select the **Q**uit command from the main Print menu without issuing the **P**age command, the final footer does not print. You can, however, reissue the /**P**rint **P**rinter command and select **P**age. In this case, the footer will print.

285

Changing the Page Layout

Before you change the page-layout defaults, be aware of the current settings. 1-2-3 initially assumes 8 1/2-by-11-inch paper, a printer output of 6 lines per inch, and the default length of a page at 66 lines. 1-2-3 reserves 2 lines at the top and bottom of each page for the top and bottom margins. Also, 1-2-3 automatically reserves 3 lines at the top and 3 lines at the bottom for headers and footers. The header or footer takes 1 line, and 2 lines are for spacing before or after the main text.

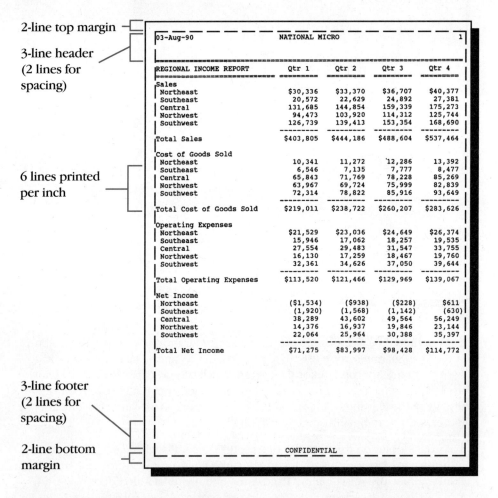

2-line top margin

3-line header
(2 lines for spacing)

6 lines printed per inch

3-line footer
(2 lines for spacing)

2-line bottom margin

03-Aug-90		NATIONAL MICRO		1
REGIONAL INCOME REPORT	Qtr 1	Qtr 2	Qtr 3	Qtr 4
Sales				
Northeast	$30,336	$33,370	$36,707	$40,377
Southeast	20,572	22,629	24,892	27,381
Central	131,685	144,854	159,339	175,273
Northwest	94,473	103,920	114,312	125,744
Southwest	126,739	139,413	153,354	168,690
Total Sales	$403,805	$444,186	$488,604	$537,464
Cost of Goods Sold				
Northeast	10,341	11,272	12,286	13,392
Southeast	6,546	7,135	7,777	8,477
Central	65,843	71,769	78,228	85,269
Northwest	63,967	69,724	75,999	82,839
Southwest	72,314	78,822	85,916	93,649
Total Cost of Goods Sold	$219,011	$238,722	$260,207	$283,626
Operating Expenses				
Northeast	$21,529	$23,036	$24,649	$26,374
Southeast	15,946	17,062	18,257	19,535
Central	27,554	29,483	31,547	33,755
Northwest	16,130	17,259	18,467	19,760
Southwest	32,361	34,626	37,050	39,644
Total Operating Expenses	$113,520	$121,466	$129,969	$139,067
Net Income				
Northeast	($1,534)	($938)	($228)	$611
Southeast	(1,920)	(1,568)	(1,142)	(630)
Central	38,289	43,602	49,564	56,249
Northwest	14,376	16,937	19,846	23,144
Southwest	22,064	25,964	30,388	35,397
Total Net Income	$71,275	$83,997	$98,428	$114,772

CONFIDENTIAL

If you want to check the default settings for margins and page length, select /Worksheet Global Default Status.

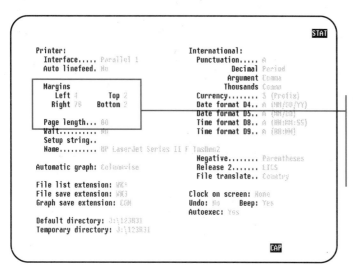

The Default
Settings sheet
appears on-screen,
showing the
current margins
and page length.

To change the page layout of the current worksheet, follow these steps:

1. Select **/Print Printer Options Margins**.

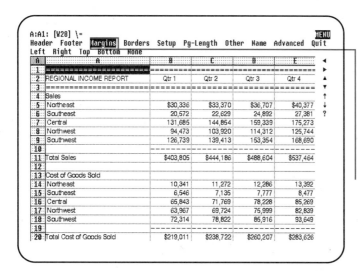

The **Margins**
option allows you
to change the size
of the margins in
the printed report.

2. Select **Left**, **Right**, **Top**, **Bottom**, or **None** from the **Margins** menu.

3. In response to the prompt to enter the margin, type a value within the indicated range and press ⏎Enter.

When you select **Left**, 1-2-3 asks you to enter a new left margin setting from 0 through 1000 characters. To change the right margin, select **Right** and enter a value from 0 through 1000 at the `Enter Right Margin:` prompt. For the top and bottom margins, select **Top** or **Bottom** and enter a margin line specification from 0 through 240.

Be sure that you set left and right margins consistent with the width of your paper and the printer's pitch (characters per inch). The right margin must be greater than the left margin. Make sure that settings for the top and bottom margins are consistent with the paper's length and the established number of lines per inch. 1-2-3 shows the options and messages in table 8.2 when you change margin settings.

Table 8.2
Selections for Changing Margin Settings

Selection	Message
Left	`Enter Left Margin (0..1000):xx`
Right	`Enter Right Margin (0..1000):xx`
Top	`Enter Top Margin (0..240):xx`
Bottom	`Enter Bottom Margin (0..240):xx`
None	Sets left, top, and bottom margins to 0; sets right margin to 1000

The `xx` at the end of each line indicates the current setting, which you can change. Notice that the **None** option of the **Margins** menu resets the left, top, and bottom margins to zero, and the right margin to 1000.

To maximize the output on every printed page of a large worksheet, you can use the **/Print Printer Options Other Unformatted** command. This command ignores margins, headers, and footers. This chapter covers this command in the section "Preparing Output for Other Programs." You can also use setup strings that condense print and increase the number of lines per inch.

Enhancing Your Reports

After you print a draft worksheet report, you may want to change the font, spacing, or orientation of your worksheet. You may want to add a graph to the worksheet and print a range with the graph. These same enhancements are also available in Wysiwyg. Wysiwyg has the advantage of allowing you to see your enhancements on the screen, plus it offers additional options. Refer to Chapter 9 for information on formatting your spreadsheets with Wysiwyg.

Printer Options

Some printers do not support all the advanced options. You can use /**Print Printer S**ample to print a sample printout that shows which of the advanced options your printer supports. This sample includes the following information:

- A list of your current print settings.
- A small predefined worksheet printed with the current print options, except **B**orders.
- Printer capabilities, including fonts 1 through 8, colors 1 through 8, and options for pitch and line spacing.
- A sample graph using the current graph options plus samples of font options and text sizes for graphs.

To print a sample of what your printer can do:

1. Select /**Print Printer S**ample **G**o.
2. Select **Q**uit to return to READY mode.

Squeezing a Worksheet to One Page

For some reports you need to put a lot of information on one page. Many annual budgets and projections require that you work with 12 months. You cannot print all twelve months of a worksheet if you use the standard print settings. To squeeze a lot on one page, you can change the pitch (size of print), line-spacing, and orientation (vertical or horizontal).

The pitch affects character size and thus the number of characters printed on each line. The choices available with the **P**itch option are **S**tandard, **C**ompressed, and **E**xpanded. Again, the actual effect of each of these options depends on your printer. Typical pitch settings are 5 characters per inch (cpi) for **E**xpanded, 10 cpi for **S**tandard, and 17 cpi for **C**ompressed. You do not see the pitch change on the screen. Wysiwyg, on the other hand, does show you type sizes on the screen.

To print a large worksheet on one page, follow these steps:

1. Select /**Print Printer O**ptions **A**dvanced **L**ayout.

1-2-3 shows four options after you choose **Layout**. You use all these options in this example.

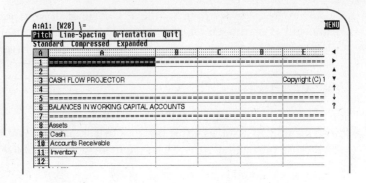

2. To change the character size, select **Pitch**.

3. Select **Standard** for normal size characters, **Compressed** for small characters, or **Expanded** for large characters.

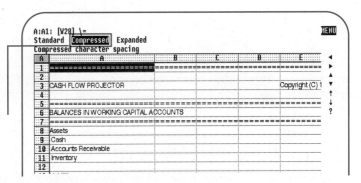

In this example, select **Compressed**.

Note: If you select compressed pitch, you probably should change the line spacing to **Compressed** also.

4. Select **Line-Spacing**.

5. Select **Compressed** to print small characters. For many printers, compressed line spacing is 8 lines per inch. Selecting **Standard** returns to normal line spacing. Many printers use 6 lines per inch.

6. Choose **Compressed** for this example.

8

Finally, you can change the orientation of printing on the paper.

1. Select **Orientation**.

2. To print lines in the usual manner, with the page situated vertically, select **Portrait**. Select **Landscape** to print so you arrange the page horizontally, and the lines of text print sideways on the page.

Not all printers support **Landscape** mode, although all laser printers do. If your printer cannot print in **Landscape**, selecting this mode has no effect on the output. When you select **Landscape** mode, 1-2-3 does not automatically adjust margins and page length. You must change these settings manually to reflect the new orientation.

The worksheet page printed with compressed line spacing and pitch with landscape orientation.

8

Selecting Fonts

With the /**Print Printer Options Advanced Fonts** option, you can specify the fonts, or type styles, to print on different sections of each page. 1-2-3 offers eight different fonts, numbered as shown here:

Font 1	Normal serif
Font 2	Bold serif
Font 3	Italic serif
Font 4	Bold italic serif
Font 5	Normal sans serif
Font 6	Bold sans serif
Font 7	Italic sans serif
Font 8	Bold italic sans serif

You can see what these fonts look like by using the /**Print Printer Sample** command mentioned earlier in this chapter. The number of these fonts available to you depends on your printer. Some printers have all eight fonts, and other printers have only one or two. You can specify different fonts for different areas of the report.

To select fonts, follow these steps:

1. Select /**Print Printer Options Advanced Fonts.**

The control panel shows which areas of the worksheet you can change.

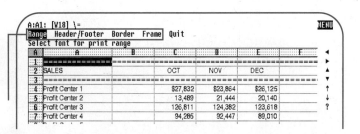

8

2. Select one of the following: **Range**, **Header/Footer**, **Border**, or **Frame**.

3. 1-2-3 next displays the numbers 1 through 8 corresponding to the preceding fonts. Choose the desired font.

4. If desired, repeat Steps 2 and 3 to select other parts of the worksheet.

5. Select **Quit** three times to return to the **Print** menu.

6. If necessary, select other options. Select **Align** **G**o **P**age **Quit** to print and return to READY mode.

If you don't specify any fonts, or if your printer does not support the specified font, 1-2-3 uses font 1 for all sections of the report.

Printing a Listing of Cell Contents

You can spend hours developing and debugging a model worksheet and additional time entering and verifying data. You should safeguard your work by making backup copies of your important files on disk. You can also print a listing of the cell contents of important worksheets. Be aware, however, that this print job can eat up lots of time (and paper) if you have a large worksheet.

You can produce printed documentation of cell contents by selecting **/Print Printer Options Other**. Then select either **Cell-Formulas** or **As**-Displayed. Choosing **Cell-Formulas** produces a list with one cell per line showing the cell format, the width of the cell (if different from the default), the cell-protection status, and the contents of cells (including any formulas) in the print range. With **As**-Displayed, the data prints as it is on-screen.

To print a cell-by-cell listing of the contents of a particular range, follow these steps:

1. Select **/Print Printer Options Other**.

2. Select **Cell-Formulas** to print a listing of formulas in cells, or select **As**-Displayed to print the range as it appears on-screen.

8

293

```
A:A45: [W28] 'Gross Profit on Sales                          MENU
As-Displayed  Cell-Formulas  Formatted  Unformatted  Blank-Header
List entries, one per line
```

	A	B	C	D	E	
42						◄
43	REGIONAL RATIO ANALYSIS	Jan	Feb	Mar	Apr	▶
44						▲
45	Gross Profit on Sales					▼
46	Northeast	65.9%	66.2%	66.5%	66.8%	↑
47	Southeast	68.2%	68.5%	68.8%	69.0%	↓
48	Central	50.0%	50.5%	50.9%	51.4%	?
49	Northwest	32.3%	32.9%	33.5%	34.1%	
50	Southwest	42.9%	43.5%	44.0%	44.5%	
51	Total	45.8%	46.3%	46.7%	47.2%	
52						
53	Return on Sales					
54	Northeast	−5.1%	−2.8%	−0.6%	1.5%	
55	Southeast	−9.3%	−6.9%	−4.6%	−2.3%	
56	Central	29.1%	30.1%	31.1%	32.1%	
57	Northwest	15.2%	16.3%	17.4%	18.4%	
58	Southwest	17.4%	18.6%	19.8%	21.0%	
59	Total	17.7%	18.9%	20.1%	21.4%	
60						
61						

In this example, select Cell-Formulas.

3. To return to the main **Print** menu, select **Quit**.

4. Select **Range**, highlight the range of cells you want printed, and then press ⏎Enter.

```
A:E59: (P1) +E38/E11                                         POINT
Enter print range: A:A45..A:E59
```

	A	B	C	D	E	
42						◄
43	REGIONAL RATIO ANALYSIS	Jan	Feb	Mar	Apr	▶
44						▲
45	Gross Profit on Sales					▼
46	Northeast	65.9%	66.2%	66.5%	66.8%	↑
47	Southeast	68.2%	68.5%	68.8%	69.0%	↓
48	Central	50.0%	50.5%	50.9%	51.4%	?
49	Northwest	32.3%	32.9%	33.5%	34.1%	
50	Southwest	42.9%	43.5%	44.0%	44.5%	
51	Total	45.8%	46.3%	46.7%	47.2%	
52						
53	Return on Sales					
54	Northeast	−5.1%	−2.8%	−0.6%	1.5%	
55	Southeast	−9.3%	−6.9%	−4.6%	−2.3%	
56	Central	29.1%	30.1%	31.1%	32.1%	
57	Northwest	15.2%	16.3%	17.4%	18.4%	
58	Southwest	17.4%	18.6%	19.8%	21.0%	
59	Total	17.7%	18.9%	20.1%	21.4%	
60						
61						

In this example, highlight the range A45..E59 as the range to print and press ⏎Enter.

5. Select **Align Go Page Quit**.

1-2-3 lists each entry in the resulting printout in the following format.

294

Each entry begins with the location of the cell.

The entry ends with the actual contents of the cell, in this case a formula.

A:C47: (P1) [W11] (C6-C15)/C6

If the format of the cell is different from the default global format, 1-2-3 prints within parentheses a notation for the cell's format.

If the column width of the cell is different from the default global column width, 1-2-3 indicates within square brackets the column width.

```
A:A45: [W28] 'Gross Profit on Sales
A:A46: [W28] ' Northeast
A:B46: (P1) (B5-B14)/B5
A:C46: (P1) [W11] (C5-C14)/C5
A:D46: (P1) [W11] (D5-D14)/D5
A:E46: (P1) (E5-E14)/E5
A:A47: [W28] ' Southeast
A:B47: (P1) (B6-B15)/B6
A:C47: (P1) [W11] (C6-C15)/C6
A:D47: (P1) [W11] (D6-D15)/D6
A:E47: (P1) (E6-E15)/E6
A:A48: [W28] ' Central
A:B48: (P1) (B7-B16)/B7
A:C48: (P1) [W11] (C7-C16)/C7
A:D48: (P1) [W11] (D7-D16)/D7
A:E48: (P1) (E7-E16)/E7
A:A49: [W28] ' Northwest
A:B49: (P1) (B8-B17)/B8
A:C49: (P1) [W11] (C8-C17)/C8
A:D49: (P1) [W11] (D8-D17)/D8
A:E49: (P1) (E8-E17)/E8
A:A50: [W28] ' Southwest
A:B50: (P1) (B9-B18)/B9
A:C50: (P1) [W11] (C9-C18)/C9
A:D50: (P1) [W11] (D9-D18)/D9
A:E50: (P1) (E9-E18)/E9
A:A51: [W28] ' Total
A:B51: (P1) (B11-B20)/B11
A:C51: (P1) [W11] (C11-C20)/C11
A:D51: (P1) [W11] (D11-D20)/D11
A:E51: (P1) (E11-E20)/E11
A:A53: [W28] 'Return on Sales
A:A54: [W28] ' Northeast
A:B54: (P1) +B32/B5
A:C54: (P1) [W11] +C32/C5
A:D54: (P1) [W11] +D32/D5
A:E54: (P1) +E32/E5
A:A55: [W28] ' Southeast
A:B55: (P1) +B33/B6
A:C55: (P1) [W11] +C33/C6
A:D55: (P1) [W11] +D33/D6
A:E55: (P1) +E33/E6
A:A56: [W28] ' Central
A:B56: (P1) +B34/B7
A:C56: (P1) [W11] +C34/C7
A:D56: (P1) [W11] +D34/D7
A:E56: (P1) +E34/E7
A:A57: [W28] ' Northwest
A:B57: (P1) +B35/B8
A:C57: (P1) [W11] +C35/C8
A:D57: (P1) [W11] +D35/D8
A:E57: (P1) +E35/E8
A:A58: [W28] ' Southwest
A:B58: (P1) +B36/B9
```

1-2-3 prints the contents of each cell, moving horizontally across each row of the print range.

8

295

Naming and Saving the Current Print Settings

If you have a large worksheet, you may want to print different areas of the worksheet with different print options. Instead of resetting the options for each range or creating complex print macros, you can save your print settings.

To save the print settings, follow these steps:

1. Select /**Print Printer Options Name**.

The following menu appears. In this example select **Create**.

```
A:A1: [W18] \=                                          MENU
Use  Create  Delete  Reset  Table
Create a print settings name
A          A             B      C        D        E       F
1 =============================================================
2 SALES                        OCT      NOV      DEC
3 =============================================================
4 Profit Center 1              $27,832  $23,864  $26,125
5 Profit Center 2              13,489   21,444   20,140
6 Profit Center 3              126,811  124,382  123,618
7 Profit Center 4              94,285   92,447   89,010
```

8

2. Select **Create** to save your print options and range.

3. Type a name for your settings. The name can contain up to 15 characters and can include any combination of letters, numbers, and symbols—except two less-than symbols (<<). If you type a print-settings name already in use, 1-2-3 replaces the original settings associated with that name with the current settings.

4. To return to READY mode, select **Quit** twice.

To use a named print setting, follow these steps:

1. Select /**Print Printer Options Name Use**.

2. Type or highlight the print settings name, and press ⏎Enter.

   If there are many print settings, press F3 to see a full list.

Make sure you save the worksheet with /**File Save** to save the print-settings names with the worksheet.

Clearing the Print Options

When you select **Print** options, 1-2-3 automatically saves the settings you specify with the worksheet when you select /**File Save**. Saving the settings with the worksheet for a future print job is a good practice, rather than clearing them after each printing. You can then quickly make minor changes to the existing settings.

At times, however, you would benefit by clearing all or some of the print settings. You can do this with the /**Print Printer Clear** command. For example, you may want to print a report in the same worksheet from which you printed earlier, but specify a different print range. You can use /**Print Printer Clear Range** to eliminate only the range setting. All other print settings remain intact. The /**Print Printer Clear All** command can prove to be helpful when a report isn't printing properly.

To clear some or all print settings, follow these steps:

1. Select /**Print Printer Clear**.

```
A:A45: [W28] 'Gross Profit on Sales                          MENU
All  Range  Borders  Format  Image  Device
Return all printer settings to defaults
  A                A             B       C       D       E       ◄
 42 ================================================================  ►
 43 REGIONAL RATIO ANALYSIS     Jan     Feb     Mar     Apr        ▲
 44 ================================================================  ▼
 45 Gross Profit on Sales                                           ↑
 46 Northeast                   65.9%   66.2%   66.5%   66.8%       ↓
 47 Southeast                   68.2%   68.5%   68.8%   69.0%       ?
 48 Central                     50.0%   50.5%   50.9%   51.4%
 49 Northwest                   32.3%   32.9%   33.5%   34.1%
 50 Southwest                   42.9%   43.5%   44.0%   44.5%
 51 Total                       45.8%   46.3%   46.7%   47.2%
 52
 53 Return on Sales
 54 Northeast                   -5.1%   -2.8%   -0.6%    1.5%
 55 Southeast                   -9.3%   -6.9%   -4.6%   -2.3%
 56 Central                     29.1%   30.1%   31.1%   32.1%
 57 Northwest                   15.2%   16.3%   17.4%   18.4%
 58 Southwest                   17.4%   18.6%   19.8%   21.0%
 59 Total                       17.7%   18.9%   20.1%   21.4%
 60
 61
```

1-2-3 displays the menu selections for clearing **Print** options.

2. Select **All**, **Range**, **Borders**, **Format**, **Image**, or **Device**. Table 8.3 describes each selection.

Table 8.3
Selections on the /Print Printer Clear Menu

Selection	Description
All	Clears every **Print** option, including the print range.
Range	Removes only the previous print-range specification.
Borders	Cancels only **Columns** and **Rows** specified as borders.
Format	Returns **Margins**, **Pg-Length**, and **Setup** string settings to the default settings displayed in the /**Worksheet Global Default** screen.
Image	Clears graphs selected for printing.
Device	Returns device name and interface to defaults.

Preparing Output for Other Programs

8

Many word processing and other software packages import ASCII text files. You can successfully export 1-2-3 files to other programs if you select several **Print** command sequences that eliminate unwanted print options. The primary command you use during this procedure is /**Print File Options Other Unformatted**. This section shows you how to use this command to create a PRN file that you can later import to another program.

To prepare output for other programs, follow these steps:

1. Select /**Print File** to print to a disk rather than to a printer.

2. Specify a file name with up to eight characters to direct output to a PRN file rather than to a printer. Then press ⏎Enter .

In this example, type **a:\salesrpt** and press ⏎Enter to direct the output to a PRN file named SALESRPT on drive A.

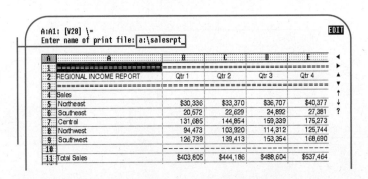

3. Select **Range**, specify the range you want to send to the PRN file, and press ⏎Enter.

In this example, select **Range**, highlight the range A1..E11, and press ⏎Enter.

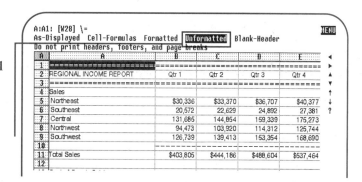

```
A:E11: (C0) @SUM(E5..E9)                                    POINT
Enter print range: A:A1..A:E11
```

	A	B	C	D	E
2	REGIONAL INCOME REPORT	Qtr 1	Qtr 2	Qtr 3	Qtr 4
4	Sales				
5	Northeast	$30,336	$33,370	$36,707	$40,377
6	Southeast	20,572	22,629	24,892	27,381
7	Central	131,685	144,854	159,339	175,273
8	Northwest	94,473	103,920	114,312	125,744
9	Southwest	126,739	139,413	153,354	168,690
10					
11	Total Sales	$403,805	$444,186	$488,604	$537,464
12					
13	Cost of Goods Sold				
14	Northeast	10,341	11,272	12,286	13,392
15	Southeast	6,546	7,135	7,777	8,477
16	Central	65,843	71,769	78,228	85,269
17	Northwest	63,967	69,724	75,999	82,839
18	Southwest	72,314	78,822	85,916	93,649
19					
20	Total Cost of Goods Sold	$219,011	$238,722	$260,207	$283,626

4. Select **Options Other Unformatted**.

The Unformatted option removes all headers, footers, and page breaks from a print operation.

```
A:A1: [W28] \=                                             MENU
As-Displayed  Cell-Formulas  Formatted  Unformatted  Blank-Header
Do not print headers, footers, and page breaks
```

	A	B	C	D	E
2	REGIONAL INCOME REPORT	Qtr 1	Qtr 2	Qtr 3	Qtr 4
4	Sales				
5	Northeast	$30,336	$33,370	$36,707	$40,377
6	Southeast	20,572	22,629	24,892	27,381
7	Central	131,685	144,854	159,339	175,273
8	Northwest	94,473	103,920	114,312	125,744
9	Southwest	126,739	139,413	153,354	168,690
10					
11	Total Sales	$403,805	$444,186	$488,604	$537,464
12					

8

5. Select **Quit** to return to the main Print menu.
6. To create the PRN file on disk, select **Go**.

Note: The **Align** and **Page** commands are not necessary when you create a PRN file. You do not use printer paper for this command.

7. To return to READY mode, select **Quit**.
8. Follow the instructions in your word processing or other software package to import the specially-prepared 1-2-3 disk files.

Summary

This chapter showed you how to print reports by selecting the /Print command from 1-2-3's main menu. You can use the /Print Printer command to print a report to a printer, or the /Print File command to create a PRN or encoded file on disk that you or someone else can print later.

You learned how to print a document of one page or less. You learned how to add borders to a multipage report and to hide worksheet segments within the print range. You also learned how to control paper movement with the Line, Page, and Align options. Additionally, you learned how to create page breaks within a worksheet.

The chapter showed ways to enhance printouts. You can add headers and footers that can include the date and a page number. You can also change the layout of a page by adjusting the margins and the page length. Other ways to enhance printouts include compressing the print and changing fonts.

Specifically, you learned the following key information about 1-2-3:

■ The /Print Printer command prints reports on a printer. The /Print File filename command "prints" a range to a file that you can import to other software packages.

■ The /Print Encoded command prints a range to a file as well. However, the commands to control the printer are also in the file. You can later print this file from your operating system, and it will contain all your printing enhancements.

■ If you have everything defined for your print range and options, use /Print Printer Align Go Page Quit. This command sets the printer at the top of the page, prints your worksheet range, moves the paper back to the top of the page, and returns to READY mode.

■ The /Print Printer Options Borders command enables you to print specified rows or columns on each page of a printed report.

■ You can print multiple ranges using the same /Print Printer Range command. Separate multiple ranges with commas.

■ When you are printing reports, you can hide specific rows, columns, or ranges. Hide columns by selecting /Worksheet Column Hide after you specify a print range. Hide rows by entering the symbol for nonprinting—two vertical bars (||)—in the first cell of the row. Hide ranges with the command /Range Format Hidden.

■ The **/Print Printer Line** command advances the paper one line in the printer. The **/Print Printer Page** command advances the paper to the top of the next page.

■ The **/Print Printer Align** command makes sure that printing begins at the top of all succeeding pages after the first. Before printing, always make sure that you have correctly positioned your printer paper.

■ Stop all printing with the **/Print Cancel** command. To stop printing temporarily, use **/Print Suspend**. To restart printing after temporarily stopping it or after a printer error message, use **/Print Resume**.

■ If you want to add a header or footer, use **/Print Printer Options Header** or **Footer**. To add a page number include a # in the header or footer. To add today's date, include an @.

■ The **/Print Printer Options Margins** command changes the left, right, top, or bottom margin for your printout.

■ To print a sample of your printer fonts and other capabilities, use the **/Print Printer Sample** command.

■ To squeeze a large worksheet onto one page use **/Print Printer Options Advance Layout** command. The **Pitch** option makes your text smaller or larger. The **Line-Spacing** option makes the space between lines smaller. The **Orientation** option enables you to print your text sideways on some printers.

■ The **/Print Printer Options Other Cell-Formulas** command prints a cell-by-cell listing of a specified range. The listing includes the cell's location, format, width, protection status, and contents (including formulas). The **/Print Printer Options Other As-Displayed** command prints cell contents as they appear on-screen.

■ If you want to save your range and print options, use **/Print Printer Options Name**.

■ The **/Print Printer Clear** command clears some or all of a worksheet's print settings. **/Print Printer Clear Range** clears only the specified print range. **/Print Printer Clear All** clears all settings, including the print range, borders, margins, and other settings.

■ **/Print File Options Other Unformatted** allows extra lines to print on the page by dropping margins and page breaks from the printout.

The next chapter shows you how to use the Wysiwyg add-in program to enhance the appearance of your printed output. You learn how to incorporate different sizes and styles of typefaces, shading, outlining, grids, and much more.

8

Printing with Wysiwyg

9

How you present yourself and your work determines your ability to convince other people. To be successful, people keep fit, smile, and dress for success.

1-2-3 now offers an option to "dress up" your work. Lotus calls this option Wysiwyg, an acronym for "What-You-See-Is-What-You-Get." This add-in offers a spreadsheet publishing choice to users of 1-2-3 Release 3.1. In this environment, the screen reflects fancy formatting (for example, lines, shading, fonts). Also, the spreadsheet prints exactly as it appears on-screen. Built into Wysiwyg is the capability to use a mouse to move the cell pointer, access the 1-2-3 and Wysiwyg menus, and select ranges.

Wysiwyg enables you to produce printed 1-2-3 reports that incorporate a variety of type fonts, lines, shadings, and other formatting features such as boldface, italics, underlining, and color. You can also change the appearance of text and graphics on the monitor for easier viewing and editing. Through menu choices, you can quickly change between portrait and landscape modes for certain printers; add worksheet column, row, and sheet indicators to your printout; add a grid; and compress your range so that it will automatically fit on one page.

In addition to enhanced text formatting, Wysiwyg enables you to embed 1-2-3 graphs in your printouts and use a graphics editor to embellish your graphs. Chapter 12 covers the graphing aspects of Wysiwyg.

Key Terms in This Chapter

Typeface	The design of a character set, such as Swiss or Dutch.
Font	A character set displaying a particular size and style of typeface, such as 12-point Swiss.
Point size	The size of a particular font. One point is equal to 1/72 of an inch; therefore, 12-point Swiss is about 1/6 of an inch high.
Soft fonts	Soft fonts are provided with Wysiwyg. These include various sizes and styles of Swiss, Dutch, Courier, and a symbol font set.
Wysiwyg	"What-You-See-Is-What-You-Get." The capability to see on-screen graphical changes (fonts, outlining, bold) as you make them on the spreadsheet. The 1-2-3 Release 3.1 Wysiwyg add-in provides this capability.

Using the Mouse

9

To use a mouse with 1-2-3 Release 3.1, you need a mouse, mouse software, and a graphics monitor and graphics card that support a mouse. Also, Wysiwyg must be loaded into memory. You can use a mouse to select commands and files, specify ranges, and move the cell pointer within a worksheet or between multiple worksheets and files. In the examples throughout this chapter, notice that the 1-2-3 commands always begin with a slash (/), and the Wysiwyg commands always begin with a colon (:). Refer to the following sections of the specified chapters for further information on using the mouse.

- Chapter 2—"Understanding Mouse Terminology"
- Chapter 3—"Mouse Control of the Cell Pointer"
     "Using the Mouse To Select Menu Commands"
- Chapter 4—"Using the Mouse To Specify Ranges"

Comparing Reports Printed with 1-2-3 and Wysiwyg

If you compare a worksheet printed with 1-2-3 /**P**rint commands and one printed with Wysiwyg, you see a dramatic difference.

```
LaserPro Corporation
Balance Sheet
October 1, 1990


ASSETS


                                This Year   Last Year    Change
    Current Assets
    Cash                           247,886     126,473      96%
    Accounts receivable            863,652     524,570      65%
    Inventory                       79,071      53,790      47%
    Prepaid expenses                 9,257      11,718     -21%
    Investments                    108,577      31,934     240%
            Total Current Assets 1,308,443     748,485      75%

    Fixed Assets
    Machinery and equipment        209,906     158,730      32%
    Vehicles                       429,505     243,793      76%
    Office furniture                50,240      36,406      38%
    (Accumulated depreciation)    (101,098)    (64,394)     57%
            Total Fixed Assets     588,553     374,535      57%
                                $1,896,996  $1,123,020      69%


LIABILITIES AND SHAREHOLDERS' EQUITY


                                This Year   Last Year    Change
    Current Liabilities
    Accounts payable trade         426,041     332,845      28%
    Notes payable                   45,327      23,486      93%
    Accrued liabilities             34,614      26,026      33%
    Income taxes payable            88,645      51,840      71%
            Total Current Liabilities 594,627  434,197      37%

    Noncurrent Liabilities
    Long-term debt                 488,822     349,253      40%
    Deferred federal tax           147,844      92,101      61%
            Total Noncurrent Liabilities 636,666 441,354    44%

    Shareholders' equity
    Common stock                     1,000       1,000       0%
    Opening retained earnings      246,469      82,531     199%
    Profit (loss) for the period   418,234     163,938     155%
            Total Shareholders' Equity 665,703  247,469    169%
                                $1,896,996  $1,123,020      69%
```

1-2-3's /**P**rint **P**rinter command created this report.

Wysiwyg created
this report.

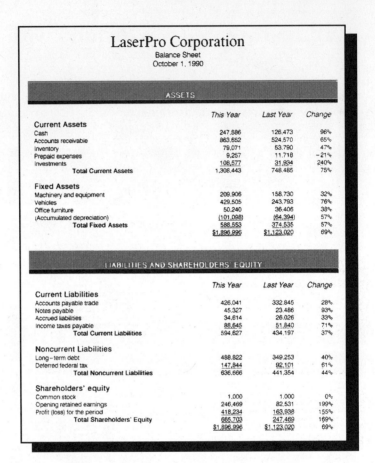

9

Understanding How 1-2-3 and Wysiwyg Work Together

1-2-3 Release 3.1 integrates more closely with Wysiwyg than Allways integrates with Release 2.2. You do not need to switch between the graphical and the standard interface because there is now only one interface: the graphical. When you start Wysiwyg, the screen looks similar to the following figures. You are in READY mode. You can now move the cell pointer, make cell entries, bring up the menu with the slash key, and do many more things that are discussed later.

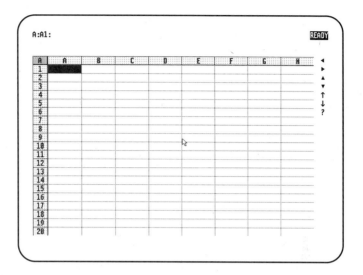

The Worksheet
screen with
Wysiwyg loaded.

In Wysiwyg, you have two menus available to you. As always, the slash key
displays the standard 1-2-3 menu. To display the Wysiwyg menu, press the
colon (:). Use Esc to back out of any displayed menu.

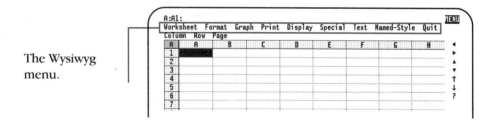

The Wysiwyg
menu.

9

Another way to display the menus is with the mouse. A menu automatically
appears when you place the mouse pointer in the control panel. The menu that
displays depends on which menu you used last; to switch to the other menu,
press the right mouse button. The right mouse button switches you back and
forth between the two menus.

Wysiwyg menus work the same way as 1-2-3 menus: select a command by typing
the first letter or by highlighting it and pressing Enter. Each of the Wysiwyg
options is explained in this chapter.

Saving Your Wysiwyg Formatting

Wysiwyg stores the enhanced formatting information in its own file, separate from the worksheet file. The Wysiwyg file has the same first name as your 1-2-3 file, but with an FM3 extension. For example, if you save a worksheet file called BUDGET.WK3 with Wysiwyg attached, Wysiwyg saves an associated BUDGET.FM3 file. This file contains all the formatting enhancements selected with Wysiwyg.

Wysiwyg saves enhanced formatting only when you use the 1-2-3 /File Save command to save the current 1-2-3 worksheet. If you choose Detach (Alt-F10), you erase Wysiwyg from memory and therefore can no longer save enhanced formatting. If you detach Wysiwyg before you save the worksheet, the program does not update your FM3 file and you may lose much of your special formatting work.

Do not modify the structure of a Wysiwyg-formatted spreadsheet without attaching Wysiwyg. If you delete, insert, or move anything, the formatting will not match the same cells the next time you attach Wysiwyg.

Learning To Format with Wysiwyg

The heart of Wysiwyg's power is its capability to add professional formatting touches. The 1-2-3 formats—numeric display and label alignment—carry through automatically to Wysiwyg. Wysiwyg's formats determine the printed typeface, character size, boldface, and other stylistic features such as lines and shading.

Wysiwyg's additional formats provide many ways to enhance the appearance of printed text. To assign a Wysiwyg format to a cell or range, use the Wysiwyg :Format command. To determine the format of a cell, move the cell pointer to the cell. The format displays at the top of the screen, next to the current-cell address. If you use Wysiwyg in graphics mode (the default), you actually see the formatting on the screen.

Selecting from a Variety of Fonts

One of the highlights of Wysiwyg is its capability to use different fonts. A font consists of a typeface (for example, Times Roman) and a point size. A *point* is a unit of measurement used in publishing, equal to 1/72 of an inch. The larger the point size, the larger the type. Your choice of fonts depends on your printer; Wysiwyg can use any font your printer can print.

Wysiwyg comes with four soft fonts: Swiss, Dutch, Courier, and XSymbol. A *soft font* is a file on disk that specifies to a printer how to make a font. Your program sends soft fonts to the printer's memory before it prints the document, so the printer can use the information to print the document. If you have a dot-matrix printer, Wysiwyg uses its graphics mode to produce these fonts. If you have a laser printer, Wysiwyg downloads these four fonts automatically to your printer when you use them. Your printer, however, may not have enough memory for many different fonts or larger point sizes.

If your printer provides additional fonts, these fonts also are available to Wysiwyg. The Hewlett-Packard LaserJet comes with two built-in fonts (Courier and Line Printer), and you can purchase dozens of cartridges to access additional fonts.

Each worksheet can use up to eight different fonts. Wysiwyg stores these eight fonts in a *font set*. The font list displayed in the following figure is the default font set, comprised primarily of Swiss and Dutch fonts.

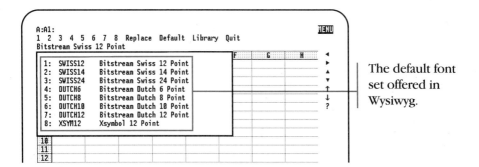

The default font set offered in Wysiwyg.

9

With Wysiwyg, you can format each cell or range of cells with a different font, and you can use up to eight fonts for a single worksheet. By default, however, Wysiwyg assigns all cells to font 1. The following figure shows examples of the default fonts.

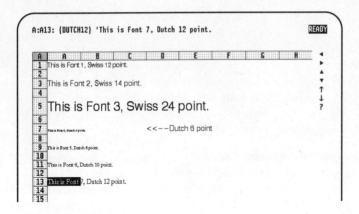

Examples of Wysiwyg's default fonts.

Changing the Font for a Range of the Worksheet

You assign a font to a cell or range with the Wysiwyg :Format Font command. Follow these steps:

1. Select :Format.

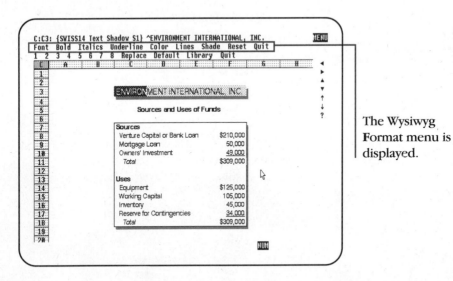

The Wysiwyg Format menu is displayed.

2. Select Font.

3. Type the number of the font desired.

4. Indicate the range where you want the font by highlighting the range (as you would in 1-2-3); then press ⏎Enter.

9

If necessary, Wysiwyg adjusts the height of the row to conform to the tallest point size present.

Choosing Alternative Fonts for the Entire Worksheet

If you want to replace all occurrences of one font with another, regardless of where they occur in the worksheet, use the command sequence **:Format Font Replace**. This command lists the fonts from which you can choose.

To change one font used throughout the worksheet to a different one, follow these steps:

1. Select **:Format Font Replace**.
2. Type the number of the font to change and press ↵Enter.
3. Select the new typeface from the following menu:

   ```
   Swiss  Dutch  Courier  XSymbol  Other
   ```
4. Type the new point size and press ↵Enter.

Two factors determine the available typeface and point sizes. First, typeface and point size depend on which fonts you generated when you installed 1-2-3. Second, they depend on which fonts your printer supports (including soft fonts and cartridges). If you select a font your printer cannot use, Wysiwyg will substitute a similar typeface.

9

A range of fonts including point sizes from 3 to 72, font cartridges, and downloadable fonts.

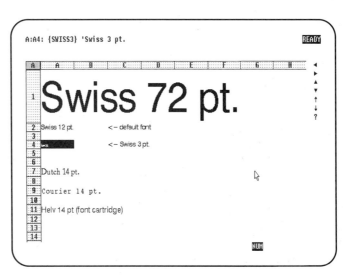

The XSymbol font contains *dingbats*, special characters such as arrows and circled numbers. Figure 10 shows different letters and numbers formatted with the XSymbol font. For example, if you enter a lowercase *a* in a cell and format it to XSymbol font, the screen displays a right arrow.

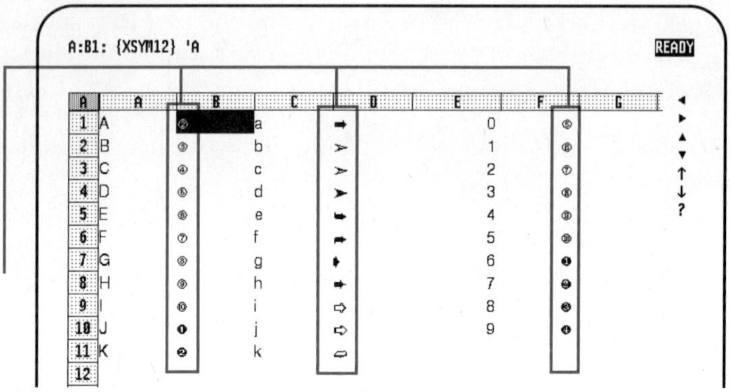

Examples of the XSymbol font characters (dingbats).

All cells automatically display font 1. Thus, when you replace font 1 with a different font, all cells not assigned to other font numbers change to the new font 1.

After experimenting with Wysiwyg, you may decide that a particular group of fonts is the one you normally want to use. Wysiwyg lets you store a group of font selections in a file so you can access those fonts later.

To store a set of fonts in a file, follow these steps:

1. Select :Format Font Library Save.
2. Type the name of the file and press ↵Enter. Wysiwyg saves your file with an AF3 extension.

To recall these groups of fonts, use the :Format Font Library Retrieve command.

If you find that you frequently retrieve the same font library, make it the default font set. To do this, retrieve the font library you want as the default and select :Format Font Default Update.

Using Shading

The :Format Shade command enables you to highlight important areas on the printed worksheet. The net income row and heading in the following figure stand out because of the background shading.

312

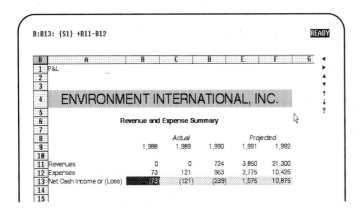

Headings and important values are emphasized with dark and light shades.

Using Light and Dark Shading

If you use light or dark shading on cells with data, the contents will remain visible through the shading. To shade a range with light shading, use the **:Format Shade Light** command; for dark shading, use the **:Format Shade Dark** command.

To highlight or accent portions of a worksheet with light or dark shading, follow these steps:

1. Select **:Format Shade**.

9

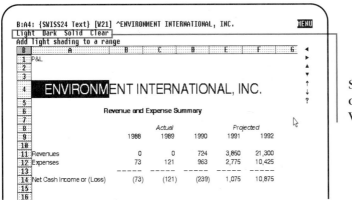

Shading options offered in Wysiwyg.

2. If you want light shading, select **Light**. If you want dark shading, select **Dark**.

3. Highlight the range you want to shade and press ⏎Enter .

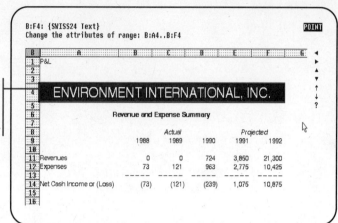

In this example, highlight the range A4..F4 and press ↵Enter.

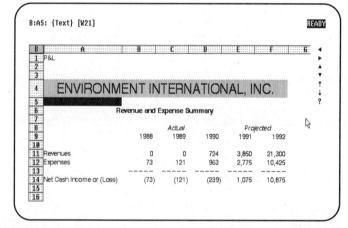

The shading appears on-screen.

9

Using Solid Shading

Use the **Solid** shade only on blank cells to create solid lines. You cannot see the cell contents if you assign **Solid** to cells containing data. When you want to create a thick, dark line, select **:Format Shade Solid.** Then use **:Worksheet Row Set-Height** to shrink the height of the row to the desired line thickness.

To add solid shading, follow these steps:

1. Select **:Format Shade Solid.**

2. Highlight the range you want to shade and press ↵Enter.

314

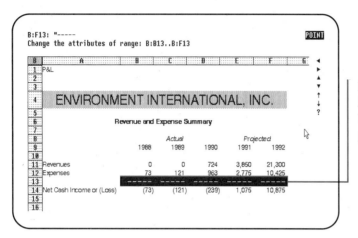

In this example, highlight the range B13..F13 and press ⏎Enter.

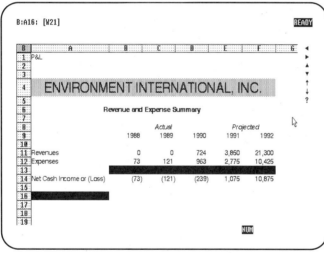

The result of solid shading shows on-screen.

9

To change the height of the row where solid shading occurs, follow these steps:

1. Select :**W**orksheet **R**ow **S**et-Height.

2. At the prompt `Select the rows to set height to:` highlight one cell from each row to change height.

3. At the prompt `Enter row height:`, use ⬆ to shorten the height of the row and see this change displayed on-screen.

4. Press ⏎Enter to accept the height.

In this example, press ↑ until the control panel displays a 2; then press ⏎Enter.

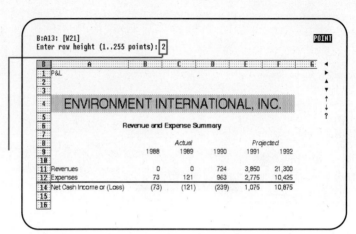

The row height of row 13 has changed to 2 points (the default is 14 points).

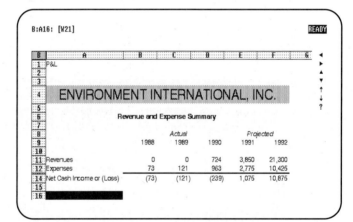

To change the height of a row using a mouse, follow these steps:

1. Move the mouse arrow to the line below the row indicator in the worksheet frame.

In this example, point to the line between rows 13 and 14.

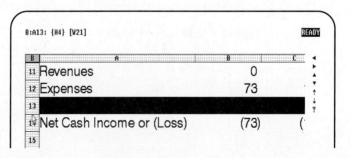

316

2. Click the left mouse button and drag the horizontal line up or down.

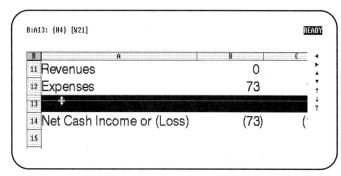

Move the mouse pointer up to decrease the row height.

3. Release the left mouse button.

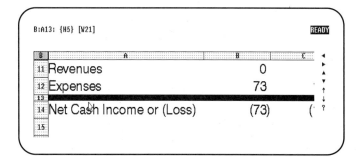

The changed row height, shown with a zoomed display.

9

Removing Existing Shading

You remove existing shading by using the command :Format Shade Clear and indicating the desired range.

To remove existing shading, follow these steps:

1. Select :Format Shade Clear.
2. Highlight the range from which you want to remove shading and press ⏎Enter.

Using Underlining and Boldface

You can use Wysiwyg to add underlining and boldface to cell entries. The :Format Underline and :Format Bold commands, discussed in the sections that follow, are useful for emphasizing important areas of the worksheet and increasing the visual impact of printed reports.

Using Underlining

Three styles of underlining are available in Wysiwyg: single, double, and wide. Wysiwyg's underlining capability is superior to the limited underlining available in 1-2-3, which merely repeats the minus sign or equal sign in a separate cell. Wysiwyg gives you the kind of solid underlining you can create on paper with a pencil and ruler. Use the **:Format Underline** command to select the type of underlining you want and highlight the range of cells to underline at the prompt.

To underline a range, follow these steps:

1. Select **:Format Underline**.
2. Select **Single**, **Double**, or **Wide**.
3. Highlight or type the range(s) to underline and press ⏎**Enter**.

In this example, type **C7, C13, F11, F18** and press ⏎**Enter**.

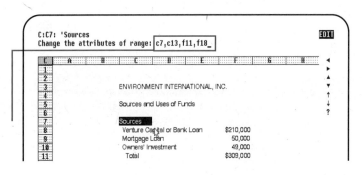

9

The result of single underlining is shown on-screen.

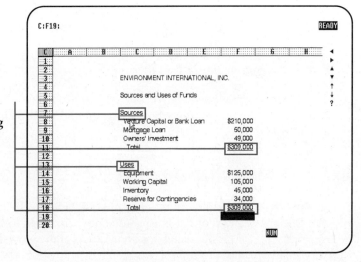

To remove existing underlining, use the command **:Format Underline Clear.**

Using Boldface

For emphasis, you may want to make the contents of some cells darker than other cells. With Wysiwyg, you can choose any cell or range of cells you want to appear darker. When you use light or dark shading in cells with data, you can see the contents more clearly if the characters are bold. Use the **:Format Bold** command to select bold characters. Then highlight the range of cells to appear in bold type at the prompt.

To create boldface characters, follow these steps:

1. Select **:Format Bold Set.**

2. Highlight or type the ranges where you want boldface to appear, and then press ⏎Enter.

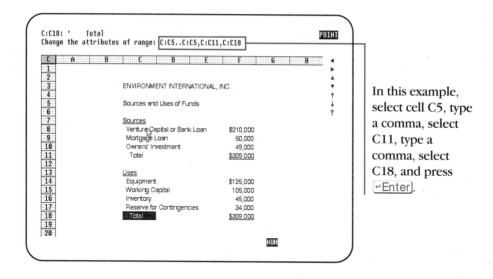

In this example, select cell C5, type a comma, select C11, type a comma, select C18, and press ⏎Enter.

To remove existing boldface, use the command **:Format Bold Clear.**

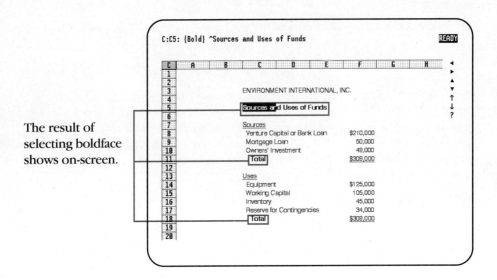

The result of selecting boldface shows on-screen.

Using Lines to Outline Cells or Create Grid Lines

With Wysiwyg, you have a variety of ways to use lines to enclose or separate parts of the worksheet. Access the options for outlining particular cells with the **:Format Lines** command. If you want to show the boundaries of all cells on the worksheet, you can add grid lines by using the **:Print Settings Grid** command.

Outlining Cells

When you select **:Format Lines**, you see the options **Outline, Left, Right, Top, Bottom, All, Double, Wide, Clear,** and **Shadow.** Usually, you surround all cells in a given range by selecting **All** or draw lines around the perimeter of a range by choosing **Outline.** To create a three-dimensional appearance, choose **Shadow.** If you want to put a single cell in a box, you can use either **:Format Lines Outline** or **:Format Lines All.** A shaded range will be more clearly defined if you surround it by using **:Format Lines Outline.** Remove existing lines with **:Format Lines Clear.** The control panel prompts you for the kinds of lines you want cleared.

To draw lines on all sides of the cells in a range, follow these steps:

1. Select **:Format Lines All.**

2. Highlight the range of cells that you want to contain lines around each cell, and then press ↵Enter].

To draw lines on the perimeter (outline) of the cells in a range, follow these steps:

1. Select **:Format Lines Outline**.

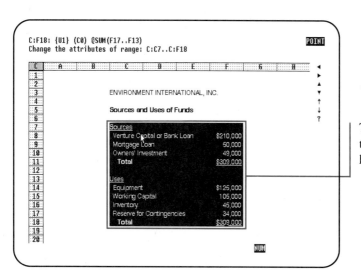

The range of cells to be outlined is highlighted.

9

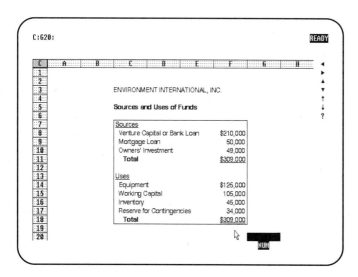

The information is outlined in a block.

2. Highlight the range of cells to outline, and then press ↵Enter.

To draw a shadow around a range and create a three-dimensional appearance, follow these steps:

1. Select **:Format Lines Shadow Set**.

2. Highlight the range of cells to shadow, and then press ↵Enter.

The range C7..F18 is highlighted.

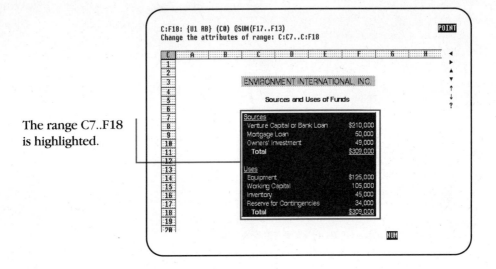

The result of selecting **Shadow** appears on-screen.

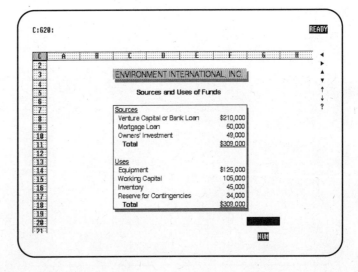

To clear the shadow, use the **:Format Lines Shadow Clear** command.

Creating Grid Lines

You can surround every cell in the worksheet with lines if you select **:Format Lines All** and highlight all cells. Although this process displays cell boundaries clearly, the result can appear cluttered.

You can display grid lines on-screen by using the **:Display Options Grid Yes** command. This command, however, will not print the grid lines.

To print cell boundaries without letting the lines dominate the text, select the command **:Print Settings Grid**. This command draws lightly-dotted lines for all column and row separations. You cannot use grid lines for a selected range of cells; the **:Print Settings Grid** command affects the entire worksheet.

To create grid lines throughout the worksheet, follow these steps:

1. Select **:Print Settings**.

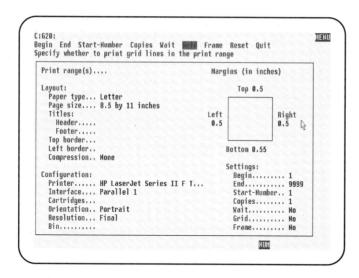

The Wysiwyg print settings sheet appears.

2. Select **Grid**.

3. Select **Yes** if you want the grid lines to print in your printed report; otherwise, select **No**.

4. To exit, select **Quit** twice.

Grid lines surround all cells in the worksheet, including labels that cross cell boundaries and graphs added to the worksheet.

Changing the Size of the Image On-Screen

By shrinking the display of your worksheet on-screen, you get a larger view of your worksheet and can see more cells. By magnifying the display, you can see the image more clearly. This is helpful if you have eye problems or if you are showing your display to a group of people. Using the **:Display Zoom** command, you can shrink the image on-screen so characters are as small as 25 percent of their usual size, or you can magnify images so characters expand up to 400 percent of normal size. The **:Display Zoom** command has no effect on printed output.

To change the size of the image on-screen, follow these steps:

1. Select **:Display Zoom**.

2. Select the size you want from among the following options:

   Tiny, Small, Normal, Large, or **Huge**

   Or

   Select **Manual** and type a number from 25 to 400 (1/4 normal size up to 4 times normal size).

3. Select **Quit** to return to a modified screen size.

The **Tiny** option displays the image on-screen at 63% of normal size.

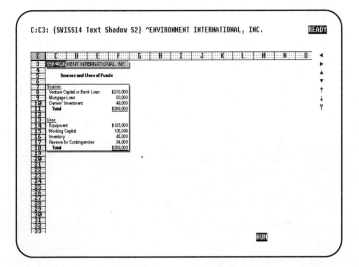

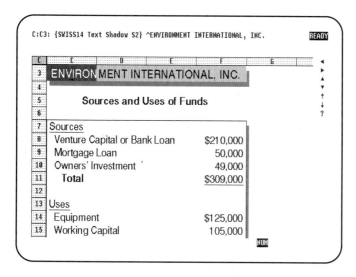

The **Huge** option displays the image on-screen at 150% of normal size.

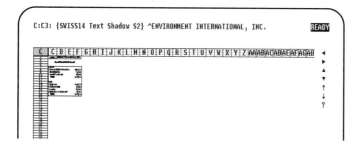

The **Manual** option lets you choose the size of the on-screen image from 25%...

9

...to 400% of normal size.

Formatting Sequences

The options on the **:**Format menu enable you to format cells and ranges. To format individual characters within a cell, you can use *formatting sequences.* Using these sequences, you can bold or italicize a single word in a cell, for example. Formatting sequences are codes you enter as you are entering or editing text in the control panel. The codes appear in the control panel, but Wysiwyg replaces the codes with the actual formatting when you press Enter.

To format a word within a cell:

1. Press F2 (Edit) and position the cursor under the first character to be formatted.

2. Press Ctrl A (for attribute). A solid triangle appears within the control panel.

3. Type the one- or two-character code for the attribute. Table 9.1 lists these codes. Be sure to type the correct upper- or lowercase characters.

4. To end the formatting sequence, press Ctrl N. An upside-down solid triangle appears within the control panel.

Table 9.1
Character Codes for Attributes

Code	Description	Code	Description	Code	Description
b	Bold	1c	Default Color	1F	Font 1
i	Italics	2c	Red	2F	Font 2
u	Superscript	3c	Green	3F	Font 3
d	Subscript	4c	Dark Blue	4F	Font 4
o	Outline	5c	Cyan	5F	Font 5
x	Flip X-axis	6c	Yellow	6F	Font 6
y	Flip Y-axis	7c	Magenta	7F	Font 7
		8c	Reverse Colors	8F	Font 8
1_	Single Underline				
2_	Double Underline				
3_	Wide Underline				
4_	Box Around Characters				

To specify multiple attributes, press Ctrl-A and the first attribute code, followed by Ctrl-A and the second code. For example, to bold and italicize a word, press

326

Ctrl-A and type **b**, and then press Ctrl-A and type **i**. At the end of the word, press Ctrl-N to cancel all formatting sequences. If you just want to cancel one of the attributes, press Ctrl-E followed by the attribute code you want to end (for example, **i** for italic).

Managing Your Formats

Because formatting is the heart of Wysiwyg, the program offers several commands for dealing with the formats assigned to your cells. You can copy and move formats—not the cell contents, but the formats associated with the cell. You can assign a name to the set of formatting instructions in a cell, and then apply this format to any range. You can save *all* the formats associated with the file and then apply this format to another file.

Copying Formats

If you want to format one cell or range with the same highlighting features as another formatted cell or range, you can use the **:Special Copy** command to copy the formatting instructions. For example, if you have formatted a range to 14-point Swiss, in boldface with shading and an outline, you can save a lot of time by copying the format to another range rather than using four separate **:Format** commands. The command copies formats only, not cell contents. 1-2-3's /Copy command copies cell contents and formats (with Wysiwyg attached). **:Special Copy** copies the following formats: font, boldface, italics, underline, shade, color, and lines. To copy formats from one file to another, use the **/File Open** command to retrieve each file before invoking **:Special Copy**. Use your file-movement commands to indicate ranges in other files.

To copy a format from one range to another range of cells, follow these steps:

1. Select **:Special Copy**.
2. Highlight the range of cells you want to copy *from* and press ⏎Enter.
3. Highlight the range of cells you want to copy *to* and press ⏎Enter.

Named-Styles

Another way to apply a format from one cell to another is by creating and using named-styles. You should create named-styles for the formats you use frequently. Suppose, for example, that your spreadsheet contains 10 subheadings and you want them to be in 14-point Swiss bold with a heavy shade. To ease formatting and ensure consistency, you can name this particular formatting style HEAD and then apply this style to all headings.

327

Another advantage to using named-styles is that you can make format changes rapidly. If you decide that you want your headings to have a light shade instead of a heavy one, you need to change the format of only one cell.

To define a style, format a cell with the desired attributes and then follow these steps:

1. Select **:**Named-Style **D**efine.

2. Choose any number from 1 to 8.

Type **1** to choose the first style to define.

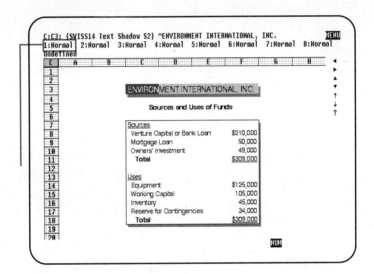

3. Highlight the cell you want as the defined style and then press ⏎Enter.

4. Type the name of the style and press ⏎Enter. The description appears on the third line of the display panel when you select the named-style.

To apply a format style to a cell or range, follow these steps:

1. Select **:**Named-Style.

2. Choose the style you want from the resulting menu.

3. Highlight the range of cells to receive the style, and then press ⏎Enter.

9

Typing Long Text in Wysiwyg

Many people use 1-2-3 to type short letters and memos. Traditionally, typing and editing in a spreadsheet was much more cumbersome than typing in a word processor—until Wysiwyg came along. You can now type directly onto the spreadsheet, and Wysiwyg automatically word-wraps when you get to the end of the line. You can position the cursor on any character in the text range, and edit the characters—insert, delete, overtype, or format them.

In addition to typing letters and memos, you can use **:Text Edit** to type a paragraph or two of descriptive information about the purpose of a spreadsheet.

Typing or Correcting Text

You can use the **:Text Edit** command to modify existing spreadsheet labels or to type new text. When you select **:Text Edit**, the control panel prompts you for a text range. Be sure to include the complete width and length of the range you want to edit. If you want to insert text, you need to include blank rows or columns in your text range. Otherwise, you see the error message `Text input range full`. If this happens, press Esc twice: once to clear the error, and the second time to return to READY mode. Then redefine your text range.

To define a range to accept text, follow these steps:

1. Select **:Text Edit**.

2. Highlight the range of cells to receive text, and then press `↵Enter`.

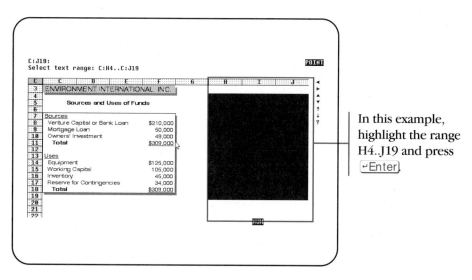

In this example, highlight the range H4..J19 and press `↵Enter`.

329

Several important changes occur when you are in the text editor. First, the cell pointer disappears and becomes a small vertical-line cursor. The arrow keys move the cursor within the defined text range. Second, the mode indicator displays LABEL. Third, once you start typing or moving the cursor, the control panel displays the following information: the cell with the current line of text, the cursor's row and column number position, and the line's alignment (left-aligned, centered, etc.). The row number corresponds to the row in the defined text range, not the actual spreadsheet row. For example, if spreadsheet row 4 is the first row in the current text range, the row number is 1. The column number refers to the number of characters over from the beginning of the line.

Wysiwyg's text editor.

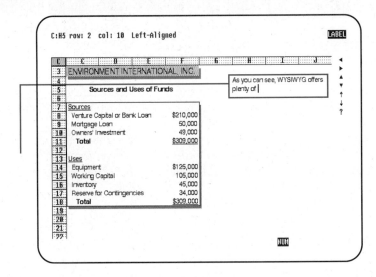

As you type new text, the words automatically wrap to the next line. When you want to start a new paragraph, you have three choices, depending on how you want the text to look:

- Press ⏎Enter twice, leaving a blank line between paragraphs.
- Press ⏎Enter once, and press the spacebar one or more times at the beginning of the paragraph.
- Press Ctrl⏎Enter to insert a paragraph symbol.

Table 9.2 lists the cursor movement and editing keys you can use in :Text Edit. Many of these keys are similar to the ones you use in 1-2-3's EDIT mode.

Table 9.2
:Text Edit Cursor Movements and Editing Keys

Key	Description
Ctrl ←	Beginning of the previous word.
Ctrl →	End of the next word.
PgDn	Next screen.
PgUp	Previous screen.
Home	Beginning of line.
Home Home	Beginning of paragraph.
End	End of line.
End End	End of paragraph.
← Backspace	Deletes character to the left of the cursor.
Del	Deletes character to the right of the cursor.
Ins	Toggles between insert mode (the default) and overtype mode.
↵ Enter	Begins a new line.
Ctrl ↵ Enter	Begins a new paragraph.
F3	Displays a format menu.
Esc	Returns to READY mode.

When you finish typing and editing the text, press Esc to exit out of the text editor. In READY mode, you can see that Wysiwyg entered each line of text into cells in the first column of the text range.

Formatting Characters

Earlier in this chapter you learned how to use formatting sequences to assign attributes to individual characters in a cell. (Press Ctrl-A and a code, and then press Ctrl-N to cancel the attribute.) The text editor offers an easier way to format characters—with the F3 key. You don't need to remember codes because pressing F3 displays a menu.

331

To add formatting attributes, follow these steps:

1. Select **:Text Edit**.
2. Highlight the range of cells to modify, and then press ⏎Enter. Be sure to include the entire width of the long labels, not just the column you type them into.

In this example, highlight range H4..J19 and press ⏎Enter.

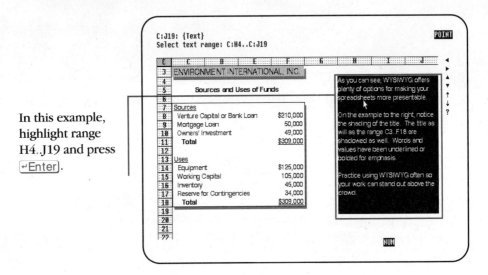

9

3. Place the cursor to the left of the first character you want to format.
4. Press F3.

The font attributes menu appears in the control panel when you press F3.

332

5. Choose the desired attribute from the resulting menu:

Selection	Description
Font	Changes the font.
Bold	Bolds the text.
Italics	Italicizes the text.
Underline	Draws a single underline under the text.
Color	Chooses a color for the text.
+	Superscripts the text.
−	Subscripts the text.
Outline	Traces the outside of the letter forms.

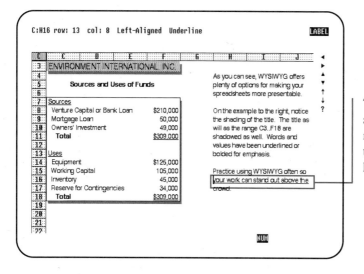

C:H16 row: 13 col: 8 Left-Aligned Underline |LABEL|

ENVIRONMENT INTERNATIONAL, INC.

Sources and Uses of Funds

Sources	
Venture Capital or Bank Loan	$210,000
Mortgage Loan	50,000
Owners' Investment	49,000
Total	$309,000

Uses	
Equipment	$125,000
Working Capital	105,000
Inventory	45,000
Reserve for Contingencies	34,000
Total	$309,000

As you can see, WYSIWYG offers plenty of options for making your spreadsheets more presentable.

On the example to the right, notice the shading of the title. The title as will as the range C3..F18 are shadowed as well. Words and values have been underlined or bolded for emphasis.

Practice using WYSIWYG often so your work can stand out above the crowd.

NUM

The attribute affects the data right of the cursor to the end of the line.

9

Normal	Removes any formatting.

6. To indicate where you want the attribute to stop, place the cursor to the right of the last character and press F3 .

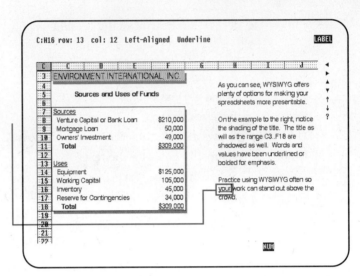

C:H16 row: 13 col: 12 Left-Aligned Underline   LABEL

3	ENVIRONMENT INTERNATIONAL, INC.					

The sample result: Wysiwyg only underlined the word "your."

ENVIRONMENT INTERNATIONAL, INC.

Sources and Uses of Funds

Sources
Venture Capital or Bank Loan $210,000
Mortgage Loan   50,000
Owners' Investment   49,000
Total $309,000

Uses
Equipment $125,000
Working Capital   105,000
Inventory   45,000
Reserve for Contingencies   34,000
Total $309,000

As you can see, WYSIWYG offers plenty of options for making your spreadsheets more presentable.

On the example to the right, notice the shading of the title. The title as will as the range C3..F18 are shadowed as well. Words and values have been underlined or bolded for emphasis.

Practice using WYSIWYG often so your work can stand out above the crowd.

NUM

7. Press N to remove the highlighting from the rest of the line.

Because some of the attributes change the size of characters, paragraphs may no longer be neatly aligned after you format. When this happens, use the **:Text Reformat** command to adjust the paragraphs.

Wysiwyg does not limit character formatting to existing text; you can also apply attributes as you type new text in text edit mode. Simply press F3 and select the format before you begin typing. When you want to discontinue the attribute, press F3 and choose **Normal**.

Aligning Labels

Wysiwyg's **:Text Align** command is an elaborate version of 1-2-3's **/Range Label** command. 1-2-3's command aligns a label to the left, right or center within the current column width. If the label exceeds the column width, 1-2-3 aligns it on the left. Wysiwyg's command aligns a label within a specified range—you can center a label across a range of cells to center it over the worksheet.

To align a range of text, follow these steps:

1. Select **:Text Align**.
2. Choose **Left**, **Right**, **Center**, or **Even**.

    Left is the default alignment. Even stretches the text between the left and the right edge of the specified range. Wysiwyg inserts spaces between words to create the smooth margins.

334

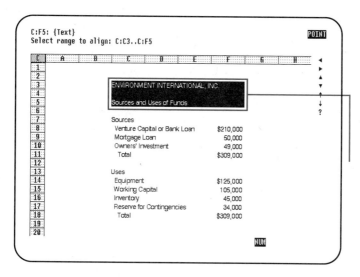

In this example,
the range C3..F5 is
highlighted.

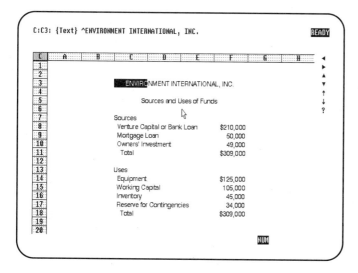

9

The result of
centering the text
in a range.

3. Highlight the range of cells to align text, and then press ⏎Enter.

Wysiwyg uses the following symbols to identify each type of alignment:

' Left

" Right

^ Center

| Even

335

These symbols match the label alignment symbols inserted with the /**R**ange Label command. The symbols have different functions, however, when the cell is formatted as text in Wysiwyg. You can insert these symbols manually in 1-2-3's EDIT mode, as long as the cell is formatted as text in Wysiwyg.

When you are editing in Wysiwyg's text editor, the control panel displays the alignment of the current line (left-aligned, centered, etc.).

Reformatting Paragraphs

One of the advantages to using the text editor is that you can easily correct typing mistakes, reword a passage, or insert additional text. Once you start editing and formatting, however, your paragraphs will be out of alignment.

Text in this example requires reformatting to correct alignment.

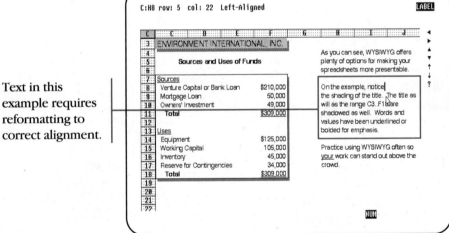

To reformat a paragraph, follow these steps:

1. If necessary, return to READY mode by pressing Esc.
2. Select **:T**ext **R**eformat.
3. Wysiwyg automatically highlights the range you last indicated in the **:T**ext **E**dit command. If this range is acceptable, press ↵Enter.
4. To indicate a different range, press Esc or ←Backspace, and then highlight the new range.

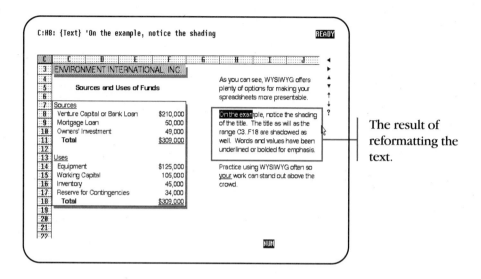

The result of reformatting the text.

Another reason to use the **:Text R**eformat command is to align the text into more columns. Suppose, for example, that the range currently spans four columns and you want it to extend to six. To make longer lines of text, simply include these extra columns in your reformat range.

Completing the Printing Process

After you finish formatting a report with Wysiwyg, you can easily print it with the **:Print G**o command. Before you print, you must specify a print range with the **:Print R**ange command; then select **G**o from the Wysiwyg **:Print** menu to begin printing. If you choose to print your report at a later time, you can instead select **:Print F**ile, which creates an encoded file on disk with the ENC extension. Print the file using the DOS COPY command (for example, **COPY REVENUE/B LPT1**).

To print a report created with Wysiwyg, follow these steps:

1. Select **:Print R**ange.
2. Select **S**et to specify the print range, or select **C**lear to reset the current print range.
3. Highlight the range you want to print and press ⏎Enter. Wysiwyg displays the print range boundaries and page breaks as dashed lines on-screen.
4. Select **G**o to begin printing.

337

Preview Printing to the Screen

The **:Print Preview** option gives you an idea of what your worksheet looks like before you commit it to paper. This option displays your print range, one page at a time. Press any key to display subsequent pages and to return to the **:Print** menu. Although you will not be able to read every character on the screen, you get a picture of your overall page layout and page breaks.

To preview your document, follow these steps:

1. Select the print range and the layout and settings you want.
2. Select **:Print**.
3. To preview the document, select **Preview**.
4. If multiple pages exist, press ⏎Enter to go to the next page.

Esc returns you to the **:Print** menu.

Forcing a Print Range to One Page

The **:Print Layout Compression Automatic** option offers an ideal way to fit a large worksheet onto one page. Rather than guess at the font size needed to print a report on a single page, you can use this option. Wysiwyg will then determine how much it needs to reduce the font size.

To compress the print range to fit on one page, follow these steps:

1. Select **:Print Layout Compression**.
2. To fit the range on one page, select **Automatic**.
3. To return to the **:Print** menu, select **Quit**.

You can use additional Wysiwyg **:Print Layout** commands to choose the paper size, change margins, add headers and footers, and add print borders to the printout.

The Wysiwyg **:Print Configuration** commands enable you to change the current printer and interface. Depending on your selected printer, other **Configuration** options may be available, including orientation (portrait or landscape) of your printout, the graphics resolution, the font cartridges you use, and the paper-feed type.

Use the **:Print Settings** commands to select which pages of a multipage report to print, the page number of the first page, the number of copies to print, whether to print the worksheet grid and frame, and whether to pause the printer for a paper change before printing pages.

9

Summary

In this chapter you learned how to use Wysiwyg to enhance your printed 1-2-3 worksheets. You can add boldface, italics, shading, underlining, grids, outlines, word-wrapped text, and symbols to your printed reports. These enhancements, which appear on-screen while you are formatting the worksheet, let you visualize how the report will appear when printed. Also, you can use different type sizes and styles to emphasize and enhance the text in your report.

Specifically, you learned the following key information about 1-2-3:

- To attach **Wysiwyg**, you use the (Alt)(F10) add-in key, select **L**oad, and choose **W**ysiwyg.

- To display the separate Wysiwyg menu, press (:).

- The **:F**ormat Font command enables you to change the font for a particular range in the worksheet. If you want to use a different font throughout the entire worksheet, you can do so with the **:F**ormat Font **R**eplace command.

- The **:F**ormat Lines command draws lines around the perimeter of a range, as well as lines in the left, right, top, or bottom of a range. An additional option enables you to create a drop shadow for a range, producing a three-dimensional effect.

- You can set grid lines to print or display on your screen. To print grid lines, choose the **:P**rint Settings Grid command. To display grid lines on-screen only, choose the **:D**isplay Options Grid command.

- The **:D**isplay Zoom command can shrink or magnify images on the screen so characters appear much smaller or larger than normal size. This command does not affect the printed output.

- The **:S**pecial Copy command enables you to copy formatting from one cell to another cell or range of cells. Alternatively, you can use the **:F**ormat Font Library command to save or retrieve formatting.

- The **:T**ext Edit command enables you to type text in your worksheet using word-wrap, and gives you the ability to enhance individual words of a cell. Once in **:T**ext Edit mode, you can press (F3) to highlight text.

- The **:T**ext Align command can align text in a cell or range of cells. **:T**ext Reformat is used to reformat a range of labels into paragraph form.

- The **:P**rint Range command enables you to select the range to print from Wysiwyg. The **G**o option on the Wysiwyg **:P**rint menu prints the specified range to the printer. The **P**review option enables you to see an on-screen preview of the document before it prints.

9

Managing Files

I n Chapter 3, you learned some of the basic file management tasks, including naming, saving, and retrieving files. This chapter covers some of the other valuable procedures for managing files. For example, you learn how to protect files with passwords so unauthorized users cannot access the files. Only those who know the current password can change or delete a file.

This chapter also covers saving and retrieving parts of files. You learn how to extract a section of data from one worksheet to a separate worksheet. Additionally, you learn how to combine parts of several files into one master file. This capability is useful for consolidating data from similar worksheets. Individual cells can contain formulas that reference information in another worksheet on disk. 1-2-3 automatically updates these linked cells when you retrieve a file containing the links.

You also learn how to list different types of files on-screen. You can change the default drive and directory (either permanently or temporarily for the current 1-2-3 session). You can delete worksheets and other 1-2-3 files. Finally, you learn how to import files from outside programs into 1-2-3 using 1-2-3's Translate utility.

Key Terms in This Chapter

Password	A string of up to 15 characters used to limit access to worksheet files.
File linking	A 1-2-3 feature that enables you to use formulas in the current worksheet to refer to values in other worksheets.
ASCII file	A text (or print) file, created in another program, that 1-2-3 can import into a worksheet with the /File Import command.
Template	An empty master file with labels and formulas but no data. Use a template to create new worksheets or combine data from multiple files.
File reservation	A file protection system that allows only one user at a time to save changes to a shared file in a multiuser network.
Read-only	A file which can be viewed only; changes to the original file cannot be saved.

Using the Mouse

To use a mouse with 1-2-3 Release 3.1, you need a mouse, mouse software, and a graphics monitor and graphics card that support a mouse. Also, Wysiwyg must be loaded into memory. You can use a mouse to select commands and files, specify ranges, and move the cell pointer within a worksheet or between multiple worksheets and files. In the examples throughout this chapter, notice that the 1-2-3 commands always begin with a slash (/), and the Wysiwyg commands always begin with a colon (:). Refer to the following sections of the specified chapters for further information on using the mouse:

- Chapter 2—"Understanding Mouse Terminology"
- Chapter 3—"Mouse Control of the Cell Pointer"
    "Using the Mouse To Select Menu Commands"
- Chapter 4—"Using the Mouse To Specify Ranges"

10

Protecting Files with Passwords

You can protect your files by using 1-2-3's password-protection system. By specifying passwords when you save files, you can prevent access to the protected files by unauthorized users. The only persons who can retrieve the protected files are those who know the passwords. This feature is particularly useful for confidential information such as sales and payroll data.

Creating a Password

You can create a password with the /File Save command. To assign a password to a worksheet, follow these steps when saving a file:

1. Select /File Save.

2. When the prompt Enter name of file to save: appears, type the file name, leave a space, type P, and press ↵Enter.

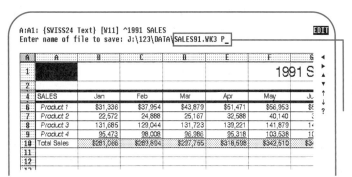

In this example, SALES91 receives a password.

3. When the prompt Enter password: appears, type your password and press ↵Enter.

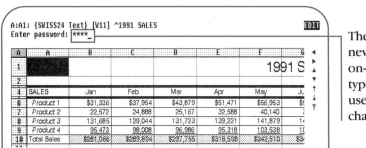

The password never appears on-screen. As you type, asterisks are used to hide characters.

10

343

4. When the prompt `Verify password:` appears, type the password once more and press ⏎Enter.

At this point, 1-2-3 saves the file with the new password. Only those who know the password can now retrieve the file.

You can enter any character in a 1-2-3 password, which can contain as many as 15 characters. You must be careful, however, because 1-2-3 accepts only the password you first entered. Uppercase or lowercase letters must be exactly the same. For example, if you entered **pdfund** as your password, 1-2-3 will not retrieve the file if you type **PDFUND** or **PDfund**. Be sure to remember your password or write it down.

The first and second passwords must match exactly (including case) or you have to start the procedure again.

```
A:A1: {SWISS24 Text} [W11] ^1991 SALES                        EDIT
Enter password: ****                  Verify password: ****_
```

A	A	B	C	D	E	F	G
1				.		1991 S	
2							
4	SALES	Jan	Feb	Mar	Apr	May	Ju
6	Product 1	$31,336	$37,954	$43,879	$51,471	$56,953	$5
7	Product 2	22,572	24,888	25,167	32,588	40,140	3
8	Product 3	131,685	129,044	131,723	139,221	141,879	14
9	Product 4	95,473	98,008	96,986	95,318	103,538	10
10	Total Sales	$281,066	$289,894	$297,755	$318,598	$342,510	$3
11							
12							

Retrieving a Password-Protected File

To open a protected file, you use the /**F**ile **R**etrieve command and type the password. To retrieve a file protected with a password, follow these steps:

1. Select /**F**ile **R**etrieve.
2. Select the file to retrieve by highlighting or typing the file name, and then press ⏎Enter.
3. When the prompt `Enter password:` appears, type your password exactly as you created it; then press ⏎Enter.

Asterisks hide your password as you type.

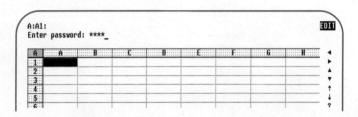

```
A:A1:                                                          EDIT
Enter password: ****_
```

A	A	B	C	D	E	F	G	H
1								
2								
3								
4								
5								
6								

If you enter the password correctly, the worksheet appears. If you enter the wrong password, however, the words Incorrect password appear in the screen's lower left corner, and the mode indicator flashes ERROR. Press Esc or Enter to return to a blank worksheet.

Deleting a Password

You can delete a password by first retrieving the file with the password you want to delete. When you are ready to save the file, select the /File Save command and erase the [PASSWORD PROTECTED] message.

To delete password protection from a file, follow these steps:

   1. Select /File Save.

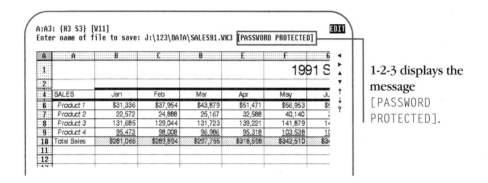

1-2-3 displays the message [PASSWORD PROTECTED].

   2. When the prompt Enter name of file to save: appears, erase [PASSWORD PROTECTED] by pressing ◆Backspace or Esc.

   3. Press ↵Enter to save the file without the password.

Changing a Password

To change a password, first delete the existing password and then enter a new one. To change a password, follow these steps:

   1. Select /File Save.

   2. When the prompt Enter name of file to save: appears, erase [PASSWORD PROTECTED] by pressing ◆Backspace or Esc.

10

3. Type the file name, leave a space, type ⟨P⟩, and press ⟨⏎Enter⟩.

4. When the prompt `Enter password:` appears, type the password and press ⟨⏎Enter⟩.

5. At the prompt `Verify password:`, type the password once more and press ⟨⏎Enter⟩. 1-2-3 saves the file with the new password.

Saving and Retrieving Partial Files

Sometimes you want to store only part of a worksheet (a range of cells, for instance) in a separate file on disk. For example, you can use the /File Xtract command to extract payments from an expense report or revenues from an income statement. Extracting is also useful for breaking up worksheet files that are too large to store on a single disk.

Conversely, you may have several worksheets with similar information. Suppose that you own a store in which each department is its own profit center. At the end of the month, you want to retrieve a partial file from each department's worksheet and combine the files to get the overall picture of the store's profit and loss. You can use the /File Combine command to perform this operation.

Extracting Data

With the /File Xtract command, you can save formulas or the current values of formulas in a range on a worksheet. Both options (Formulas and Values) create a separate worksheet file that you can reload in 1-2-3 with the /File Retrieve command.

The /File Xtract command requires that you specify the portion of the worksheet you want to save. The range can be as small as a cell or as large as the entire worksheet.

To copy a part of your worksheet to a separate file, follow these steps:

1. Select /File Xtract.

2. To extract data and preserve any formulas in the extract range, select Formulas; or to extract data and convert formulas to values, select Values.

10

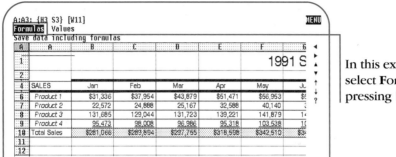

In this example, select **Formulas** by pressing F.

3. When the prompt Enter name of file to extract to: appears, type a name for the file to hold the extracted data and press ⏎Enter.

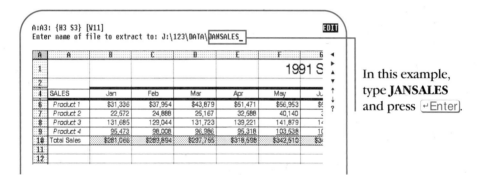

In this example, type **JANSALES** and press ⏎Enter.

4. When the prompt Enter extract range: appears, highlight the range you want to extract and press ⏎Enter.

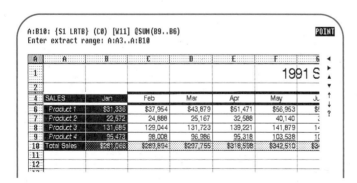

In this example, highlight the range A3..B10 and press ⏎Enter.

10

347

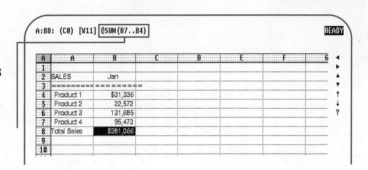

1-2-3 retains the
formula in cell B8
(displayed in the
control panel) in
the new file.

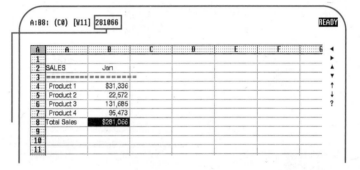

In this example,
select /File Xtract
Values. 1-2-3
converts the
formula in B8 to a
value.

If you save only the current values with /File Xtract Values, remember that the
resulting worksheet file will contain numbers but no formulas. The /File Xtract
Formulas command preserves any formulas that are in the extract range.

When you select the /File Xtract Values command, you can lock the current
values in a worksheet. Think of this process as taking a snapshot of the current
worksheet. You can then reload the new, values-only file into the worksheet and
quickly perform operations that do not require formulas (such as printing and
graphing). Before using /File Xtract Values, however, be sure to press Calc (F9) if
the CALC indicator appears at the bottom of the screen to be sure that 1-2-3 will
extract the correct formula values.

Combining Files

Another task you may need to perform is to copy ranges of cells from other
worksheets and place them in strategic spots in your current worksheet. For
example, if you work in a large firm, you may want to combine quarterly sales
information by region into one consolidated worksheet.

10

A simple technique for this kind of consolidation is to start with a copy of an empty master file, or template. A template can contain exactly the same labels as the combined worksheets, but the area containing the specific data values is blank. When you start with a blank template, you can copy the first quarterly sales worksheet to the template, leaving the original worksheet untouched. Copying a range of cells also can be helpful when you want to combine divisional data in a single consolidated worksheet.

The command used to combine data from different files is /File Combine. The Copy option of this command copies the worksheet or range on top of the current worksheet. The Add option adds the values from the combined worksheet or range to the values in the current worksheet. The Subtract option decreases the values in the current worksheet by the values in the combined worksheet or range.

To combine data from different files, follow these steps:

1. Retrieve the blank template file into which you want to combine files with /File Retrieve.

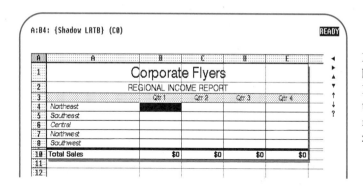

In this example, because the range B4..E8 is blank, all the formulas in row 10 evaluate to zero.

10

2. Position the cell pointer on the first cell of the range to receive the combined data.

3. Select /File Combine.

4. Select Copy to copy a worksheet or range from another file to the existing worksheet or select Add to add the incoming values in a worksheet or range to the values in the existing worksheet or range. To decrease the existing values in a worksheet or range by the values in an incoming worksheet or range, select Subtract.

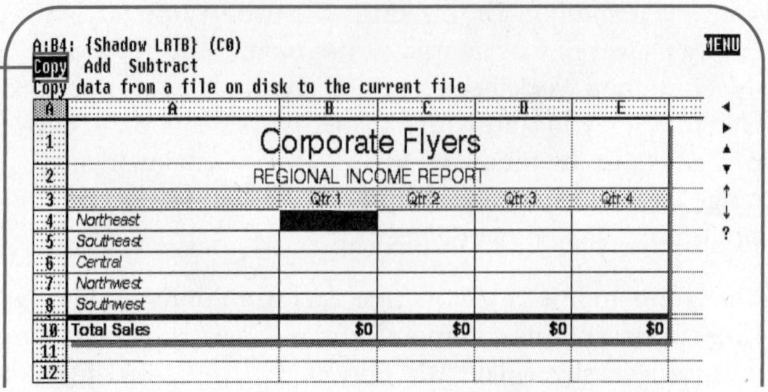

```
A:B4: {Shadow LRTB} (C0)                                    MENU
Copy  Add  Subtract
Copy data from a file on disk to the current file
```

In this example,
select Copy.

5. If you want to copy an entire incoming file, choose Entire-File. To copy a specific range from an incoming file, choose Named/Specified-Range.

```
A:B4: {Shadow LRTB} (C0)                                    MENU
Entire-File  Named/Specified-Range
Incorporate specified range from a file into the current file
```

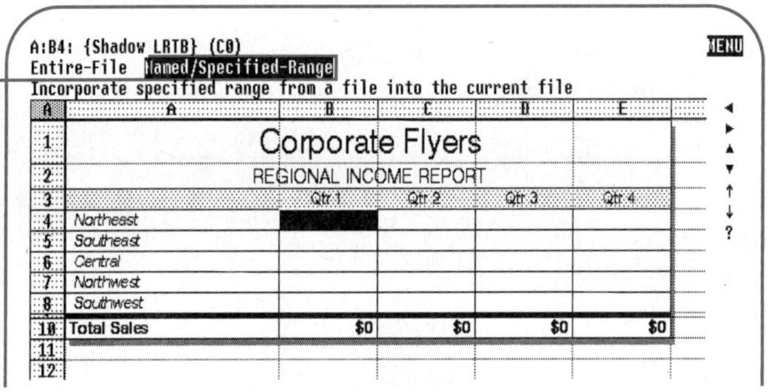

In this example,
select Named/
Specified-Range.

6. Type the range name or location of the incoming range and press ↵Enter. (If you select the Entire-File option, 1-2-3 does not prompt you to enter a range.)

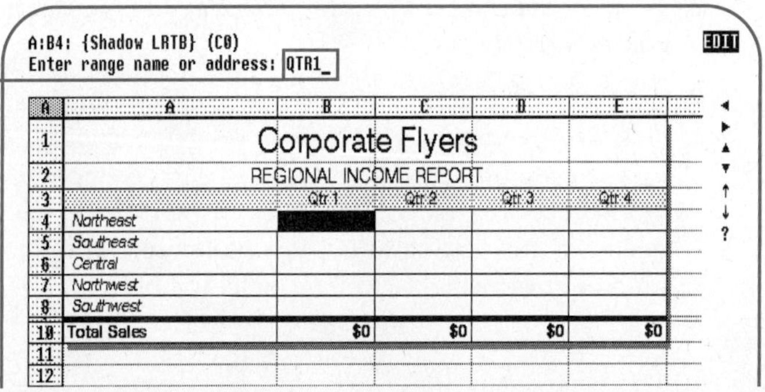

```
A:B4: {Shadow LRTB} (C0)                                    EDIT
Enter range name or address: QTR1_
```

In this example,
type the range
name QTR1 and
press ↵Enter.

350

7. When the prompt `Enter name of file to combine:` appears, indicate the name of the file containing the data and press `⏎Enter`.

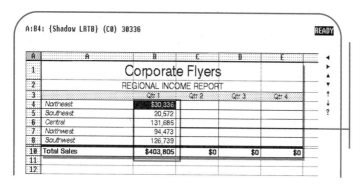

The first quarter data is now in the range B4..B8. 1-2-3 automatically updates the formula in cell B10.

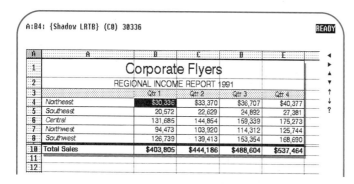

After you combine data for all quarters, the template is filled. The formulas in row 10 display values.

The Copy option of /File Combine pulls in an entire worksheet or named range and causes the new contents to write over the corresponding cells in the current worksheet. The Copy command does not affect cells in the current worksheet that correspond to blank cells in the target file. (Note the important distinction between blank cells and cells containing a space in the target file or range.)

10

In this example, the **Add** option was selected. The values in the center worksheet (the worksheet to be combined) were added to the values in the corresponding cells of the top worksheet (the current worksheet) to create a worksheet of combined values.

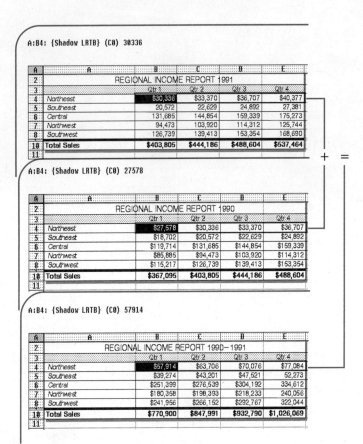

A:B4: {Shadow LRTB} (C0) 30336

A	A	B	C	D	E
2		REGIONAL INCOME REPORT 1991			
3		Qtr 1	Qtr 2	Qtr 3	Qtr 4
4	Northeast	$30,336	$33,370	$36,707	$40,377
5	Southeast	20,572	22,629	24,892	27,381
6	Central	131,685	144,854	159,339	175,273
7	Northwest	94,473	103,920	114,312	125,744
8	Southwest	126,739	139,413	153,354	168,690
10	Total Sales	$403,805	$444,186	$488,604	$537,464
11					

A:B4: {Shadow LRTB} (C0) 27578

A	A	B	C	D	E
2		REGIONAL INCOME REPORT 1990			
3		Qtr 1	Qtr 2	Qtr 3	Qtr 4
4	Northeast	$27,578	$30,336	$33,370	$36,707
5	Southeast	$18,702	$20,572	$22,629	$24,892
6	Central	$119,714	$131,685	$144,854	$159,339
7	Northwest	$85,885	$94,473	$103,920	$114,312
8	Southwest	$115,217	$126,739	$139,413	$153,354
10	Total Sales	$367,095	$403,805	$444,186	$488,604
11					

A:B4: {Shadow LRTB} (C0) 57914

A	A	B	C	D	E
2		REGIONAL INCOME REPORT 1990–1991			
3		Qtr 1	Qtr 2	Qtr 3	Qtr 4
4	Northeast	$57,914	$63,706	$70,076	$77,084
5	Southeast	$39,274	$43,201	$47,521	52,273
6	Central	$251,399	$276,539	$304,192	334,612
7	Northwest	$180,358	$198,393	$218,233	240,056
8	Southwest	$241,956	$266,152	$292,767	322,044
10	Total Sales	$770,900	$847,991	$932,790	$1,026,069
11					

+ =

10

Add pulls in the values from another worksheet or range and adds these values to the corresponding cells in the current worksheet. The **Add** command affects only blank worksheet cells or cells containing numeric values. In the current worksheet, cells that contain formulas or labels do not change.

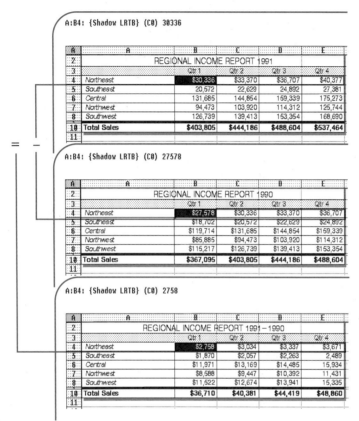

A:B4: {Shadow LRTB} (C0) 30336

A	A	B	C	D	E
2	REGIONAL INCOME REPORT 1991				
3		Qtr 1	Qtr 2	Qtr 3	Qtr 4
4	Northeast	$30,336	$33,370	$36,707	$40,377
5	Southeast	20,572	22,629	24,892	27,381
6	Central	131,685	144,854	159,339	175,273
7	Northwest	94,473	103,920	114,312	125,744
8	Southwest	126,739	139,413	153,354	168,690
10	Total Sales	$403,805	$444,186	$488,604	$537,464
11					

A:B4: {Shadow LRTB} (C0) 27578

A	A	B	C	D	E
2	REGIONAL INCOME REPORT 1990				
3		Qtr 1	Qtr 2	Qtr 3	Qtr 4
4	Northeast	$27,578	$30,336	$33,370	$36,707
5	Southeast	$18,702	$20,572	$22,629	$24,892
6	Central	$119,714	$131,685	$144,854	$159,339
7	Northwest	$85,885	$94,473	$103,920	$114,312
8	Southwest	$115,217	$126,739	$139,413	$153,354
10	Total Sales	$367,095	$403,805	$444,186	$488,604
11					

A:B4: {Shadow LRTB} (C0) 2758

A	A	B	C	D	E
2	REGIONAL INCOME REPORT 1991 – 1990				
3		Qtr 1	Qtr 2	Qtr 3	Qtr 4
4	Northeast	$2,758	$3,034	$3,337	$3,671
5	Southeast	$1,870	$2,057	$2,263	2,489
6	Central	$11,971	$13,169	$14,485	15,934
7	Northwest	$8,588	$9,447	$10,392	11,431
8	Southwest	$11,522	$12,674	$13,941	15,335
10	Total Sales	$36,710	$40,381	$44,419	$48,860
11					

In this example, select the **S**ubtract option. 1-2-3 subtracted the values in the center worksheet from the values in the corresponding cells in the top worksheet to create a worksheet of combined values.

Subtract pulls in an entire worksheet or a named range and subtracts the values from the corresponding cells in the current worksheet. When an existing cell is blank, 1-2-3 subtracts the incoming value. Like **A**dd, **S**ubtract affects only blank cells or cells that contain numeric values. In the current worksheet, cells containing formulas or labels do not change.

Managing Multiple Worksheets and Files

An alternative to /**F**ile **X**tract is to use /**C**opy or /**R**ange **V**alue with more than one file loaded in your computer's memory. You can also use formulas to link cells in multiple worksheets instead of the /**F**ile **C**ombine commands.

If you want to remove all files after you have several in memory, use /Worksheet Erase. To remove only a single file from memory, use the /Worksheet Delete File command.

Opening a New File with a Worksheet in Memory

You can load many files in memory simultaneously, including existing files and new, unnamed files. (1-2-3 limits you to 256 worksheets or the worksheets your computer's memory can hold.)

To open a new worksheet with a worksheet already in memory, follow these steps:

1. Select /**F**ile **N**ew.

2. Select **B**efore to load a file in front of your current worksheet or select **A**fter to load a file behind your current worksheet.

In this example, select **A**fter.

```
A:A1: {SWISS24 Text} [W11] ^1991 SALES                      MENU
Before After
Read a file into memory behind the current file
```

	A	B	C	D	E	F	G
1							1991 S
2							
4	SALES	Jan	Feb	Mar	Apr	May	Ju
6	Product 1	$31,336	$37,954	$43,879	$51,471	$56,953	$5
7	Product 2	22,572	24,888	25,167	32,588	40,140	3
8	Product 3	131,685	129,044	131,723	139,221	141,879	14
9	Product 4	95,473	98,008	96,986	95,318	103,538	10
10	Total Sales	$281,066	$289,894	$297,755	$318,598	$342,510	$3
11							

3. The prompt `Enter name of file to create:` appears, followed by a default file name. Type a new name or accept the current one and press ⏎Enter.

1-2-3's default file name is FILE0001.WK3.

```
A:A1: {SWISS24 Text} [W11] ^1991 SALES                      EDIT
Enter name of file to create: J:\123\DATA\FILE0001.WK3
```

	A	B	C	D	E	F	G
1							1991 S
2							
4	SALES	Jan	Feb	Mar	Apr	May	Ju
6	Product 1	$31,336	$37,954	$43,879	$51,471	$56,953	$5
7	Product 2	22,572	24,888	25,167	32,588	40,140	3
8	Product 3	131,685	129,044	131,723	139,221	141,879	14
9	Product 4	95,473	98,008	96,986	95,318	103,538	10
10	Total Sales	$281,066	$289,894	$297,755	$318,598	$342,510	$3
11							

10

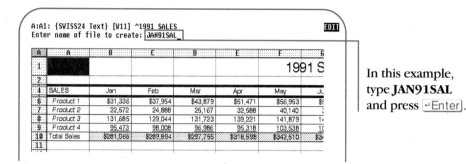

A:A1: {SWISS24 Text} [W11] ^1991 SALES   **EDIT**
Enter name of file to create: JAN91SAL

	A	B	C	D	E	F	G
1						1991 S	
2							
4	SALES	Jan	Feb	Mar	Apr	May	Ju
6	Product 1	$31,336	$37,954	$43,879	$51,471	$56,953	$
7	Product 2	22,572	24,888	25,167	32,588	40,140	
8	Product 3	131,685	129,044	131,723	139,221	141,879	1
9	Product 4	95,473	98,008	96,986	95,318	103,538	1
10	Total Sales	$281,066	$289,894	$297,755	$318,598	$342,510	$3
11							

In this example, type **JAN91SAL** and press ⏎Enter.

Your cell pointer is in the new file. If you want to return to the worksheet you started from, press Ctrl-PgUp if you chose to place the new worksheet **A**fter the current worksheet. If you chose **B**efore, press Ctrl-PgDn.

Opening an Existing File with a Worksheet in Memory

To open an existing worksheet with one already in memory, follow these steps:

1. Select /**F**ile **O**pen.

2. Select **B**efore to load a file in front of your current worksheet, or **A**fter to load a file behind your current worksheet.

3. Type or highlight the file name and press ⏎Enter.

4. Your cell pointer is in the new file. If you want to return to the worksheet you started from, press Ctrl PgUp if you chose **A**fter, or Ctrl PgDn if you chose **B**efore.

Viewing More than One Worksheet at a Time

When you have several files in memory, you may want to see multiple worksheets at one time. You can use the /**W**orksheet **W**indow **H**orizontal or **V**ertical command and move the cell pointer to a second worksheet. If you want to see up to three worksheets at one time, select /**W**orksheet **W**indow **P**erspective.

When you move to another worksheet by pressing Ctrl-PgUp or Ctrl-PgDn, 1-2-3 displays the new file name in the bottom left corner of the screen.

To remove the **P**erspective window, use the /**W**orksheet **W**indow **C**lear command.

10

While you are
in the JAN91SAL
worksheet, select
/**W**orksheet
Window
Perspective.

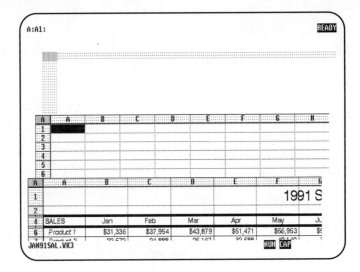

The cell pointer
remains in the
JAN91SAL
worksheet.
Because there are
only two sheets in
memory, Wysiwyg
displays a shadow
for the third sheet.

10

Press Ctrl PgUp to
move to the
SALES91 file.
Notice that the
lower left corner
now displays the
file name
SALES91.WK3.

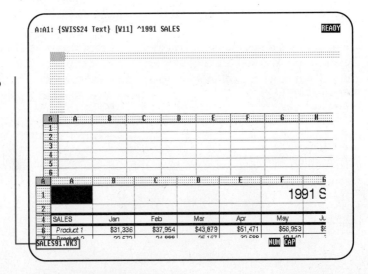

356

Copying a Range from One File in Memory to Another

Copying a range from one file to another loaded file is similar to copying a range from one part of a worksheet to another. The major difference is that you use the worksheet direction keys such as Ctrl-PgUp and Ctrl-PgDn and the file direction keys such as Ctrl-End. See Chapter 3 for a complete description of the direction keys.

Use the /Copy command to copy values and formulas to another file in memory. If you just want to convert all formulas to values (as in the /File Xtract Values command), use the /Range Value command.

To copy a range to another file in memory, follow these steps:

1. Move the cell pointer to the beginning of the source range.

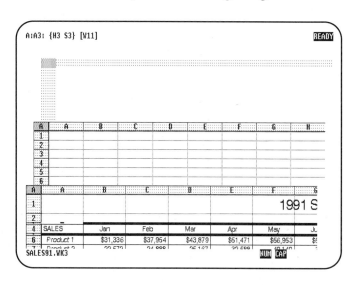

In this example, move the cell pointer to A3 in the SALES91 file.

2. Select /Copy.

3. 1-2-3 prompts you for the source range with the `Enter range to copy FROM:` prompt. Type or highlight the source range and press `↵Enter`.

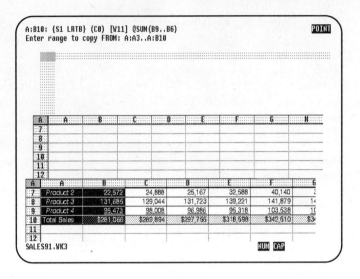

In this example,
select the range
A3..B10 and press
⏎Enter .

4. Move the cell pointer to the upper left corner of the target range. (Use
   direction keys to move between the worksheets.)

10

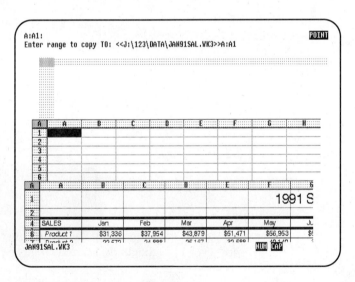

In this example,
press Ctrl PgUp to
move to the next
worksheet; then
move to cell A1.

5. Press ⏎Enter to complete the copy.

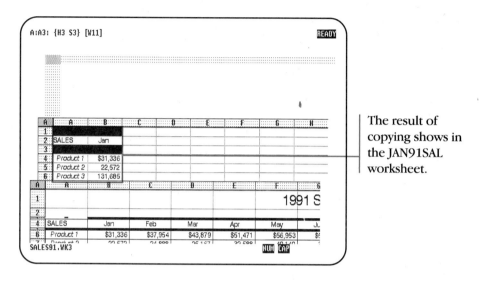

The result of copying shows in the JAN91SAL worksheet.

Saving All Files in Memory

In addition to saving each file, you can save all files in memory at one time.

To save all files, follow these steps:

1. Select /**F**ile **S**ave.

2. 1-2-3 displays the prompt Enter name of file to save: with the default [ALL MODIFIED FILES]. Press ⏎Enter to save all files with their current file names.

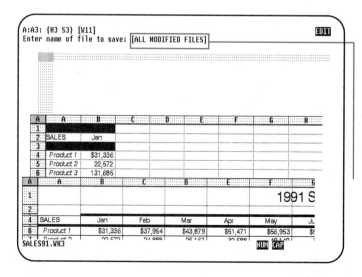

The default is [ALL MODIFIED FILES]. Save both SALES91 and JAN91SAL by pressing ⏎Enter.

3. If you already saved any of the files, 1-2-3 prompts you to `Cancel`, `Replace`, or `Backup`. Choose **R**eplace to erase the files on disk and replace them with the worksheets in memory. Choose **B**ackup to make a copy of the files on disk (add a BAK extension) and save the worksheets in memory with WK3 extensions.

4. If you want to save only the file at the cell pointer, press `Esc` at the `Enter name of file to save:` prompt, and then press `↵Enter`.

Linking Cells between Files

1-2-3 enables you to use formulas to link a range in one worksheet to a cell in another. The cell that receives the information is the target cell. The range that sends the information is the source range. You can save linked cells with /**F**ile **S**ave; 1-2-3 automatically updates the linked formulas when you retrieve the file. (Cell linking is unavailable with versions before 1-2-3 Release 2.2. Cell linking to a range is unavailable with versions before Release 3.0.)

Use /**F**ile **C**ombine when you want to copy information from file to file. The cell linkage feature, however, is automatic and requires no active use of commands.

Establishing a Link

1-2-3 performs links within the target cell, using a special kind of formula. The formula begins with a plus sign (+), followed by two less-than symbols (<<). Next, enter the name of the source file (including the directory name if the file is not in the current directory). Then type two greater-than symbols (>>). Finally, add the address or range name of the source cell.

To establish a link between cells in different worksheets, follow these steps:

1. With the cell pointer in the target cell, press `+`.

2. Press `<` twice to place two less-than symbols in the file link formula.

3. Type the name of the source file (including the directory name if the file is not in the current directory). If the file uses the default WK3 extension, you do not need to type the extension. In this example, the source file for target cell B8 is MIAMI.WK3.

10

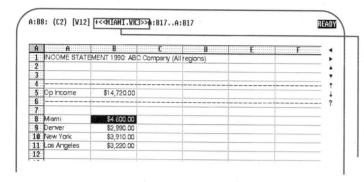

The target file is the income statement worksheet for all regions. This file uses existing information from each region's file.

4. Press $\boxed{>}$ twice to place two greater-than symbols in the formula.

5. Type the address or range name of the source cell; then press $\boxed{\text{←Enter}}$. In this example, the source cell for target cell B8 is cell B17 of MIAMI.WK3.

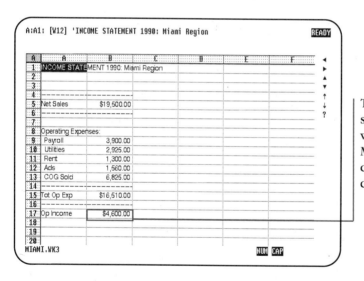

The income statement worksheet for the Miami region contains a source cell: B17.

When the linking formula is complete, data is copied immediately from the source cell to the target cell.

For the link to become permanent and automatic (occurring with every /File **Retrieve**), use /File **S**ave to save the target worksheet.

10

When you alter a source cell, 1-2-3 does not immediately copy its new contents to the linked target cell or cells. In fact, a source cell may go through many changes and you can save the file many times, yet the target cell might not reflect any of these interim values. 1-2-3 only updates the contents of the target cell when you retrieve the target file, or when you issue the /**File Admin Link-Refresh** command.

This last example linked one cell from the source file to one cell in the target file. 1-2-3 Release 3.0 and higher allows you to link to a *range* in the source file. To link to a range of another worksheet, type the range name or address after the greater-than symbols in the file-linking formula.

The entry @SUM<<MIAMI>>A:B9..A:B13) in the current example means that B8 is to contain the sum of the range B9..B13 on sheet A of the file MIAMI.WK3 in the current directory.

The target file, a summary of operating expenses for all regions, uses a range from the Miami file.

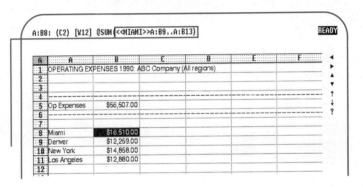

Listing Linked Files

The command /**File List Linked** provides a list of all files linked to the current worksheet. The /**File List Linked** command does not give you the addresses of either the target cells or source cells.

To list the files linked to the current worksheet, select /**File List Linked**. The resulting screen lists all other files that have links to the current file.

In this example, four files are linked to the current file.

Refreshing Links

If you use 1-2-3 in a network or multiuser environment, someone else may alter files that contain source cells for the worksheet you are using. In this case, you may want periodic updating of your target cells. Use the **/File Admin Link-Refresh** command to update all target cells in the worksheet to reflect the current contents of source cells.

To update or "refresh" the cells linked to the current worksheet, select **/File Admin Link-Refresh**.

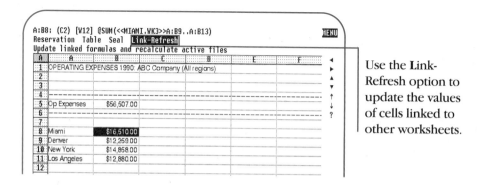

Use the Link-Refresh option to update the values of cells linked to other worksheets.

Listing Different Types of Files

1-2-3 can list all the names of a certain type of file in the current drive and directory with the **/File List** command. When you list files, you can specify worksheet, print, or graph files; any type of files; files in memory; or linked files.

To display a list of files on the current drive and directory, follow these steps:

1. Select **/File List**.
2. Select the type of file you want to list: **Worksheet**, **Print**, **Graph**, **Other**, **Active**, or **Linked**.

After you choose an option, 1-2-3 displays the list of files.

To list only worksheet files (files with a WK3 or WK1 extension), choose **Worksheet**. To list only print files (files with a PRN extension), choose **Print**. Select **Graph** to list only graph files (files with a PIC extension). Choose **Other** to list all types of files (files with any extension). To list all files open in memory, choose **Active**. To list only files linked to the current worksheet, choose **Linked**.

10

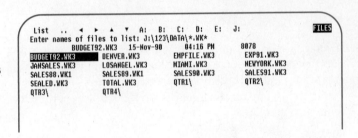

In this example, 1-2-3 displays all WK1 and WK3 files in the current directory after you select **W**orksheet.

Specifying a Drive and Directory

Use the /**W**orksheet **G**lobal **D**efault **D**irectory or the /**F**ile **D**irectory commands to change the drive and directory. The default directory is the one containing the 1-2-3 program files. /**W**orksheet **G**lobal **D**efault **D**irectory can change the default drive and directory to one that contains your data files. /**F**ile **D**irectory, on the other hand, changes the drive and directory temporarily for only the current worksheet session.

To change the default directory, follow these steps:

1. Select /**W**orksheet **G**lobal **D**efault **D**irectory. The control panel shows the current default directory.

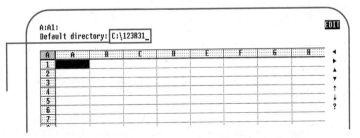

In this example, C:\123R31 is the default directory.

2. Press Esc or use ◆Backspace to clear the current default directory.

3. Type the new default directory name and press ↵Enter. Remember to precede the directory name with the drive letter, a colon (:), and a backslash (\ ).

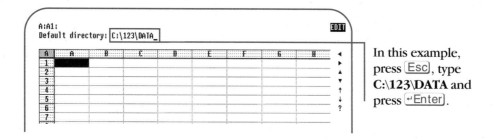

In this example, press ⎡Esc⎤, type **C:\123\DATA** and press ⎡↵Enter⎤.

4. Select **Update**. This command updates a program file that allows 1-2-3 to use the new default directory in future sessions.

5. Select **Quit** to return to READY mode.

With a hard disk, you can use the default directory setting to your advantage. As in the preceding example, you can set the default directory to C:\123\DATA. When you want to retrieve a file, 1-2-3 displays all the subdirectories and files within the C:\123\DATA directory. If you select a subdirectory from the list, 1-2-3 displays the subdirectories and files stored in that directory so you can make a choice. Setting the default directory this way saves time if you use worksheets in different subdirectories.

If you are working with files in a different directory than the one you normally use, you can change the directory temporarily with the /**File Directory** command. This command overrides the default directory for the current session only.

To change the current directory temporarily, follow these steps:

1. Select /**File Directory**. The control panel shows the current directory.

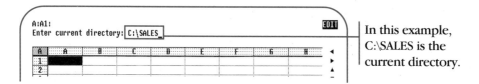

In this example, C:\SALES is the current directory.

2. Type the new directory name (the current directory name automatically clears when you start typing). Remember to precede the directory name with the drive letter.

3. Press ⎡↵Enter⎤.

10

In this example, type **C:\EXPENSES** and press ⏎Enter.

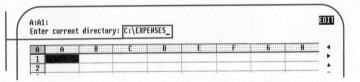

1-2-3 changes the directory for the current session only. The next time you access 1-2-3, the default directory again becomes the current directory.

Deleting Files

When you save files to a floppy disk, you sometimes find that the disk is full. To alert you, 1-2-3 displays the message `Disk full` in the screen's lower left corner, and the mode indicator flashes `ERROR`. You must either swap disks or delete one or more of the files occupying space on the disk to save the current file.

You have two ways to delete stored files in 1-2-3. First, you can use the /File **Erase** command within 1-2-3. Second, you can access DOS with the /System command and erase the file at the DOS level with the ERASE or DEL (delete) command.

To delete a file from within 1-2-3, follow these steps:

1. Select /File **Erase**.
2. Select the type of file you want to erase: **Worksheet**, **Print**, **Graph**, or **Other**. To erase a worksheet file (a file with a WK1 or WK3 extension), choose **Worksheet**. To erase a print file (a file with a PRN extension), choose **Print**. To erase a graph file (a file with a PIC extension), choose **Graph**. To erase any type of file, choose **Other**.

In this example, choose **Worksheet** by pressing Ⓦ.

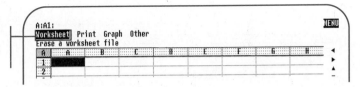

Depending on your choice, 1-2-3 displays files with the appropriate extensions.

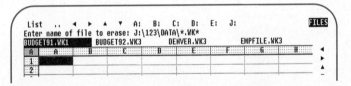

3. Press [F3] (Name) to display a full-screen listing of files.

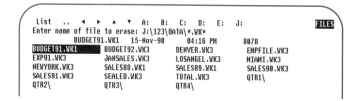

In this example, a full-screen listing shows all worksheet files.

4. Highlight the file you want to erase, or type its name; then press [↵Enter].

You can use the wild-card characters described in Chapter 3 to display all the files of a certain type that you want to delete. These characters are the same familiar wild-card characters used for DOS and other commands throughout 1-2-3. The following list shows some examples of using wild-card characters:

*   Matches the remaining characters of a file name. For example, C* matches CHICAGO, CASHFLOW, and CENTERS.

?   Matches all characters in a single position in a filename. For example, SALES8? matches SALES88 and SALES89, but not SALES90 or SALES.

Be careful when you use the /File Erase command. After you delete a file, you cannot recover it with 1-2-3. Always double-check before you delete a file.

Importing Files into 1-2-3

A powerful 1-2-3 feature is its capability to transfer data between 1-2-3 and other programs. To perform a transfer, use the /File Import and /Print File Options Other Unformatted commands, and the Translate utility. See Chapter 8 for a discussion of the Unformatted print option.

Importing ASCII Text Files

Use the /File Import command to copy standard ASCII files to specific locations in the current worksheet. For example, PRN (print) files are standard ASCII text files created to print after the current 1-2-3 session. Other standard ASCII files include those produced by various word processing, BASIC, and database programs. These programs, like 1-2-3, can produce and retrieve ASCII files.

To import an ASCII text file to 1-2-3, follow these steps:

1. Select /**File Import**.
2. Select **Text** or **Numbers**.

   Use the **Text** option for importing an ASCII file created by your word processor. Use the **Numbers** option when you import delimited files–ASCII files that contain separator characters to distinguish items of data.

If you select **Text**, 1-2-3 displays all PRN files in the current directory.

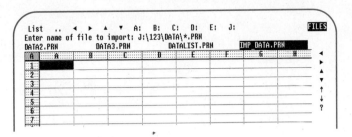

```
List    ..  ◄   ►   ▲   ▼   A:  B:  C:  D:  E:  J:                    FILES
Enter name of file to import: J:\123\DATA\*.PRN
DATA2.PRN              DATA3.PRN              DATALIST.PRN    IMP_DATA.PRN
A         A        B        C        D        E        F        G        H      ◄
1                                                                                 ►
2                                                                                 ▲
3                                                                                 ▼
4                                                                                 ↑
5                                                                                 ↓
6                                                                                 ?
7
```

3. To display files in a different drive or directory, type the appropriate drive and directory.
4. Type wild-card characters (* or ?) and extensions as needed; then press ↵Enter to display the desired files.
5. Highlight the name of the text file you want to import; then press ↵Enter.

10

1-2-3 imported the ASCII text file.

```
A:A1: '         PARTY BUDGET                                          READY

A         A        B        C        D        E        F        G        H      ◄
1                  PARTY BUDGET                                                   ►
2         Beverages                                                               ▲
3         2 Coke            $7.00   $14.00                                        ▼
4         2 Pepsi           $6.50   $13.00                                        ↑
5         3 Seven-Up        $7.50   $22.50                                        ↓
6         4 Sprite          $7.00   $28.00                                        ?
7         3 Diet Coke       $8.00   $24.00
8         3 Diet Pepsi      $8.00   $24.00
9                                   $125.50 Total
10
```

If you select /**File Import Numbers**, 1-2-3 places labels and numbers—separated by commas, colons, semicolons, or spaces—into separate columns. If you import a file with the **Numbers** option, 1-2-3 imports only those column headings which are surrounded by quotation marks.

If you have Wysiwyg loaded, imported text files may appear out of alignment. To make sure that text characters line up, change the font to a nonproportional font such as Courier with the **:Format Font** command.

Importing Files from Other Programs

Use the Translate utility to import files into 1-2-3 from dBASE II, dBASE III, Multiplan (SYLK), and VisiCalc. Also use the utility to export 1-2-3 files to dBASE II, dBASE III, and DIF formats. (Many presentation-graphics packages use DIF files.)

This utility provides good communication with dBASE, including dBASE IV (which the menu does not list but which you can access by selecting dBASE III and III+). The Translate utility also provides translation capabilities among all Lotus products, allowing free interchange of worksheets between Symphony and earlier releases of 1-2-3.

To use the Translate utility, follow these steps:

1. Select **Translate** from the 1-2-3 Access System menu.

2. Select the format (program) from which you want to translate by highlighting your selection; then press ⏎Enter.

3. Select the format (program) to which you want to translate by highlighting your selection; then press ⏎Enter.

4. Based on your choice of format, a list of files appears. (As a format choice, for example, you can choose *.WK3 for 1-2-3 Release 3.0 or higher, or *.DBF for a dBASE file.)

5. Select the file name you want to translate by highlighting the file name and pressing ⏎Enter, or pressing Esc to edit the subdirectory or file name.

10

369

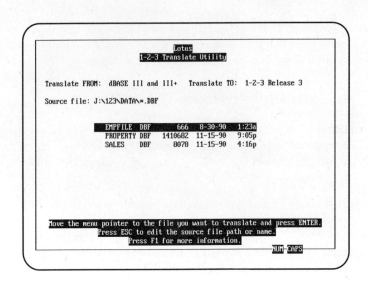

In this example,
highlight
EMPFILE.DBF and
press ⏎Enter.

6. When the file name is correct, press ⏎Enter.

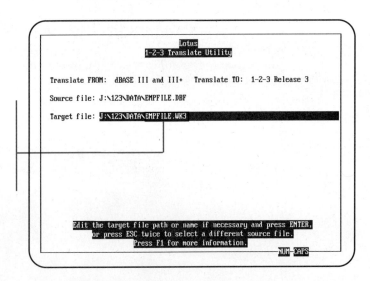

10

In this example,
press ⏎Enter to
accept
EMPFILE.WK3 as
the translated
filename.

7. At the resulting menu, select **Yes** to proceed with the translation.

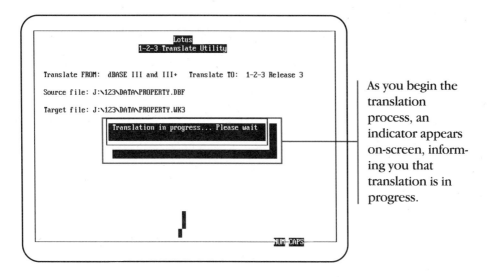

As you begin the translation process, an indicator appears on-screen, informing you that translation is in progress.

8. When the translation is complete, press Esc twice to reach a menu giving you the option to leave the Translate utility. To exit, select **Yes**.

Writing a List of Files into the Worksheet

1-2-3 uses the **/File Admin Table** command to create a table of information about files on disk, active files, or files linked to the current file. This table appears in a specified range in the worksheet.

The **Table** command lists varied information about the files, depending on the type of file you select. Make certain that the specified location in the worksheet is blank. 1-2-3 writes over the existing data to create the table. The following breakdown shows the information you can find:

- When you select **Worksheet**, **Print**, **Graph**, or **Other** options, 1-2-3 lists basic information about each file. You see listed the names and extension of each file, the last date and time each file was saved, and its disk size in bytes.

- **Linked** displays basic file information along with the path and the file name of each linked file.

- When you select **Active**, 1-2-3 displays basic file information and the number of worksheets in each file. If you have changed the file, a 0 appears in the sixth column, a 1 appears if you haven't. In the seventh column, a 1 appears if you have the file's reservation and 0 appears if you don't.

10

371

To write a table of information in the worksheet, follow these steps:

1. Select /**File Admin Table**.

2. Select the type of file you want to list: **Worksheet**, **Print**, **Graph**, **Other**, **Active** or **Linked**. To list only worksheet files (files with a WK1 or WK3 extension), choose **Worksheet**. To list only print files (files with a PRN extension), choose **Print**. To list only graph files (files with a PIC extension), choose **Graph**. To list all types of files (files with any extension), choose **Other**. To list all files open in memory, choose **Active**. To list only files linked to the current worksheet, choose **Linked**.

3. Type the drive and directory and press ⏎Enter.

In this example, to list the default directory, press ⏎Enter.

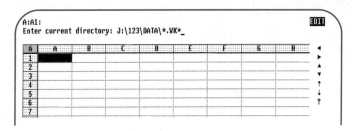

```
A:A1:                                                              EDIT
Enter current directory: J:\123\DATA\*.WK*_
```

4. Type or highlight the address of the top left corner of the range where the directory will appear and press ⏎Enter. 1-2-3 displays the list of files.

This screen is the result of /**File Admin Table Worksheet** command.

```
A:A1:  'BUDGET92.WK3                                              READY

      A          B        C         D       E     F     G     H
 1  BUDGET92    33192   0.67794     8078
 2  DENVER.WI   33214   0.737662    1039
 3  EMPFILE.WI  33158   0.882639    1400
 4  LOSANGEL.   33217   0.737662    1039
 5  MIAMI.WK3   33222   0.737153    1038
 6  NEWYORK.\   33207   0.737662    1039
 7  QS10-23.W   33292   0.760532    1317
 8  SALES88.W   32592   0.67794   155589
 9  SALES89.W   32942   0.67794   244418
10  SALES90.W   33337   0.67794   233341
11  SALES91.W   33692   0.67794   278911
12  TOTAL.WK3   33242   0.760394    1317
13  QTR1\       33192   0.76456   <DIR>
14  QTR2\       33192   0.764583  <DIR>
15  QTR3\       33192   0.764606  <DIR>
16  QTR4\       33192   0.764653  <DIR>
17
18
19
20                                                          NUM CAP
```

10

For the information to be clear, you may need to increase the width of columns with the /Worksheet Column Set-Width command. You should also format the second column with /Range Format Date and the third column with /Range Format Date Time.

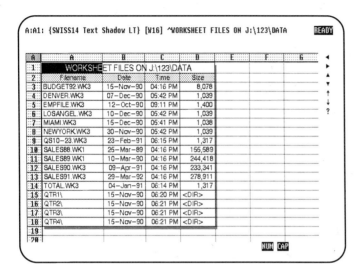

This example shows the result of /File Admin Table Worksheet after formatting.

Protecting Your File from Unwanted Changes

Sometimes you want others to update your file, but not to make changes to hidden and protected information. For example, you want someone to input data, but not to deal with protected formulas and hidden macros. Use /File Admin Seal in this situation.

The commands that are then protected from change include:

- /File Admin Reservation Setting
- /Graph Name [Create, Delete, Reset]
- /Print [File, Encoded] Options Name [Create, Delete, Reset]
- /Range [Format, Label, Prot, Unprot]
- /Range Name [Create, Delete, Labels, Reset, Undefine]
- /Range Name Note [Create, Delete, Reset]
- /Worksheet Column Hide
- /Worksheet Global [Col-Width, Format, Group, Label, Prot, Zero]

10

373

To seal the file so that no one can use these commands until unsealed with a password, follow these steps:

1. Select /**F**ile **A**dmin **S**eal.
2. To allow only users with the password to use this command, select **F**ile. To save the reservation setting with a password, select **R**eservation-Setting.
3. Type a password and press ⏎Enter. Your password does not appear on the screen.
4. Type your password again to verify it and press ⏎Enter.
5. Use /**F**ile **S**ave to save the sealed file.

To unseal a file, use the /**F**ile **A**dmin **S**eal **D**isable command. Type your password at the prompt.

Summary

Knowing how to manage files is essential for the efficient use of 1-2-3. Aside from the basic tasks of naming, saving, and retrieving files you learned in Chapter 3, you need to perform other file-management tasks. This chapter showed you how to protect files with passwords. You also learned how to save partial files when you want to extract or combine portions of a worksheet. You can list and delete files with ease if you know how to specify drives, subdirectories, and file names accurately. You can even import files from other software programs. You also learned how to work with files that are part of a network environment.

Specifically, you learned the following key information about 1-2-3:

■ You can add passwords to your files with the /**F**ile **S**ave command so that only those who know the exact password can retrieve your file.

■ The /**F**ile **X**tract command enables you to save part of the worksheet file. You can save either the formulas existing in a range of cells or the current values of the formulas in the range.

■ The /**F**ile **C**ombine command enables you to combine data from different files. You can copy the source worksheet or range on top of the current worksheet. You can also add or subtract values from the combined worksheet or range with the values in the current worksheet.

■ The /**F**ile **O**pen and /**F**ile **N**ew commands enable you to have more than one file in memory. You can use the /**C**opy command to copy information between open files in memory.

10

■ The /File List Linked command provides a listing of all files linked to the current worksheet.

■ The /File Admin Link-Refresh command updates all target cells in the current worksheet to reflect the current contents of the source cells. This command is particularly helpful for users on a network.

■ You can use the /Worksheet Global Default Directory and the /File Directory to change the current drive and directory. The latter command affects only the current session of 1-2-3.

■ The /File Erase command deletes stored files from within 1-2-3. You can also delete files by accessing DOS with the /System command. Then you erase the files at the DOS level with the ERASE or DEL command.

■ The /File Import command allows the transfer of data between 1-2-3 and other programs. Use this command to copy standard ASCII files to specific locations in the current worksheet.

■ Use the Translate utility, available from the 1-2-3 Access System menu, for converting other programs to 1-2-3's format.

■ The /File Admin Table command enables you to write a list of file information in your worksheet.

The next chapter shows you how to create graphs within 1-2-3. You learn about the graph creation process and how to select graph types and data ranges. Also included are steps to enhance the appearance of a graph and to save a graph to disk for later printing.

10

Creating and Printing Graphs

E ven if 1-2-3 provided only spreadsheet capabilities, the program would be extremely powerful. More information can be quickly assembled and tabulated electronically than can possibly be developed manually. But despite the importance of keeping detailed worksheets that show real or projected data, that information can be worthless if you can't readily understand it.

To help decision-makers who are pressed for time or unable to draw conclusions from countless rows of numeric data, and who may benefit from seeing key figures displayed graphically, 1-2-3 offers graphics capabilities. The program has seven types of basic business graphs as well as options for enhancing the graphs' appearance. You can quickly design and alter graphs as worksheet data changes. This capability means that graphs may be changed almost as fast as 1-2-3 recalculates the data.

An overview of creating a graph

Selecting a graph type

Specifying a data series range

Enhancing the appearance of a graph

Saving graphs on disk

Printing graphs

11

Key Terms in This Chapter

Graph type The manner in which data is represented graphically.

X-axis   The horizontal bottom edge of a graph.

Y-axis   The vertical left edge of a graph. 1-2-3 also allows you to create graphs with a y-axis on the vertical right edge of a graph.

Origin   The intersection of the x- and y-axes.

Legend   The description of the shading, color, or symbols assigned to data ranges in line or bar graphs. The legend appears across the bottom of the graph.

Tick marks The small marks on the axes of a graph which indicate the increments between the minimum and maximum graph values.

Using the Mouse

To use a mouse with 1-2-3 Release 3.1, you need a mouse, mouse software, and a graphics monitor and graphics card that support a mouse. Also, Wysiwyg must be loaded into memory. You can use a mouse to select commands and files, specify ranges, and move the cell pointer within a worksheet or between multiple worksheets and files. In the examples throughout this chapter, notice that the 1-2-3 commands always begin with a slash (/), and the Wysiwyg commands always begin with a colon (:). Refer to the following sections of the specified chapters for further information on using the mouse.

- Chapter 2— "Understanding Mouse Terminology"
- Chapter 3— "Mouse Control of the Cell Pointer"
     "Using the Mouse To Select Menu Commands"
- Chapter 4— "Using the Mouse To Specify Ranges"

You create graphs with 1-2-3's /Graph commands. Although the program has a number of options, you need to specify only a graph type and a single data range to create a basic graph. After providing the required information, you select the

View option from the /Graph menu. This command plots the graph to the screen, temporarily replacing the spreadsheet until a key is pressed.

You can perform true graphics "what if" analyses with 1-2-3. In fact, you can use the Graph (F10) key to replot a graph after making changes to the worksheet, without having to redefine the graph with the /Graph commands. This replotting immediately shows the effects of changes on the current graph.

In this chapter, you learn to create a basic graph, to select seven types of graphs from the data on your worksheet, and to enhance your graphs. You also learn to name and save your graphs in a worksheet file that you can retrieve and modify at any time. The last part of the chapter shows you how to print graphs.

Graphing commands are also available in Wysiwyg. However, the options on the :Graph menu are primarily for further enhancing the graphs you create from 1-2-3's /Graph menu. Wysiwyg contains a built-in graph editor that you can use to annotate your graphs. With Wysiwyg, you can also insert a graph in any spreadsheet range; draw arrows, lines, circles, and other shapes; and print graphs and spreadsheet data on the same page. Chapter 12 covers how to use the Wysiwyg :Graph commands to enhance your 1-2-3 graphs.

An Overview of Creating a Graph

Before creating your first graph, you must determine whether your hardware supports viewing and printing graphs, whether your 1-2-3 software is correctly installed for graphics, and whether the worksheet on-screen contains data you want to graph. And you should understand which type of graph is best suited for presenting specific numeric data in picture form.

You can use 1-2-3's graphing capabilities to create and view a graph, store its specifications for later use, and print the graph. Creating and storing a graph requires only that you have the 1-2-3 software installed on your equipment, that you correctly select options from the /Graph menu, and that you save these options with the associated worksheet file.

Hardware Requirements

To view a graph on-screen, you need a graphics monitor or a monitor with a graphics-display adapter. Without this monitor, you can construct and save a 1-2-3 graph, but you must print the graph to view it. To print a graph, you need a graphics printer supported by 1-2-3.

11

The Graph Creation Process

To create a 1-2-3 graph, begin by selecting the /Graph command while the worksheet containing the data you want to graph is displayed.

Selecting /Graph produces a menu of options for creating graphs.

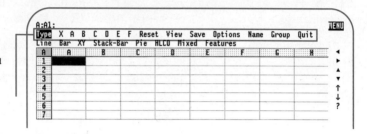

Each option on the /Graph menu is described in table 11.1.

Table 11.1
Selections on the /Graph Menu

Selection	Description
Type	Provides options for creating seven types of graphs: line, bar, XY, stacked bar, pie, HLCO, or mixed.
X	Specifies the range to be used as x-axis labels or values, or labels of pie slices.
A through F	Specifies the ranges containing the numeric data to be graphed.
Reset	Clears the current graph settings.
View	Displays a full-screen view of the current graph.
Save	Saves a graph in the file format needed for using the graph with other programs.
Options	Provides choices for labeling, enhancing, or customizing a graph.
Name	Lets you assign a name to one or more graphs and store the graph settings so that you can redisplay the graph(s) whenever you retrieve the worksheet file.

380

Table 11.1 (continued)

Selection	Description
Group	Defines a range of contiguous cells to be the X and A through F ranges.
Quit	Quits the /Graph menu and returns the worksheet to READY mode.

You use some of these commands every time you create a graph. Other commands (particularly some commands available through **Options**) are used less frequently; you use these commands when you need to enhance or customize your graph. If you do not need to enhance or customize the graph, creating a graph that displays nothing more than data points is easy. Only four steps are required to produce a simple graph. To create a simple graph, follow these steps:

1. Select the type of graph (if different from the default type, which is Line) by using the /Graph **T**ype command.

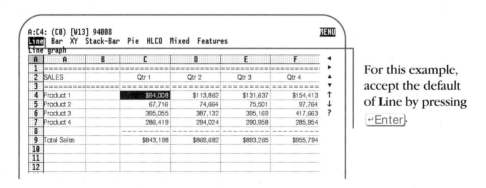

For this example, accept the default of **Line** by pressing
⏎Enter.

2. Indicate the data ranges from your worksheet that you want to graph by selecting one or more of the **A—F** options from the /Graph menu.

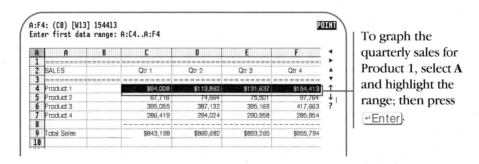

To graph the quarterly sales for Product 1, select **A** and highlight the range; then press
⏎Enter.

11

3. Use the **X** option from the /Graph menu to indicate the data range for labeling the tick marks along the x-axis in a line, bar, or stacked-bar graph; for labeling each part of a pie graph; or for plotting the independent variable in an XY graph.

For example, select **X** and highlight the labels Qtr 1 through Qtr 4 in row 2; then press ↵Enter.

```
A:F2: [W13] ^Qtr 4                                              POINT
Enter x-axis range: A:C2..A:F2

  A      A         B         C          D          E          F      ◄
  1  =============================================================  ►
  2  SALES                  Qtr 1      Qtr 2      Qtr 3      Qtr 4   ▲
  3  =============================================================  ▼
  4  Product 1              $94,008   $113,862   $131,637   $154,413  ↑
  5  Product 2              67,716     74,664     75,501     97,764   ↓
  6  Product 3             395,055    387,132    395,169    417,663   ?
  7  Product 4             286,419    294,024    290,958    285,954
  8                      -------    -------    -------    -------
  9  Total Sales         $843,198   $869,682   $893,265   $955,794
 10
```

You can combine steps 2 and 3 into a one-step operation by using the /Graph Group command to set all data ranges at once. This option is described later in the chapter.

4. Display the graph on the screen by selecting the **View** command from the /Graph menu or by pressing F10 (Graph) when in READY mode.

The resulting line graph, the default graph type, illustrates the default features for this type of graph.

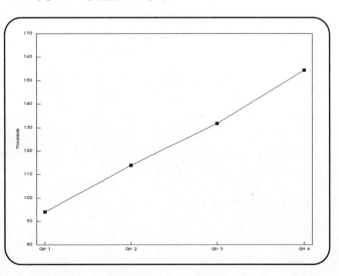

Press any key to return to the worksheet.

After you have created a basic graph using the preceding four steps, you can choose from among numerous options to change the graph type and add titles, labels, grid lines, and legends. The following graph, for example, has been enhanced in a number of ways.

11

Because 1-2-3 sets a scale based on minimum and maximum values, the program automatically displays a numeric indicator, such as Thousands, along the y-axis.

The y-axis measures the amount along the vertical axis.

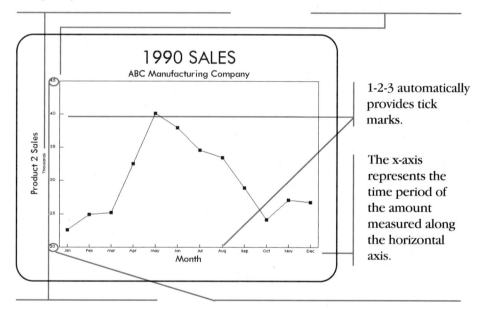

1-2-3 automatically provides tick marks.

The x-axis represents the time period of the amount measured along the horizontal axis.

1-2-3 automatically scales the adjacent numbers on the y-axis, based on the minimum and maximum values of the graphed data.

The origin of the x- and y-axes. Notice that if the origin on the graph is not zero, the upward trend will seem larger than it really is. Use an origin of zero to provide a more accurate picture of the trend.

11

You learn more about the many ways you can enhance a graph later in this chapter. Specifically, you learn how to select the graph type you need and how to indicate which data from your worksheet you want to appear on the graph.

Selecting a Graph Type

1-2-3's graphic capabilities increase the program's power by giving you a way to represent your data visually, when deciphering that type of information from columns of numbers would be difficult. 1-2-3 offers seven basic graph types: line, bar, XY, stacked bar, pie, HLCO (high-low-close-open), and mixed.

A line graph is best used for showing numeric data across time.

For example, you can track the sales trend of several products with a line graph.

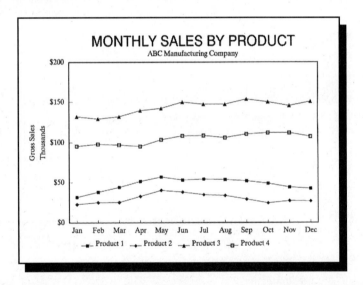

11

A bar graph, often comparing two or more data items, shows the trend of numeric data across time.

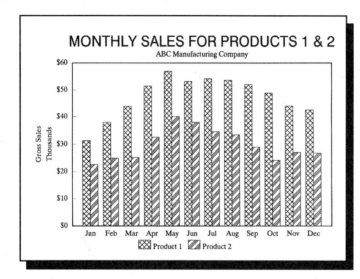

For example, you can track the progress of two or more products with a bar graph.

An XY graph compares one numeric data series to another across time, to determine whether one set of values (the dependent variable) depends on the other (the independent variable).

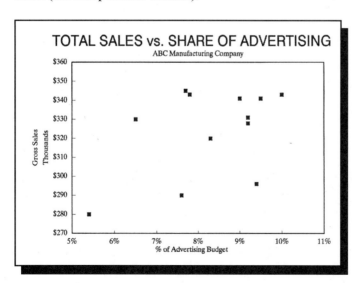

Use an XY graph, for example, to plot total sales and percent of advertising to assess whether sales data appears to depend on the share of advertising.

11

A stacked-bar graph shows two or more data series that total 100 percent of a specific numeric category. (Do not use this type of graph if your data contains negative numbers.)

Use a stacked-bar graph, for example, to graph data series for four products (displayed one above the other) to depict the proportion each represents of total product sales throughout the year.

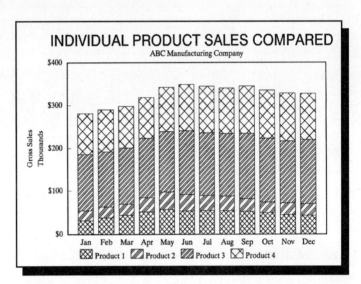

A pie graph is used to graph only one data series in which the components total 100 percent of a specific numeric category. (Do not use this type of graph if your data contains negative numbers.)

Use a pie graph, for example, to graph the percentage of total sales by month.

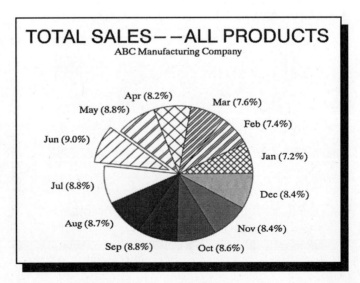

An HLCO (high-low-close-open) graph can be used to graph stock trends—showing changes in the high, low, closing, and opening prices over time. HLCO graphs can be used for tracking other data trends as well, such as sales information.

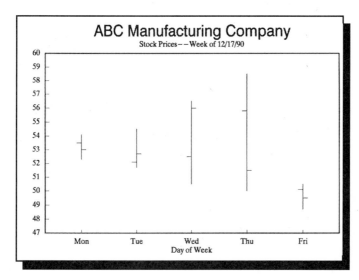

Use an HLCO graph, for example, to show the high, low, closing, and opening prices of a particular stock.

A mixed graph combines a bar graph and a line graph to display two types of data. These graphs contain two Y-axes—on the left and right sides of the graph.

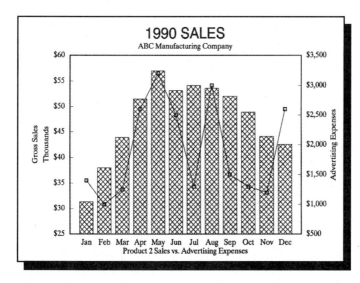

Use a mixed graph, for example, to show two types of data, such as sales and advertising expenses.

11

Selecting one of the seven available graph types is easy. When you select **Type** from the /Graph menu, 1-2-3 displays the following options:

Line   Bar   XY   Stack-Bar   Pie   HLCO   Mixed Features

By selecting one of these options, you set that graph type and automatically return to the /Graph menu. Note that the final option, **Features**, allows you to create variations of a basic graph type—such as horizontal (rather than vertical) bars.

To understand which type will best display specific numeric data, you must know something about plotting points on a graph. All graphs (except pie graphs) have two axes: the x-axis (the horizontal bottom edge) and the y-axis (the vertical left edge). (Note that in 1-2-3, you can also create a graph with another y-axis—on the vertical right edge of the graph.) 1-2-3 automatically provides tick marks for the axes. The program also scales the adjacent numbers on the y-axis, based on the minimum and maximum figures included in the plotted data range(s).

Every point plotted on a graph has a unique location (x,y): *x* represents the time period or the amount measured along the horizontal axis; *y* measures the corresponding amount along the vertical axis. The intersection of the x-axis and the y-axis is called the *origin*. To avoid the misinterpretation of graph results and to make graphs easier to compare, use a zero origin in your graphs. Later in this chapter, you learn how to manually change the upper or lower limits of the scale initially set by 1-2-3.

Of the seven 1-2-3 graph types, all but the pie graph display both x- and y-axes. Line, bar, stacked-bar, HLCO, and mixed graphs display numbers (centered on the tick marks) along the y-axis only. The XY graph displays numbers on both axes.

Specifying Data Ranges

Because more than one type of graph can accomplish the desired presentation, you need to consider what data ranges you want to graph and the relationships among data you want to show. To create a graph, you must specify the range(s) of cells from the current worksheet to be used as data series.

To enter a data series from the /Graph menu, choose from the options **X, A, B, C, D, E, F,** or **Group**.

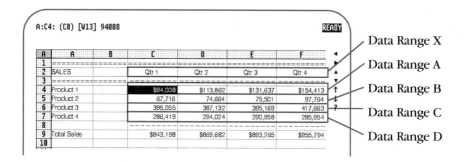

You have the option of defining each data range on the worksheet separately or defining all the data ranges you want to plot at one time. To define one data range at a time, you use the **X** and **A—F** options from the /**G**raph menu. If all the ranges you want to plot are contiguous (next to each other without any intervening rows or columns), you can use the **G**roup option to define all the ranges at once.

Defining One Data Range at a Time

If the ranges you want to plot are located in various parts of the worksheet—that is, the ranges are not all contiguous—you must define one range at a time. You can do so by choosing from among the options **X** and **A—F**.

To specify the data ranges containing x-axis and y-axis data, follow these steps:

1. Select /**G**raph.
2. Choose from the following selections the ranges for x- or y-axis data or labels:

Selection	Description
X	Enters the x-axis label range. These are labels such as Jan., Feb., Mar., and so on. Creates labels for pie graph wedges and for line, bar, and stacked-bar graphs.
A	Enters the first y-axis data range. **A** is the only *data* range used by a pie graph.
B	Enters the second y-axis data range. Identifies pie graph shading values and any slices to be exploded.
C through **F**	Enters the third through sixth y-axis data ranges.

11

When you select one of the **X** or **A—F** options, 1-2-3 prompts you for the cell or range of cells containing the data you want to graph. You cannot enter data directly at the prompt.

3. Highlight the data range and press ⏎Enter.

In this example, highlight the **A** range C4..F4 and press ⏎Enter.

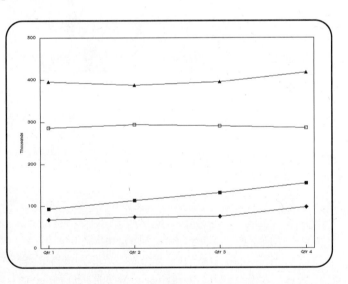

```
A:F4: (C0) [W13] 154413                                    POINT
Enter first data range: A:C4..A:F4
```

A	A	B	C	D	E	F
1						
2	SALES		Qtr 1	Qtr 2	Qtr 3	Qtr 4
3						
4	Product 1		$94,008	$113,862	$131,637	$154,413
5	Product 2		67,716	74,664	75,501	97,764
6	Product 3		395,055	387,132	395,169	417,863
7	Product 4		286,419	294,024	290,958	285,954
8						
9	Total Sales		$843,198	$869,682	$893,265	$955,794
10						

4. To view the graph, select **View.**

Although this line graph shows four data series, you can enter as many as six data series when you access the /Graph menu choices **A** through **F** separately.

You can specify the ranges in any order; the range selected will always correspond to the letter assigned in the selection process. Use the **X** option to plot the time or amount measured along the x-axis. The data points in each data series are marked by a unique symbol.

390

11

These six symbols, which correspond to specific data ranges from A through F, are displayed in table 11.2. Shading within bar, stacked-bar, pie, and mixed graphs is covered in the following pages.

Table 11.2
Data Range Symbols for Line Graphs

Data Range	Line Graph Symbol
A	▪
B	◆
C	▲
D	▭
E	◇
F	△

With bar, stacked-bar, or mixed graphs, you can also enter as many as six data series when you access separately the /Graph menu choices **A—F**.

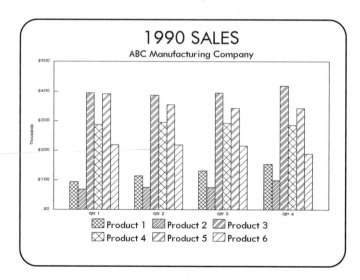

In a bar graph, multiple data ranges appear on the graph from left to right in order of data ranges A through F.

11

In a stacked-bar graph, multiple data ranges appear on the graph from bottom to top in order of data ranges A through F.

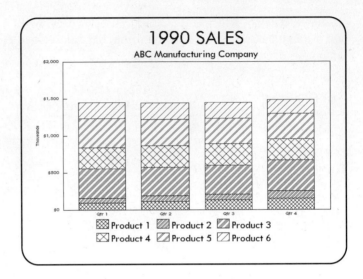

In bar, stacked-bar, and mixed graphs, the **X** option lets you indicate the time or amount measured along the x-axis. Every data series displayed in monochrome (one color) has unique shading. Data series displayed in color are assigned up to six different colors. Refer to table 11.3 for an explanation of the patterns and colors used in bar, stacked-bar, and mixed graphs.

Table 11.3
Data Range Patterns and Colors for Bar Graphs

Data Range	Bar Graph Pattern	Bar Graph Color
A	▨	Red
B	▨	Green
C	▨	Blue
D	⊠	Yellow
E	▨	Magenta
F	▱	Light Blue

11

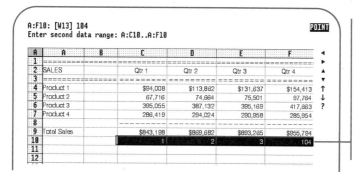

With XY graphs, to enter the data series being plotted as the independent variable, select **X** from the /Graph menu and specify the range.

Plot at least one dependent variable (you would usually select **A**). The unique symbols that mark the data points depend on which data series (**A—F**) is selected.

With pie graphs, choose **X** to identify each piece of the pie. Then enter only one data series by selecting **A** from the /Graph menu. Other than the **X** and **A** options, the only other option in the **X** and **A—F** selections you need for creating a pie graph is **B**. By selecting **B**, you can shade and "explode" pieces of the pie.

To shade pieces of the pie graph, select a range of cells containing values between 1 and 8—corresponding to data range **A** of the graph.

To explode a piece of the pie, add 100 to this number. Select **B** from the menu and highlight the range of numbers.

11

The pie graph
shows some of the
different types of
shading and one
exploded slice.

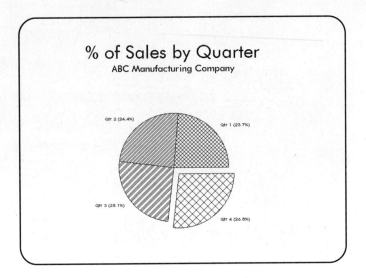

Defining All Data Ranges at Once

If the **X** and the **A—F** ranges are in one contiguous range, you can use the /Graph
Group command to define all the ranges at once. The command /Graph Group
gives you a quick way to define the **X** and **A—F** ranges without having to specify
them individually. For this option to work properly, the cells for the **X** range
must be immediately to the left of—or immediately above—the cells of the **A**
range. The cells for ranges **B** through **F**, if present, are adjacent one by one to the
A range. Once you have defined the location of the range, the command prompts
you for a "columnwise" or "rowwise" orientation.

To select all the data ranges for a graph, **X** and **A—F**, when data is in adjacent
rows and columns are in consecutive order, follow these steps:

1. Select /Graph **Type**.

   Choose a graph type from the seven selections provided.

2. Select **Group**.

3. Specify the range that contains **X** and one or more **A** through **F** data
   ranges, and then press ⏎Enter. The rows or columns must be adjacent
   and in the order X, A, B, C, and so on.

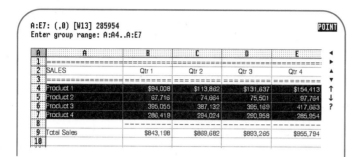

For this example, specify the group range as A4..E7 and press ⏎Enter.

4. Select **Columnwise** if the data ranges are in columns, or select **Rowwise** if the data ranges are in rows.

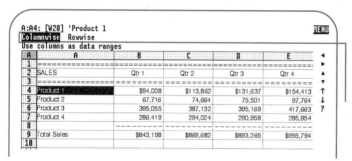

For this example, select **Columnwise**.

5. Select **View**.

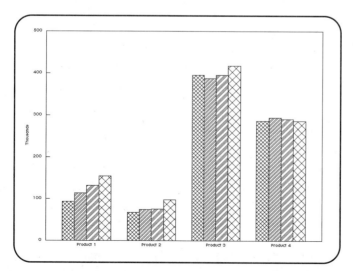

This graph shows the result of selecting **Columnwise** orientation with the **/Graph Group** command.

Creating Automatic Graphs

1-2-3's automatic graph feature enables you to create certain types of graphs with a single keystroke. For an automatic graph, the position of the cell pointer—not the settings of the /Graph **X** and /Graph **A** through **F** options—determines which data is included in the graph. Before creating an automatic graph, you must clear the /Graph **X** and /Graph **A** through **F** settings (with the /Graph **R**eset **R**anges command) and the cell pointer must be in a section of the worksheet that can be interpreted as an automatic graph (explained later in this section).

If these conditions are satisfied, displaying an automatic graph requires only that you position the cell pointer anywhere within the spreadsheet data range and press Graph (F10) or select /Graph **V**iew.

The following criteria for an automatic graph range can be met by many common arrangements of data in a worksheet:

- An automatic graph range must contain data that can be divided, by either rows or columns, into the X and A through F ranges for the graph.

- An automatic graph range must be separated by at least two blank rows and columns from other data in the worksheet.

- The data in an automatic graph range must be arranged by columns or rows with the X data range first, the A data range second, and so on. The first row or column in the range can contain labels.

1-2-3 divides an automatic graph range into rows or columns depending on the setting of /Worksheet **G**lobal **D**efault **G**raph, which can be set to **C**olumnwise or **R**owwise. Use **R**owwise when each data range is located in a row; use **C**olumnwise when each data range is in a column. The type of graph created depends on the setting of /Graph **T**ype; if no setting has been made, the default graph type, **L**ine, is created.

An automatic graph makes use of all current /Graph menu selections, such as **T**ype, **F**eatures, and **O**ptions. The only part of an automatic graph that is "automatic" is the assignment of data ranges. Once an automatic graph exists, it can be treated as any other graph—named, saved, printed, and so on.

Enhancing the Appearance of a Graph

After you have created a basic graph using the simple four-step procedure described earlier in this chapter, you can improve the appearance of your graphs and produce final-quality output suitable for business presentations. By selecting from the /Graph **O**ptions menu, you can enhance a graph by adding descriptive labels and numbers, and by changing the default graph display items.

396

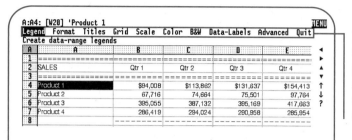

To improve the appearance of a graph, select /Graph Options to access the menu shown here.

Each of the selections on the /Graph Options menu is described in table 11.4.

Table 11.4
Selections on the /Graph Options Menu

Selection	Description
Legend	Specifies descriptions to link symbols, shadings, or colors to specific y-axis data ranges.
Format	Adds lines and/or symbols to connect or represent data points.
Titles	Adds graph titles, axis titles, and footnotes to a graph.
Grid	Adds horizontal and/or vertical lines within a graph.
Scale	Controls the division and format of values along the x-axis or y-axis.
Color	Causes a graph to be displayed and printed in color, if the proper equipment is available.
B&W	Changes the graph display and printing from color to monochrome (black and white).
Data-Labels	Adds labels identifying different data points within the graph.
Advanced	Specifies colors, fonts, and hatch patterns for a graph.
Quit	Returns you to the /Graph menu.

11

The following sections of this chapter describe and illustrate how you can create basic graphs by using only a few commands. You also learn how to use additional commands from the /Graph Options menu to create presentation-quality graphs.

As you add enhancements to your graphs, check the results frequently. Select **Quit** to leave the /Graph Options menu and return to the /Graph menu. Then select **View** to check the most recent version of the graph. Press any key to exit the graph display and restore the /Graph menu to the screen.

To view the current graph while in READY mode, press the Graph (F10) key, which instantly redraws the graph with any updated worksheet data. You can use the Graph (F10) key to "toggle" between the worksheet and the graph.

Using the Titles Option

If you select /Graph Options Titles, the following options are displayed in the control panel:

   First Second X-Axis Y-Axis 2Y-Axis Note Other-Note

You can enter one or two centered titles at the top of the graph, a title below the x-axis, a title to the left of the y-axis and to the right of the second y-axis, and two lines of footnotes at the bottom of the graph.

The titles that can be added are displayed in these designated locations.

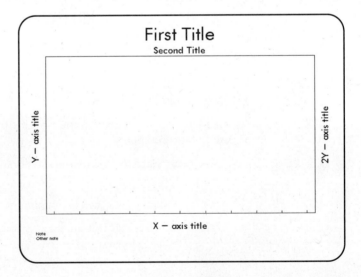

You can enter titles by typing a new description, by specifying a range name, or by referencing the cell location of a label or a number already in the worksheet. Although all titles appear on-screen in the same print style, you can select up to three different fonts to be printed.

To add titles to a graph (after you have chosen the graph type and entered data ranges), complete the following steps:

1. Select /Graph Options Titles.

2. From the Titles menu, choose from the following selections, type the title, and press ⏎Enter :

Selection	Description
First	Displays a title on the top line of a graph.
Second	Displays a title on the second line of a graph.
X-Axis	Displays a title below the x-axis.
Y-Axis	Displays a title to the left of the left y-axis.
2Y-Axis	Displays a title to the right of the right y-axis.
Note	Displays the first footnote line in the lower left corner of the graph.
Other-Note	Displays the second footnote line in the lower left corner of the graph.

Note: The **X-Axis** and **Y-Axis** titles do not apply when you construct a pie graph.

3. To view the graph with titles displayed, select **Quit View**.

To edit a title, use the command sequence that you used for creating the title, /Graph Options Titles. The existing text, cell reference, or range name will appear in the control panel, ready for editing. To modify a title, use the left- and right-arrow keys, the Backspace key, or the Esc key. If you want to eliminate a title entirely, press Esc and then press Enter.

Entering Labels within a Graph

After you have graphed a data series, you can enter values or labels to explain each point plotted on a bar, line, or XY graph. For example, you can label points on a line graph illustrating sales figures with the specific values for each point.

11

To add labels to be displayed within a graph, follow these steps:

1. Select /**Graph Options Data-Labels**.

2. Specify the data series (**A, B, C, D, E, F,** or **Group**) to which the data labels apply.

In a line graph that includes only one data range, choose **A** to assign labels to the range.

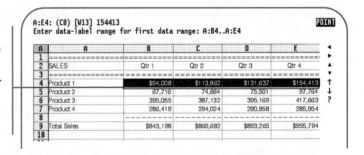

3. Enter the range containing the text or values you want to use as labels for the graph and press ↵Enter .

To label data points in the sales graph, highlight the range containing the sales figures and press ↵Enter .

Note: Instead of typing the labels (as you typed the titles), you must specify each data-label range by pointing to an existing range in the worksheet, providing cell coordinates, or specifying a previously-determined range name.

4. Indicate the location of the data labels by selecting from the menu options **Center, Left, Above, Right,** and **Below.** You may need to experiment with two or more positions for data labels to determine which position is best for your graph.

5. To view the graph with data labels displayed, select **Quit Quit View.**

400

11

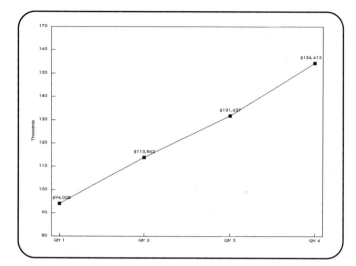

This graph shows the result of choosing the **A**bove option for the location of data labels.

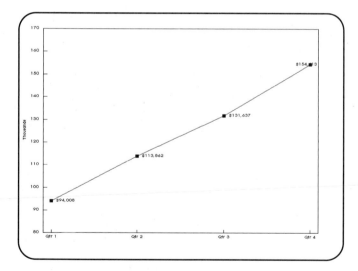

This graph shows the result of choosing the **R**ight option for the location of data labels.

If you graph more than one data series, attach the data labels to the data series with the largest figures. Then select **A**bove to position the data labels above the data points plotted. To enter text or numbers as the plotted points, use the **C**enter option with line graphs that display **N**either lines nor symbols.

11

To edit either the range or position of the data label, use the same command sequence you used to create the data label. Edit the current range or specify a different position.

To eliminate data labels that have been specified, you must issue the command you used to specify the data labels, and highlight or type the address of a blank cell or the name of a blank range in the worksheet.

Using the Legend Option

Whenever a graph contains more than one set of data, you need to be able to distinguish between those sets. If you are using a color monitor and select **Color** from the /Graph menu, 1-2-3 differentiates data series with color. If the **B&W** (monochrome) option is in effect, the data series in line and XY graphs are marked with special symbols.

If you intend to print the graph on a black-and-white printer, even if you have a color monitor, choose **B&W** before saving the graph. A graph saved under the **Color** option will print all ranges on a black-and-white printer as solid blocks of black. You might pick a data series (**A**, **B**, **C**, **D**, **E**, **F**, or **Group**) based on certain symbols, shadings, or colors represented, or to avoid using certain combinations of symbols or shadings. You may want to experiment with the different combinations to discover which you like best.

To provide explanatory text for data that is represented by symbols or shadings, use the /Graph Options Legend command to display legends below the x-axis. To add a legend to your graph, follow these steps:

1. Select /**Graph Options**.

2. Select **Legend**.

3. Select **A** to specify the legend for the first data range.

4. At the prompt `Enter legend for first data range:`, type ⃞\; then type the cell address containing the label and press ⃞Enter, or simply type the label and press ⃞Enter.

For this example, type **\A4** and press ⃞Enter.

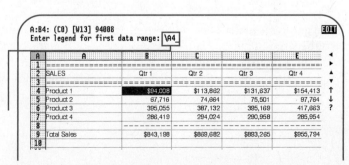

5. Repeat steps 2 through 4 for each data range contained in your graph.

6. To view the graph with a legend displayed, select **Quit View**.

You can use the command **/Graph Options Legend Range** to select the legend in one step, if the text to appear in the legend is in adjacent cells in the worksheet. In the previous example, you would type or highlight the range A4..A7 and press Enter (after the **/Graph Options Legend Range** command).

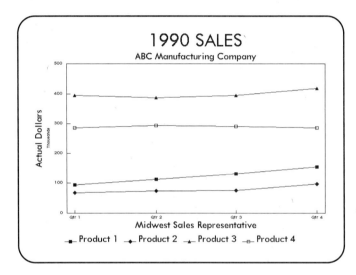

After you have entered all legends and then viewed the graph, the legends appear below the x-axis. As shown, different data ranges in line and XY graphs are distinguished by symbols.

If you want to edit a legend, use the same command sequence you used to create it. The existing text, cell reference, or range name will appear in the control panel, ready for you to edit. To eliminate a legend, press Esc and then press Enter.

As with the **/Graph Group** command and the **/Graph Options Data-Labels** command, the **Legend** option lets you define the placement of all legends at once. Because this range is one-dimensional, you are not prompted for row or column orientation.

11

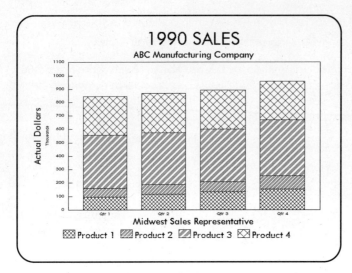

The legends for the different data ranges in bar and stacked-bar graphs are marked with unique shadings.

Specifying Connecting Lines or Symbols

The **F**ormat option of the /**G**raph **O**ptions menu, which is used to display connecting lines and/or symbols on a line-type graph, can be used for line, XY, HLCO, and mixed graphs.

To add connecting lines and/or symbols, follow these steps:

1. Select /**G**raph **O**ptions **F**ormat.

   1-2-3 displays a menu with these options:

   Graph A B C D E F Quit

2. Assign lines and/or symbols to the whole graph (**Graph**), or assign lines and/or symbols to individual data ranges (**A—F**).

3. Select from the following options on the displayed menu:

Selection	Description
Lines	Connects data points by lines alone.
Symbols	Displays only symbols.
Both	Displays both lines and symbols. This is the default setting for a line graph.
Neither	Displays only data labels. Remember that the data labels must be added with the /**G**raph **O**ptions **D**ata-Labels command.

404

Area   Fills the space between the specified line and either the line below it or the x-axis.

4. To view the graph with the specified format, select **Quit Quit View.**

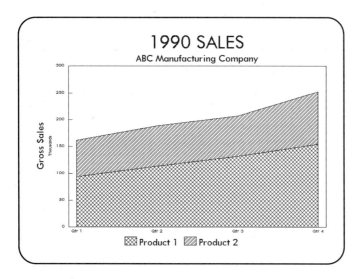

This example shows the result of using the **Area** option with two data ranges.

To restore the default format setting for the sample line graph, select **/Graph Options Format A B**oth. Returning to the **/G**raph menu and selecting View displays the graph in its original form.

Setting a Background Grid

Ordinarily, you use the default background (clear—without a grid) for your graphs. Sometimes you may want to impose a grid on a graph so that the data-point amounts are easier to read. To add a grid to your graph, follow these steps:

1. Select **/Graph Options Grid.**

2. Select the type of grid you want from the following options on the displayed menu:

Selection	Description
Horizontal	Displays horizontal grid lines. Grid lines are spaced according to the tick marks on one or both of the y-axes (specified with the **Y-A**xis option).
Vertical	Displays vertical grid lines. Grid lines are spaced according to the tick marks on the x-axis.

11

Both	Displays a graph with both horizontal and vertical grid lines.
Clear	Removes all grid lines from the current graph.
Y-Axis	Determines placement of horizontal grid lines.

3. To view the graph with grid lines displayed, select **Quit View**.

This example shows the result of using the **Horizontal** option to display grid lines.

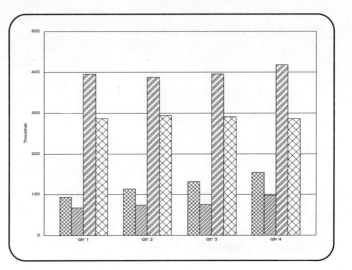

Changing Axis Scale Settings

You can use the /**Graph Options Scale** command to alter three distinct default settings associated with the values displayed along a graph's x- and y-axes. These settings let you change the upper and lower limits of the y-axis scale (both y-axes, if two are used), change the format of y-axis values, and suppress the y-axis scale indicator(s). In addition, you can use this option to change the number of labels displayed along the x-axis.

Changing the Upper and Lower Limits of the Y-Axis Scale

When you create a line, XY, bar, or stacked-bar graph, 1-2-3 automatically sets scale limits displayed on the y-axis, taking into account the smallest and largest numbers in the data ranges plotted. (For XY graphs only, 1-2-3 also establishes x-axis scale values.)

406

You can change the upper and lower scale limits. You cannot, however, determine the size of the increment between the maximum and minimum values. (This increment is indicated by tick marks.)

To change the scale of values displayed along the y-axis of a graph, follow these steps:

1. Select /**Graph** **O**ptions **S**cale.

2. From the resulting menu, select the **Y**-Scale option if you want to change the y-axis scale. If you want to modify the scale of a second y-axis, select **2Y**-Scale. Select the **X**-Scale option to change the x-axis scale on an XY graph.

```
A:C5: (,0) 22572                                              MENU
Automatic Manual  Lower  Upper  Format  Indicator  Type  Exponent  Width  Quit
Scale according to specified lower and upper limits
    A         A        B        C        D        E        F        G        H
1  =======  =======  =======  =======  =======  =======  =======  =======
2  SALES                       Jan      Feb      Mar      Apr      May      Jun
3  =======  =======  =======  =======  =======  =======  =======  =======
4  Product 1                 $31,336  $37,954  $43,879  $51,471  $56,953  $53,145
5  Product 2                  22,572   24,888   25,167   32,588   40,140   37,970
6  Product 3                 131,685  129,044  131,723  139,221  141,879  149,803
7  Product 4                  95,473   98,008   96,986   95,318  103,538  108,146
8                            -------  -------  -------  -------  -------  -------
9  Total Sales              $281,066 $289,894 $297,755 $318,598 $342,510 $349,064
10
```

1-2-3 displays the menu you use to adjust the scale.

3. Select **Manual** to change from 1-2-3's automatic scaling to your own scaling. The same menu remains on the screen.

4. Select **Lower** to assign the lower value of the scale. Type the value to be used as the lower limit and press [↵Enter].

   For example, select **Lower,** and then press [↵Enter] to accept the default of 0.

5. Select **Upper** to assign the upper value of the scale. Type the value to be used as the upper limit and press [↵Enter].

   For example, select **Upper,** type **50000,** and press [↵Enter].

6. To view the graph with different y-axis limits, select **Quit Quit View.**

11

The graph now appears with the specified y-axis lower and upper limits of 0 and 50,000, respectively.

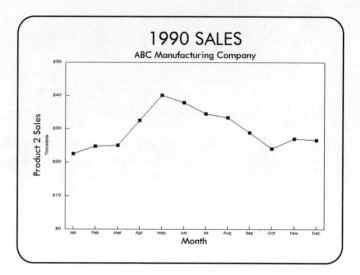

You can later select /Graph Options Scale **Y**-Scale **Automatic** if you choose to restore the default upper and lower y-axis limits.

If you elect to establish manual limits, remember two basic rules: (1) you must specify both upper and lower settings, and (2) the upper limit must be larger than the lower limit. You can use negative figures for scale values only in line and XY graphs. The lower limit in a bar, stacked-bar, or mixed graph is zero.

Select /Graph Options Scale **X**-Scale only when the graph type is XY. The **F**ormat, **I**ndicator, and **M**anual scale capabilities are not applicable to pie graphs.

Changing the Format of Y-Axis Values

1-2-3 automatically sets the format of the scale values to General. 1-2-3 does not automatically display dollar signs, commas, and decimal points along the y-axis. To change the format of the values on the y-axis (or x-axis for XY graphs), select the /Graph Options Scale **Y**-Scale (or **X**-Scale or **2Y**-Scale) **F**ormat command. When you choose Format, 1-2-3 displays the same options that are displayed when you use /**R**ange **F**ormat or /**W**orksheet **G**lobal **F**ormat.

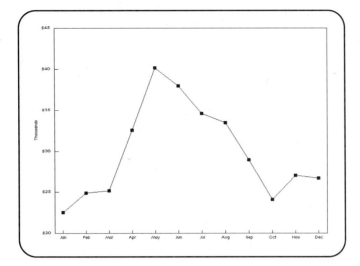

The values formatted as currency on the y-axis scale were produced with the /**Graph Options Scale Y-Scale Format Currency** command.

Modifying the Scale Indicator

The scale indicator indicates the magnitude of the values displayed along the y-axis (and the 2Y-axis, if used) when a graph is created. On an XY graph, an indicator also appears along the x-axis.

You can change the indicator, or you can suppress its display. To understand why you might want to suppress the display of the indicator, imagine a worksheet that contains data with truncated trailing zeros (for example, a sales figure of 94,008,000 that has been entered in the worksheet as 94,008). Graphing the truncated figures will produce the y-axis indicator *Thousands*, but you need *Millions*. In this case, you modify the indicator to display the appropriate text.

To modify either the y-axis or x-axis scale indicator, follow these steps:

1. Select /**Graph Options Scale**.
2. Select the **Y-Scale** option to suppress the y-axis scale indicator. Select the **X-Scale** option to suppress the x-axis scale indicator on an XY graph. Select the **2Y-Scale** option to suppress the scale indicator of the second y-axis.
3. Select **Indicator Manual**.

11

4. At the prompt `Enter indicator text:`, type the appropriate indicator and press `Enter`.

In this example, type **Millions** and press `Enter`.

```
A:B4: (C0) [W13] 94008
Enter indicator text: Millions_                                    EDIT
```

A	A	B	C	D	E
1	=================	=========	=========	=========	=========
2	SALES	Qtr 1	Qtr 2	Qtr 3	Qtr 4
3	=================	=========	=========	=========	=========
4	Product 1	$94,008	$113,862	$131,637	$154,413
5	Product 2	67,716	74,664	75,501	97,764
6	Product 3	395,055	387,132	395,169	417,663
7	Product 4	286,419	294,024	290,958	285,954
8					
9	Total Sales	$843,198	$869,682	$893,285	$955,794
10					

5. To view the graph with the modified indicator, select **Quit Quit View**.

The y-axis scale indicator now displays `Millions`.

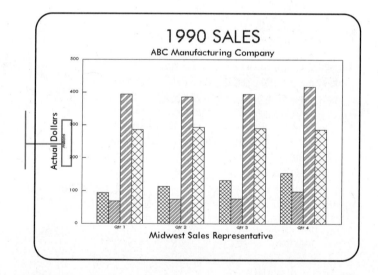

Spacing the Display of X-Axis Labels

Use the **/Graph Options Scale Skip** command to determine the spacing and number of labels along the x-axis. For example, this command can be used to change the x-axis labels from displaying every month to displaying every other month. The default setting of 1 shows every label. If you set the skip factor to 3, every third label is shown.

410

If the labels are so long that they crowd together or overlap, use the **Skip** option to improve the appearance of the graph. You will seldom need to set the factor higher than 3 or 4.

Adding a Second Y-Axis Scale

1-2-3 can create graphs that have two separate y-axes with different scales. The second y-axis, called the 2Y-axis, is displayed on the right side of the graph. By using dual y-axes, you can include on the same graph data sets that encompass widely different ranges of values.

When you assign data ranges to graph ranges A through F in the /**Graph** menu, the ranges automatically are assigned to the first y-axis. The /**Graph Type Features 2Y-Ranges** command is used to create a 2Y-axis.

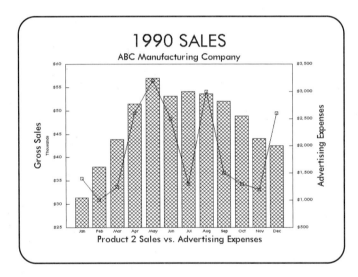

This screen displays an example of a graph with dual y-axes.

Saving Graphs on Disk

To create a disk file of a graph to be used with other programs, use the /**Graph Save** command. This command creates a file with the extension PIC or CGM—depending on the current setting of the /**Worksheet Global Default Graph** command. To save the graph specifications along with the underlying worksheet, first use the /**Graph Name Create** command to name the graph, and then save the worksheet to retain the graph settings by using /**File Save**.

11

Suppose that you have constructed a graph you want to store for subsequent printing or importing through another program, such as a word-processing program. After you verify that the graph type chosen is appropriate for your presentation needs, that the graph data ranges have been specified accurately, and that all desired enhancements have been added, use **/Graph Save** to create a PIC or CGM file on disk.

To save a graph as a PIC or CGM file so that it can be used with other programs, follow these steps:

1. Select **/Graph Save**.

   1-2-3 prompts you for a file name and displays (across the top of the screen) a list of the PIC or CGM files in the current directory.

2. Type a new file name (as many as eight characters long), or use → or ← to highlight a name already listed; then press ↵Enter.

   Note: You can press F3 to display a full-screen listing of existing graph names.

3. If you chose an existing name from the list, select **Replace** to overwrite the old file, or select **Cancel** to avoid overwriting the old file. 1-2-3 automatically adds the PIC extension to the file name for you.

After you have saved the graph settings for printing, you can follow instructions provided with the other program for using the 1-2-3 graph with that program.

Saving Graph Settings

If you want to view on-screen a graph that you created in an earlier graphing session, you must have given the graph a name when you originally constructed the graph. You also must have saved the worksheet, unless the same worksheet is still active. To name a graph, you issue the **/Graph Name Create** command. Use the **/Graph Name** options to save the graph along with the underlying worksheet or to retrieve or delete a named graph you have saved.

Only one graph at a time can be the current graph. If you want to save a graph that you have just completed (for subsequent recall to the screen) as well as build a new graph, you must first issue the **/Graph Name Create** command. The only way to store a graph for later screen display is to issue this command, which instructs 1-2-3 to remember the specifications used to define the current graph. If you do not name a graph and subsequently either reset the graph or change the specifications, you cannot restore the original graph without having to rebuild it.

11

To use the graph name settings, follow these steps:

1. Select /**Graph Name**.

2. Select from the following options the graph naming activity you want to perform:

Selection	Description
Create	Creates a name for the currently-defined graph so that you can later access and modify the graph.
Use	Displays a graph whose settings have already been saved with /**Graph Name Create**. This option allows you to recall any named graph from within the active worksheet.
Delete	Erases an individual graph name and the settings associated with that graph.
Reset	Erases all graph names.
Table	Produces a listing of all graph names, their types (pie, bar, and so on), and titles (the top line of the graph). Use caution to avoid writing over existing data.

3. If you selected **Create** in step 2, type a new name (up to 15 characters in length), and then press ⏎Enter. If you selected **Use** or **Delete**, use →or ←to highlight in the list the name of the graph you want (press F3 to view a full-screen list of names); then press ⏎Enter. If you selected **Table**, highlight the desired location of the graph name table and press ⏎Enter.

Note: If you want graph names to be stored with their worksheets, remember to save the worksheet file by using /**File Save** after creating the names.

Printing Graphs

The first part of this chapter showed you how to create 1-2-3 graphs that are displayed on-screen. The remainder of this chapter shows you how to create printed copies that can be distributed to colleagues, used in business presentations, or filed for future reference. You will learn how to modify the quality, size, and orientation of printed graphs. In addition, you learn how to include one or more graphs in a printed report.

11

Another way to print graphs is through the Wysiwyg **:Graph Add** and **:Print** commands. Chapter 12 includes information on this process.

Installing a Printer to Print Graphs

To print a graph, you must have installed a graphics-capable printer during installation, and have it connected to your computer and on-line. If you installed only one printer, you are ready to go.

If you installed more than one graphics-capable printer, you can select the one to be used for graph printing. Issue the **/Print Printer Options Advanced Device Name** command and choose a printer. To see which printer is associated with which number, highlight the numbers and read the descriptions. You can determine the currently selected printer with **/Worksheet Global Default Status**, which presents a screen display of various default settings, including the selected printer.

Printing a Graph with Default Settings

Assuming that your printer is properly installed and connected, printing a graph with the default settings is simple. You print graphs from the **/Print** menu. A graph, or a report containing a graph, can be sent directly to the printer or to an encoded disk file for later printing. To print immediately, select **/Print Printer**. To send output to an encoded file, select **/Print Encoded**, then enter the desired file name. Chapter 8 includes detailed information on creating and using encoded files.

To print the current graph or a named graph with the default settings, follow these steps:

1. Select **/Print Printer** or **/Print Encoded**.

   Note: To print a graph immediately, you must select **/Print Printer**.

2. Select **Image**.

3. Select **Current** or **Named-Graph**.

   The **Current** option prints the current graph—that is, the graph that is displayed on-screen by selecting **/Graph View** or pressing `F10` (Graph).

   The **Named-Graph** option prints a graph you have saved with **/Graph Name Create**. If you select **Named-Graph**, highlight the desired name from the list presented and press `↵Enter`. You can select a named graph from any active file.

414

11

4. After specifying the image to print, you are returned to the /Print **Printer** (or /**Print Encoded**) menu. Make sure that the printer is on-line. Position the paper, then select **Align** from the menu.

5. Select **Go** to start printing, then select **Quit** to return to your worksheet.

   You can continue working on the worksheet while a graph is printing, even specifying additional graphs and reports to print. If you do so, the additions are placed in 1-2-3's print queue and printed in the order specified.

Changing the Appearance of Printed Graphs

Most aspects of a graph's appearance are decided when you initially design the graph for screen display. For example, colors, fonts, text size, and hatch patterns are specified as you create the graph on the screen. You cannot modify these features during printing. Note, however, that the final appearance of the printed graph may differ somewhat from its appearance on-screen, particularly with regard to fonts and, if using a color printer, colors. The printed appearance of fonts and colors depends to a large extent on the specifics of your printer. As you learned in Chapter 8, you can select /**Print Printer Sample Go** to print a sample worksheet and sample graph containing graph, color, and font examples. Keep this sample worksheet available for reference when you create your next graph.

Some aspects of a graph's appearance are specified when you are ready to print the graph. Selecting /**Print Printer** (or **Encoded**) **Options Advanced Image** displays the following menu options:

   Rotate   Image-Sz   Density   Quit

These options are described in detail in the following sections.

Rotating Graphs

The **Rotate** option of the /**Print Printer** (or **Encoded**) **Options Advanced Image** menu determines whether your graph is printed upright on the page or sideways. A **No/Yes** menu results when you select **Rotate**. The **No** option, which is the default setting, prints graphs upright on the page. The **Yes** option prints graphs rotated 90 degrees counterclockwise. If your printer cannot rotate graphs, selecting **Yes** has no effect.

11

When you rotate a graph, its size depends on your **Image-Sz** settings (discussed in the next section). When you use the default **Margin-Fill** size, the graph's 4:3 (width:length) ratio does not change when the graph is rotated, but the right-left margin space is considered the length rather than the width. When using the **Length-Fill** size setting, the length you specified is considered the width when the graph is rotated.

The **Rotate** option affects only graphs and does not affect the orientation used to print worksheet data. To rotate both worksheet data and graphs, select **/Print Printer (or Encoded) Options Advanced Layout Orientation Landscape**. This command sequence has an effect only if supported by your printer.

Changing the Size and Shape of a Graph

The **Image-Sz** option of the **/Print Printer (or Encoded) Options Advanced Image** menu is used to specify the size and shape of printed graphs. The default graph shape is a rectangle with a 4:3 (width:length) ratio; the default size is a graph that fills the width of the page between the margins. By using the default page margin settings, you get a graph that is approximately 6 1/2 inches wide and 5 inches high.

The options that result when you select **Image-Sz** are described as follows:

Length-Fill	You enter a graph length in standard lines (6 per inch). 1-2-3 creates the largest possible graph using that length, while maintaining the default 4:3 (width:length) ratio.
Margin-Fill	1-2-3 creates a graph of the default shape that fills the page between the left and right margins. This is the default **Image-Sz** setting.
Reshape	You enter a graph length in standard lines (6 per inch) and a graph width in standard characters (10 per inch). 1-2-3 creates a graph of the specified size and shape. If the specified width or length exceeds the page size, 1-2-3 resizes the graph to fit on the page.

If you have previously printed a data range or another graph on part of a page, select **/Print Printer Page** to make the next graph print on a new page. If you do not advance the paper to the next page, and the graph does not fit on the remaining portion of the page, 1-2-3 automatically advances to the next page before starting the new graph.

11

To print the largest possible graph on its own page, select the **Reshape** option, and then enter a length and width that exceed the dimensions of the page. 1-2-3 resizes the graph to the largest size that fits on a page.

When **Length-Fill** or **Reshape** has been selected and a graph length is entered that is longer than a page, 1-2-3 prints the largest possible graph, centering it both vertically and horizontally on the page. With **Margin-Fill**, the graph is centered horizontally but not vertically.

Changing the Print Quality of a Graph

The **Density** option of the /**Print Printer** (or **Encoded**) **Options Advanced Image** menu offers you two choices: **Draft** or **Final**. **Draft** produces a lower-density printout with an image that is not as dark as **Final**. On some printers, graphs in **Draft** density are printed significantly faster than those in **Final** density. **Draft** density also puts less wear on printer ribbons and toner cartridges. While you are experimenting to see how your graphs look on paper, use **Draft** density; then switch to **Final** for the final printed copy.

Note: 1-2-3 supports only one density on some printers. In this case, the **Density** option has no effect.

Saving Graph Print Settings

Keep in mind that graph size settings are not saved with the graph. You can, however, save them as a named print setting. To save print settings, you select /**Print Printer** (or **Encoded**) **Options Name Create**. You are then prompted for a name to assign to the current print settings. Type in a descriptive name of up to eight characters and press Enter. The print settings are saved under that name when you save the worksheet with /**File Save**.

The next time you want to print a graph with these settings, you can recall them by selecting /**Print Printer** (or **Encoded**) **Options Name Use**, highlighting the desired name, and then press Enter.

Including Graphs in Reports

Printing your graphs on separate pages from the worksheet data and then collating them to produce a report is a simple matter. A more effective approach, however, is to have a graph and its supporting data on the same page. If your graph size supports this arrangement, you can accomplish this easily with 1-2-3. You can use two techniques to print worksheet data and graphs on a single page.

11

In the first technique, you specify *both* the graph and the text as part of the same print job. As mentioned in Chapter 8 on printing reports, this step is performed by including the name of the graph, preceded by an asterisk, as part of the print range. This method works with all types of printers.

A second technique you can use to print worksheet data and graphs on the same page is offered in Wysiwyg. You first use the **:Graph Add** command to insert the graph into a spreadsheet range. You then use the **:Print Range Set** command and highlight the worksheet data and the graph. See Chapter 12 for details on this procedure.

Summary

This chapter has shown you how to create graphs. You learned the basic steps for creating a graph, and how to select any one of 1-2-3's seven types of graphs: line, XY, bar, stacked-bar, pie, HLCO, and mixed.

You learned, too, how to improve the appearance of graphs by adding titles, data labels, legends, grids, and formatting; assigning connecting lines and symbols; and altering the scaling of the x- and y-axes.

So that you could use graphs with another program, the chapter showed you how to create a PIC or CGM file on disk. You also learned how to print graphs with the default settings, rotate and size printed graphs, and print graphs on the same page as worksheet data.

Specifically, you learned the following key information about 1-2-3:

- The 1-2-3 /Graph menu creates graphs associated with data in the 1-2-3 worksheet.

- The /Graph **T**ype command enables you to select from seven different types of graphs. Which graph type is most appropriate depends on your data and your graphing needs.

- You can choose the data ranges to be displayed in a graph with the /Graph **X** and /Graph **A** through **F** commands. The /Graph **G**roup command allows you to select all data ranges at once, as long as they form a contiguous block of cells in the worksheet.

- The /Graph **O**ptions command allows you to select from many different options that can be used to enhance the appearance of your graph. You can use this command to add data labels, titles, a legend, and a grid to your graph, as well as change the scale of the axes.

■ The /Graph Save command saves the graph as a PIC or CGM file on disk. This file can then be used with other programs, such as word processing programs.

■ The /Graph Name command enables you to use existing graph specifications, create a new graph name, delete a graph name, reset all graph names, and display a table of graph names in the worksheet.

■ To modify a graph in a later session of 1-2-3, you must use the /Graph Name Create command and then save the file with /File Save. Otherwise, your graph specifications will be lost, even if a PIC or CGM file has been created with /Graph Save.

■ The /Print Printer (or Encoded) Image Current (or Named-Graph Align Go) command prints the current (or specified) graph with the default settings.

■ The Rotate option of the /Print Printer (or Encoded) Options Advanced Image menu determines whether your graph is printed upright on the page or sideways. The Image-Sz option is used to specify the size and shape of printed graphs.

■ The Density option of the /Print Printer (or Encoded) Options Advanced Image menu allows you to print graphs of two different densities: Draft or Final. Use the Final option only when you are ready to print the final copy of your graph.

■ Use the /Print Printer (or Encoded) Options Name Create command to save print settings (including the graph size settings) so that they can be used again. You must then issue the /File Save command to store the settings with the file.

11

Enhancing and Printing Graphs in Wysiwyg

12

In the last chapter you learned how to create and print business graphs with 1-2-3's /Graph and /Print commands. As you see in this chapter, Wysiwyg offers its own set of graphing commands. However, the Wysiwyg :Graph commands are not for creating graphs—they are primarily for embellishing graphs you create in 1-2-3 and other graphic programs. (You can even create your own drawings.) A graphics editor lets you add geometric shapes, rotate and flip objects, and perform other advanced operations.

Adding a Graph

Replacing a Graph

Repositioning a Graph

Using the Graphics Editor

12

Key Terms in This Chapter

Graphic	A current graph, named graph, PIC file, Metafile, or blank placeholder you add to your worksheet with **:Graph Add**.
Graphics editing window	A screen that appears when you select **:Graph Edit**, enabling you to add and change objects on your graphic.
Selection indicators	Small boxes that appear on the edges of an object selected for editing.
Selected objects	Objects that you can change together.
Bounding box	A rectangle shown on the screen in the graphics editor mode that outlines an object you move or change.

Using the Mouse

To use a mouse with 1-2-3 Release 3.1, you need a mouse, mouse software, and a graphics monitor and graphics card that support a mouse. Also, Wysiwyg must be loaded into memory. You can use a mouse to select commands and files, specify ranges, and move the cell pointer within a worksheet or between multiple worksheets and files. In the examples throughout this chapter, notice that the 1-2-3 commands always begin with a slash (/), and the Wysiwyg commands always begin with a colon (**:**). Refer to the following sections of the specified chapters for further information on using the mouse:

- Chapter 2—"Understanding Mouse Terminology"
- Chapter 3—"Mouse Control of the Cell Pointer"
  "Using the Mouse To Select Menu Commands"
- Chapter 4—"Using the Mouse To Specify Ranges"

Adding a Graph

Before you can include a 1-2-3 graph in a Wysiwyg-formatted report, you must add the graph to the worksheet with the **:Graph Add** command. With this command, you define the worksheet range where you want the graph to appear—you actually see the graph in the worksheet.

To add a graph into the worksheet, follow these steps:

1. Select **:Graph Add**.

2. Select **Current** to insert the current 1-2-3 graph (the same graph that appears when you press F10).

   Or

   Select **Named** to insert a 1-2-3 graph that you named with the **/Graph Name Create** command.

   Or

   Select **PIC** to insert a 1-2-3 graph created with the **/Graph Save** Command. The file has the extension PIC.

   Or

   Select **Metafile** to insert a Metafile graphic. 1-2-3 Release 3 or an external graphics package created this file, and it has the extension CGM.

   Or

   Select **Blank** to insert an empty placeholder. Use this option if you have not yet created the graph, but want to reserve space for it. You also can use it to create your own graphic drawing.

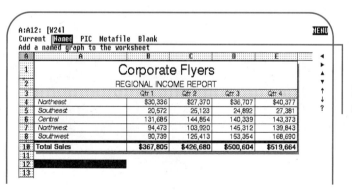

In this example, choose **Named**.

Choose the **Current** option only if the worksheet contains a single graph. If the worksheet has multiple graphs, 1-2-3 replaces the graph with the new current graph every time you use the command **/Graph Name Use**. When the worksheet contains more than one graph, you can save time by naming the graph before adding it.

3. If you choose **Named**, **PIC**, or **Metafile**, Wysiwyg prompts you for the name of the graph. Type the name or move the cursor to one of the graphs listed; and then press ↵Enter.

In this example, choose the named graph REG INCOME by moving the cursor to the right and pressing ↵Enter.

```
A:A12: [W24]                                              NAMES
Select a named graph:
CENTRAL         REG INCOME     SALES-QTR1      SALES-QTR2
```

	A	B	C	D	E
1			Corporate Flyers		
2		REGIONAL INCOME REPORT			
3		Qtr 1	Qtr 2	Qtr 3	Qtr 4
4	Northeast	$30,336	$27,370	$36,707	$40,377
5	Southeast	20,572	25,123	24,892	27,381
6	Central	131,685	144,854	140,339	143,373
7	Northwest	94,473	103,920	145,312	139,843
8	Southwest	90,739	125,413	153,354	168,690
10	Total Sales	$367,805	$426,680	$500,604	$519,664
11					
12					
13					

4. When the prompt Enter the graphic display range: appears, indicate the range to accept the graph.

```
A:E25:                                                    POINT
Enter the graphic display range: A:A12..A:E25
```

	A	B	C	D	E
7	Northwest	94,473	103,920	145,312	139,843
8	Southwest	90,739	125,413	153,354	168,690
10	Total Sales	$367,805	$426,680	$500,604	$519,664

```
                                                    NUM CAP
```

In this example, press . (period) to anchor the range at A12. Move the cell pointer to E25. Then press ↵Enter.

5. To exit the Wysiwyg menu, select **Quit**.

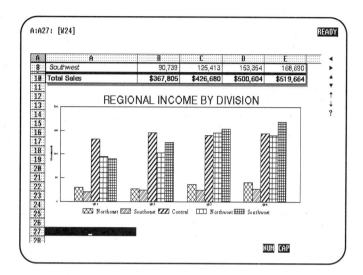

The graph appears in the worksheet.

Before you add a graph to the middle of a worksheet report, insert blank rows or columns where you want the graph to appear. Otherwise the graph overlays worksheet data. The graph range should include only blank cells, so be sure that you insert enough rows and columns to make the graph the size you want.

Replacing a Graph

If you add the wrong graph or you create a graph you want in that same-sized range, you can replace the existing graph with another. You do not need to remove one graph before adding another in the same location.

To replace a graph, follow these steps:

1. Select **:Graph Settings Graph**.

2. Indicate the graph you want to replace by moving the cell pointer to one cell in the graph range. If your cell pointer is not near the graph, you can press F3 (Name) and select the graph name from a list.

3. Select type of graphic (**Current, Named, PIC, Metafile,** or **Blank**).

4. If you choose **Named, PIC,** or **Metafile,** Wysiwyg prompts you for the name of the graph.

5. Type the name or move the cursor to one of the graphs listed; and then press ↵Enter.

425

12

Any enhancements (such as annotations) to the initial graph also appear in the new graph. If you don't want these enhancements in the new graph, use **:Graph Remove** to delete the initial graph. Insert the new graph with **:Graph Add**.

Repositioning a Graph

After adding a graph, you may realize that the range isn't appropriate for your graph, or you may want it positioned in a different area of the worksheet. The **:Graph** menu offers several commands for changing your graph's position. You can move, resize, or remove the graph.

If your spreadsheet is large or has many graphs, you can use the **:Graph Goto** command to move to a graph before editing it. To go to a graph on your worksheet, follow these steps:

1. Select **:Graph Goto**.
2. Move the cursor to select the graphic name from the list. (Press F3 (Name) to see a full-screen list.)
3. Press Enter .

Moving a Graph

To move a graph from one spreadsheet location to another, use the **:Graph Move** command. This command retains the graph's original size and shape (number of rows and columns). The only change is the graph's position in the spreadsheet.

To move a graph on the worksheet, follow these steps:

1. Select **:Graph Move**.
2. Move the cursor to select the graphic name from the list. (Press F3 (Name) to see a full-screen list.)
3. Press Enter .
4. Type the range name or move the cell pointer to the upper-left corner of the target range and press Enter . (You needn't highlight the entire range.)

Resizing a Graph

After you add a graph, you may realize that the range you specified is either too large or too small for your graph. The **:Graph Settings Range** command lets you resize an existing graph.

To change the size of a graph, follow these steps:

1. Select **:Graph Settings Range**.

2. Indicate the graph you want to resize. Move the cell pointer to one cell in the graph range or press F3 and select the graph name from a list. 1-2-3 highlights the current graph range.

3. Type the new range, or move the cell pointer to highlight a larger or smaller area. If you want to specify a new range to be different from the existing one, press Esc or ◆Backspace. Then move the cursor and specify the new range.

4. Press ◄Enter after you have set the new range.

Removing a Graph

To erase a graph from the worksheet report, follow these steps:

1. Select **:Graph Remove**.

2. Indicate the graph you want to remove. Move the cell pointer to a cell in the graph range or press F3 and select the graph name from the list.

Using the Graphics Editor

Included in Wysiwyg is a graphics editor that enables you to add and manipulate graphic objects. Using this text editor you can add text, arrows, boxes, and other geometric shapes. After adding these objects, you can modify, rearrange, duplicate, and transform them.

To place a graph in the graphics editing window, follow these steps:

1. Select **:Graph Edit**.

2. Indicate the graph you want to change. Move the cell pointer to one cell in the graph range, or press F3 and select the graph name from the list.

To use a mouse to place the graph, follow these steps:

1. Call up the Wysiwyg menu by moving the mouse pointer to the top of the screen. If the 1-2-3 menu appears, click the right mouse button for the Wysiwyg menu.

427

2. Click the left mouse button on **Graph**.

3. Click the left mouse button on **Edit**.

4. Place the mouse pointer on the graphic, and double-click the left mouse button.

The graphics editing window.

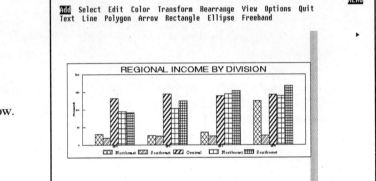

When you are in the graphics editing window, you are almost in a different world. You see only your graphic—not your worksheet. This lets you concentrate on your task at hand: enhancing your graphic. Furthermore, the editing menu permanently remains at the top of the screen; the Esc key or right mouse button does not clear the menu. The only way to exit out of the graphics editor is to choose the **Q**uit menu option or press Ctrl-Break.

The Undo command does not work on options in the **:**Graph **E**dit menu.

Adding Objects

Wysiwyg lets you add the following types of objects to your graphic: text, lines, polygons, arrows, rectangles, and ellipses. You can also draw freehand. These objects help you add text to explain your charts. For example, you can add a brief explanation why a data point is unusually high or low. The following figure demonstrates how text, an arrow, and an ellipse point out a value on the graph.

428

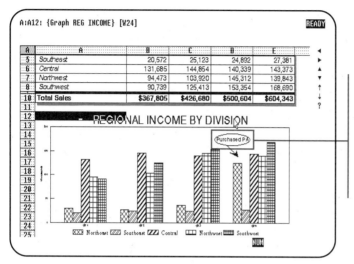

A graph annotated with the graphics editor, showing how text, an arrow, and an ellipse point out a value on the graph.

Adding Text to the Chart

You do not type the text directly on the graph. Instead, you add the text in two steps. Type the text at the Text: prompt at the top of the screen. Then position the complete phrase where you like. The text phrase can be up to 512 characters long.

To add text to your graph, follow these steps:

    1. From the **:G**raph **E**dit menu, select **A**dd **T**ext.

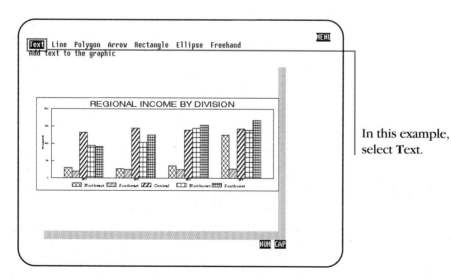

In this example, select **T**ext.

2. Type the text you want. To insert the contents of a cell, press ⬚\⬚ followed by the cell's coordinates or range name.

12

Type **Purchased PA**, and press ⬚↵Enter⬚.

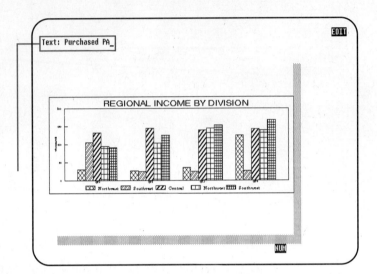

3. Position the cursor where you want the text to go. Either move the cursor with the arrow keys and press ⬚↵Enter⬚ or move the cursor with the mouse and click the left mouse button.

Note: The arrow keys move in such small increments that you will probably prefer to use the mouse if you have one.

For this example, place Purchased PA above the first bar in quarter 4.

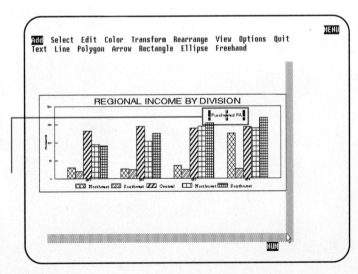

Small, filled-in squares, called selection indicators, surround the text. These boxes mean that you selected the object and can perform another operation on it (such as move it, change its font, and so forth). To change the font, use the **Edit Font** command. To change the content of the text, use the **Edit Text** command.

The text you add can include formatting sequences (for example, bold, italic, outline, fonts). See the section "Formatting Sequences" in Chapter 10 for further information.

Adding Lines and Arrows

The process of drawing lines and arrows is the same. The only difference is the arrow's arrowhead at the second point of the line.

To draw a line or arrow, follow these steps:

1. From the **:Graph Edit** menu, select **Add**.
2. Select **Line** or **Arrow**.
3. The screen prompts you to `Move to the first point`. Use the arrow keys to move the pointer to one end of the line.
4. Press the space bar to anchor this point.
5. The screen prompts you to `Stretch the line to the next point`. Use the arrow keys to move the pointer to the other end of the line.
6. Press `⏎Enter` to complete the line.

To use a mouse to draw a line or arrow, follow these steps:

1. From the **:Graph Edit** menu, click on **Add** with the left mouse button.
2. Click the left mouse button on **Line** or **Arrow**.

12

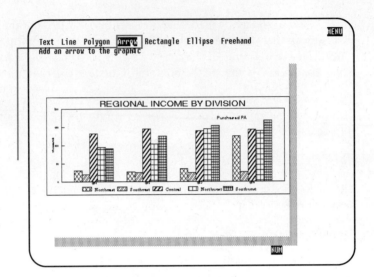

For this example,
click on **Arrow.**

3. Move the mouse cursor to the first point and click the left mouse button.

4. At the stretch prompt, move the mouse cursor to the next point and click the left mouse button twice to complete the line.

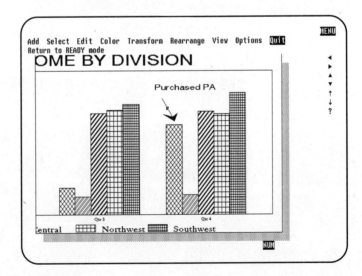

The line is completed.

The line or arrow shows on-screen and the selection indicator appears in the center of the line. If you are adding an arrow, the arrowhead points from the end of the line (the second point you indicated). To switch the direction of the arrow, use the **Edit Arrowheads** option. To change the line width, use the **Edit Width** option.

You can connect several lines by pressing the space bar or clicking the left mouse button for each line ending. When you finish drawing lines, click twice or press Enter.

When drawing horizontal, vertical, or diagonal lines, you notice that drawing straight lines is difficult; the lines look somewhat jagged. To prevent this jagged look, press and hold down the Shift key before you anchor the last point. The line segment automatically snaps to 45-degree angles, allowing you to draw perfectly straight lines.

Adding Polygons to the Chart

A polygon is a multisided object. The object can have as many connecting lines as you want. With Wysiwyg commands, you can connect the last line drawn to the first line. The steps for creating a polygon are similar to creating lines and arrows:

1. From the **:Graph Edit** menu, select **Add Polygon**.
2. The screen prompts you to `Move to the first point`. Use the mouse or arrow keys to move the pointer to one end of the line.
3. Press the left mouse button or space bar to anchor this point.
4. The screen prompts you to `Stretch the line to the next point`. Use the mouse or arrow keys to move the pointer to the opposite end of the first line.
5. Press the left mouse button or space bar to anchor this point.
6. Repeat steps 4 and 5 for each point of the polygon.
7. Click the left mouse button twice, or press ⏎Enter to complete the polygon.

Adding Rectangles and Ellipses

Use the **Rectangle** and **Ellipse** commands to enclose text and other objects on your graphic. For example, the following figure shows a rectangle and ellipse surrounding text.

12

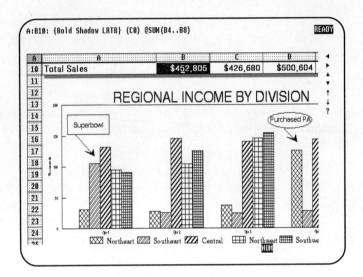

This shows a graph annotated with text, a rectangle, and an ellipse.

To draw rectangles and ellipses with the keyboard, follow these steps:

1. Select **:Graph Edit Add**.
2. Select **Rectangle** or **Ellipse**.
3. Place the cursor on the upper left corner of the area where you want the object to go.
4. Press the space bar to anchor the corner.
5. Use the arrow keys to stretch the box to its desired size. (A box appears regardless of whether you are drawing a rectangle or ellipse. This is the bounding box.)
6. Press ⏎Enter.

To draw rectangles and ellipses with a mouse, follow these steps:

1. From the **:Graph Edit Add** menu, click the left button on **Rectangle** or **Ellipse**.
2. Click and hold the left mouse button in the upper left corner of the object.
3. Drag the mouse to create the desired size.
4. Release the button. Wysiwyg draws the shape you chose.

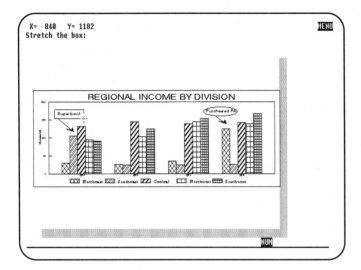

Whether you are creating a rectangle or an ellipse, a rectangle (the bounding box) appears until you release the mouse.

The middle of each side of the rectangle or ellipse has selection indicators. To change the type of line (solid, dashed, or dotted) used in the rectangle or ellipse, use the **Edit Line-Style** command.

To create a circle when you choose **Ellipse**, or a square when you chose **Rectangle**, hold the Shift key before you set the object size. The object may not appear perfectly circular or square on-screen, but will print out accurately.

Adding Objects Freehand

When you use the Freehand option, it is like drawing with a pencil on the screen. Unless you have artistic ability, freehand drawing looks like freehand scribbling; therefore, you may want to leave this option to the professionals.

12

Freehand drawing
(scribbling).

You must have a mouse to draw freehand. To draw freehand, follow these steps:

1. From the **:Graph Edit Add** menu, select **Freehand**.
2. Place the cursor where you want to begin drawing.
3. Click and hold the left mouse button, and move the mouse to draw.
4. Release the mouse button when you finish drawing a segment of the graphic.

Each segment of the freehand drawing displays a selection indicator. To change the type of line (solid, dash, or dotted), use the **Edit Line-Style** command.

Selecting Objects

There is much you can do to your objects after you add them to your graphic. For example, you can change the line-style and font. You can also move, delete, or copy the objects. Whatever you wish to change, you must first select the object. If you just added the object, Wysiwyg selects it automatically. Selection indicators, small filled-in boxes, show that you selected the object or objects.

Normally, you select the object before issuing a command. If you issue a command without selecting an object, Wysiwyg prompts you to point to what you want.

Selecting Objects with the Mouse

To select one object with the mouse, follow these steps:

1. With the main **:Graph Edit** menu displayed, move the mouse cursor to the object.
2. Click the left mouse button.

Check the selection indicators to make sure that they are around the object you want to change. If two objects are close together, you may need to click several times. Wysiwyg selects the correct object.

Sometimes you want to select more than one object. For example, you may want to change the font of all the text you have added.

To select multiple objects with the mouse, follow these steps:

1. With the main **:Graph Edit** menu displayed, move the mouse cursor to the object.
2. Hold down the ⧰Shift key as you click the left mouse button on each object. If you accidentally select the wrong object, keep the ⧰Shift key down and click on the object again.

Selecting Objects with the Menu

To select a single object with the keyboard, use the **:Graph Edit Select** menu option and choose **One**.

To select one object with the menu, follow these steps:

1. Choose **:Graph Edit Select One**.
2. Wysiwyg then prompts you to `Point to desired object`. Use the arrow keys to move the cursor to the object and press ↵Enter.
3. The selection indicators appear on the object.

Another way to select an object is with the **:Graph Edit Select Cycle** command.

To select multiple objects with the menu, follow these steps:

1. From the **:Graph Edit** menu, choose **Select**.
2. Select **Cycle**.
3. To move to an object, press an arrow key. The object displays small boxes that are similar to selection indicators, but the boxes are hollow.

12

4. To select or deselect the object, press the space bar.

5. Repeat steps 3 and 4 until you have selected all the objects you want.

6. Press ⏎Enter.

Mouse users may want to use the **Cycle** option if they are having trouble selecting an object that is close to another object. You may not be able to identify an object with a click of the mouse. The **Cycle** option enables you to select or skip every object in the graphic.

The **Select** menu offers several other ways to select objects. **All** selects all the objects you have added except the graphic itself. **None** selects everything—the objects and your graphic. **Graph** selects only your underlying graphic. **More/Less** lets you select an additional object or deselect one of the currently selected objects. If you point to an unselected object, Wysiwyg selects it. If you already selected the object, Wysiwyg removes the selection.

Editing Text on the Graph

The **Text** option on the Using the Graphics Editor **:Graph Edit** menu lets you edit text you added with the **Add Text** command. You cannot edit text (titles and legends, for example) that was part of the worksheet graph, PIC, or Metafile graphic you inserted. You can select text before or during the editing process. If you select text before editing, skip step 3.

To begin editing text on the graph, follow these steps:

1. From the **:Graph Edit** menu, select **Edit**.

2. Select **Text**.

3. If you have not pre-selected text, Wysiwyg displays the prompt Select text to edit. Move to the text to edit; then press ⏎Enter. A copy of the text appears at the top of the screen.

To correct or insert text on the graph, follow these steps:

1. Move the cursor and type text to be inserted.

2. Press Ins to type over text.

3. Press Del to delete the character at the cursor.

4. Press ⬅Backspace to delete the character before the cursor.

5. Press End to move to the end of the line.

6. Press Home to move to the beginning of the line.

7. When you finish editing the graph, press ⏎Enter. The correct text appears on-screen.

438

Adding Patterns and Colors

The Color option on the **:Graph Edit** menu enables you to assign colors or patterns to the following areas of your graphic:

Selection	Description
Lines	Lines, arrows, and object outlines.
Inside	The space inside the rectangle, ellipse, or polygon.
Text	Text added with **Add Text** (not legends or titles you entered with **/Graph** commands).
Background	The area behind the graphic.

To change the color of lines or text, follow these steps:

1. From the **:Graph Edit** menu, select Color.
2. Select **Lines** or **Text**.
3. Choose from a menu of the following colors:

Black	**White**	**Red**	**Green**	**Dark-Blue**
Cyan	**Yellow**	**Magenta**	**Hidden**	

4. If you have not pre-selected lines or text, Wysiwyg displays the prompt `Select objects to colorize`. Move to the line or text to appear in color, and press `⏎Enter`.

To change the color or pattern inside objects, follow these steps:

1. From the **:Graph Edit** menu, select Color.
2. Select **Inside**.
3. A color palette displays on your color monitor. Monochrome monitors use a palette of different patterns. Type the number, or click on the desired color/pattern.
4. If you have not pre-selected lines or text, Wysiwyg displays the prompt `Select objects to colorize.`
5. Move to the object where you want the change, and press `⏎Enter`.

12

439

12

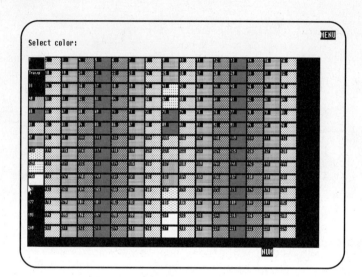

If you have a
monochrome
monitor, the
palette displays
patterns.

To change the background color, follow these steps:

1. From the **:G**raph **E**dit menu, select **C**olor.

2. Select **B**ackground.

3. A color palette appears on your screen. Monochrome monitors display a palette of different patterns.

4. Type the number and press ⏎Enter, or click on the color/pattern you want.

Changing Colors of Graph Elements

To change the colors or patterns of any elements in your 1-2-3 graph, you can use either color mapping or the /Graph Options Advanced command.

The **:G**raph **E**dit **C**olor **M**ap option allows you to change the fill colors and patterns of the underlying graphic. For example, suppose you don't like a bar's green shading. You can use color mapping to adjust this shade or to use a different pattern. You cannot use this option to change the color of the lines or text.

You can change up to 16 different colors. The **M**ap menu shows the 16 choices with the numbers 1 through 9 and the letters A through G. How do you know which color in your chart corresponds to which letter or number on the menu? Unfortunately, trial and error is the answer. Wysiwyg does not tell you which

440

color goes with which menu choice until after you choose the letter or number. If you want to change the green bar, you have to try A through 9 until you see green on the color map.

To change a graph color or pattern, follow these steps:

1. From the **:Graph Edit** menu, select **Color**.
2. Select **Map**.
3. Select a number from 1 to 9 or a letter from A to G. A color palette appears on your color monitor. Monochrome monitors display a palette of different patterns. The palette shows the current color/pattern with a box.
4. Type the number or click on the desired color/pattern. If you change your mind, press Esc and try another letter or number.

If you have a color monitor and a black-and-white printer, you may want to view the graph in black and white before you print. This allows you to see the contrast when the colors translate into gray shades. Use the **:Display Mode B&W** command to change to a black-and-white display.

Rearranging Objects

The **Rearrange** option on the **:Graph Edit** menu lets you delete, copy, and move objects you added to your graphic with **:Graph Edit Add**. Before you choose one of the **Rearrange** options, select the object(s) you want to rearrange. See "Selecting Objects" earlier in this chapter for details on preselecting objects with the mouse or the **Select** menu.

Deleting and Restoring Objects

The **Rearrange Delete** option removes the selected object(s) from the graphic. Be careful; Wysiwyg does not ask you to confirm your intention to delete. However, you can retrieve the last deleted object or group of objects with the **Rearrange Restore** command.

To delete selected objects, follow these steps:

1. Select objects using one of the procedures in the "Select Objects" section in this chapter.
2. From the **:Graph Edit** menu, select **Rearrange**.
3. Select **Delete**.

441

As an alternative to using the **Rearrange Delete** command, you can simply select the object and press Del.

To restore the objects you deleted (last deletion only):

1. From the **:Graph Edit** menu, select **Rearrange**.
2. Select **Restore**.

Suppose, for example, that you select three objects at once and then choose **Rearrange Delete**. Wysiwyg deletes all three objects. If you choose **Rearrange Restore**, Wysiwyg retrieves all three objects into their original locations. However, if you select and delete a line, and then select and delete a rectangle, you cannot restore the deleted line.

Press the ⌊Ins⌋ key on your numeric keypad to restore the most recently deleted object(s). Do not select any objects when you press ⌊Ins⌋, or Wysiwyg will copy the selected object.

Moving Objects

To reposition an object, follow these steps:

1. From the **:Graph Edit** menu, select **Rearrange**
2. Select **Move**.
3. If you haven't already done so, Wysiwyg asks you to select the objects to move. Use the arrow keys to move the cursor to the object and press ⌊↵Enter⌋.
4. After you make your selection, a copy of your object appears inside a dotted rectangle (the bounding box). A hand also appears inside the bounding box, indicating you are moving the object.
5. Use the arrow keys to move the bounding box to the target location; then press ⌊↵Enter⌋.

To use a mouse to move an object, follow these steps:

1. From the **:Graph Edit** menu, move to the object.
2. If necessary, click the left mouse button to select the object.
3. Click and hold the left mouse button on the object.
4. While holding down the left mouse button, drag the object to the desired location.

Copying Objects

After you create an object, you may want to copy it to another location on your worksheet. Using the **:Graph Edit Rearrange Copy** command ensures that two or more objects have the same size, color, line-styles, and rotation options. For example, if you create a shaded rectangle with wide lines, the copy of the rectangle is also shaded and has wide lines.

12

To copy an object, follow these steps:

1. From the **:Graph Edit** menu, select **Rearrange**.
2. Select **Copy**.
3. If you preselected an object before you chose the **Rearrange Copy** command, Wysiwyg places a duplicate slightly to the right and below the original object. If you did not select an object before you chose the **Copy** command, Wysiwyg prompts you to select the objects to copy.

Note that the **Copy** command does not prompt you for a target location. You must use the **Rearrange Move** command to put the object into place. Thus, copying is a two-step process.

Rather than using the **Rearrange Copy** command, you can simply select the object and press the Ins key. Like the **Copy** command, Ins places the duplicated object next to the original. You have to use the **Move** command to put the object into position. If you don't have an object selected when you press Ins, Wysiwyg restores the last deleted object.

Sizing an Object

You can change the size (height and width) of any added objects except text. To change the text size, specify a different font with the **Edit Font** command.

To change the size of an object, follow these steps:

1. From the **:Graph Edit** menu, select **Transform**.
2. Select **Size**.
3. Wysiwyg surrounds the selected object with a bounding box. Wysiwyg anchors the upper-left corner of the box, and the cursor is in the lower-right corner. Change the size of the object by pressing the arrow keys until the bounding box is the desired size.
4. When the desired size is reached, press ↵Enter.

443

Rotating an Object

The **Transform** menu offers two ways to rotate an object. The **Quarter-Turn** option rotates the selected object(s) in 90-degree increments. Wysiwyg makes the turns in a counter-clockwise direction.

If you need to rotate an object in increments other than 90 degrees, use the **Transform R**otate option. You can rotate the selected object(s) to any angle.

To rotate selected objects by any amount, follow these steps:

1. From the **:Graph E**dit menu, select **Transform**.
2. Select **R**otate.
3. An axis extends from the center of the object to outside the bounding box. Think of this axis as a handle that pulls the object in the direction you press the arrow keys. As you rotate, the original object remains intact, and a copy of the object rotates.

In this example, use ↑ and ← to rotate the object.

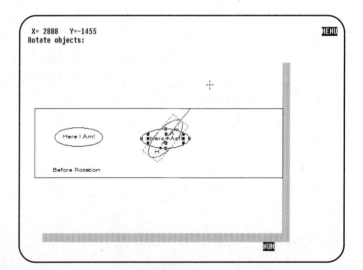

4. Press **↵Enter** to finish the rotation. Wysiwyg replaces the original with the rotated copy.

12

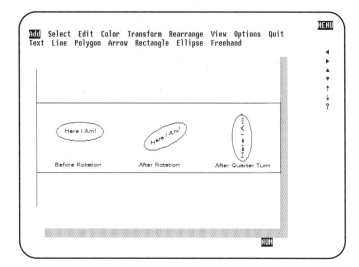

This example shows a figure and text rotated with the **Transform Rotate** and **Transform Quarter-Turn** options.

Some printers can only print text rotated in 90-degree increments. The HP LaserJet Series printers and PostScript printers can print text at any angle.

Summary

This chapter showed you how to use Wysiwyg's graphing commands and options. At the simplest level, you can insert a graph to include it with a Wysiwyg-formatted report. You can then take the 1-2-3 graph and add comments to point out key data values. At another level, you can use the graphics editor to create your own graphic drawings with text and geometric objects.

Specifically, you learned the following key information about 1-2-3:

- To add a graph to a worksheet range, use **:Graph Add**.
- To replace a graph on the worksheet with a different graph, use **:Graph Settings Graph**.
- The **:Graph Move** command allows you to move a graph to a different position on the worksheet.
- To change the size of a graph on a worksheet, use **:Graph Settings Range**.
- To delete a graph from a worksheet range, use **:Graph Remove**.
- The graphics editor enables you to add and modify objects on a graph. These objects include text, lines, arrows, rectangles, and ellipses.

12

■ To reach the graphics editor window, select **:Graph Edit**. The graph will appear on-screen with a new menu. To return to the worksheet, select **Quit**.

■ Add objects to a graph with the **:Graph Edit Add** command. Then choose **Text, Line, Polygon, Arrow, Rectangle, Ellipse,** or **Freehand**.

■ To select objects using the mouse in the **:Graph Edit** window, click the left mouse button on the object. To select multiple objects, hold down the Shift key as you select.

■ To select objects using the menu in the **:Graph Edit** window, choose **Select**. The **One** option allows you to select one item. The **Cycle** option allows you to select multiple items.

■ When you want to edit text you have added to the graph, choose the **:Graph Edit Edit Text** command.

■ The **:Graph Edit Color** command allows you to change colors of text and objects you added to the graph, the graph background, and the original parts of a graph.

■ The **Rearrange Delete** option on the **:Graph Edit** menu allow you to delete selected objects. The **Rearrange Restore** option allows you to restore the objects if necessary.

■ To move an object on a graph, choose **:Graph Edit Move**.

■ To copy an object on the graph, choose **:Graph Edit Rearrange Copy**.

■ The **:Graph Edit Transform** command enables you to **Size** or **Rotate** an object.

Managing Data

13

In addition to the electronic spreadsheet and business graphics, 1-2-3 provides a third element: data management. 1-2-3's database feature is fast, easy to access, and relatively simple to use.

You can easily access the 1-2-3 database because Lotus Development Corporation has made the entire database visible from the worksheet. You can view the contents of the whole database by using worksheet windows and direction keys to scroll through the database.

The relative ease of use is a result of integrating data management with the program's spreadsheet and graphics functions. The procedures for adding, changing, and deleting items in a database are the same as those for manipulating cells within a worksheet. Creating graphs from ranges in a database is as easy as creating them in a worksheet.

Capabilities of the 1-2-3 Database

Planning and building a database

Modifying a database

Sorting database records

Searching for records

Working with external databases

13

Key Terms in This Chapter

Database	A collection of data organized so you can list, sort, or search its contents.
Field	One information item, such as an address or a name.
Field name	Labels in the first row of a database that identify the contents of each field or column.
Record	A collection of associated fields. In 1-2-3, a record is a row of cells within a database.
Key field	A column (or field) that determines sorting order for rows in a database.
Input range database	The range of the database on which 1-2-3 performs database operations.
Output range	The range to which 1-2-3 copies data when extracted from the database.
Criteria	The range of the database in which you enter range search criteria.
External database	A database file from another program such as dBASE that you can link to 1-2-3.

Using the Mouse

To use a mouse with 1-2-3 Release 3.1, you need a mouse, mouse software, and a graphics monitor and graphics card that support a mouse. Also, Wysiwyg must be loaded into memory. You can use a mouse to select commands and files, specify ranges, and move the cell pointer within a worksheet or between multiple worksheets and files. In the examples throughout this chapter, notice that the 1-2-3 commands always begin with a slash (/), and the Wysiwyg commands always begin with a colon (:). Refer to the following sections of the specified chapters for further information on using the mouse:

- Chapter 2 — "Understanding Mouse Terminology"
- Chapter 3 — "Mouse Control of the Cell Pointer"

    "Using the Mouse To Select Menu Commands"
- Chapter 4 — "Using the Mouse To Specify Ranges"

What Is a Database?

A database is a collection of data organized so you can list, sort, or search its contents. The list of data may contain any kind of information, from addresses to tax-deductible payments. A Rolodex is one form of a database. Other examples of databases include address books and a file cabinet of employee records.

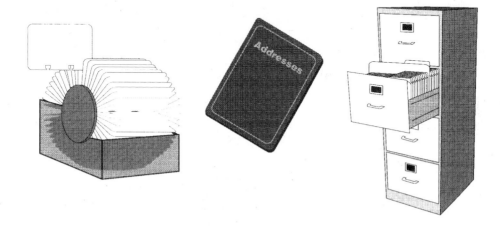

In 1-2-3, the word *database* means a range of cells that spans at least one column and more than one row. This definition, however, does not distinguish between a database and any other range of cells on a worksheet. Because a database is actually a list, its manner of organization distinguishes it from an ordinary range. As a list must be organized to be useful, you have to arrange a database so the information is easy to access.

The smallest unit in a database is a field, or single data item. For example, if you were to develop an information database of customer accounts that are overdue, you might include the following fields of information:

Customer Last Name	Area Code
Customer First Name	Telephone Number
Street	Account Number
City	Payment Due Date
State	Date Paid
ZIP Code	Amount Due

A database record is a collection of associated fields. For example, the accumulation of all data about one customer forms one record. In 1-2-3, a record is a row of cells within a database, and a field is one type of information, such as City.

You must set up a database so you can access the information it contains. Retrieval of information usually involves relying on key fields. A database key field is any field (or column) on which you base a list, sort, or search operation. For example, you can use the ZIP code as a key field to sort the data in the overdue accounts database. Then you could assign contact representatives to specific geographic areas.

A database field name

A database key field

A database record

A database field

A database input range

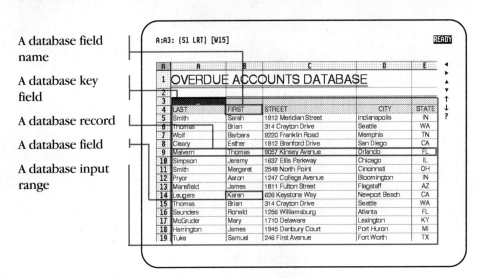

Capabilities of the 1-2-3 Database

Building a database in 1-2-3 is no different from building any other worksheet table. After you build the database, you can perform a variety of functions on it. You can accomplish some of the tasks on a 1-2-3 database with standard 1-2-3 commands. For example, you can add records and fields using simple worksheet commands such as /Worksheet Insert. Editing data in the database is the same as editing worksheet cells. Highlight the cell, press Edit (F2), and correct it.

You can also sort data. You sort with a primary, a secondary, or additional keys, in ascending or descending order. In addition, you can perform various mathematical analyses on a field of data over a specified range of records. For example, you can count the number of items in a database that match a set of criteria. You can compute a mean, variance, or standard deviation. You can also

450

find the maximum or minimum value in the range. The capability to perform statistical analysis on a database is an advanced feature for database management systems on any microcomputer.

Other database operations specifically require database commands, such as /Data Query Find and /Data Query Unique. Data commands can help you search the database and remove duplications.

You have several options for defining selection criteria with 1-2-3. The criteria range can contain up to 256 cells across the worksheet, with each cell containing criteria. You can use numbers, text, and complex formulas as criteria.

1-2-3 also has a special set of statistical functions that operate only on information stored in the database. Like the /Data Query commands, the statistical functions use criteria to determine on which records they operate. The database functions include @DCOUNT, @DSUM, @DAVG, @DVAR, @DVARS, @DSTD, @DSTDS, @DGET, @DQUERY, @DMAX, and @DMIN.

Understanding the Data Menu

You use the Data menu for many of 1-2-3's data management tasks. All other options from the 1-2-3 main menu work as well on databases as they do on worksheets. When you select /Data from the 1-2-3 main menu, the control panel displays the following options:

  Fill Table Sort Query Distribution Matrix Regression Parse External

Table 13.1 describes each of these options.

Table 13.1
Selections on the /Data Menu

Selection	Description
Fill	Fills a specified range with values. You can choose the increment by which 1-2-3 increases or decreases successive numbers or dates.
Table	Substitutes different values for a variable used in a formula; often used for "what if" analyses.
Sort	Organizes the database in ascending or descending order based on one or two specified key fields.
Query	Offers different options for performing search operations and manipulating the found data items.

13

Table 13.1 (continued)

Selection	Description
Distribution	Finds how often specific data occurs in a database.
Matrix	Lets you solve systems of simultaneous linear equations and manipulate the resulting solutions.
Regression	Performs multiple regression analysis on X and Y values.
Parse	Separates long labels resulting from /File Import into discrete text and numeric cell entries.
External	Lets you work with data from a database other than 1-2-3 such as dBASE III.

In the /Data menu, the Sort and Query (search) options are true data management operations. Sort allows you to specify the order in which you want the records of the database organized. For example, you can sort by number, by name, or by date. With Query, you can perform many search operations, allowing you to display quickly a specific record without having to scan a multitude of records.

Planning and Building a Database

Before you begin to create a database in 1-2-3, you should determine the categories (fields) of information you want to include. You can determine these fields by planning what kind of output you expect to produce from your data. Next, decide which area of the worksheet to use. Then create a database by specifying field names across a row. Finally, enter data in cells beneath these names, as you would for any other 1-2-3 application. Entering database contents is simple. The most critical step in creating a database is choosing your fields accurately.

Determining Required Output

1-2-3's data-retrieval techniques rely on finding data by field names. Before you begin typing the kinds of data items you think you may need, write down the output you expect from the database. You also need to consider any source documents already in use that can provide input to the file.

Before you set up the items in your database, be sure to consider how you might look for data in each field. For example, consider how you will look for a particular information item. Will you search by date? By last name? Knowing beforehand how you will use your database will save time that you would lose if you have to redesign the database.

452

After you decide on the fields, select the appropriate column width (which you can later modify) and determine whether you will enter the data as a number, label, or date.

Overdue Accounts Database		
Item	Column Width	Type of Entry
1. Customer Last Name	15	Label
2. Customer First Name	10	Label
3. Street Address	25	Label
4. City	15	Label
5. State	7	Label
6. ZIP Code	6	Label
7. Area Code	6	Number
8. Telephone Number	11	Label
9. Account Number	10	Number
10. Payment Due Date	11	Date
11. Date Paid	11	Date
12. Amount Due	12	Number

Here are some tips for planning various types of fields (columns) in your database:

- For ease in sorting, put last and first names in separate columns. Optionally, put both names in the same cell and separate the last and first names with a comma.

- Some ZIP codes begin with zero, which would not appear in the cell if you entered it as a value. Enter ZIP codes as labels by preceding them with a label prefix.

- Set up a separate area code in a different field from telephone number. This helps if you want to search, sort, or extract records by area code.

13

- Enter a telephone number as a label. This number must be a label because of the hyphen between the first three and last four digits of a telephone number. A hyphen signifies subtraction in a number entered as a value.

Be sure to plan your database carefully before you type field names, set column widths and range formats, and enter data. Although you can make changes after you set up your database, planning helps to reduce the time required for making those changes.

Positioning the Database

You can create a database as a new database file or as part of an existing worksheet. If you decide to build a database as part of an existing worksheet, choose an area where inserting or deleting lines won't affect the worksheet or another database.

If you place a database to the right of a worksheet, inserting and deleting rows may affect the worksheet.

If you place a database directly below a worksheet, inserting and deleting columns may affect the worksheet.

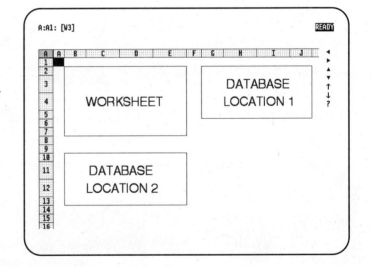

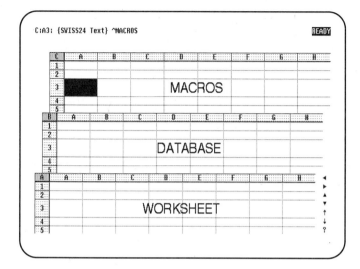

C:A3: {SWISS24 Text} ^MACROS   READY

MACROS

DATABASE

WORKSHEET

It's best to use a separate worksheet for your database. Put your worksheet, database, and macros on different sheets.

13

Entering Data

After you plan your database and decide which area of the worksheet to use, you can start entering data. Build a database by specifying field names as labels across a row. Make sure that each field name is unique and in a separate column.

You can use one or more rows for field names, but 1-2-3 processes only the bottom row. Therefore, each field name in the bottom row must be unique. After you enter the field names, enter data in cells as you would for any other 1-2-3 application. Change the column width to fit the information you enter by using the /Worksheet Column Set-Width command.

To build a 1-2-3 database, follow these steps:

1. Choose an area for your database.

   You should start with a blank worksheet. If you would rather use an existing worksheet, select an area that is out of the way of the data you have entered.

2. Enter the field names across a single row.

   The field names must be labels, even if they are numeric labels. Although you can use more than one row for the field names, 1-2-3 processes only the values that appear in the bottom row. For example, picture field name DATE DUE in a column with DATE in row 5 and DUE in row 6. 1-2-3 references only DUE as a key field in sort or query operations. Remember that all field names should be unique. Any repetition of names can be confusing.

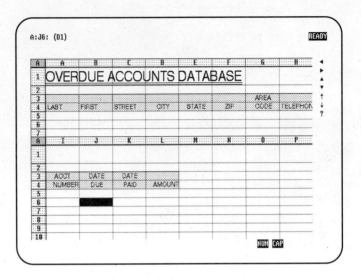

This screen shows all field names in the overdue accounts database, displayed with two windows.

3. Set the column widths and cell display formats.

   Note that whenever a right-justified column of numeric data is next to a left-justified column of label information, the data looks crowded. You can insert blank columns and adjust the column width of the blank column to change the spacing between fields.

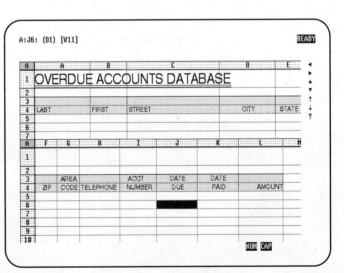

Use 1-2-3's /Worksheet Column Set-Width to control the width of columns. Use /Range Format to control the way 1-2-3 displays the data.

4. Add records to the database.

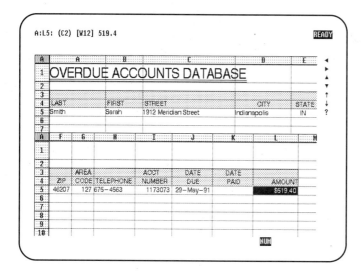

A:L5: (C2) [W12] 519.4   READY

	A	B	C	D	E
1	OVERDUE ACCOUNTS DATABASE				
2					
3					
4	LAST	FIRST	STREET	CITY	STATE
5	Smith	Sarah	1912 Meridian Street	Indianapolis	IN
6					
7					

	F	G	H	I	J	K	L	M
1								
2								
3		AREA		ACCT	DATE	DATE		
4	ZIP	CODE	TELEPHONE	NUMBER	DUE	PAID	AMOUNT	
5	46207	127	675-4563	1173073	29-May-91		$519.40	
6								
7								
8								
9								
10								

NUM

To enter the first record, move the cell pointer to the row directly below the field-names row. Then enter the data across the row in each applicable column (field).

Modifying a Database

After you collect the data and decide which field names and types, column widths, and formats to use, creating a database is easy. Thanks to 1-2-3, maintaining the accuracy of the database contents is also simple. Table 13.2 summarizes the commands you use to change a database.

Table 13.2
Commands for Modifying a Database

Action	Command
Add a record	/Worksheet Insert Row
Add a field	/Worksheet Insert Column
Delete a record	/Worksheet Delete Row
Delete a field	/Worksheet Delete Column
Edit a field	Edit (F2)

The process of changing fields in a database is the same as that for altering the contents of cells in any other application. You change the cell contents either by retyping the cell entry or by using the Edit (F2) key and editing the entry. You learn more about editing in this chapter's section titled "Editing Records During a Search."

Other 1-2-3 commands, such as those for copying, moving, and formatting cells, are the same for both database and other worksheet applications. For more information about these commands, see Chapters 4 through 6.

Inserting and Deleting Records

13

To add and delete records in a database, use the 1-2-3 commands for inserting and deleting rows. Because records correspond to rows, you begin inserting one or more records with the /Worksheet **I**nsert **R**ow command. You then fill in the various fields in each row with the appropriate data. To delete one or more rows, you use the /Worksheet **D**elete **R**ow command.

To insert one or more rows (records) in the database, follow these steps:

1. Select /Worksheet **I**nsert **R**ow.

2. When the prompt `Enter row insert range:` appears, highlight (or type the cell address of) the location where you want the row (record) to be inserted.

3. Press Enter.

When you press ↵Enter, a blank row appears, ready for you to enter a new record.

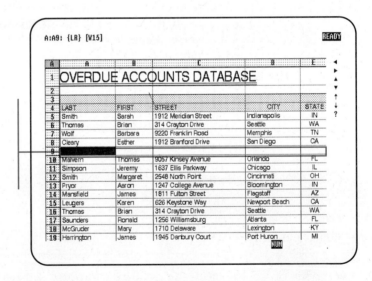

To delete one or more rows (records) from the database, follow these steps:

1. Select /Worksheet **D**elete **R**ow.

2. When the prompt `Enter range of rows to delete:` appears, highlight (or type the cell address of) the rows (records) you want to delete and press ↵Enter.

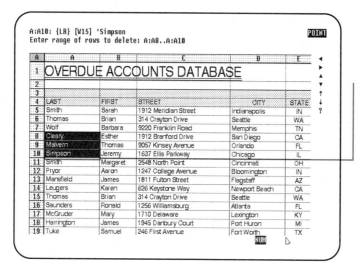

A:A10: {LR} [W15] 'Simpson
Enter range of rows to delete: A:A8..A:A10   `POINT`

	A	B	C	D	E
1	OVERDUE ACCOUNTS DATABASE				
2					
3					
4	LAST	FIRST	STREET	CITY	STATE
5	Smith	Sarah	1912 Meridian Street	Indianapolis	IN
6	Thomas	Brian	314 Crayton Drive	Seattle	WA
7	Wolf	Barbara	9220 Franklin Road	Memphis	TN
8	Cleary	Esther	1912 Branford Drive	San Diego	CA
9	Malvern	Thomas	9057 Kinsey Avenue	Orlando	FL
10	Simpson	Jeremy	1637 Ellis Parkway	Chicago	IL
11	Smith	Margaret	2548 North Point	Cincinnati	OH
12	Pryor	Aaron	1247 College Avenue	Bloomington	IN
13	Mansfield	James	1811 Fulton Street	Flagstaff	AZ
14	Leugers	Karen	626 Keystone Way	Newport Beach	CA
15	Thomas	Brian	314 Crayton Drive	Seattle	WA
16	Saunders	Ronald	1256 Williamsburg	Atlanta	FL
17	McGruder	Mary	1710 Delaware	Lexington	KY
18	Harrington	James	1945 Danbury Court	Port Huron	MI
19	Tuke	Samuel	246 First Avenue	Fort Worth	TX

NUM

In this example, to delete rows 8 through 10, highlight the rows and press ↵Enter.

A:A8: {LR} [W15] 'Smith   `READY`

	A	B	C	D	E
1	OVERDUE ACCOUNTS DATABASE				
2					
3					
4	LAST	FIRST	STREET	CITY	STATE
5	Smith	Sarah	1912 Meridian Street	Indianapolis	IN
6	Thomas	Brian	314 Crayton Drive	Seattle	WA
7	Wolf	Barbara	9220 Franklin Road	Memphis	TN
8	Smith	Margaret	2548 North Point	Cincinnati	OH
9	Pryor	Aaron	1247 College Avenue	Bloomington	IN
10	Mansfield	James	1811 Fulton Street	Flagstaff	AZ
11	Leugers	Karen	626 Keystone Way	Newport Beach	CA
12	Thomas	Brian	314 Crayton Drive	Seattle	WA
13	Saunders	Ronald	1256 Williamsburg	Atlanta	FL
14	McGruder	Mary	1710 Delaware	Lexington	KY
15	Harrington	James	1945 Danbury Court	Port Huron	MI
16	Tuke	Samuel	246 First Avenue	Fort Worth	TX
17	Wright	Amy	6327 Arlington	Des Moines	IA
18	Holland	Mark	316 Atwood Terrace	Miami	FL
19	Englert	Michael	397 Drexel Boulevard	Boston	MA

NUM

When you press ↵Enter, 1-2-3 deletes the records in the highlighted rows.

You cannot verify the range before you issue the /Worksheet Delete Row command. Therefore, be extremely careful when you specify the records to delete. If you want to remove inactive records only, first consider using the /Data Query Extract command. Described in a later section, this command enables you to store the inactive records in a separate location (or file) before you permanently delete the records.

459

Inserting and Deleting Fields

To add and delete fields in a database, use the 1-2-3 applications for inserting and deleting columns. To add one or more fields, use the /Worksheet Insert Column command. To delete one or more fields, use the /Worksheet Delete Column command.

To insert one or more new fields (columns) in the database, follow these steps:

1. Select /Worksheet Insert Column.

2. The prompt `Enter column insert range:` appears. Highlight (or type the cell address of) the location where you want the column (field) to be inserted; then press `⏎Enter`.

When you press `⏎Enter`, a blank column appears. The column is ready for you to enter new data.

A:C3: {S1 LRT}				READY
	A	B	C	D	E
1	OVERDUE ACCOUNTS DATABASE				
2					
3					
4	LAST	FIRST		STREET	CITY
5	Smith	Sarah		1912 Meridian Street	Indianapolis
6	Thomas	Brian		314 Crayton Drive	Seattle
7	Wolf	Barbara		9220 Franklin Road	Memphis
8	Cleary	Esther		1912 Branford Drive	San Diego
9	Malvern	Thomas		9057 Kinsey Avenue	Orlando
10	Simpson	Jeremy		1637 Ellis Parkway	Chicago
11	Smith	Margaret		2548 North Point	Cincinnati
12	Pryor	Aaron		1247 College Avenue	Bloomington
13	Mansfield	James		1811 Fulton Street	Flagstaff
14	Leugers	Karen		626 Keystone Way	Newport Beach
15	Thomas	Brian		314 Crayton Drive	Seattle
16	Saunders	Ronald		1256 Williamsburg	Atlanta
17	McGruder	Mary		1710 Delaware	Lexington
18	Harrington	James		1945 Danbury Court	Port Huron
19	Tuke	Samuel		246 First Avenue	Fort Worth

Because maintaining data takes up valuable memory, you can remove seldom-used data fields from the database.

To delete one or more fields (columns) from the database, follow these steps:

1. Select /Worksheet Delete Column.

2. When the `Enter range of columns to delete:` prompt appears, highlight the columns (fields) you want to delete; then press `⏎Enter`.

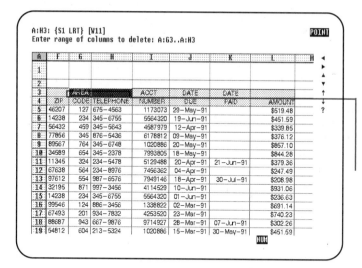

In this example, to delete columns G and H, highlight the columns and press ⏎Enter.

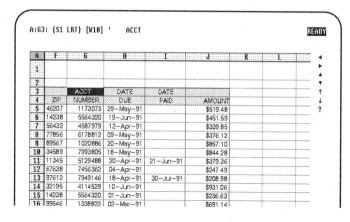

1-2-3 deletes the fields in the highlighted range.

Sorting Database Records

Storing data in a database would be meaningless if you were unable to alphabetize the data or sort it numerically. Sorting is an important function of any database. 1-2-3's data management capability lets you change the order of records by sorting them according to the contents of the fields. To sort data, you use the options available when you select /Data Sort:

Data-Range **Primary-Key** **Secondary-Key** **Extra-Key** **Reset** **Go** **Quit**

Table 13.3 describes each of these options.

Table 13.3
Selections on the /Data Sort Menu

Selection	Description
Data-Range	The range on which the sort operation occurs.
Primary-Key	The first item to organize the sort.
Secondary-Key	The second item to organize the sort.
Extra-Key	Specifies up to 253 more items to organize the sort.
Reset	Resets the sort options.
Go	Starts the search.
Quit	Exits the /Data Sort menu.

Before you issue a /Data Sort command, save the database to disk. That way, if the sort does not produce the results you expected, you can restore the file to its original order by retrieving it. To sort a database, follow these steps:

1. Select /Data Sort.

2. Select Data-Range and define the range you want to sort.

   This range must be long enough to include all the sorted records and wide enough to include all the fields in each record.

   Note: Do not include the field-names row. (If you are unfamiliar with how to define ranges or how to name them, see Chapter 4.)

   The data range does not have to include all rows in the database. However, it must include all fields (columns) to maintain the proper contents of each record. If some of the database records already have the organization you want, or if you don't want to sort all records, you can sort a portion.

3. Specify the key field(s) for the sort. Then specify ascending or descending order for each key field.

   Key fields are the columns to which you attach the highest precedence when 1-2-3 sorts the database. The column (or field) with the highest precedence is the Primary-Key. The field with the next highest precedence is the Secondary-Key. Fields with descending precedence are Extra-Keys. You must always set a Primary-Key. Setting the Secondary-Key and Extra-Keys is optional.

4. Select Go to perform the sort.

The One-Key Sort

One of the simplest examples of a database sorted according to a primary key is the white pages of the telephone book. All the records in the white pages are in ascending alphabetical order using the name as the primary key.

Suppose, for example, that you want to reorder records alphabetically on the LAST name field. To perform a one-key sort operation, follow these steps:

1. Select /**D**ata **S**ort **D**ata-Range.

2. The prompt `Enter data range:` appears. Highlight (or type) the cell addresses, or enter the range name for the range you want to sort; then press ⏎Enter.

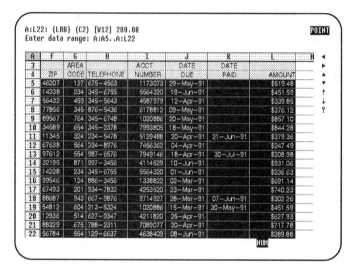

In this example, highlight the range for the entire database, A5..L22 (excluding the field names in rows 3 and 4) and press ⏎Enter.

3. From the **S**ort menu, select **P**rimary-Key.

4. Type or point to any cell in the column containing the primary-key field on which you want to sort; then press ⏎Enter.

13

In this example, to sort the database by the LAST (last name) field, highlight any cell in column A; then press ↵Enter.

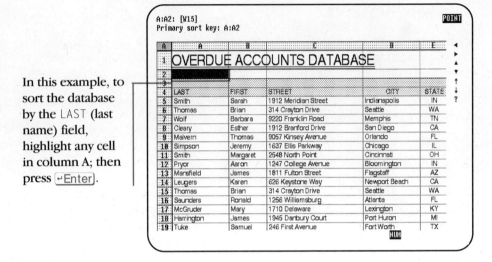

5. Type **A** or **D** to indicate whether you want your database sorted in ascending or descending order; then press ↵Enter.

In this example, type **A** to sort the database so 1-2-3 alphabetizes the last names from A to Z.

6. When the **S**ort menu returns, select **G**o to have 1-2-3 sort the database.

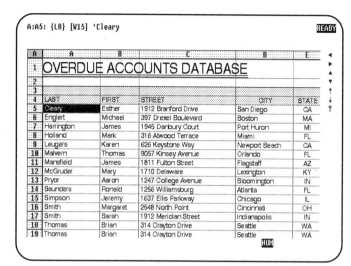

The database now displays the result of the one-key sort on the LAST field.

13

The Two-Key Sort

A two-key database sort uses both a primary and secondary key. The yellow pages sort records first according to business type (the primary key) and then by business name (the secondary key). Another example of a two-key sort (first by one key and then by another key within the first sort order) is an addresses database. First the address database sorts by state and then by city within state. Suppose, for example, that you want to perform a two-key sort on an overdue accounts database. First, you sort records according to due date. Then, when more than one record has the same due date, you sort further according to account number.

To perform a two-key sort operation, follow these steps:

1. Select /**D**ata **S**ort **D**ata-Range.
2. The prompt Enter Data-Range: appears. Highlight (or type) the cell addresses, or enter the range name for the range you want to sort; then press [↵Enter].

   For this example, highlight the range A5..L22 and press [↵Enter].
3. From the **S**ort menu, select **P**rimary-Key to indicate the first field on which you want the data sorted.
4. Type or highlight any cell in the column containing the primary-key field on which you want to sort; then press [↵Enter].

13

In this example, to
first sort the
database by the
DATE DUE column,
highlight any cell
in column J.

```
A:J1: [W11]                                          POINT
Primary sort key: A:J1
```

ZIP	AREA CODE	TELEPHONE	ACCT NUMBER	DATE DUE	DATE PAID	AMOUNT
77856	345	876-5436	6178812	09-May-91		$376.12
56784	554	129-6637	4638409	08-Jun-91		$289.88
88687	943	667-9876	9714927	28-Mar-91	07-Jun-91	$302.26
88329	675	788-2311	7089077	20-Apr-91		$717.78
32195	871	997-3456	4114529	10-Jun-91		$931.06
89567	764	345-6748	1020886	20-May-91		$857.10
97612	554	987-6576	7949146	18-Apr-91	30-Jul-91	$208.98
67493	201	934-7832	4253520	23-Mar-91		$740.23
67638	564	234-8976	7456362	04-Apr-91		$247.49
99546	124	886-3456	1338822	02-Mar-91		$691.14
34589	654	345-2378	7993805	18-May-91		$844.28
11345	324	234-5478	5129488	20-Apr-91	21-Jun-91	$379.36
46207	127	675-4563	1173073	29-May-91		$519.48
14238	234	345-6755	5564320	01-Jun-91		$236.63
14238	234	345-6755	5564320	19-Jun-91		$451.59

5. Indicate the sort order by typing **A** for ascending or **D** for descending;
   then press ↵Enter.

   For this example, type **A** to sort the database so 1-2-3 arranges the due
   dates from earliest to most recent.

6. Select Secondary-Key to have the data sorted a second time within the
   primary sort order.

7. Type or highlight any cell in the column containing the secondary-key
   field on which you want to sort; then press ↵Enter.

```
A:I1: [W10]                                          POINT
Secondary sort key: A:I1
```

To sort according
to ACCT NUMBER
after sorting by
DUE DATE,
highlight any cell
in column I and
press ↵Enter.

ZIP	AREA CODE	TELEPHONE	ACCT NUMBER	DATE DUE	DATE PAID	AMOUNT
77856	345	876-5436	6178812	09-May-91		$376.12
56784	554	129-6637	4638409	08-Jun-91		$289.88
88687	943	667-9876	9714927	28-Mar-91	07-Jun-91	$302.26
88329	675	788-2311	7089077	20-Apr-91		$717.78
32195	871	997-3456	4114529	10-Jun-91		$931.06
89567	764	345-6748	1020886	20-May-91		$857.10
97612	554	987-6576	7949146	18-Apr-91	30-Jul-91	$208.98
67493	201	934-7832	4253520	23-Mar-91		$740.23
67638	564	234-8976	7456362	04-Apr-91		$247.49
99546	124	886-3456	1338822	02-Mar-91		$691.14
34589	654	345-2378	7993805	18-May-91		$844.28
11345	324	234-5478	5129488	20-Apr-91	21-Jun-91	$379.36
46207	127	675-4563	1173073	29-May-91		$519.48
14238	234	345-6755	5564320	01-Jun-91		$236.63
14238	234	345-6755	5564320	19-Jun-91		$451.59

8. Indicate the sort order by typing **A** for ascending or **D** for descending; then press ⏎Enter.

   For this example, type **A** for **A**scending.

9. Select **G**o to have 1-2-3 sort the database.

A	F	G	H	I	J	K	L	M
		AREA		ACCT	DATE	DATE		
	ZIP	CODE	TELEPHONE	NUMBER	DUE	PAID	AMOUNT	
5	99546	124	886–3456	1338822	02–Mar–91		$691.14	
6	54812	604	213–5324	1020886	15–Mar–91	30–May–91	$451.59	
7	67493	201	934–7832	4253520	23–Mar–91		$740.23	
8	88687	943	667–9876	9714927	28–Mar–91	07–Jun–91	$302.26	
9	67638	564	234–8976	7456362	04–Apr–91		$247.49	
10	56432	459	345–5643	4587979	12–Apr–91		$339.85	
11	97612	554	987–6576	7949146	18–Apr–91	30–Jul–91	$208.98	
12	11345	324	234–5478	5129488	20–Apr–91	21–Jun–91	$379.36	
13	88329	675	788–2311	7089077	20–Apr–91		$717.78	
14	12936	514	627–9347	4211820	25–Apr–91		$627.93	
15	77856	345	876–5436	6178812	09–May–91		$376.12	
16	34589	654	345–2378	7993805	18–May–91		$844.28	
17	89567	764	345–6748	1020886	20–May–91		$857.10	
18	46207	127	675–4563	1173073	29–May–91		$519.48	
19	14238	234	345–6755	5564320	01–Jun–91		$236.63	

The database now displays the result of the two-key sort on the DATE DUE and ACCT NUMBER fields. 1-2-3 sorts accounts that are due on the same day according to their account numbers.

If you need to sort on more than two fields, use the **Extra-Key** option on the /**D**ata **S**ort menu. For example, you may need to sort by State, City, and Zip code. You can sort on up to 255 key fields, including the primary and secondary sort keys.

Tips for Sorting Database Records

Here are a few tips to help you sort database records more successfully.

Tip 1:   Don't include blank rows in your data range before you sort the database.

If you accidentally include one or more blank rows in your data range, the blank rows appear at the top of your data range. Remember to include only rows with data when specifying the data range.

13

Blanks have precedence over all other characters in a sort. Therefore, blank rows included in the sort data range appear at the top of the sorted database.

```
A:A5: {LR} [W15]                                        READY

   A        A            B            C                    D              E
   1  OVERDUE ACCOUNTS DATABASE
   2
   3
   4  LAST       FIRST        STREET                    CITY           STATE
   5
   6
   7
   8  Cleary     Esther       1912 Branford Drive       San Diego      CA
   9  Englert    Michael      397 Drexel Boulevard      Boston         MA
  10  Harrington James        1945 Danbury Court        Port Huron     MI
  11  Holland    Mark         316 Atwood Terrace        Miami          FL
  12  Leugers    Karen        626 Keystone Way          Newport Beach  CA
  13  Malvern    Thomas       9057 Kinsey Avenue        Orlando        FL
  14  Mansfield  James        1811 Fulton Street        Flagstaff      AZ
  15  McGruder   Mary         1710 Delaware             Lexington      KY
  16  Pryor      Aaron        1247 College Avenue       Bloomington    IN
  17  Saunders   Ronald       1256 Williamsburg         Atlanta        FL
  18  Simpson    Jeremy       1637 Ellis Parkway        Chicago        IL
  19  Smith      Margaret     2548 North Point          Cincinnati     OH
                                                               NUM
```

Tip 2: Use the /Worksheet Insert Column and /Data Fill commands to create a "counter" field. With this field you can easily re-sort the database to its original order.

After you sort the original contents of the database on any field, you cannot restore the records to their original order. To avoid mistakes and restore the records to the original order, add a counter column to the database before any sort. Include the counter column in the sort range. You can restore the original order by re-sorting on the counter field. The counter field assigns a number to each record so you can restore the records to their original order.

To create a counter field, follow these steps:

1. Insert a blank column by selecting /Worksheet Insert Column. You can reduce the column width of this new column with the /Worksheet Column Set-Width command.

2. Select /Data Fill.

3. Within the blank column, highlight the rows of your database (or the records you want to sort) where you wish to enter counter numbers; then press ⏎Enter.

4. Press 1 and ⏎Enter for Start, and then press 1 and ⏎Enter for Step. Next, press ⏎Enter to accept the default Stop value.

   Note: Although the default Stop value of 8192 is larger than it needs to be, 1-2-3 uses only the numbers necessary to fill the specified range.

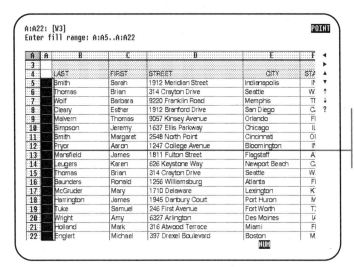

In this example, highlight the range A5..A22 and press [↵Enter].

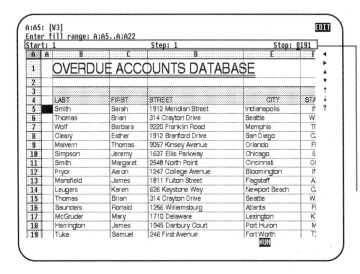

After indicating the /**D**ata **F**ill range, 1-2-3 prompts you for the **S**tart, **S**tep (increment), and **S**top numbers.

13

1-2-3 fills the range with consecutive numbers, beginning with 1 and ending with the number of the last highlighted row.

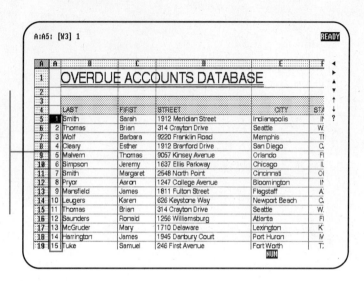

When you sort the database, include the counter column in your data range. To re-sort the database to its original order, use the counter field as your primary-key field.

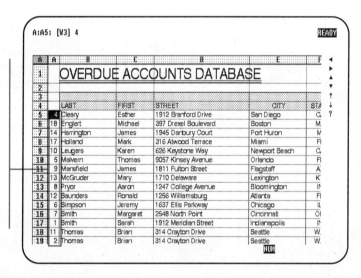

Tip 3: Add records to the end of the database. Then expand the sort range to include the new records.

You can add a record to an alphabetized name-and-address database without having to insert the record manually. Simply add the record to the bottom of the current database, expand the sort data range, and then sort again by last name.

Searching for Records

You have learned how to use the /Data Sort command to reorganize information by sorting records according to key fields. In this section, you learn how to use /Data Query to search for records. You can then edit, extract, or delete those records.

Looking for records that meet one condition is the simplest form of searching a 1-2-3 database. In an inventory database, for example, you can determine when to reorder items. Use a search operation to find any records with an on-hand quantity of fewer than four units. Once you find the information you want, you can extract or copy the found records from the database to another empty section of the worksheet. For example, you can extract all records with a future purchase order date and print the newly extracted area as a record of pending purchases.

With 1-2-3's search operations, you also have the option of looking for only the first occurrence of a specified field value. This allows you to develop a unique list of field entries. For example, you can search and extract a list of the different units of measure. Then you can delete all inventory records for which quantity on-hand equals zero (if you don't want to reorder these items).

Minimum Search Requirements

The /Data Query command lets you search for and extract data that meets specific criteria. After you choose /Data Query, 1-2-3 displays a menu of nine options for performing search and extract operations:

Input Criteria Output Find Extract Unique Del Modify Reset Quit

Table 13.4 describes these options.

Table 13.4
Selections on the /Data Query Menu

Selection	Description
Input	Specifies the location of the search area.
Criteria	The conditions to search the database.
Output	The range where you want to locate the records extracted from the database.
Find	Finds records based on specified criteria.

471

Table 13.4 (continued)

Selection	Description
Extract	Copies from the database the records matching the specified criteria and places them in the output range.
Unique	Eliminates duplicate records in the output range.
Del	Removes from the input range records that match the specified criteria.
Modify	Inserts or replaces records in the input range with records from the output range.
Reset	Resets the input, criteria, and output ranges.
Quit	Returns 1-2-3 to READY mode.

The first three options specify ranges applicable to the search operation. **Input** and **Criteria** give the locations of the search area and the search conditions. You must specify both in all **Query** operations. You specify the output range with the **Output** option. The output range is necessary when you select a /Data Query command that copies records to an area outside the database.

The next five options of the /Data Query menu perform a variety of search functions. Find moves down through a database and positions the cell pointer on records that match given criteria. You can enter or change data in the records as you move the cell pointer through them. Extract creates copies, in a specified area of the worksheet, of all or some of the fields in certain records that match given criteria. Unique is similar to Extract, but ignores duplicates as 1-2-3 copies entries to the output range. Delete erases from a database all the records that match the given criteria and closes the remaining gaps. Modify replaces or inserts records into the input range that you changed or edited in the output range.

The last two options of the /Data Query menu are **Reset** and **Quit**. They signal the end of the current search operation. **Reset** removes all previous search-related ranges so you can specify a different search location, condition, and output range (if applicable). **Quit** restores 1-2-3 to READY mode.

Searching for Specific Records

If you want to search for one or several records that meet certain criteria, you need to use three commands from the /Data Query menu: **Input, Criteria**, and **Find**. Suppose, for example, that you want to search a database containing a list of customers with overdue accounts to find a specific customer. The following sections describe the procedure.

Defining the Input Range

The input range for the /Data Query command is the range of records you want to search. The specified area does not have to include the entire database. Whether you search all or only part of a database, you must include the field-names row in the input range. (In contrast, remember that you do not include the field names in a sort operation.) If field names occupy space on more than one row, specify only the bottom row to start the input range. Do not use a blank row or a dashed line to separate the field names from the database records.

Select /Data Query Input, and then specify the range by typing or highlighting the range, or by typing an assigned range name. You do not have to specify the range again in later query operations unless the search area changes.

The input range for the database containing a list of overdue accounts includes the entire database and the field names. To define the input range containing the records to search, follow these steps:

1. Select /Data Query Input.

2. The prompt `Enter input range:` appears. Specify the range by typing or highlighting the range, or by typing an assigned range name; then press `↵Enter`.

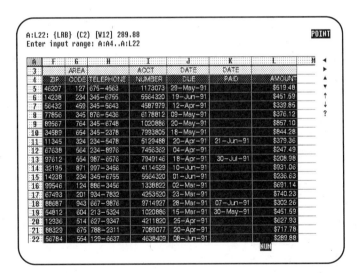

In this example, highlight the range A4..L22 and press `↵Enter`.

3. To return to READY mode, select **Quit**.

13

473

After you have defined the input range, the next step in a data query operation is to define the criteria range. The next section covers this procedure.

Defining the Criteria Range

To search for data that meets certain conditions, or criteria, you must set up a special range called a criteria range. First find an empty area of the worksheet for your criteria range. Then use the /Data Query Criteria command.

You can use numbers, labels, or formulas as criteria. A criteria range can be up to 256 columns wide and two or more rows long. The first row must contain the field names of the search criteria, such as STATE in the previous example. The rows below the unique field names contain the actual criteria, such as OH. The field names of the input range and the criteria range must match exactly.

To keep the criteria range separate from the input range, put your criteria range on a different sheet. This protects both ranges from accidental erasing of rows or columns. To add a worksheet use the /Worksheet Insert Sheet command.

Suppose that in an overdue accounts database, you want to identify all records for customers with the last name Smith. To define the criteria range containing the search conditions, follow these steps:

1. Begin by locating an area of the worksheet where you can enter the criteria on which you want to search the database. Type the label **CRITERIA RANGE** to mark the area; then press ⏎Enter.

In this example, move to cell A1 of worksheet B, type **CRITERIA RANGE**; then press ⏎Enter.

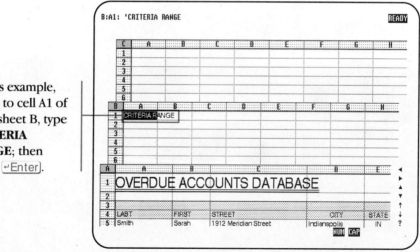

474

2. Copy the exact field names of your database to the section of the worksheet where you want to locate the criteria range.

   Note: You do not have to include each field name in the criteria range. However, you should copy all field names, because you may choose to enter criteria based on different field names at a later time.

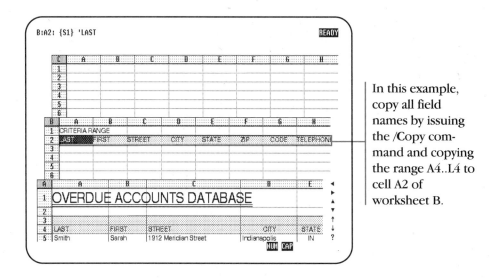

In this example, copy all field names by issuing the /Copy command and copying the range A4..L4 to cell A2 of worksheet B.

3. Type the search criteria just below a field name and press ↵Enter.

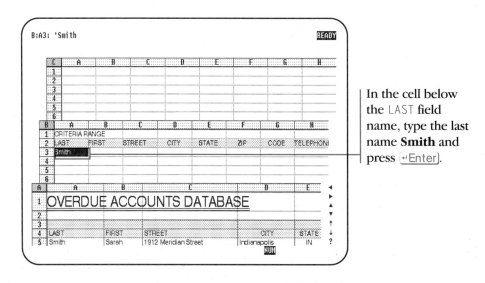

In the cell below the LAST field name, type the last name **Smith** and press ↵Enter.

4. Select /**Data Query Criteria**.

5. The prompt `Enter criteria range:` appears. Highlight or type the range of cells containing the field names and specific criteria; then press ⏎Enter.

In this example, highlight the range B:A2..B:L3 and press ⏎Enter.

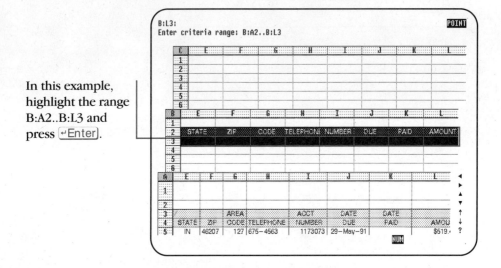

6. To return to READY mode, select **Quit**.

The next step involves searching for (but not copying) the specified records. The next section covers this step.

Finding Records That Meet the Criteria

After you enter the input and criteria ranges, you have completed the minimum requirements for executing a **Find** or **Delete** command. Be sure to enter the specific field names above the conditions in the worksheet (in READY mode) before you use /**Data Query Criteria**.

To search for records that meet the criteria you have specified, follow these steps:

1. Select /**Data Query Find**.

A highlight bar rests on the first record (in the input range) that meets the conditions specified in the criteria range. Notice that the mode indicator changes to FIND during the search.

476

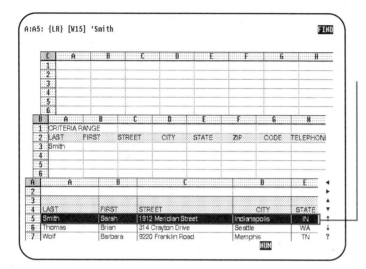

In this example, the highlight bar rests on the first record that includes `Smith` in the LAST field, in row 5 of the worksheet.

2. Press ⬇ to move the highlight bar to the next record that meets the specified criteria. You can continue pressing ⬇ until 1-2-3 highlights the last record that meets the search conditions.

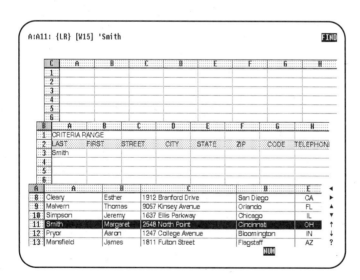

In this example, the highlight bar moves to row 11, the next occurrence of `Smith` in the LAST field of the database.

3. When you want to end the search, press ⏎Enter or Esc to return to the /Data Query menu.

4. To return to READY mode, select **Quit**.

13

Use the down- and up-arrow keys to position the highlight bar on the next and previous records that meet the search criteria. You can use the Home and End keys to position the highlight bar on the first and last records in the database. This is so even if those records do not fit the search criteria.

In FIND mode, use the right- and left-arrow keys to move the single-character flashing cursor to different fields in the current highlighted record. Then enter new values or use the Edit (F2) key to update the current values in the field. The next section discusses editing while in FIND mode.

Editing Records During a Search

If you need to change a record while conducting a search, you can switch from FIND to EDIT mode temporarily. Then you can edit the record and return to searching for other records. Suppose, for example, that you want to update a record in an overdue accounts database. Follow these steps to edit a record during a search:

1. To begin the search operation, select /**D**ata **Q**uery **F**ind.

2. In FIND mode, press → or ← until the blinking cursor is in the cell where you want to edit data.

3. When the blinking cursor is in the cell you want to edit, press F2 (Edit) to change from FIND to EDIT mode. The cell contents (if any) appear in the control panel.

4. Type new data, or edit existing data by pressing F2 (Edit); then press ↵Enter.

In this example, type new data in the DATE PAID column; then press ↵Enter.

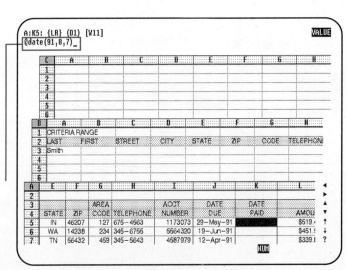

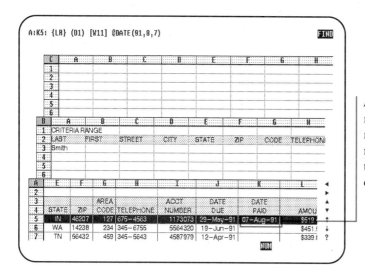

After you edit the record, 1-2-3 returns to FIND mode and displays the new or edited data.

13

Listing All Specified Records

The /Data Query Find command has limited use, especially in a large database. The command must scroll through the entire file if you want to view each record that meets the specified criteria. As an alternative to the **Find** command, you can use the **Extract** command. This command copies to a blank area of the worksheet only those records that meet specified conditions. Before you issue the command, you must define the blank area of the worksheet as an output range. You can view a list of all the extracted records or print the range of the newly extracted records. You can even use the /File Xtract command to copy only the extracted record range to a new file on disk.

Defining the Output Range

Choose a blank area in the worksheet as the output range to receive records copied in an extract operation. In the first row of the output range, type the names of only those fields whose contents you want to extract. You do not have to type these names in the same order as they appear in the database.

The field names in both the criteria and output ranges must match exactly the corresponding field names in the input range. If you enter a database field name incorrectly in the output range, an extract operation based on that field name does not work. For example, FIRSTNAME does not work instead of FIRST. To avoid mismatch errors, use the /Copy command to copy the database field names to the criteria and output ranges.

13

You can create an open-ended output range by entering only the field-names row as the range. The output range, in this case, can be any size, according to how many records meet the criteria. Or you can set the exact size of the extract area so no data located below the area is accidentally overwritten.

To keep the output range separate from the criteria range and input ranges, put your output range on a different worksheet. This protects all ranges from accidental erasing of rows or columns. To add a worksheet, use the /Worksheet Insert Sheet command.

To define the output range where 1-2-3 will copy records meeting the specified criteria, follow these steps:

1. Begin by locating an area of the worksheet where you want to copy the records meeting the criteria. Type the label **OUTPUT RANGE** and press ⏎Enter to mark the area.

2. Copy the exact field names of your database to the section of the worksheet where you want to locate the output range.

   Note: You do not have to extract entire records or maintain the order of field names in the output range. If you do not need to see information for every field in the output range, copy only the desired field names.

In this example, copy all field names by issuing the /Copy command and copying the range A4..L4 to cell C:A2 on sheet C.

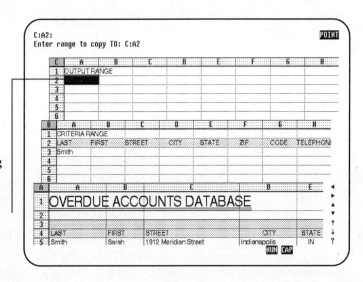

3. Select /Data Query Output.

4. The prompt Enter output range: appears. Highlight the range where you want to copy the records and press ⏎Enter. You can indicate either an unlimited range or a range limited to a specific block of cells.

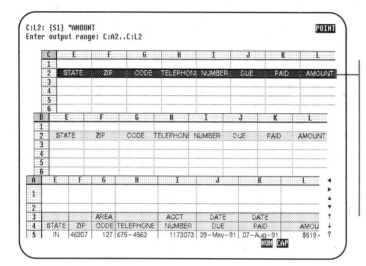

To enter an unlimited output range, highlight only the cells containing field names. In this example, highlight the range C:A2..C:L2 and press ↵Enter.

13

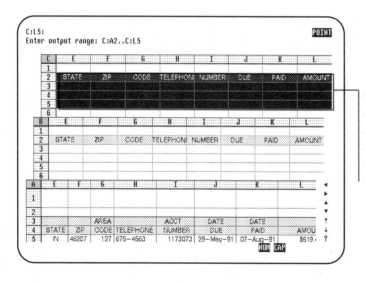

To enter a limited output range, specify additional rows below the field-names row and press ↵Enter.

5. To return to READY mode, select **Quit**.

An open-ended output range does not limit the number of incoming records. To create an open-ended range, specify only the row containing the output field names as the output range. Keep in mind that an extract operation first removes all existing data from the output range. If you use only the field-names row, 1-2-3 destroys all data below that row (down to row 8192). Therefore, be sure that you don't have data below the row of field names if you choose an open-ended output range. To avoid errors, use a separate worksheet for the output range.

To limit the size of the output range, enter the upper left to lower right cell coordinates of the entire output range. The first row in the specified range must contain the field names. The remaining rows must accommodate the maximum number of records you expect to receive from the extract operation. Use this method when you want to keep additional data that is below the extract area. If you do not allow enough room in the fixed-length output area, the extract operation aborts and 1-2-3 displays `Too many records`. Nevertheless, 1-2-3 fills the output area with as many records as will fit.

Executing the Extract Command

Before you can execute the /Data Query Extract command, you must type the search conditions in the criteria range of the worksheet. You must also copy the output field names to the output range in the worksheet. Finally, you must specify the input, criteria, and output ranges with the /Data Query commands.

To extract (or copy) to the output range records that meet the specified criteria, follow these steps:

1. Select /Data Query Extract.

   1-2-3 copies all records that meet the specified criteria in the criteria range to the output area. 1-2-3 keeps the same order as the input range.

In this example, 1-2-3 copied all records in the LAST field that correspond to the search criteria of Smith to the output range.

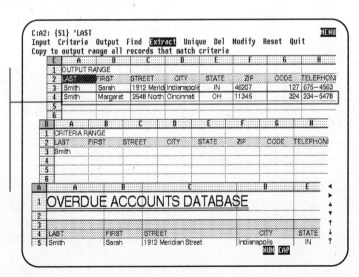

2. To return to READY mode, select **Quit**.

To speed up the process, you can set up standard input, criteria, and output ranges, and then store the range names for these locations. You can set up a single criteria range that encompasses all the key fields on which you might search. By establishing such a range, you save the time needed to re-specify a criteria range for each extract on different field names.

When 1-2-3 is in READY mode, you can press the Query (F7) key to repeat the most recent query operation (**Extract**, to repeat in this example). This would eliminate the need to select /**Data Query Extract** again after changing the criteria range. Use the shortcut method only when you do not want to change the locations of the input, criteria, and output ranges.

Copying Extracted Records to a New File

If you want to copy extracted records to their own special file, follow these steps:

1. Select /**File Xtract**.
2. Select either **Formulas** or **Values**, depending on whether the data contains formulas you want retained in the new file.
3. Type the name you want to give to the new file and press ⏎Enter.
4. Highlight the range or type the range address of the records you want to copy to a new file; then press ⏎Enter.

    For example, highlight the range C:A2..C:L4 and press ⏎Enter.

1-2-3 creates a new file containing the data from your extract range. To access this file, you must issue the /**File Retrieve** command and specify the new file name.

Creating More Complex Criteria Ranges

In addition to searching for an "exact match" of a specified label within a field of labels, 1-2-3 permits a wide variety of other types of record searches. For example, you can search for an exact match in numeric fields. In addition, you can choose a search criteria that only partially matches the contents of specified fields. You can include formulas in your search criteria. You can also use multiple criteria that involve searching for specified conditions in more than one field.

483

Using Wild Cards in Criteria Ranges

Depending on the complexity of your database operations, you may need to be a bit more creative when you are specifying criteria ranges in 1-2-3. For that reason, 1-2-3 allows you to use wild cards and formulas in criteria ranges. The following are some examples that show how you can use wild cards in search operations:

Enter	To find
N?	NC, NJ, and NY
BO?L?	BOWLE, but not BOWL
BO?L*	BOWLE, BOWL, BOLLESON, and BOELING
SAN*	SANTA BARBARA and SAN FRANCISCO
SAN *	SAN FRANCISCO and SAN DIEGO, but not SANTA BARBARA
~N*	Strings (in specified fields) that do *not* begin with the letter N

You can use 1-2-3's wild cards for matching labels in database operations. The characters ?, *, and ~ have special meanings when used in the criteria range. The ? character instructs 1-2-3 to accept any single character in that specific position. Only use ? to find fields of the same length. Use the * character to tell 1-2-3 to accept any and all characters that follow. You can use * on field contents of unequal length. By placing a tilde (~) at the beginning of a search condition, you tell 1-2-3 to accept all values *except* those that follow.

~IN is in the STATE field of the criteria range. The output range on worksheet C after an **Extract** includes all records that do *not* match IN (Indiana).

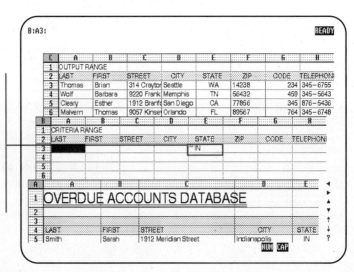

Use the ? and * wild-card characters when you are unsure of the spelling used in field contents. Be sure that the results of any extract operation that uses a wild card are what you need. And be extremely careful when you use wild cards with a /Data Query Del command (discussed later in this chapter). If you are not careful, you may remove more records than you intend.

13

Entering Formulas in Criteria Ranges

To set up formulas that query numeric fields in the database, you can use the following relational (or logical) operators:

>	Greater than
<	Less than
=	Equal to
>=	Greater than or equal to
<=	Less than or equal to
<>	Not equal to

You may need to type a label prefix before the operator. For example, to enter the less-than sign, type an ' (apostrophe) followed by the less-than sign (<).

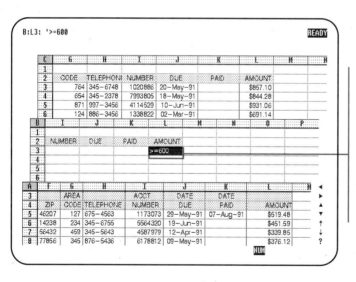

The formula >=600 is in the AMOUNT field of the criteria range. The output range after an Extract includes all records with an amount due greater than or equal to $600.

Specifying Multiple Criteria

So far, you have seen how to base a **Find** or **Extract** operation on only one criterion. In this section, you learn how to use multiple criteria for your queries. When you maintain a criteria range that includes all (or many) field names, you can quickly extract records based on alternative conditions. You also can continue to add more conditions.

You can set up multiple criteria in which the search must meet *all* the criteria or any *one* criterion. For example, searching a music department's library for sheet music requiring both drums *and* trumpets is likely to produce fewer selections than searching for music appropriate for drums *or* trumpets. You can indicate two or more criteria by specifying the conditions in separate fields of the criteria row immediately below the field names. The search must meet all criteria.

After an Extract, the output range shows all customers with ZIP codes that begin with 3 and who owe at least $600.

Using multiple criteria in a single row of the criteria range tells 1-2-3 to "search for the records that meet this *and* that criterion." Notice that the search criteria are in a single row immediately below the field-names row.

In contrast, criteria placed on different rows find or extract records based on this field condition *or* that field condition. You can also search on one or more fields using this type of multiple criteria.

Searching a single field for more than one condition is the simplest use of criteria entered on separate rows. For example, you can extract from the overdue accounts database only those records with state abbreviations of IN or TX.

486

To perform this search, under the STATE criteria field, type one condition immediately below the other. Be sure to use the /**D**ata **Q**uery **C**riteria command to expand the definition of the criteria range to include the additional row.

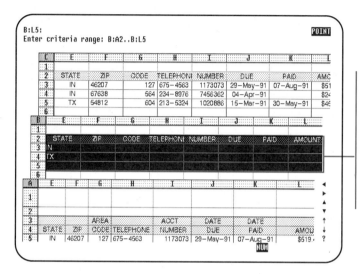

In this example, first change the criteria range to include more than one row. Then enter criteria in separate rows to find all accounts in Indiana or Texas.

Notice that each condition is in a separate row under the field-names row. The output range shows the result of an **Extract**.

You can also specify multiple criteria on different rows with two or more different criteria fields. Building on the preceding example, suppose you want to find the records with the states IN or TX or with overdue amounts of at least $600.

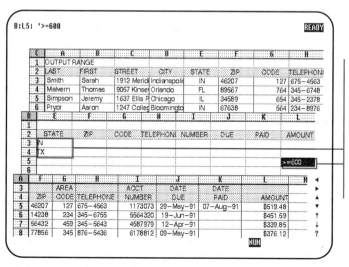

Use multiple criteria on different rows to find the items that have either IN or TX in the STATE field, or have overdue amounts of at least $600.

487

As shown, when you issue the **Extract** command, the records that meet either condition appear in the output range.

If you are careful when you specify conditions, you can mix both multiple fields and multiple rows within the criteria range. Follow the format of placing *all* criteria to meet at once in a single row immediately below the criteria field-names row. To find records that match *any* criteria, place criteria specifications in separate rows. Because using multiple criteria may sometimes get confusing, test the logic of your criteria on a small sample of records and verify the results. Then you can proceed to search all your records according to the multiple criteria.

Using Special Operators

To combine search conditions within a single field, use the special operators #AND# and #OR#. Use the special operator #NOT# to negate a search condition. Use #AND# or #OR# to search on two or more conditions within the same field. For example, suppose that you want to extract all records with Indiana (IN) and Texas (TX) in the STATE field, but not California (CA).

Use the #AND#, #OR#, and #NOT# operators to enter (in one field) conditions that you could enter another way (usually in at least two fields). For example, you can enter the following in a single cell of the STATE field in the criteria range as an alternative to entering each condition on a separate line:

+STATE="IN"#OR#STATE="TX"

The reference to STATE in the formula shows that you are searching the STATE field located in column E. Use #NOT# at the beginning of a condition to negate that condition. For example, you can find records that do not have CA listed in the STATE field by typing #NOT#CA in the criteria range.

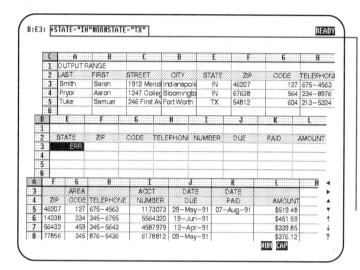

Here enter the formula condition in cell B:E3, as shown in the control panel. Rows 3 through 5 on worksheet C display the extracted records.

13

Performing Other Types of Searches

In addition to **Find** and **Extract**, you can use the **/Data Query** menu's **Unique**, **Delete**, and **Modify** to perform searches. By issuing the **Unique** command, you can produce (in the output range) a copy of only the first occurrence of a record that meets the specified criteria. The **Delete** command allows you to update the contents of your 1-2-3 database by deleting all records that meet the specified criteria. After entering the search conditions, you need to specify only the input and criteria ranges before you issue the **Delete** command. The **Modify** command allows you to extract data to the output range, edit it and put the edited records back into the input range. You can also add records to the output range, and **Modify** adds the records to the input range.

Searching for Unique Records

Ordinarily, you use the **Unique** command to copy into the output area only a small portion of each record that meets the criteria. For example, if you want a list of states represented in the overdue accounts database, set an output range that includes only the STATE field. To search all records, leave blank the row below the field-names row in the criteria range. Then define the input, criteria, and output ranges and select **/Data Query Unique**. In the following example, the output range includes only the STATE field. The row below the field-names row in the criteria range is blank.

To copy to the output range unique records that meet the criteria you have specified, follow these steps:

1. Select /**Data Query Unique**.

    1-2-3 copies all records that meet the specified criteria in the criteria range to the output area. The order is the same as in the input range.

In this example, issuing the Unique command produces a list of the different states represented in the database.

```
D:A2: 'STATE                                                    MENU
Input  Criteria  Output  Find  Extract  Unique  Del  Modify  Reset  Quit
Copy to output range all nonduplicate records that match criteria
     A         B          C         D         E        F        G        H
 1  OUTPUT RANGE FOR DATA QUERY UNIQUE
 2  STATE
 3        AZ
 4        CA
 5        FL
 6        IA
 7        IL
 8        IN
 9        KY
10        MA
11        MI
12        OH
13        TN
14        TX
15        WA
16
17
18
19
20                                                           NUM CAP
```

2. To return to READY mode, select **Quit**.

Deleting Specified Records

As discussed earlier, you can use the /**Worksheet Delete Row** command to remove records from a worksheet. An alternative approach is to use the /**Data Query Del** command to remove from the database unwanted records matching a specified criteria. Before you select **Del** from the /**Data Query** menu, specify the range of records to search (the input range) and the conditions for the deletion (the criteria).

Be extremely careful when you issue the **Del** command. To give you the opportunity to verify that you indeed want the **Del** command, 1-2-3 asks you to select **Cancel** or **Del**. Choose **Cancel** to abort the **Del** command. Select **Delete** to verify that you want to execute the delete operation.

Although 1-2-3 asks if you want to delete records, you can't view the records that match the criteria you specified. For this reason, use /**File Save** to make a copy of the database before deleting records. Or you can use the **Extract** command to copy the records you plan to delete and view them. When you are sure you want to remove the records from the database, proceed with the delete operation.

In the following example, 1-2-3 deletes the records in the overdue accounts database that have an entry in the DATE PAID column. The first row of the DATE PAID column in the criteria range contains the following formula:

    +PAID<>""

To delete records that meet specified criteria, follow these steps:

1. Select **/Data Query Del** (Delete).

2. Select **Cancel**, or **Del** to proceed with the command. In this example, select **Del**. 1-2-3 acts on the **Delete** command without displaying the records to delete.

```
A:K2: [W11]                                                    READY

A     E      F      G        H          I        J         K        L
                         AREA                          DATE
1
2
3                        AREA                   DATE      DATE
4   STATE   ZIP    CODE  TELEPHONE   NUMBER    DUE       PAID      AMOU
5    WA    14238    234  345-6755    5564320  19-Jun-91            $451.
6    TN    56432    459  345-5643    4587979  12-Apr-91            $339.
7    CA    77856    345  876-5436    6178812  09-May-91           $376.
8    FL    89567    764  345-6748    1020886  20-May-91           $857.
9    IL    34589    654  345-2378    7993805  18-May-91           $844.
10   IN    67638    564  234-8976    7456362  04-Apr-91           $247.
11   CA    32195    871  997-3456    4114529  10-Jun-91           $931.(
12   WA    14238    234  345-6755    5564320  01-Jun-91           $236.(
13   FL    99546    124  886-3456    1338822  02-Mar-91           $691.
14   KY    67493    201  934-7832    4253520  23-Mar-91           $740.
15   IA    12936    514  627-9347    4211820  25-Apr-91           $627.
16   FL    88329    675  788-2311    7089077  20-Apr-91           $717.
17   MA    56784    554  129-6637    4638409  08-Jun-91           $289.
18
19
                                                      NUM  CAP
```

1-2-3 deleted all records with an entry in the DATE PAID column of the database.

3. To return to READY mode, select **Quit**.

Working with External Databases

1-2-3's **/Data External** commands access data in tables in an external database. An external table is a file that a database program other than 1-2-3 creates and maintains. An example is dBASE III. Once you establish a connection or link between 1-2-3 and an external table, you can perform the following tasks:

13

- Use /**Data** **Query** commands to find and manipulate data in the external table. Then you can work with that data in the worksheet.

- Use formulas and database functions to calculate information from data in the external table.

- Create a new external table that contains data from the worksheet or from an existing external table.

When you select /**Data External**, the following menu appears:

Use List Create Delete Other Reset Quit

Table 13.5 describes these options.

Table 13.5
Selections on the /Data External Menu

Selection	Description
Use	Sets up a connection to an external table.
List	Displays the names of the tables in an external database, or lists the names of the fields in an external table.
Create	Sets up a new table in an external database. Copies data from a worksheet data table or another external table to the new table.
Delete	Deletes a table from an external database.
Other	Includes three functions. **Refresh** updates the table. **Command** sends commands to the external database program. **Translation** uses a different character set.
Reset	Breaks the connection to an external table.
Quit	Returns to READY mode.

Networks and database programs used on networks usually include controls to limit access to database files. These same controls apply when using 1-2-3 to access external database files. Your screen, for example, may prompt you to enter your user ID and password. If so, type them, press Enter, and then continue with your 1-2-3 commands. You have your usual access to the network files. If you encounter problems, see your network administrator.

Understanding External Database Terms

Data management in 1-2-3 is powerful and flexible because of Release 3's capacity to use data from tables in external databases. Before you begin working with this feature, you should be familiar with several terms.

A database driver is a program that serves as an interface between 1-2-3 and an external database. The driver allows 1-2-3 to transfer data to and from the tables in the database. You need a separate database driver for each external database format you use.

An external database is simply the path where the external tables reside.

A table name identifies the external table with which you want to work. You must enter the full table name before you can access the table from 1-2-3. The full table name consists of three or four parts in the following order:

1. The name of the database driver.
2. The name of the external database (path).
3. An owner name or user ID, if required by the database program.
4. The name of the table in the database, or a 1-2-3 range name that you assigned to the table.

Using an Existing External Table

Using the data in an external table does not differ much from using a worksheet database. The major difference is that you need to set up a connection to the external table before you use it. Then you must break the connection when you finish.

To use an existing external table, follow these steps:

1. Select /Data External Use.
2. A list of existing database drivers appears. Highlight your choice, and press ⏎Enter.

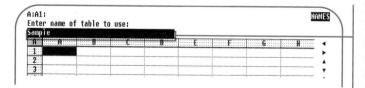 In this example, highlight the sample database driver for dBASE III, and press ⏎Enter.

3. A list of existing databases appears. Highlight your choice and press ⏎Enter.

If you use the sample driver, the name of the external database is the path of a directory.

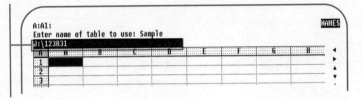

4. A list of table names appears. To see a full-screen list, press F3. Highlight your choice and press ⏎Enter.

In this example, type **CUSTOMER** to choose the database file CUSTOMER.DBF.

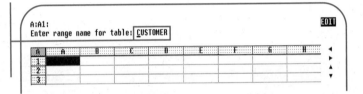

5. 1-2-3 displays the prompt Enter range name for the table:. Accept the default name or type a new one and press ⏎Enter.

6. To return to READY mode, select **Quit**.

By using the range name assigned to the table, you can treat the external table like any other database. You can use /**Data Query Extract** and database functions such as @DSUM.

Listing the Fields in the External Database

If you need to manipulate the external database, you probably need a list of fields from that database. This list is helpful if you want to extract information from the database or use database functions.

To list the fields in the external database, follow these steps:

1. Select /**Data External List Fields**.

2. Highlight the range name of your table, and press ⏎Enter.

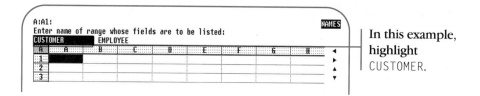

In this example, highlight CUSTOMER.

3. Type or move the cursor where you want the field names and press ⏎Enter.

   Note: The field names write over any existing information in cells. Make sure you move to an empty place on the worksheet.

1-2-3 lists the field names and information about each field in the worksheet.

4. To return to READY mode, select **Quit**.

The list consists of six columns and as many rows as there are fields in the table. Each row in the list contains information about one field in the table. The contents of the columns are the following:

Column	Contents
1	Field name
2	Field data type
3	Field width in characters
4	Column label
5	Field description
6	Field-creation string

If the external table does not use column labels, field descriptions, or field-creation strings, these columns contain NA.

Converting the Field List to a Horizontal Format

To use the field name list in /Data Query and database function commands, you need to arrange the field names in one row.

To arrange the field name list, follow these steps:

1. Select /Range Trans (Transpose).
2. Highlight the first column of field names, and press ↵Enter.

In this example, select /Range Trans, highlight A1..A10, and press ↵Enter.

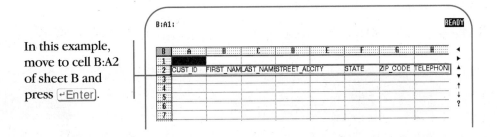

3. At the `Enter TO range for transpose:` prompt, type or move the cell pointer to the location to receive the field names; then press ↵Enter.

In this example, move to cell B:A2 of sheet B and press ↵Enter.

If you want to see all the information in each column, use the /Worksheet Column Set-Width command. Change the column widths on the worksheet to the character width shown in the third column of the field name list.

Extracting Information from the External Database

To list specific records from the database, you follow the same procedures already discussed for extracting information from a database on the worksheet. You need to define the input range as the range name of the database table. Build the criteria and output ranges from field names you retrieved with /Data External List Fields and /Range Trans.

To extract specific information from the external database, follow these steps:

1. Define the input range by selecting /Data Query Input and typing the range name of your database table; then press ⏎Enter).

    Note: If you want to see a list of all range names, including data tables, press F3).

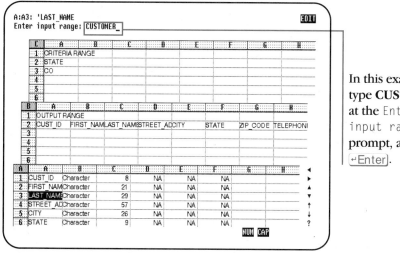

In this example, type **CUSTOMER** at the Enter input range: prompt, and press ⏎Enter).

2. Define the criteria range by selecting **Criteria** and highlighting your criteria range; then press ⏎Enter).

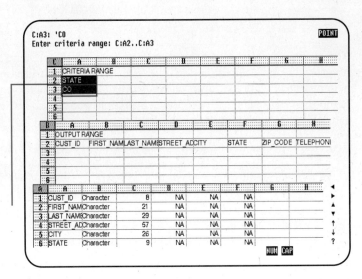

Highlight
C:A2..C:A3 and
press ⏎Enter.
Note that the
criteria range is
only one field and
that the cell in A3
has a label.

3. Define the output range by selecting **Output** and highlighting your output range; then press ⏎Enter.

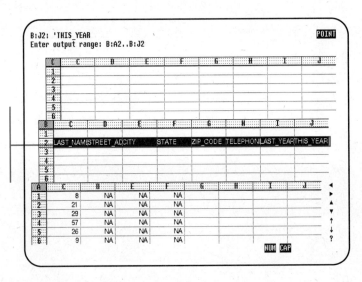

In this example,
highlight
B:A2..B:J2 as the
output range and
press ⏎Enter.

4. To extract the information, select **Extract**.

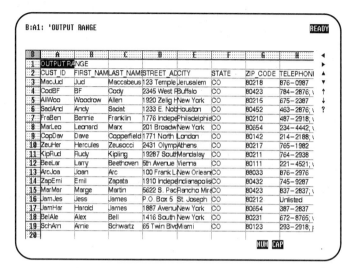

13

The output
appears in the
output range.

If you want to extract other records from the database, change the criteria and use the /**Data Query Extract** command again. Alternately, use F7 to repeat the query. You can also use the external database in a database function by defining the input range as the database table name.

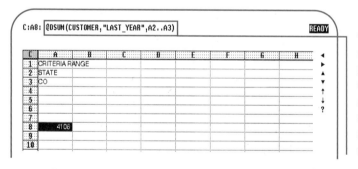

The formula sums
the LAST_YEAR
field in the
CUSTOMER
database (in
dBASE III) for
any STATE with
an entry of CO.

Disconnecting 1-2-3 and the External Table

/**Data External Reset** severs the connection between 1-2-3 and an external table. After you break the connection, the range name of the table becomes undefined. Any worksheet formulas or queries that use that range name may produce errors.

To disconnect the external table, follow these steps:

1. Select /**Data External Reset**.
2. Highlight the name of range and press ⏎Enter.
3. To return to READY mode, select **Quit**.

13   Summary

Although 1-2-3 is used frequently for spreadsheet applications, you can also use 1-2-3 for many types of database applications. You create a 1-2-3 database within the column-row worksheet. You also use the same cell pointer and direction keys as you used for other applications. Therefore, you don't have to learn a completely different program when you want to work with a database.

The /**Data** command on 1-2-3's main menu leads to commands for performing common database applications. These include sorting data, searching for records that meet specific criteria, extracting records from the main database, and linking to another database program. Sorting in 1-2-3 is fast and easy, and you can sort on up to 255 fields. When searching for and extracting records, you must create an input range that contains the field names and all records you want to search. You must also create a criteria range to specify the search conditions. When extracting records from a 1-2-3 database, you must also define the output range where you want to copy the extracted data.

Search conditions in a 1-2-3 database can be text strings or numbers, but can also be much more complicated. More complicated conditions on which to search a 1-2-3 database can include formulas as well as conditions that involve multiple criteria.

Specifically, you learned the following key information about 1-2-3:

- A *database* consists of records and fields. In 1-2-3, a *record* is a row of cells in the database. A *field* is one type of information within the record, such as a ZIP code.

- 1-2-3's /**Data** menu contains most of the commands you commonly use to manage and manipulate databases. However, you can also use worksheet options from the 1-2-3 main menu to manage databases.

- An ideal location for a database is on a blank worksheet. Inserting and deleting rows and columns won't affect other applications. Use the /**Worksheet Insert Sheet** command to create a blank worksheet.

- Use /Worksheet Insert Row and /Worksheet Delete Row to add or delete records (rows) in the database. Similarly, use /Worksheet Insert Column and /Worksheet Delete Column to add or delete fields (columns) in the database.

- /Data Sort allows you to change the order of records by sorting them according to the contents of specified key fields. In 1-2-3, you can sort with a primary, secondary, and up to 253 extra keys, in ascending or descending order.

- Use the /Data Query command to set up a database or to search a database for records matching a specified criteria. Before starting a search, you must first specify an input range and a criteria range with the commands /Data Query Input and /Data Query Criteria, respectively. When using the Extract and Unique options of this command, you must also specify an output range with the /Data Query Output command.

- The /Data Query Find command positions the cell pointer on records matching a given criteria. You can change records as you move the cell pointer.

- The /Data Query Extract command copies records (or specified portions of records) matching a given criteria to another area of the worksheet.

- Use the wild-card characters ?, *, and ~ for more complex search operations. You can also enter formulas in criteria ranges, as well as multiple criteria involving two or more fields.

- The /Data Query Unique command also copies records to an output range. However, it does not copy duplicate entries based on fields specified in the criteria range.

- The /Data Query Del (Delete) command erases from a database the records that match conditions specified in the criteria range. 1-2-3 asks for confirmation before deleting the records.

- The /Data External command allows you to link to a file from a different database such as dBASE.

- Use /Data External Use to set up the link and name the range you use to refer to the external database.

- Use /Data External List Fields and /Range Trans (Transpose) to organize field names for your output and criteria ranges.

- Extract data from your external database with /Data Query Extract after defining the input range as the database table range name.

You have learned about 1-2-3's worksheet, graphics, and data management capabilities. You can now go on to the last chapter, which introduces 1-2-3 macros. Macros allow you to perform simple or complex routine operations by pressing a few keys.

501

Understanding Macros

In addition to the capabilities available from the commands in 1-2-3's main menu, another feature makes 1-2-3 the most popular spreadsheet program available today. Macros and the advanced macro commands enable you to automate and customize your applications, and thus reduce tasks requiring multiple keystrokes to a two-keystroke operation. Just press two keys and 1-2-3 does the rest, whether you're formatting a range, creating a graph, or printing a worksheet. You also can control and customize worksheet applications by using 1-2-3's advanced macro commands. These 50 built-in commands give you a greater range of control over your 1-2-3 applications.

You can think of simple keystroke macros as the building blocks for advanced macro command programs. When you add advanced macro commands to simple keystroke macros, you can control and automate many of the actions required to build and update 1-2-3 worksheets. At the most sophisticated level, you can use 1-2-3's advanced macro commands as a full-fledged programming language for developing custom business applications.

Planning macros

Positioning macros in the worksheet

Documenting and naming macros

Using the macro Record feature

Executing macros

Using an automatic macro

Debugging and editing macros

Creating a macro library

14

Key Terms in This Chapter

Macro	A series of stored keystrokes or commands that 1-2-3 carries out when you press two or more keys.
Program	A list of instructions in a computer programming language, such as 1-2-3's advanced macro commands, which tells the computer what to do.
Advanced macro commands	More than 50 built-in 1-2-3 commands that are not accessible through the 1-2-3 menu system.
Tilde (~)	The symbol used in a macro to signify the Enter keystroke.
Key names	Representations of keyboard keys used in macros. Enclose key names in braces: for example {EDIT}.
Documented macro or program	A macro or program that contains information explaining each step in the macro or program.
Record feature	Records keystrokes, enables copying of keystrokes into a worksheet cell as a label, and automatically creates a macro.
Bug	An error in a macro or program.
Debugging	The process of identifying and fixing errors in a macro or program.

In this chapter, you find an introduction to the concept and application of macros. You also will find some simple keystroke macros, which you can retrieve as necessary. For more detailed information on macros and the advanced macro commands, consult Que's *Using 1-2-3 Release 3.1*, 2nd Edition, or *1-2-3 Macro Library*, 3rd Edition.

Using the Mouse

To use a mouse with 1-2-3 Release 3.1, you need a mouse, mouse software, and a graphics monitor and graphics card that support a mouse. Also, Wysiwyg must be loaded into memory. You can use a mouse to select commands and files, specify ranges, and move the cell pointer within a worksheet or between multiple worksheets and files. In the examples throughout this chapter, notice that the 1-2-3 commands always begin with a slash (/), and the Wysiwyg commands always begin with a colon (:). Refer to the following sections of the specified chapters for further information on using the mouse:

14

- Chapter 2— "Understanding Mouse Terminology"
- Chapter 3— "Mouse Control of the Cell Pointer"
        "Using the Mouse To Select Menu Commands"
- Chapter 4— "Using the Mouse To Specify Ranges"

What Is a Macro?

A macro, in its most basic form, is a collection of stored keystrokes that you can replay at any time. These keystrokes can be commands or simple text and numeric entries. Macros provide an alternative to typing data and commands from the keyboard. Macros therefore can save you time by automating frequently performed tasks.

```
B:B3:  {Shadow T}  [W11]  '/rfc0~~                                    READY

      A              A                  B        C        D        E
   2  REGIONAL INCOME REPORT         Qtr 1    Qtr 2    Qtr 3    Qtr 4
   4  Sales
   5  Northeast                    $30,336  $33,370  $36,707  $40,377
   6  Southeast                     20,572   22,629   24,892   27,381
   7  Central                      131,685  144,854  159,339  175,273
   8  Northwest                     94,473  103,920  114,312  125,744
   9  Southwest                    126,739  139,413  163,354  168,690
      A              B                  C        D        E        F
   1                          MACROS
   2
   3  \c       /rfc0~ ~       Format currency, 0 decimals
   4
   5  \p       /rfp0~ ~       Format percent, 0 decimals
   6
   7  \w       /wcs{?} ~      Set column width
   8
   9  \SAVE    /fs{?} ~       Save file
  10
  11  \ADD     @SUM({?}) ~    Sum the specified range
  12                                                          NUM CAP
```

This screen shows five simple keystroke macros in the window on the bottom (sheet B). The window on top displays worksheet data (sheet A).

A simple macro, for example, can automate the sequence of seven keystrokes which format a cell in **Currency** format with zero decimal places.

You can execute the seven keystrokes in cell B:B3 by pressing two keys, Alt and **C**.

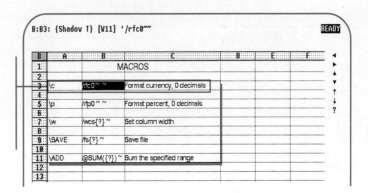

```
B:B3: {Shadow T} [W11] '/rfc0~~                                    READY
```

	A	B	C	D	E	F
1		MACROS				
2						
3	\c	/rfc0~ ~	Format currency, 0 decimals			
4						
5	\p	/rfp0~ ~	Format percent, 0 decimals			
6						
7	\w	/wcs{?}~	Set column width			
8						
9	\SAVE	/fs{?}~	Save file			
10						
11	\ADD	@SUM({?})~	Sum the specified range			
12						
13						

You can name macros in two different ways. One way is to use the backslash key (\) and a single letter. Execute an Alt-letter macro by holding down the Alt key and pressing the letter that identifies the macro. This is the only method available for use with versions of 1-2-3 before Release 2.2. In Release 3, you can name macros by using descriptive names of up to 15 characters in length. Access these macros by pressing Run (Alt-F3). When the list of macro names appears, highlight the one you want to use and press Enter.

The Elements of Macros

1-2-3 macros follow a specific format, whether they are simple keystroke macros or macros that perform complex tasks. A macro is nothing more than a specially-named text cell. Create all macros by entering into a worksheet cell the keystrokes (or representations of those keystrokes) to store. Suppose that you want to create a simple macro that will format the current cell to appear in **Currency** format with no decimal places. The macro looks like this:

```
'/rfc0~~
```

The following are the macro elements for the formatting macro, along with descriptions of the actions that result when 1-2-3 executes each element:

Macro Element	Action
'	Tells 1-2-3 that the information which follows is a label.
/	Calls up the 1-2-3 menu.
r	Selects **R**ange.
f	Selects **F**ormat.
c	Selects **C**urrency.
0	Tells 1-2-3 to suppress the display of digits to the right of the decimal point.
~~	Functions as two Enter keystrokes. (Each tilde acts as one Enter keystroke.)

You enter this macro into the worksheet in exactly the same way you would enter any other label. Type a label prefix followed by the characters in the label. The label prefix (displayed only in the control panel) informs 1-2-3 to treat what follows as a label. Every macro that starts with a nontext character (/, \, +, –, or a number) must begin with a label prefix. If you did not use a prefix, 1-2-3 would automatically interpret the next character as a command to execute immediately, instead of a label stored in the cell. Any of the three 1-2-3 label prefixes (', ", or ^) will work.

The next four characters in the macro represent the command used to create the desired format. After all, /rfc is simply shorthand for /**R**ange **F**ormat **C**urrency. The 0 (zero) tells 1-2-3 that you want no digits displayed to the right of the decimal point. If you were entering this command from the keyboard, you would type the 0 in response to a prompt.

At the end of the macro are two characters called *tildes*. When used in a macro, a tilde (~) represents the Enter key. In this case, the two tildes signal 1-2-3 to press the Enter key twice: to accept the number of decimal places, and to select the current cell as the range to format.

Other elements used in macros include range names and cell addresses. Although you can use these two elements interchangeably, you should use range names instead of cell addresses whenever possible. Range names are better; if you move data included in specified ranges, or insert or delete rows and columns, the range names adjust automatically and the macro continues to refer to the correct cells and ranges. Cell references used in macros do not adjust to any changes made in the worksheet and you must change them manually.

14

14

Some macro examples in this chapter include the {?} command. The {?} is actually a type of advanced macro command. Use it to pause the macro so you can type information, such as a file name, from the keyboard. The macro continues executing when you press the Enter key. For example, a macro that sets column widths can include the {?} command to let you type the new column width when the macro pauses. Then you can press Enter to complete execution of the macro.

Characters in macro commands are not case-sensitive. You can use capitalization wherever you want. For readability, however, this book uses lowercase letters in macros to indicate commands. Range names and key names are in uppercase letters.

Macro Key Names and Special Keys

1-2-3 uses other symbols besides the tilde (~) to stand for keystrokes. You can add to the formatting example key names and special keys that highlight a range as if you were using /Range Format.

The added part of the macro anchors the range and highlights all occupied cells to the right in the current row.

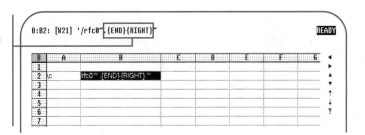

This revised macro is similar to the preceding one, except that the .{END}{RIGHT} command causes the cell pointer to move. You can use this version of the macro to format an entire row instead of just one cell.

Once again, notice the apostrophe (') at the beginning of the macro (displayed in the control panel) and the tilde (~) at the end. Notice also the phrase .{END}{RIGHT} in the macro. The period (.) anchors the cell pointer. The {END} key name stands for the End key on the keyboard. The {RIGHT} key name represents the right-arrow key. This phrase has the same effect in the macro as these three keys would have if you pressed them in sequence from the keyboard. The cell pointer moves to the next boundary between blank and occupied cells in the row.

Use representations like these to signify key names and special keys on the keyboard. In every case, enclose the key name in braces. For example, {UP} represents the up-arrow key. {ESC} stands for the Esc (Escape) key. {GRAPH} represents the F10 function key.

Tables 14.1 through 14.5 provide lists of macro key names and special keys grouped according to their uses. They include function keys, direction keys, editing keys, and special keys.

14

Table 14.1
Macro Key Names for Function Keys

Function Key	Key Name	Action
Help (F1)	{HELP}	Accesses 1-2-3's on-line help system.
Edit (F2)	{EDIT}	Edits the contents of the current cell.
Name (F3)	{NAME}	Displays a list of range names in the current worksheet.
Abs (F4)	{ABS}	Converts a relative reference to absolute, or an absolute reference to relative.
GoTo (F5)	{GOTO}	Jumps the cell pointer to the specified cell address or range name.
Window (F6)	{WINDOW}	Moves the cell pointer to the other side of a split screen.
Query (F7)	{QUERY}	Repeats the most recent /Data Query operation.
Table (F8)	{TABLE}	Repeats the most recent table operation.
Calc (F9)	{CALC}	Recalculates the worksheet.
Graph (F10)	{GRAPH}	Redraws the current graph on-screen.
Zoom (Alt-F6)	{ZOOM}	Enlarges or shrinks current window.

14

Table 14.2
Macro Key Names for Direction Keys

Direction Key	Key Name	Action
Up arrow (↑)	{UP} or {U}	Moves the cell pointer up one row.
Down arrow (↓)	{DOWN} or {D}	Moves the cell pointer down one row.
Left arrow (←)	{LEFT} or {L}	Moves the cell pointer left one column.
Right arrow (→)	{RIGHT} or {R}	Moves the cell pointer right one column.
Shift-Tab or Ctrl- ←	{BIGLEFT}	Moves the cell pointer left one screen.
Tab or Ctrl- →	{BIGRIGHT}	Moves the cell pointer right one screen.
PgUp or Page Up	{PGUP}	Moves the cell pointer up one screen.
PgDn or Page Down	{PGDN}	Moves the cell pointer down one screen.
Home	{HOME}	Moves the cell pointer to cell A1. If /Worksheet Titles is activated, to the top left cell outside the titles area.
End	{END}	Used with {UP}, {DOWN}, {LEFT}, or {RIGHT}. The cell pointer will move in the indicated direction to the next boundary between blank cells and cells that hold data. Also used with {HOME} to move the cell pointer to the lower right corner of the worksheet.

510

Table 14.3
Macro Key Names for Direction Keys Used in Multiple Worksheets

Direction Key	Key Name	Action
Next Sheet (Ctrl-PgUp)	{NEXTSHEET} or {NS}	Moves the cell pointer to the next worksheet (from A: to B:).
Previous Sheet (Ctrl-PgDn)	{PREVSHEET} or {PS}	Moves the cell pointer to the previous sheet (from B: to A:)
First Cell(Ctrl-Home)	{FIRSTCELL} or {FC}	Moves cell pointer to cell A:A1 of current worksheet.
Last Cell (End, Ctrl-Home)	{LASTCELL} or {LC}	Moves cell pointer to last cell of current worksheet.
File (Ctrl-End)	{FILE}	Used with Home, End, Ctrl-PgUp, and Ctrl-PgDn to move the cell pointer to another file loaded in memory.
Next File (Ctrl-End, Ctrl-PgUp)	{NEXTFILE} or {NS}	Moves the cell pointer to the next file.
Previous File (Ctrl-End, Ctrl-PgDn)	{PREVFILE} or {PF}	Moves cell pointer to the previous file.
First File (Ctrl-End, Home)	{FIRSTFILE} or {FF}	Moves cell pointer to the first file.
Last File (Ctrl-End, End)	{LASTFILE} or {LF}	Moves cell pointer to the last file.

14

Table 14.4
Macro Key Names for Editing Keys

Editing Key	Key Name	Action
Delete (Del)	{DELETE} or {DEL}	Used with {EDIT} to delete a single character from a cell entry.
Insert (Ins)	{INSERT} or {INS}	Toggles between insert and overtype modes when you are editing a cell.
Esc	{ESCAPE} or {ESC}	Signifies the Esc key.
Backspace	{BACKSPACE} or {BS}	Signifies the Backspace key.
Ctrl-Break	{BREAK}	Clears command and returns to READY mode.
No equivalent	{CLEARENTRY} or {CE}	Clears entry in EDIT mode.

Table 14.5
Macro Key Names for Special Keys

Special Key	Key Name	Action
/ (menu)	/	Causes the command menu to appear.
Enter	~	Signifies the Enter key.
~ (Tilde)	{~}	Causes a tilde to appear in the worksheet.
{ (Open brace)	{{}	Causes an opening brace to appear in the worksheet.
} (Close brace)	{}}	Causes a closing brace to appear in the worksheet.

Note: A few keys or key combinations do not have a key name to identify them. These include Shift, Caps Lock, Num Lock, Scroll Lock, Print Screen, Compose (Alt-F1), Step (Alt-F2), Run (Alt-F3), and Undo (Alt-F4). You cannot represent any of these keys or key combinations within macros.

512

To specify more than one use of a key name, you can include repetition factors inside the braces. For example, you can use the following statements in macros:

Statement	Action
{PGUP 3}	Press the PgUp key three times in a row.
{L 4}	Press the left-arrow key four times.
{RIGHT JUMP}	Press the right-arrow key the number of times indicated by the value in the cell named JUMP.

Planning Macros

A simple keystroke macro can be thought of as a substitute for keyboard commands. Because of this, the best way to plan a macro is to step through the series of instructions one keystroke at a time. Perform this exercise before you start creating the macro. Take notes about each step as you proceed with the commands on-screen, then translate the keystrokes that you've written into a macro that conforms to the rules discussed in this chapter.

Stepping through an operation at the keyboard is an easy way to build simple macros. The more experience you have with 1-2-3 commands, the easier it becomes to "think through" the keystrokes you need to use in a macro.

For more complex macros, the best approach is to break them into smaller macros that execute in a series. Each small macro performs one simple operation, and the series of simple operations together performs the desired application.

This approach starts with the result of an application. What is the application supposed to do or produce? What form must the results take? If you start with the desired results and work backward, you decrease the risk of producing the wrong results with your macro.

Next, consider input. What data do you need? What data is available and in what form? How much work will it take to go from data to results?

Finally, look at the process. How do you analyze available data and, using 1-2-3, produce the desired results? How can you divide calculations into a series of tasks, each of which can have a simple macro?

This "divide-and-conquer" method breaks a complex task into smaller and simpler pieces. It is the key to successful development of macros and complex worksheets. Although this method entails some initial work, you will be able to detect and correct errors more easily because you can locate them in a smaller section of the macro.

14

513

Positioning Macros in the Worksheet

Usually, you should place macros outside the area occupied by data on your worksheet. This practice helps you avoid accidentally overwriting or erasing part of a macro as you create your model.

In Releases 3 and 3.1, you can position macros on a separate sheet of your worksheet. Use the /Worksheet Insert Sheet command to add a sheet.

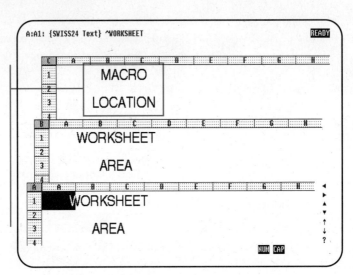

This positioning lessens the chance that you will accidentally include the macro's range in worksheet operations. With this placement, deleting rows or columns in the worksheet area will not affect the cells in the macro location.

1-2-3 has no rule that says you must place your macros in the same place in every worksheet. You may, however, want to make a habit of always placing your macros on the last worksheet of a file. You will then always know where to look in your applications for the macros if you need to change them. The last sheet is also easy to reach with the End Ctrl-Home key combination.

You can assign the range name MACROS to the area containing the macros. Using a range name allows you to move to the macro area quickly with the GoTo (F5) key.

Documenting Macros

Professional programmers usually write documented programs. This term means that the program contains comments which help to explain each step in the program. In BASIC, these comments are in REM (for REMark) statements. For example, in the following program, the REM statements explain the actions taken by the other statements.

```
10   REM This program adds two numbers
20   REM Enter first number
30   INPUT A
40   REM Enter second number
50   INPUT B
60   REM Add numbers together
70   C=A+B
80   REM Display result
90   Print C
```

14

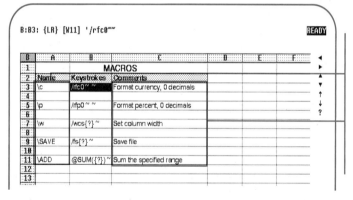

Document your 1-2-3 macros by placing comments in the column to the right of the macro steps. Place the name of the macro to the left of the macro steps.

Including comments in your macros will make them far easier to use. Comments are especially useful when you have created complex macros that are important to the worksheet's overall design. Suppose that you have created a complex macro but have not looked at it for a month. Then you decide that you want to change the macro. Without built-in comments, you might have a difficult time remembering what each step of the macro does.

Naming Macros

You must give a macro a name before you can execute it.

Name a macro by using a backslash (\) followed by a single letter. Alternatively, you can name a macro with a descriptive name, like a typical range name.

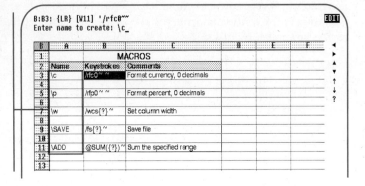

If you choose to use the single-letter naming convention, select a character that in some way helps describe the macro. For example, you could use \c to name a macro that formats a range as currency.

To assign a name to a macro, follow these steps:

1. Select /**R**ange **N**ame **C**reate.

2. Type `\` and a single letter, and then press `⏎Enter`; or type a descriptive name of up to 15 characters and press `⏎Enter`.

   For this example, type `\` `c`, and then press `⏎Enter`.

3. The prompt `Enter range:` appears. Highlight (or type the cell addresses of) the range where you entered macro commands, and then press `⏎Enter`.

In this example, highlight cell B:B3 and press `⏎Enter`.

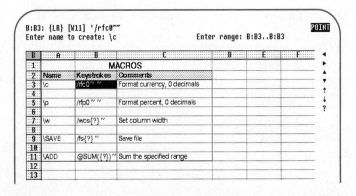

This book and the 1-2-3 documentation place the name of the macro in the cell to the immediate left of the macro's first command. If you follow this format, you can use the command **/Range Name Labels Right**. Specify the range containing the macro names to assign these names to the macros in the adjacent column. This approach works with descriptive and Alt-letter macro names. This command also ensures that you include the name of the macro within the worksheet for easy identification. The **/Range Name Labels Right** command is also useful for naming several macros at once. Otherwise, you would have to name them individually with **/Range Name Create**.

The advantage of using a single letter for a macro name is that you can activate the macro more quickly from the keyboard. A disadvantage is that a single-letter name doesn't offer as much flexibility in describing what the macro does. Therefore, remembering the name and purpose of a specific macro may be difficult.

In versions of 1-2-3 before Release 2.2, single-letter names are the only names you can use for macros. Releases 2.2 and later, however, allow you to assign descriptive names (up to 15 characters in length) to ranges containing macros. To avoid confusing macro names with other range names, you can also begin descriptive macro names with the backslash (\) character. For example, in this chapter, illustrated macros include one named \SAVE, which you can use to save files. Another macro is \ADD, which uses the @SUM function to add a specified range of values.

Note: 1-2-3 lets you assign a third type of name to a macro. You can use the name \0 (backslash zero) to create an automatic macro. Automatic macros are discussed later in this chapter.

Using the Macro Record Feature

A powerful new feature provided in Release 3 of 1-2-3 records keystrokes and allows you to copy the keystrokes into a worksheet cell as labels. You can then create a macro from these labels.

The Record feature works by displaying information from a special storage area in your computer's memory called the *record buffer*. The record buffer is not large, however, so copy your keystrokes from the buffer often. 1-2-3 uses shortcuts when possible. If you press the right-arrow key 10 times, you might guess that the record buffer records the keyword {RIGHT} 10 times. Instead, 1-2-3 uses a repetition factor and the most abbreviated form of the keyword—in this case, {R 10}.

517

The column width of the range to which you copy the keystrokes affects the number of keystrokes 1-2-3 copies to each cell. To fit more keystrokes in the macro keystroke column, increase the width of the column.

Erasing the Record Buffer

The record buffer is only 512 bytes. A *byte* is roughly equal to one character. When you type the 513th character, 1-2-3 "forgets" the first character. In effect, it removes from the record buffer the oldest character to make room for the newest. Therefore, it is a good idea to erase the buffer before you record keystrokes. Erasing the buffer also helps you find the characters you need because no extra keystrokes will be in the buffer.

To erase the buffer, follow these steps:

1. Press [Alt] [F2] (Record).

The **Record** menu appears.

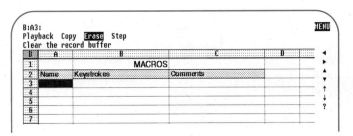

2. Select **Erase**.

Copying Keystrokes from the Record Buffer

Suppose that you want to create a macro that sets the global worksheet format to Currency with two decimal places. To make this setting manually, you select /Worksheet Global Format Currency, type **2**, and then press Enter. You can write this macro easily. 1-2-3, however, gives you an even easier way to create the macro.

To copy keystrokes from the buffer to the worksheet, follow these steps:

1. Type the keystrokes you want the macro to execute.

   For this example, type **/wgfc**, type **2**, and press [⏎Enter].

2. Press [Alt] [F2] (Record) and select **Copy**.

518

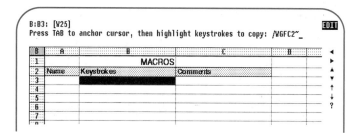

The keystrokes you typed since the beginning of the 1-2-3 session or since you last selected (Alt)(F2) **Erase** appear in the control panel.

14

3. Move the cursor to the first character you want to copy to the worksheet.

4. Press (Tab ⇄) to anchor the cursor.

5. Use the arrow keys to highlight the remaining keystrokes you want to copy from the record buffer and press (↵Enter).

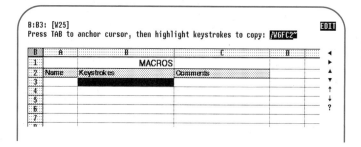

In this example, highlight all keystrokes and press (↵Enter).

6. The Select range to copy TO: prompt appears. Type or move to the cell address where you want to copy the characters and press (↵Enter).

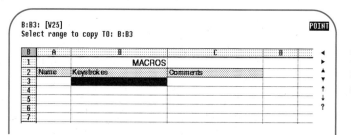

In this example, move to cell B:B3 and press (↵Enter).

519

1-2-3 records the activity of special keys in macro notation. For example, if one of the keys you press is the Window (F6) key, the record buffer will contain the macro key name {WINDOW}.

When the recorded activity represents what you want the macro to do, assign a name, such as \f, to the first cell of the macro.

Note: When naming macros, you need to name only the first cell of the macro, rather than the entire macro range.

Executing Macros

Alt-letter macros named with a backslash and a single letter are the simplest to run. If necessary, move the cell pointer to the appropriate position before you execute the macro. For example, when using a format macro, you must move the cell pointer to the cell you wish to format before running the macro.

To execute an Alt-letter macro, follow these steps:

1. Press and hold down the [Alt] key.
2. Press the letter in the macro name.
3. Release both keys.

For example, if you named a macro \a, you invoke it by pressing Alt-A. The \ symbol in the name represents the Alt key. Pressing Alt-A plays back the recorded keystrokes in the macro.

When you identify a macro with a longer descriptive name, it only takes a couple more keystrokes to execute the macro. You must first press Run (Alt-F3) to display a list of range names. Highlight the macro name and then press Enter. The list of names you see when you press Run (Alt-F3) will include range names as well as macro names. To simplify your search for macro names, begin them with a backslash.

To execute a macro with a descriptive name, follow these steps:

1. Press [Alt][F3] (Run).
2. Highlight the name of the macro you want to execute and press [↵Enter].

520

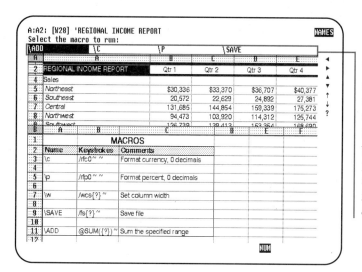

The screen displays up to four names. If you don't see the name of the macro you want to run, press F3 (Name) again to display a full-screen listing of names.

14

As soon as you issue the command to execute a macro, it starts to run. If there are no special instructions (such as a pause) and no bugs are present, the macro continues to run until finished. The macro executes each command much faster than if you tried the command manually. You can store many macro keystrokes or commands in a single cell. When 1-2-3 starts executing a macro, the program begins with the first cell and continues until it executes all the keystrokes stored there. Next, 1-2-3 moves down one cell to continue execution. If the next cell is blank, the program stops. If that cell contains more macro commands, however, 1-2-3 continues reading down the column until it finds the first blank cell.

Using an Automatic Macro

1-2-3 can create an automatic macro that will execute automatically when you load the worksheet. You create this macro just like any other. The only difference is its name. The macro that you want to execute automatically must have the name \0 (backslash zero). You can use only one automatic macro in a worksheet.

For example, you can use an automatic macro to position the cell pointer at the upper left corner of a range named DATABASE. The macro can then redefine the range by anchoring the cell pointer and moving it to the right and down to include all contiguous cells. You do not press the Alt key to start the macro in this case. 1-2-3 executes the macro as soon as you retrieve the worksheet.

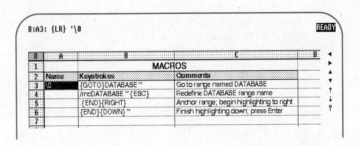

1-2-3 executes an automatic (\0) macro when you retrieve a file.

Note that you cannot execute automatic macros with the Alt-0 key combination. If you need to be able to execute the macro from the keyboard, you can use Run (Alt-F3) or you can assign the \0 macro an additional name, such as \a. You then have two identical macros on your system: one that executes automatically, and one that you can execute from the keyboard. This tip is especially useful when testing new automatic macros.

If you do not want to execute automatic macros when 1-2-3 starts, you can disable this feature. To disable these macros for all worksheets, use /Worksheet Global Default Autoexec No.

Debugging and Editing Macros

Almost no program works perfectly the first time. In nearly every case, errors cause programs to malfunction. Programmers call these problems *bugs*. Debugging is the process of eliminating bugs.

Like programs written in other programming languages, 1-2-3 macros usually need to be debugged before you can use them. 1-2-3 has a useful feature, STEP mode, that helps make debugging much simpler. When in STEP mode, 1-2-3 executes macros one step at a time. 1-2-3 literally pauses between keystrokes stored in the macro. Using this feature means that you can follow along step-by-step with the macro as it executes.

When you discover an error, you must get out of the macro and return 1-2-3 to READY mode by pressing Break. Then you can start editing the macro.

Common Errors in Macros

Like all computer programs, macros are literal creatures. They have no capability to discern an error in the code. For example, you recognize immediately that {GOTI} is a misspelling of {GOTO}. However, a macro cannot make this distinction. The macro tries to interpret the misspelled word and, being unable to, delivers an error message. Following are four reminders to help you avoid some of the most common macro errors.

- Save your worksheet before you execute a macro.
- Verify all syntax and spelling in your macros.
- Include all required tildes (~) to represent ⏎Enter keystrokes in macros.
- Use range names in macros whenever possible to avoid problems with incorrect cell references. Cell references in macros are always absolute. They never change when you make modifications to the worksheet.

If a macro is not working correctly, you can use two 1-2-3 features to help you correct worksheet and macro errors. Use the Undo (Alt-F4) feature to "undo" damage to the worksheet created by the faulty execution of a macro. Also, use STEP mode to help pinpoint the location of an error in a macro.

14

Undoing Macros

The Undo feature (not available in versions of 1-2-3 before Release 2.2) offers a significant advantage when debugging macros. When a macro doesn't work and appears to have caused major problems within the worksheet, press Undo (Alt-F4). All the steps in the macro will be undone. Remember, the Undo feature restores the worksheet as it was before the last operation. Even though it may contain many steps, 1-2-3 considers a macro as one operation.

If you want to undo a macro, make sure that the Undo feature is active before you actually execute the macro. If necessary, enable Undo with the /Worksheet **G**lobal **D**efault **O**ther **U**ndo **E**nable. The UNDO indicator should appear at the bottom of the screen. If the macro produces unsatisfactory results, do not perform another operation. Use Undo immediately to reverse the effect of the macro.

Note: There are certain commands that 1-2-3 cannot normally reverse with Undo. 1-2-3 also cannot reverse these commands within macros. For example, 1-2-3 cannot reverse a macro that includes the /**F**ile **S**ave command. Therefore, you should not rely entirely on Undo when you test macros.

To reverse the results of a macro safely, save the file before you execute a macro. Then, if necessary, you can retrieve the original file after the macro has executed.

Using STEP Mode To Debug Macros

Most programs require debugging before they can be used. If you can't locate an error in a macro, enter STEP mode and rerun the macro one step at a time. After each step, the macro pauses and waits for you to type any keystroke before continuing. Although you can use any key, you should use the space bar to step through a macro. As you step through the macro, each command appears in the control panel.

To use STEP mode to debug a macro, follow these steps:

1. Press `Alt` `F2` (Record).
2. Select **Step**.

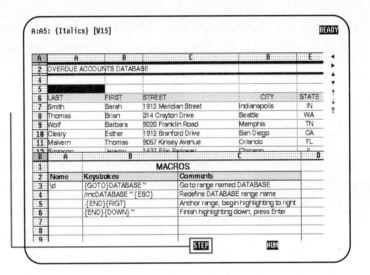

The mode indicator STEP appears at the bottom of the screen.

3. Execute the macro by pressing `Alt` followed by the letter of the macro name. Alternatively, use `Alt` `F3` to select the macro name and press `⏎Enter`.

    The STEP indicator changes to SST as soon as you execute the macro.

4. Evaluate each step of the macro, pressing the space bar after you have checked each step.

5. When you discover an error, press `Ctrl` `Break` to return 1-2-3 to READY mode.

6. When 1-2-3 is in READY mode, edit the macro. You can edit the macro while 1-2-3 displays the STEP indicator at the bottom of the screen.

7. To exit STEP mode, press `Alt` `F2` (Record) and select **Step** again.

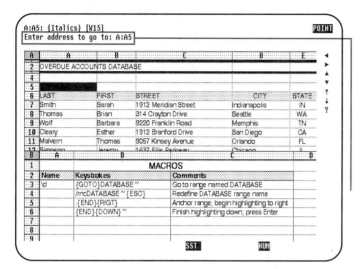

Each time you press the space bar, prompts and the results of commands appear in the control panel.

14

The bottom of the screen displays an error message. In this example, the misspelled key name in cell B:B5 caused the error.

Editing Macros

After you identify an error in a macro, you can correct the error. Fixing an error in a macro is as simple as editing the cell that contains the erroneous code. You don't need to rewrite the entire cell contents. You need only change the element in error. Although editing a complex macro can be much more challenging than editing a simple one, the concept is exactly the same.

14

Use the F2 (Edit) key to correct the cell that contains the error.

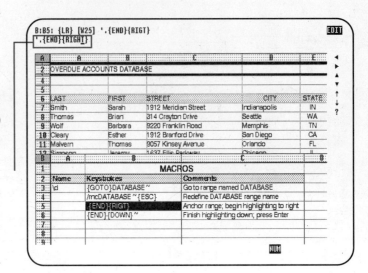

Using Macros from Another Worksheet

Once you have macros created and saved on a worksheet, you can use those macros with any worksheet. All you need to do is load the file with macros into memory with the /File Open command.

To load a file with macros into memory, follow these steps:

1. Select /File Open.
2. Choose Before to load the new file in front of the current worksheet or After to load the new file behind the current worksheet.
3. Type or highlight the name of the file with macros and press ↵Enter.

Invoke the macros with the single letter key (Alt-letter) or with the Alt F3 (Run) key. If you use the Run key, you will first need to point to the file name and then choose the macro name.

Creating a Macro Library

Once you have created macros and saved them on a worksheet, you can use these macros with many worksheets. The macros can range from simple keystroke macros to more specialized advanced macro commands. These macro libraries can save the time needed to re-create the same macros in different files. After you create a macro library file, load the file with macros into memory with the /File Open command.

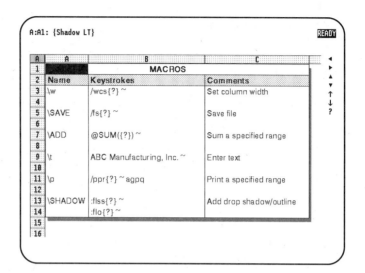

This section introduces six simple keystroke macros that you can create for use in your own macro library.

14

The sections that follow provide a brief explanation of each macro. These macros perform common tasks that would require additional keystrokes and time if performed manually. The first five macros work with previous versions of 1-2-3 as well as with Release 3.1.

A Macro That Sets Column Widths

Use the \w macro in cell B3 to change the column width of the current column. Highlight the column whose width you want to change, and then press Alt-W. The macro begins by executing the /Worksheet Column Set-Width command. Then, as a result of the {?} command, the macro pauses for input. Enter the desired character width and press Enter. 1-2-3 displays the adjusted column width.

You can modify this macro to change the column width of a range of columns by typing the following in place of the macro in cell B3:

```
'/wccs{?}~{?}~
```

This modified macro executes the command /Worksheet Column Column-Range Set-Width. It then pauses for you to enter the column range and press Enter. The macro pauses again until you type the column width and press Enter. 1-2-3 then displays the range of specified columns with the selected column width.

A Macro That Saves a File

The \SAVE macro in cell B5 saves the current file in the current directory on disk. To use this macro, press Run (Alt-F3), select \SAVE from the list of macro and range names, and then press Enter. This macro executes the /File Save command and then pauses for you to enter the desired name. After you type the name of the file and press Enter, 1-2-3 begins to save the file. If the file exists, select Replace from the resulting menu to continue saving the file.

A Macro That Sums a Specified Range

The \ADD macro in cell B7 uses the @SUM function to add values from a specified range. To use this macro, first highlight the cell to contain the result of the formula. Then press Run (Alt- F3), select \ADD from the list of macro and range names, and press Enter. The macro pauses for you to highlight a range of cells that you want to sum. After you select the range and press Enter, the screen displays the formula result.

A Macro That Enters Text

The \t macro in cell B9 enters a long text label into the current cell. Press Alt-T to execute the macro, and 1-2-3 automatically enters the specified label into the highlighted cell. This macro is straightforward, but very useful for entering any long label that commonly appears throughout the worksheet.

A Macro That Prints a Specified Range

The \p macro in cell B11 prints a range you specify to the printer and advances the paper to the top of the next page. To run this macro, press Alt-P. The macro executes the /Print Printer Range command. It then pauses for you to specify the desired print range. Highlight the range you want to print and press Enter. Then Align Go Page Quit aligns the paper, prints the range, advances the paper to the top of the page, and returns 1-2-3 to READY mode.

If you normally print the same range from a particular worksheet, you can name this print range with /Range Name Create. Then you can use this name in place of {?} in the Alt-P macro. For example, to print a range named PAGE1, use the following macro in place of the macro in cell B11:

```
'/pprPAGE1~agpq
```

If you use this print macro, remember to redefine the range named PAGE1 whenever you add new data to the print range. If you have multiple named ranges to print, you can copy this cell and change the range references. This macro would print ranges named PAGE1, PAGE2, and PAGE3.

```
'/pprPAGE1~agpq
'/pprPAGE2~agpq
'/pprPAGE3~agpq
```

A Macro That Adds a Drop Shadow

Use the \SHADOW macro in B13 to add a drop shadow and outline around a range you specify. To use this macro, press Alt-F3 and select \SHADOW from the list of range names. Then outline the range for the shadow and select the range for the outline. Notice that each line of the macro starts with a colon (:). This invokes the Wysiwyg menu and chooses the **Format Shadow** and **Format Outline** commands.

Summary

This chapter provided the basic information you need to begin creating your own simple keystroke macros. These macros are tools you can use to save time, reduce repetition, and automate your worksheet applications. The chapter identified each of the steps necessary to create macros. It also described ways to document, name, and execute macros. You learned that the Record feature allows you to create macros by recording keyboard activity. You also learned about automatic (\0) macros, as well as about methods to debug and edit your simple keystroke macros.

Specifically, you learned the following key information about 1-2-3:

- The elements of macros include actual command keystrokes, key names, range names and cell addresses, and the advanced macro commands.
- In 1-2-3 macros, tilde (~) represents the Enter key.
- Enclose macro key names, which represent keyboard keys, within braces, such as {EDIT}. Key names are available for the function keys, direction keys, editing keys, and special keys.
- You can specify more than one use of a key name by including repetition factors within the braces separated by a space. An example is {DOWN 5}.

■ Position macros outside of the main area of your worksheet. To find your macros quickly, place them on the last sheet of your worksheet.

■ Always document your 1-2-3 macros. An easy way to do this is to include comments in the cells to the right of the macro steps. Type the macro name in the cells to the left of macro steps.

■ You can name macros in two different ways. You can use backslash (\) followed by a single letter or use a descriptive name of up to 15 characters. Use the /Range Name Create or /Range Name Labels Right command to name your macros.

■ The Record feature of 1-2-3 Release 3 lets you create macros automatically by recording your keystrokes and storing them in a specified range. Use Record (Alt-F2) Copy to copy the keystrokes from the record buffer to the worksheet.

■ To execute Alt-letter macros, press the Alt key and letter key assigned to the macro at the same time. Execute macros with descriptive names by pressing Run (Alt-F3), selecting the macro name, and pressing Enter.

■ Automatic (\0) macros execute automatically when you retrieve a file. You can only use one automatic macro in each worksheet.

■ Access 1-2-3's STEP mode by pressing Record (Alt-F2) and selecting Step. Use Step to find macro errors by proceeding through a macro one step at a time. You can use the Undo feature sometimes to reverse the effect of a macro if the macro has caused errors in the worksheet.

■ Edit macros just like any cell entries in the worksheet. Press Edit (F2) and correct each cell containing the error. Rewriting the entire contents of these cells is not necessary.

■ A macro library is a collection of two or more macros saved in a separate file and used with several different files. Use /File Open to put the library in memory.

Installing 1-2-3 Release 3.1

The Install program for 1-2-3 Release 3.1 makes installation almost automatic. After you start the program, follow the on-screen instructions. You must install Release 3.1 on a hard disk; the Install program is designed for hard-disk installation. You cannot run Release 3.1 from a floppy disk.

The Install program begins by creating several subdirectories on your hard disk. Then the program copies the program files to the appropriate subdirectory. The program also asks you to select the type of video display you have, as well as the type of printer. Before you install Release 3.1, verify the brand and model of your printer. The program can detect the type of video display you use. Finally, the Install program generates the font files needed to use the Wysiwyg add-in.

Installation takes about 20 minutes; you need another 20 minutes to generate the basic font set for the Wysiwyg feature. When you are ready to begin, turn on your computer and follow the instructions in this appendix.

Checking DOS Configuration

Before you install 1-2-3 Release 3.1 to run under DOS, you must complete a preliminary step: you must make sure that DOS is configured adequately to run 1-2-3. To do so, check your CONFIG.SYS file for the FILES statement. CONFIG.SYS is found on your start-up hard disk in the root directory. Type **TYPE C:\CONFIG.SYS** and press Enter to see the contents of CONFIG.SYS (assuming that drive C is your start-up hard disk). The screen displays something like the following:

```
FILES=25
BUFFERS=20
DEVICE=C:\DOS\ANSI.SYS
```

The FILES statement tells DOS how many files can be open at once. The minimum number of files you should have is 20 (FILES=20). If you do not have a FILES statement or if the number of files is less than 20, change the CONFIG.SYS file. You can edit CONFIG.SYS with any text editor, such as EDLIN, or with a word processing software that can save files as ASCII unformatted text.

To use 1-2-3 Release 3.1 with Microsoft Windows 3.0, your system must have at least 4.25M of free Windows memory. To determine how much memory you have available, at the "Windows Program Manager," choose "Help" and then choose "About Program Manager."

To use 1-2-3 Release 3.1 with Windows 3.0 in 386 Enhanced mode, you must modify your AUTOEXEC.BAT file. By using a text editor that modifies ASCII files, add the path C:\123R3 statement to the end of your path statement as follows:

PATH = C:\DOS;C:\DOS\BATCH;C:\123R3

You can also regulate the amount of memory available to 1-2-3 once in Windows by adding the following statement to your AUTOEXEC.BAT file:

SET 123MEMSIZE=m

Set m as 500 for average size spreadsheets. If you create large spreadsheets, set m equal to the total amount of memory in your system, minus 2000. In other words, if your system has 6M of memory, set m equal to 4000. The m cannot be smaller than 100, and it cannot be greater than the total amount of memory installed in your system.

If you modify the CONFIG.SYS or AUTOEXEC.BAT file, be sure to restart your computer. A change in CONFIG.SYS or AUTOEXEC.BAT does not modify DOS until you reload DOS. Restart your computer after you modify the CONFIG.SYS or AUTOEXEC.BAT file by pressing Ctrl-Alt-Del.

532

Also make sure your version of DOS is 3.0 or higher and that you have at least 1MB of memory available for 1-2-3.

Using the Install Program

The installation program provided to copy 1-2-3 Release 3.1 to your hard disk and set up the program for your hardware is easy to use. Installation is fully menu-driven; you simply make choices from menus provided on screen.

Before starting Install, check to see that you have all the disks necessary to install 1-2-3 Release 3.1. The disks required are as follows:

5 1/4-inch disk	*3 1/2-inch disks*
Disk 1 (Install)	Disk 1 (Install)
Disk 2 (Translate)	Disk 2
Disk 3	Disk 3
Disk 4	Disk 4
	Disk 5 (Translate)
	Disk 6
	Disk 7

When using Install, use the up- and down-arrow keys to select menu items. To activate a menu item, press Enter. Pressing Esc returns you to a previous screen, and pressing F9 returns you to the main menu.

As you are using Install, you may press F10 to see the current selections you have made, such as display cards, printers and so forth. You may press Help (F1) to get further information as you use Install.

After installation is complete, be sure to make backup copies of the original disks and store the originals in a safe place.

Starting the Install Program

You have many options to choose from while installing. The following sets of steps help you make correct choices as you install 1-2-3 on your hard disk.

To start installing 1-2-3 Release 3.1, follow these steps:

1. Place Disk 1 (Install) in drive A.
2. Type **A:** and press ⏎Enter to make A> the current drive.

533

3. At the A> prompt, type **INSTALL** and press ⏎Enter .

   The first screen you see is 1-2-3's Welcome screen. Read the information on-screen.

4. Press ⏎Enter to continue the installation and register your disks.

Registering Your Original Disks

To make your disks usable, you must register them by entering and saving your name and company name on the Install disk. Each time you start 1-2-3, your name, company name, and program serial number are displayed.

To register your disks, follow these steps:

1. At the Your name: prompt, type in your name and press ⏎Enter .

2. At the Company name: prompt, type in your company's name and press ⏎Enter . If this is your personal copy of 1-2-3, type your name again and press ⏎Enter . You can press ⏎Enter to move from field to field to make any corrections.

3. When both entries are correct, press the Ins key.

4. A Confirmation box appears on-screen. Type **Y** and press ⏎Enter if your name and company name are correct. If you must make changes, type **N** and press ⏎Enter . If you press **N**, return to step 1.

Choosing Files To Copy

The next series of steps prepares Install to begin copying files to your hard disk. In these steps, you answer a series of **Yes/No** questions to copy the Translate utility and Wysiwyg files. Also, you specify the hard disk to copy 1-2-3 to, as well as the directory to use.

To begin copying files to your hard disk, follow these steps:

1. At the TRANSFERRING THE TRANSLATE UTILITY screen, type **Y** to transfer Translate files, or **N** to skip copying Translate files.

2. Press ⏎Enter to continue.

3. At the TRANSFERRING WYSIWYG FILES screen, type **Y** to transfer Wysiwyg, or **N** to skip copying Wysiwyg files.

4. Press ⏎Enter to continue.

5. At the SPECIFYING YOUR HARD-DISK DRIVE screen, type the letter of the desired hard disk drive. Type **C** for drive C.

534

6. Press ⏎Enter to continue.

7. Type the directory to copy 1-2-3 to, or accept the default directory of
   C:\123R3.

8. Press ⏎Enter to continue.

   After you specify the directory to copy 1-2-3 to, Install tests to see if the
   directory exists. If the directory does not exist, Install will ask if you
   want to create the directory.

9. If you see the Confirmation box, type **Y** to create the directory, or **N** to
   type a new directory name. Press ⏎Enter after your answer.

Install begins copying all necessary files to your hard drive. As installation
progresses, on-screen prompts ask for successive disks. Pay close attention to the
disk that is requested. Replace the existing 1-2-3 disk in the drive with the disk
requested. Press Enter after placing the new disk in the drive.

Configuring 1-2-3 for Your Computer

After the program copies the system files, you must configure 1-2-3 for your
computer. Configuring 1-2-3 means specifying the type of display you use and the
printer attached to your computer.

To configure 1-2-3 for your system, follow these steps:

1. Press ⏎Enter at the FILE TRANSFER SUCCESSFUL screen.

2. From the MAIN MENU, select First-Time Installation and press
   ⏎Enter .

3. Note the type of display detected on the SCREEN DISPLAY DETECTION
   screen.

4. Press ⏎Enter to select the type of display card installed in your computer.

5. The correct display card should be highlighted in the SCREEN
   SELECTION screen. If not, select the correct display-card type.

6. Press ⏎Enter to continue.

   If your display card has only one display mode, skip to step 9.

7. Select the correct display mode using the arrow keys.

   For example, a VGA display has the following modes: 80x25 color,
   80x34 color, 80x60 color, 80x25 monochrome, 80x34 monochrome,
   and 80x60 monochrome. Using the arrow keys, select the mode that
   best fits your type of work.

8. Press ⏎Enter after you have selected the correct display mode.

9. At the `PRINTER SELECTION` screen, select `Yes` and press `↵Enter` to install a printer. Select `No` and press `↵Enter` to bypass installing a printer. If you select No, skip to step 16.

10. From the list of printer manufacturers, select your brand of printer.

    If your printer manufacturer does not show up in the list, check your printer manual. Your printer may be compatible with one of the manufacturers listed. If so, select the compatible printer manufacturer. If your printer does not emulate one of the printers listed, select `Generic`.

11. Press `↵Enter` to select the printer model.

12. Select the model of your printer from the menu listed.

    Again, if your printer is not listed, select the model your printer emulates. If your printer supports font cartridges, a screen appears so that you may select the correct font cartridge; continue with step 13. If, however, your printer does not use font cartridges, skip to step 15.

13. If your printer supports font cartridges, then either select the font cartridge you have installed, or select `No cartridge` if you do not use a font cartridge.

14. Press `↵Enter` to continue.

15. Select `Yes` and press `↵Enter` if you have another printer to install; then return to step 9. Select `No` and press `↵Enter` when you have installed all printers.

16. At the screen `NAMING YOUR DCF` select `No` and press `↵Enter` to save the driver configuration file.

    A file called 123.DCF is created that contains your configuration. Each time you start 1-2-3, this file is read for the configuration. If you select `Yes` and press `↵Enter`, you must name the DCF file. Because this is the first-time installation, you should let Install create the default DCF.

    Begin placing the disks that 1-2-3 requests in your disk drive. More files will be copied to your hard disk, based on your selections as you configured 1-2-3. Do not be surprised if Install requests disks you have already used.

17. When you see that installation has been successful, press `↵Enter`.

Generating Wysiwyg Fonts

If you selected to install Wysiwyg, you may generate fonts for Wysiwyg to use. These fonts are files stored on disk that let you change the font type that you see on-screen and that you print. You can generate the Basic font set, Medium font set, or Extended font set. The font set you use depends on your hard-disk space. Selecting the Basic fonts takes the least amount of disk space, while selecting Extended fonts takes the most space.

Generating fonts takes a considerable amount of time. For example, generating the Basic font set on a 286 computer takes about 20 minutes. On a 386 computer, count on at least 5 minutes to generate the fonts.

To generate fonts and complete Install, follow these steps:

1. At the GENERATING FONTS screen, press ⏎Enter .

2. From the menu, highlight Basic, Medium, or Extended, and press ⏎Enter .

3. If you chose either Medium or Extended, select Yes and press ⏎Enter to generate fonts now. If you selected No and pressed ⏎Enter , you can generate fonts at a later time.

4. When a message appears telling you that fonts have been generated successfully, press ⏎Enter to exit Install and return to the DOS prompt.

Changing 1-2-3's Configuration

In some cases, you may want to change 1-2-3's configuration. For example, if you purchase a new printer or a new video display, you must reconfigure 1-2-3 for that equipment. Or, if your video display card offers different modes of display, you may want to install a second mode of display.

Also, if you want to create additional driver configuration files (DCFs), you must start the Install program again. You may create more than one DCF, each with a different name. When you start 1-2-3, you may specify a different DCF to load, rather than using the default 123.DCF.

Modifying Your DCF

To change a driver configuration file (DCF) or create an additional one, follow these steps:

1. Change to the drive and directory where 1-2-3 Release 3.1 is located.

   For example, if you installed 1-2-3 in the directory C:\123R3, at a DOS prompt type **C:** and press ⏎Enter . Then type **CD\123R3** and press ⏎Enter .

2. Type **INSTALL** and press ⏎Enter .

3. Press ⏎Enter again when you see the Welcome screen.

537

4. Select `Change Selected Equipment` from the `Main Menu`, and press `⏎Enter` .

   The `CHANGE SELECTED EQUIPMENT` screen's menu lists the following options:

Options	Description
Return to Main Menu	Returns to the Main menu
Modify Current DCF	Enables you to change the configuration of the current DCF (normally 123.DCF)
Choose Another DCF to Modify	Enables you to choose a different DCF to place in memory for changing
Save Changes	Saves any modifications in the current DCF to the disk
End Install Program	Exits the Install program

   You may choose to modify the current DCF, or load another DCF into memory to modify. If you plan to load a new DCF into memory to modify, continue with step 5. To modify the current DCF, skip to step 7.

5. Select `Choose Another DCF to Modify` and press `⏎Enter` .
6. At the `CHOOSE ANOTHER DCF TO MODIFY` screen, type the name of the DCF to modify and press `⏎Enter` . For example, type **C:\123R3\COLOR.DCF** if COLOR.DCF is the DCF to modify.
7. Select `Modify Current DCF` and press `⏎Enter` .

You may now change the selected display, printer or country.

Changing the Selected Display

When changing the selected display, you can select a different display card, or install a second display card. You can also change the current display mode, or select a second display mode. From 1-2-3, the /Worksheet Window Display command enables you to change displays or display modes.

To change or modify the selected display, follow these steps:

1. Select `Change Selected Display` and press `⏎Enter` .

   When the `DISPLAY` screen appears, notice that the current display card has a 1 in front of it. If you plan to replace the existing display card with a new card, continue with step 2. If you plan to add a second display card, go to step 5. If you are selecting a second display mode, go to step 7.

Note: Before adding new display cards, replacing display cards or adding a new display mode, you must be sure that you do not have two display cards or modes selected already. If you do have two selected, you must delete one by highlighting that option and pressing `Del`.

2. Select the new display card and press `↵Enter`. If the card offers different display modes, select the correct mode, and press `↵Enter`. Notice that a 2 appears in front of the new display card selection.

3. Hightlight the display card with 1 in front of it.

4. Press `Del`.

   The MODIFY CURRENT DCF screen returns.

5. Highlight the second display card and press `↵Enter`.

6. If the second display card offers different display modes, select the correct mode. Skip to step 9.

7. Select the display card with the 1 in front of it, and press `↵Enter`.

   Notice that the current display mode also has a 1 in front of it.

8. Select the second display mode.

9. Press `↵Enter` to return to the MODIFY CURRENT DCF screen.

Changing the Selected Printer

1-2-3 Release 3.1 allows up to 16 different printers to be installed. From 1-2-3's /Print Printer Options Advanced Device Name menu or Wysiwyg's **:Print** Configuration **Printer** menu, you may select the printer to print to. Using Install, you may add or delete printers listed in the DCF.

To change the selected printer, follow these steps:

1. From the MODIFY CURRENT DCF screen, select Change Selected Printer and press `↵Enter`.

2. From the list of printer manufacturers, select your brand of printer.

   If your printer manufacturer does not show up in the list, check your printer manual. Your printer may be compatible with one of the manufacturers listed. If so, select the compatible printer manufacturer. If your printer does not emulate one of the printers listed, select Generic.

3. Press `↵Enter` to select the printer manufacturer.

4. Select the model of your printer from the menu listed.

   Again, if your printer is not listed, then select the model that your printer emulates.

5. Press ⏎Enter to accept the printer model that you selected.

6. If your printer supports font cartridges, select the font cartridge that you have installed, or select No cartridge if you do not use a font cartridge.

7. Press ⏎Enter to return to the MODIFY CURRENT DCF screen.

Changing the Selected Country

Use the Change Selected Country option on the MODIFY CURRENT DCF menu to change the sorting order that 1-2-3 uses. Three options are listed in this menu:

Selection	Description
Numbers First	Numbers are sorted before letters.
Numbers Last	Letters are sorted before numbers.
ASCII	Characters are sorted according to the ASCII table.

Suppose, for example, that you have four entries:

   123 Main Street
   Adams Rib Plaza
   4 Market Place
   ADAMS RIB PLAZA

With the Numbers First option selected, sorting the four entries in ascending order results in the following:

   123 Main Street
   4 Market Place
   Adams Rib Plaza
   ADAMS RIB PLAZA

Sorting the four entries with the Numbers Last option selected results in the following:

   Adams Rib Plaza
   ADAMS RIB PLAZA
   123 Main Street
   4 Market Place

In an ASCII table, each character is assigned a numeric value. Numbers have lower numeric values than letters. Uppercase letters have a lower numeric value than lowercase letters. Therefore, sorting the entries with the ASCII option selected results in the following order:

123 Main Street

4 Market Place

ADAMS RIB PLAZA

Adams Rib Plaza

These three options give you greater flexibility in sorting data.

To change the sort order, follow these steps:

1. Select Change Selected Country and press ⏎Enter .
2. From the COUNTRY screen, highlight the option that has a 1 in front of it.
3. Press Del .
4. Select the correct order, and press ⏎Enter .

You return to the MODIFY CURRENT DCF menu.

Saving Changes

After you have made all necessary changes, you must save those changes. You either save the changes in the current DCF loaded in memory, or you can create a new DCF. Follow these steps to save changes to a DCF:

1. From the MODIFY CURRENT DCF screen, select Return to Menu and press ⏎Enter .
2. From the CHANGE SELECTED EQUIPMENT screen, select Save Changes and press ⏎Enter .

   The NAMING YOUR DCF screen is displayed. Either save the changes to the current DCF, or type a new name. If you are creating a new DCF, continue with step 3. If, however, you are saving to the current DCF, skip to step 4.
3. Replace the current DCF name with the new DCF name. For example, **C:\123R3\COLOR.DCF.**
4. Press ⏎Enter to save the changes.

   Install may need to read new files from your system disks. You first must specify the drive where you will be placing the disks.
5. At the SPECIFYING A DISKETTE DRIVE screen, type the letter of the drive that you will place the disks in and press ⏎Enter .

541

6. Place the disk requested by Install in the specified drive. More than one disk may be requested.

7. Press `⏎Enter` at the `INSTALLATION SUCCESSFUL` screen.

   If you installed Wysiwyg, you will be asked to generate fonts.

8. Press `⏎Enter` at the `GENERATING FONTS` screen.

9. Select `Basic`, `Medium`, or `Extended` to generate fonts and press `⏎Enter`.

10. If you choose either `Medium` or `Extended`, select `Yes` to generate fonts now. If you select `No`, you may generate fonts at a later time.

11. Press `⏎Enter` to return to DOS once the fonts have been generated.

Changing Wysiwyg Options

Selecting `Wysiwyg Options` from Install's Main Menu enables you to change your Wysiwyg options. The options for this menu are `Return to Main Menu`, `Generate Fonts`, `Switch Mouse Buttons`, and `Add Fonts`.

To start changing Wysiwyg options, follow these steps:

1. Change to the drive and directory where 1-2-3 Release 3.1 is located.

   For example, if you installed 1-2-3 to C:\123R3, at a DOS prompt type **C:** and press `⏎Enter`. Then type **CD\123R3** and press `⏎Enter`.

2. Type **INSTALL** and press `⏎Enter`.

3. Press `⏎Enter` when you see the Welcome screen.

4. Select `Wysiwyg Options` from the `Main Menu` screen, and press `⏎Enter`.

Generating Fonts

Wysiwyg enables you to use different typeset-style fonts. Prior to using the fonts, however, you must generate them so that they reside on your hard disk. You may choose this option if, as you were installing, you chose not to generate fonts at that time. If you only installed, for example, the Basic font set, and now you want to increase the fonts that you have available, you can install either the `Medium` or `Extended` font set.

To generate fonts, follow these steps:

1. From the `WYSIWYG OPTIONS` screen, select `Generate Fonts` and press `⏎Enter`.

2. Select `Basic`, `Medium`, or `Extended` and press `⏎Enter`.

3. If you choose either Medium or Extended, select Yes to generate fonts now. If you select No, you return to the WYSIWYG OPTIONS screen.

4. When a message appears telling you that fonts have been generated successfully, press ⏎Enter to exit Install. You return to the DOS prompt.

Switching Mouse Buttons

When Wysiwyg is installed, the left mouse button is set up as the select button. This is convenient because you use your index finger to select with the mouse. However, if you are left-handed, you may want to make the right mouse-button the select button.

To change the mouse select button, follow these steps:

1. From the WYSIWYG OPTIONS screen, select Switch Mouse Buttons and press ⏎Enter .

2. From the SWITCH MOUSE BUTTONS screen, select Left or Right as the select button.

3. Press ⏎Enter to accept the selection and return to the WYSIWYG OPTIONS screen.

Adding Fonts

1-2-3 Release 3.1 comes with several fonts that you may use with Wysiwyg. However, you may desire to increase the font library that you have available.

To add fonts, follow these steps:

1. From the WYSIWYG OPTIONS menu, select Add Fonts and press ⏎Enter .

2. At the SPECIFYING A DISKETTE DRIVE screen, type the drive letter where you insert the disks and press ⏎Enter .

3. Place the disk with the fonts to add in the specified drive and press ⏎Enter .

   After the disk fonts have been transferred, you may copy additional fonts, generate the fonts you have added, or return to the main menu without generating fonts. Continue with step 4 to add more fonts or skip to step 7 to generate fonts. Press F9 to return to the main menu without generating fonts. If you press F9, select End Install Program, then Yes to return to a DOS prompt.

4. Press [Esc] to add more fonts.

5. At the SPECIFYING A DISKETTE DRIVE screen, type the drive letter where you will insert the disks and press [↵Enter] .

6. Place the disk containing the fonts in the specified drive and press [↵Enter]. (If you have more fonts to install, return to step 4.)

7. Press [↵Enter] to generate the newly installed fonts (remember, generating fonts can take a considerable amount of time).

8. When fonts have been generated, press [↵Enter] to return to a DOS prompt. No more steps are required.

Index

H

Q

R

Computer Books From Que Mean PC Performance!

Spreadsheets

1-2-3 Database Techniques	$29.95
1-2-3 Graphics Techniques	$24.95
1-2-3 Macro Library, 3rd Edition	$39.95
1-2-3 Release 2.2 Business Applications	$39.95
1-2-3 Release 2.2 PC Tutor	$39.95
1-2-3 Release 2.2 QueCards	$19.95
1-2-3 Release 2.2 Quick Reference	$ 8.95
1-2-3 Release 2.2 QuickStart, 2nd Edition	$19.95
1-2-3 Release 2.2 Workbook and Disk	$29.95
1-2-3 Release 3 Business Applications	$39.95
1-2-3 Release 3 Workbook and Disk	$29.95
1-2-3 Release 3.1 Quick Reference	$ 8.95
1-2-3 Release 3.1 QuickStart, 2nd Edition	$19.95
1-2-3 Tips, Tricks, and Traps, 3rd Edition	$24.95
Excel Business Applications: IBM Version	$39.95
Excel Quick Reference	$ 8.95
Excel QuickStart	$19.95
Excel Tips, Tricks, and Traps	$22.95
Using 1-2-3/G	$29.95
Using 1-2-3, Special Edition	$27.95
Using 1-2-3 Release 2.2, Special Edition	$27.95
Using 1-2-3 Release 3.1, 2nd Edition	$29.95
Using Excel: IBM Version	$29.95
Using Lotus Spreadsheet for DeskMate	$22.95
Using Quattro Pro	$24.95
Using SuperCalc5, 2nd Edition	$29.95

Databases

dBASE III Plus Handbook, 2nd Edition	$24.95
dBASE III Plus Tips, Tricks, and Traps	$24.95
dBASE III Plus Workbook and Disk	$29.95
dBASE IV Applications Library, 2nd Edition	$39.95
dBASE IV Programming Techniques	$24.95
dBASE IV Quick Reference	$ 8.95
dBASE IV QuickStart	$19.95
dBASE IV Tips, Tricks, and Traps, 2nd Edition	$24.95
dBASE IV Workbook and Disk	$29.95
Using Clipper	$24.95
Using DataEase	$24.95
Using dBASE IV	$27.95
Using Paradox 3	$24.95
Using R:BASE	$29.95
Using Reflex, 2nd Edition	$24.95
Using SQL	$29.95

Business Applications

Allways Quick Reference	$ 8.95
Introduction to Business Software	$14.95
Introduction to Personal Computers	$19.95
Lotus Add-in Toolkit Guide	$29.95
Norton Utilities Quick Reference	$ 8.95
PC Tools Quick Reference, 2nd Edition	$ 8.95
Q&A Quick Reference	$ 8.95
Que's Computer User's Dictionary	$ 9.95
Que's Wizard Book	$ 9.95
Quicken Quick Reference	$ 8.95
SmartWare Tips, Tricks, and Traps 2nd Edition	$24.95
Using Computers in Business	$22.95
Using DacEasy, 2nd Edition	$24.95
Using Enable/OA	$29.95
Using Harvard Project Manager	$24.95
Using Managing Your Money, 2nd Edition	$19.95

Using Microsoft Works: IBM Version	$22.95
Using Norton Utilities	$24.95
Using PC Tools Deluxe	$24.95
Using Peachtree	$27.95
Using PFS: First Choice	$22.95
Using PROCOMM PLUS	$19.95
Using Q&A, 2nd Edition	$23.95
Using Quicken: IBM Version, 2nd Edition	$19.95
Using Smart	$22.95
Using SmartWare II	$29.95
Using Symphony, Special Edition	$29.95
Using Time Line	$24.95
Using TimeSlips	$24.95

CAD

AutoCAD Quick Reference	$ 8.95
AutoCAD Sourcebook 1991	$27.95
Using AutoCAD, 3rd Edition	$29.95
Using Generic CADD	$24.95

Word Processing

Microsoft Word 5 Quick Reference	$ 8.95
Using DisplayWrite 4, 2nd Edition	$24.95
Using LetterPerfect	$22.95
Using Microsoft Word 5.5: IBM Version, 2nd Edition	$24.95
Using MultiMate	$24.95
Using Professional Write	$22.95
Using Word for Windows	$24.95
Using WordPerfect 5	$27.95
Using WordPerfect 5.1, Special Edition	$27.95
Using WordStar, 3rd Edition	$27.95
WordPerfect PC Tutor	$39.95
WordPerfect Power Pack	$39.95
WordPerfect Quick Reference	$ 8.95
WordPerfect QuickStart	$19.95
WordPerfect 5 Workbook and Disk	$29.95
WordPerfect 5.1 Quick Reference	$ 8.95
WordPerfect 5.1 QuickStart	$19.95
WordPerfect 5.1 Tips, Tricks, and Traps	$24.95
WordPerfect 5.1 Workbook and Disk	$29.95

Hardware/Systems

DOS Tips, Tricks, and Traps	$24.95
DOS Workbook and Disk, 2nd Edition	$29.95
Fastback Quick Reference	$ 8.95
Hard Disk Quick Reference	$ 8.95
MS-DOS PC Tutor	$39.95
MS-DOS Power Pack	$39.95
MS-DOS Quick Reference	$ 8.95
MS-DOS QuickStart, 2nd Edition	$19.95
MS-DOS User's Guide, Special Edition	$29.95
Networking Personal Computers, 3rd Edition	$24.95
The Printer Bible	$29.95
Que's PC Buyer's Guide	$12.95
Understanding UNIX: A Conceptual Guide, 2nd Edition	$21.95
Upgrading and Repairing PCs	$29.95
Using DOS	$22.95
Using Microsoft Windows 3, 2nd Edition	$24.95
Using Novell NetWare	$29.95
Using OS/2	$29.95
Using PC DOS, 3rd Edition	$24.95
Using Prodigy	$19.95

Using UNIX	$29.95
Using Your Hard Disk	$29.95
Windows 3 Quick Reference	$ 8.95

Desktop Publishing/Graphics

CorelDRAW Quick Reference	$ 8.95
Harvard Graphics Quick Reference	$ 8.95
Using Animator	$24.95
Using DrawPerfect	$24.95
Using Harvard Graphics, 2nd Edition	$24.95
Using Freelance Plus	$24.95
Using PageMaker: IBM Version, 2nd Edition	$24.95
Using PFS: First Publisher, 2nd Edition	$24.95
Using Ventura Publisher, 2nd Edition	$24.95

Macintosh/Apple II

AppleWorks QuickStart	$19.95
The Big Mac Book, 2nd Edition	$29.95
Excel QuickStart	$19.95
The Little Mac Book	$ 9.95
Que's Macintosh Multimedia Handbook	$24.95
Using AppleWorks, 3rd Edition	$24.95
Using Excel: Macintosh Version	$24.95
Using FileMaker	$24.95
Using MacDraw	$24.95
Using MacroMind Director	$29.95
Using MacWrite	$24.95
Using Microsoft Word 4: Macintosh Version	$24.95
Using Microsoft Works: Macintosh Version, 2nd Edition	$24.95
Using PageMaker: Macinsoth Version, 2nd Edition	$24.95

Programming/Technical

Assembly Language Quick Reference	$ 8.95
C Programmer' sToolkit	$39.95
C Quick Reference	$ 8.95
DOS and BIOS Functions Quick Reference	$ 8.95
DOS Programmer's Reference, 2nd Edition	$29.95
Network Programming in C	$49.95
Oracle Programmer's Guide	$29.95
QuickBASIC Advanced Techniques	$24.95
Quick C Programmer's Guide	$29.95
Turbo Pascal Advanced Techniques	$24.95
Turbo Pascal Quick Reference	$ 8.95
UNIX Programmer's Quick Reference	$ 8.95
UNIX Programmer's Reference	$29.95
UNIX Shell Commands Quick Reference	$ 8.95
Using Assembly Language, 2nd Edition	$29.95
Using BASIC	$24.95
Using C	$29.95
Using QuickBASIC 4	$24.95
Using Turbo Pascal	$29.95

For More Information, Call Toll Free!

1-800-428-5331

All prices and titles subject to change without notice.
Non-U.S. prices may be higher. Printed in the U.S.A.